Some of My Best Friends Are Books

Guiding Gifted Readers from Preschool to High School

3rd Edition

Judith Wynn Halsted

Great Potential Press®

Some of My Best Friends Are Books: Guiding Gifted Readers from Preschool to High School,
3rd Edition

Edited by: Jennifer Ault
Interior Design: The Printed Page
Cover Design: Hutchison-Frey

Published by Great Potential Press, Inc.
P.O. Box 5057
Scottsdale, AZ 85261

13 12 11 10 09   5 4 3 2 1

At the time of this book's publication, all facts and figures cited are the most current available. All telephone numbers, addresses, and website URLs are accurate and active; all publications, organizations, websites, and other resources exist as described in this book; and all have been verified as of the time this book went to press. The author(s) and Great Potential Press make no warranty or guarantee concerning the information and materials given out by organizations or content found at websites, and we are not responsible for any changes that occur after this book's publication. If you find an error or believe that a resource listed here is not as described, please contact Great Potential Press.

Library of Congress Cataloging-in-Publication Data

Halsted, Judith Wynn, 1940-
    Some of my best friends are books / Judith Wynn Halsted. — 3rd ed.
      p. cm.
    ISBN-13: 978-0-910707-96-1
    ISBN-10: 0-910707-96-0
    1. Gifted children—Books and reading—United States. 2. Gifted children—
Education—United States. 3. Children's literature—Bibliography. 4.
  Young adult literature—Bibliography. 5. Bibliotherapy. I. Title.
    Z1039.G55H35 2009
    028.5'5—dc22
                                                    2009023702

Dedication

To parents, teachers, and librarians
whose work and privilege it is to reach—
and expand—both the hearts and the minds of children.

Contents

Preface

Long before the current awareness of giftedness developed, my husband and I had two small sons. By the time they were five and two, I had noticed a recurring phenomenon that first pleased and then puzzled me: when we returned from evenings out, a succession of sitters, as they accepted their pay and put on their coats, would comment on how "smart" our boys were. Eventually I realized that these sitters saw many more young children than we did. Maybe they knew something we needed to know.

And so, for one of my courses at the Graduate School of Library and Information Science at the University of Illinois, I chose to write about library services for gifted children. What I learned about giftedness confirmed the sitters' impressions. I understood that we needed to learn much more—very quickly.

As our sons progressed through elementary school, there were unproductive teacher conferences, a lack of communication with administrators, and constant efforts on our part to keep up with emerging developments. There were also some shining examples of understanding—from several teachers, a principal, public and school librarians, and two religious educators—but for the most part, we learned about the needs of gifted children much faster than educational practices evolved to meet those needs.

As public awareness about giftedness grew, the focus was on curriculum and teaching practices for gifted students—that is, the emphasis was on the classroom, not the playground. By the time our older son was in sixth grade, it was clear that, given access to a library and the Natural Science Center, he could continue his intellectual development as well without school, at least for a while. We wanted a more comprehensive educational program—one that would see him as more than a very good brain, but rather as a whole person.

When we moved to Michigan, we enrolled him in The Pathfinder School, an independent school that offered understanding and flexibility, as well as good teaching in small classes. Two years later, his younger brother's public school principal explained that, although by January our second son had solved all of the problems in his math textbook and testing showed that he was capable of higher-level work, his teacher would not allow him to move ahead. So that fall, our younger son entered Pathfinder as well. (A few years later, the Traverse City public school system initiated a gifted program.)

To cover the cost of private education, I served as the librarian, trading my hours for tuition and enjoying the challenge of working with children from preschool through high school. The founders of Pathfinder, inspired by the Roeper School in Birmingham, Michigan, hoped to develop a program for gifted students, and two years later, I became the director of that program. In this position, I attended conferences on gifted education, where I heard Dr. James T. Webb speak about the social and emotional components of gifted children—an idea whose time was finally arriving.

This book comes out of that history. In the years since our sons were small, due in part to the efforts of Jim Webb and others whose careers he has nurtured, a significant and growing body of literature about the social and emotional needs of gifted children has been made available to teachers—and to parents, who were mostly not included in debates about gifted children in the classroom and who have responded enthusiastically to invitations to join the discussion about social and emotional development. I am deeply gratified to be a small part of this evolution.

My thanks go first to Jim Webb for inviting me to write *Guiding Gifted Readers* (1988) and the editions of *Some of My Best Friends Are Books* that have followed. It is a pleasure and a privilege to work with him and others at Great Potential Press. They are engaged in good and meaningful work.

The staff of the Traverse Area District Library has been unfailingly supportive. The Circulation Department, the Reference Department, and the Youth Services Department have been especially helpful. Bernadette Groppuso, the head of Youth Services, has developed an extensive collection for children and young adults, and she has been more than generous with her time. I am grateful for the hours I have spent in the library and for the convenience of its online capabilities.

I am thankful also to Mary Beeker at the library of Northwestern Michigan College, where she teaches courses on online research. Mary introduced me to the "Invisible Web," which is discussed in Chapter 5. I hope I have described it well enough so that others will expand their research options, going beyond search engines to include databases as well.

When I mention "my local bookseller" in this book, I am referring to the staff of one of Traverse City's excellent resources, Horizon Books. My gratitude goes to all of them, and in particular to Lois Orth, who reads the children's books as they come in and who knows her patrons. Lois often greets me with recommendations for titles I might otherwise miss.

Thanks also to friends and especially to family members who have made allowances for my preoccupation with this book for the last many months. Special thanks go to my husband, David W. Halsted, who encouraged me to undertake this edition and then consistently made good on his promise to be supportive, even when the laptop came along on vacations. Always, I am grateful for the sustaining pleasure of time with our family: our sons, David and Mark; our daughters-in-law, Keely and Barbara; and our grandchildren, Christopher and Caroline, Chloe and Benjamin. They are a never-ending source of joy and wonder, and our view into the future.

Introduction

Some of My Best Friends Are Books is written for parents, teachers, librarians, and counselors of children and young people who stand out due to advanced reading ability, giftedness, or intense interests—intellectual, artistic, or musical. It proposes that by reading and discussing well-chosen books with children, adults can encourage these youngsters' optimum development in two areas—emotional and intellectual—through one pleasurable activity.

Emotional: Books can provide a focus for discussions (*non-threatening* discussions, since, after all, they are about someone else) that touch less on plot and characterization and more on feelings, values, and decision making. Parents who have tried this tell me that they find books to be wonderful bridges for communicating with their youngsters.

Intellectual: In an effort to provide our students with intellectual challenge, the well-planned use of books enables adults to create an individualized program for any youngster. A fundamental benefit of reading is its ability to keep intellectual curiosity alive. If adults feel that they need a more down-to-earth incentive to encourage reading, there is a practical benefit, too: students who spend more time reading—fiction as well as nonfiction—earn higher scores on college entrance exams.

1

The ideas presented here are recommended for children who are formally identified as gifted, but also for many others who may not be included in that category, especially:

○ the many gifted students who have not been identified

○ the bright, eager learners who are not placed in a gifted program because they do not quite meet the criteria of the local schools

○ the highly able children in school systems that lack a gifted program

○ all children who have special ability or intense interests and for that reason feel "different," whether or not they could be identified as gifted

When an adult senses a special spark in a child who is interested in reading and talking about challenging books, even if "gifted" seems not quite the right word, this book can help.

○ Teachers, seeking ways to provide challenge for gifted children in the face of funding cuts and curricular change, will find updated suggestions for using book discussion in school settings.

○ Counselors, aware that recent textbooks in counseling the gifted recommend bibliotherapy as one approach to meeting these children's psychological needs, will find detailed information on the process of bibliotherapy.

○ Librarians who assist these teachers and counselors will find new books listed, along with familiar treasures, in the annotated bibliography, which comprises about half of this book.

○ Homeschooling parents will learn how to use books as primary resources for promoting the intellectual and emotional development of their children.

○ Parents who recognize that they must become more involved in their children's education will find ways to enhance their children's educational experience with the confidence that they are doing it well.

Some of My Best Friends Are Books, 3rd Edition has three parts and is divided into eight chapters. Part One, "The Children," offers background information on the emotional and intellectual developmental needs of children of high ability.

Part Two, "The Process," begins with a chapter about typical reading patterns and the importance of reading guidance. Then, the two subsequent chapters suggest methods for discussing books with young readers—enhancing emotional development through bibliotherapy in Chapter 4, and promoting intellectual growth through a variety of ways to discuss ideas in Chapter 5.

Part Three, "The Books," offers criteria for selecting challenging books in Chapter 6, as well as a brief overview of children's literature, with special emphasis on gifted readers in Chapter 7. The final chapter—and the longest, comprising about half of the book—is the annotated bibliography, listing well over 300 books carefully selected for their usefulness in promoting the intellectual and emotional development of gifted children and young people. Indexes provide easy access to the annotated bibliography by category, author, and title. The category "Drive to Understand" has been further expanded in this edition to offer more books to meet intellectual interests and to appeal to readers who prefer nonfiction, and a new category, Resilience, has been added.

There is nothing new about the idea that children need good books or that books can be used to help children build coping skills. From the beginning, the response to this book has suggested that there *is* something new and welcome in the ideas it presents for using books with *gifted* children to help them develop optimally. As in the earlier editions, the stories presented in it are of children—or composites of children—whom I have known (with fictional names).

Here are four stories to exemplify the backgrounds of children for whom this book may be helpful.

Marcelo is a cheerful, curious, friendly, bright preschooler who talks easily with adults and seems quite mature. In fact, his teacher relies on him as the most responsible child in his group. But other children are sometimes puzzled by him. Marcelo gets frustrated when his friends can't follow what he's saying, and it bothers him that they don't share his amazed interest in the insects he brings to class. Adults, though, help him find out about insects in books, and he is beginning to read about them himself.

Steven is a smart, sullen high school junior. Social difficulties have left their marks on him, most obviously in the discrepancy between his ability and his performance. His PSAT scores qualify him to compete for a National Merit Scholarship, but his grades will keep him out of the better colleges. Teachers say that he doesn't measure up to his potential, that he refuses to do homework, and that he just doesn't study, particularly for courses that require consistent daily effort, such as French and math. Steven knows that he has mental ability that he does not use, at least not at school, but he has no idea how to "realize his potential." His teachers are concerned but do not know how to help him.

Tamika, also a high school junior, is active in sports, student government, and the school newspaper, and she keeps her grades at an honors level. Tamika is quiet about her own excellent grades and is ready to help others who don't understand as quickly. In the summer, she's a counselor at a day camp, where the campers love her. She's always available to them for ping-pong or a quiet talk. But Tamika feels truly alone sometimes. Her concerns about the future are so much more intense than her friends' that she has never attempted to discuss them with anyone.

If we were to ask both Steven's and Tamika's parents what their children were like as preschoolers, they would describe someone remarkably like Marcelo. What determines whether a "Marcelo" will, in 12 years, turn into a "Steven" or a "Tamika"?

Marcelo, Steven, and Tamika are all gifted. This giftedness adds an extra dimension to their lives, imposing on them certain developmental and intellectual tasks in addition to those all children face. This book attempts an answer to this question: *If I'm fortunate enough to start with a child like Marcelo, what can I do to help him or her develop into a confident, productive young adult who remains as happy and responsive as Marcelo is now?*

A fourth student, Beth, is a conscientious ninth grader w. organization, discipline, and genuine interest in learning help her to maintain an A- average. Requirements for the gifted program at her school are unusually high, and her test scores have not qualified her to join. But her intellectual curiosity and her voracious reading habit set her apart from her classmates who are too busy for books. Sometimes Beth wonders why she has not been selected for special classes, but she is confident that she has a bright future nevertheless. To be honest, she is often relieved not to have the pressure of being labeled a "gifted" student. But with or without the label, she is a bright, intellectually curious girl whose development depends in part on caring adults who recognize and encourage these qualities.

Challenges as They Grow

Each stage of childhood and adolescence brings a different challenge for children of high ability. Preschoolers need to develop a positive self-concept and grow toward a strong sense of self. In the early grades of elementary school, such youngsters begin to understand that people have different levels of abilities, and they must learn to value abilities that differ from their own. Although bright children need friends who share their own capabilities, they must learn to get along with all children.

In the later elementary grades, talented students often choose whether to acknowledge and follow their natural eagerness to learn or to hide their abilities in order to fit in. This is one reason why it is so important for preschoolers to develop a strong sense of self—a confidence in their own worth.

Well-adjusted gifted children enter middle school able to withstand the turmoil that typifies that age. If giftedness and intellectual curiosity are part of their self-concept, these aspects will remain intact—if temporarily submerged—as these youngsters try on various personae. Ideally, they emerge from this stage knowing their capabilities, being at ease with their classmates, and having a few close friends.

udents with this background—aware of their indi-
their responsibility for their own future—have a
and use their abilities without self-consciousness.
Marcelo at this point: he is still happy but far more
self-aware, conscious of both his abilities and his shortcomings. He
enjoys his intelligence and his curiosity and realizes that although he
is different, he is accepted by family and friends. He accepts and
values others as well. He has the confidence and resilience to take
risks, to fail, and to try again. Marcelo's healthy development is due
in large part to the fact that his parents, teachers, friends, and school
system value and nurture giftedness—whether or not they formally
identify it.

Social and Emotional Needs

In fact, many exceptionally bright youngsters are not identified
as gifted. Instead, they may be labeled "difficult" or "emotionally
immature" or "too talkative" or "withdrawn"—or even ADD/ADHD.
The unique, often intense emotional and intellectual needs of such
children may not be accepted and understood by the children themselves or by the adults around them. This is especially true of highly
gifted children. A teacher of one such child consoled his parents by
saying, "Some people aren't so good at being children. But they will
be good adults." One reason for this is that children of school age
typically cannot choose their milieu; they are forced to try to fit in or
to give up in defeat, often at great cost to their self-esteem. In contrast, adults who have succeeded in their educational path usually
have some control over their daily work environment; they can
choose to work where they are likely to find friends among their
colleagues.

The fact that work is very important to gifted children is one of
the ways in which they differ from the norm, according to psychologist Ellen Winner, who points out that, in contrast to the culture
around them, gifted children are motivated to achieve mastery, they
derive pleasure from challenge, and they often have an early sense of
what they want to do as adults. In addition, they are independent

and non-conforming, and they are often more introverted than average children, both because they are so different and because developing their talent requires time alone. Clearly, they are different, and "the social and emotional problems faced by the gifted are caused not by their being gifted but by the consequences of their being so different from others."[1]

How Books Can Help

The differences that gifted children experience require them to take different paths toward optimal emotional and intellectual development. This book recommends that the adults most concerned with the development of gifted, talented, creative children consider very seriously the potential that books and reading have for helping these children understand themselves and become all that they can be.

Books for children are plentiful, and most bright children are good readers who find them easily. It may seem, then, that *planning* to use books is unnecessary—but surprisingly often, where there is no planning, even good readers are not introduced to the pleasures of leisure reading. Teachers struggling to meet basic requirements have little time to suggest and follow through with extra reading for brighter students. Parents may find it difficult to keep track of what their children are reading. Guiding children's reading appears to be one more unaffordable luxury in an increasingly busy world.

Yet books offer compelling advantages to parents and teachers who want to nurture the minds and hearts of highly able children. Excellent books are abundant and inexpensive and are accessible sources of challenge and understanding. In fact, books should be the first choice of enrichment for bright youngsters.

Merely providing books is not enough, however. Knowledge of gifted children, discussion techniques, and children's literature will maximize the benefits that books offer. By filling the gaps in their knowledge, parents, teachers, counselors, and librarians can bring gifted children and books together more effectively. In so doing, they can help gifted children be themselves—comfortable in their present world and poised to grow into happy, productive adults.

Part One

The Children

Chapter 1

The Heart of the Child: Emotional Development

Too often, we fail to recognize that gifted children can have trouble with emotional and social development, and we assume that even if they do have problems, they have the intelligence to deal with them. Sensitive adults who work with gifted children realize that this is not true—that gifted children often are burdened with *extra* emotional and social needs and difficulties. In fact, being gifted truly complicates the usual problems of growing up.

Thomas Buescher has noted several specialized needs of gifted adolescents which go beyond the general social and emotional needs of all adolescents:[1]

O recognizing and owning their giftedness

O resolving the dissonance between their expectations of themselves and their actual performance (they must learn to accept the fact that they cannot always perform at a high level in every area)

O taking risks (the reluctance of gifted adolescents to take risks can hamper their willingness to choose appropriate but difficult classes)

○ determining how much to respond to others' expectations and how much weight to give to their own needs

○ coping with their impatience with the frequent lack of clear-cut answers, especially in personal relationships and career choices

○ meeting their inner demand for an identity while avoiding the temptation to make premature decisions (usually regarding college and career) which would limit future access to their full potential

While Buescher's work highlights the difficulties of giftedness for teenagers, his point holds true for gifted people of all ages—that is, to understand their emotional needs, we need to recognize the extras in the developmental tasks that they face.

This book highlights five broad areas in which giftedness affects development, as well as how reading and discussing selected books can nurture this maturity. One of the areas, intellectual development, is reserved for the next chapter. In this chapter, we will look at four particular aspects of social and emotional development as they pertain to gifted children:

○ establishing an identity
○ needing time alone
○ fostering and maintaining relationships with others
○ learning how to use one's ability

After a brief introduction to each of these concerns, we will consider them again in greater detail.

First, while every child must establish his or her own identity, the gifted child must recognize and accept an identity that is different from the norm and that may not be popular or acceptable to peers or even to family.

As a seventh grader, Damien has figured out that many of his ideas seem weird to his classmates and even to his parents and teachers. Entering a new school, he's determined to be quiet and to keep his hand down. No more frantic

12

arm waving when the answer is so very clear! Stifle, stifle, stifle. Stifle is the name of the game. At an age when most kids his age are establishing a sense of identity, he is denying a large part of himself. He is attempting to lose himself to melt into the crowd called "normal." Perhaps if someone had helped him to understand and accept his differences when he first became aware of them, he would be freer to acknowledge them now.

Second, while all children must learn to be alone at times, gifted children may actually *require* time alone, and they may need more of it than most other people need or can understand. Children who are gifted and talented may have to learn to cope with mixed feelings about their own need for time alone—aware that they also need time with other people and yet uncertain how to balance these divergent needs with the expectations of others.

Hannah loves to read, play the piano, and sew—all solitary activities. After a busy day with large groups of people at school, she enjoys coming home to these quiet pursuits. Her parents are worried, however, because she seldom invites friends home with her. Although Hannah is happy with her friends at school and content with her activities at home, she senses her parents' concern and wonders if there is something wrong with her. Her worries would be relieved if her parents understood her need for time alone and encouraged her to take it.

Third, all children must learn how to get along with others, and gifted children must find a few good friends and learn to value and respect others, even though others may reject them. Gifted children often speak or act with unusual intensity, and this intensity is difficult for other children to understand or accept; they may see it as "weird." In addition, people who are gifted frequently have heightened sensitivity to the comments and actions of others, so being misunderstood or rejected is more painful for them than for most other people. Thus, for gifted children, the issues of friendship—so important to their healthy development—are much more complex than they are for most children.

> *Eleven-year-old Brian talks with enthusiasm to high school students and adults, but he can find no other children his age who share his interest in biology. His sixth-grade classmates are puzzled by the intensity that marks his oral science reports, and he mistakes their lack of understanding for rejection. As a result, he is building a protective wall around himself, neither giving nor expecting friendship from people his own age. If a significant adult can help him learn to respect his classmates' social or athletic skills, as well as his own knowledge of biology—and if he can find just one or two friends who share his interest, perhaps at a community science center—he can avoid years of social isolation. Otherwise, Brian may not learn to make friends his own age until he enters college.*

Fourth, while all adolescents must make career and college decisions, gifted youngsters often have so many possibilities that choices can paralyze them. Unwilling to give anything up and unable to choose, gifted teenagers and young adults may find it difficult to take the steps that will enable them to make full use of their abilities.

> *Wei, a superior student in math and science, is considering a career in medicine. He also plays piano and guitar in a band that has performed at high school proms for the last three years. Music is so important to Wei that he wants to delay entering college while he tests his chances of finding work as a professional musician. However, he's afraid that too much time away from science and math will dull his skills and ruin his chances of getting into medical school. As he weighs the decision, college application deadlines are passing by. He's beginning to panic about his future. Some attention paid to preliminary college and career planning, beginning in his early adolescent years, would have helped Wei.*

This chapter considers the social and emotional development of gifted children by further exploring each of these four aspects of development, with a brief introduction to ways in which books can enhance that development.

Establishing an Identity

A major task of growing up is the search for one's identity. Gifted children, in order to be wholly themselves, must recognize and accept their own giftedness. But since the history of education in our country reveals a persistent strain of anti-intellectualism,[2] intellectual giftedness often seems more a burden than a blessing. Gifted children learn early—sometimes before they enter kindergarten—that many people are annoyed by and resentful of precocious and verbal children with abilities well above the norm. And so to fit giftedness willingly and comfortably into their self-concept takes a degree of maturity that must develop over time.

Who They Are

Establishing an identity is a matter of discovering who we are—of learning what it is that makes us, like the Little Prince's rose, "unique in all the world." And what gifted children discover may be a self that they know will not be popular, so they feel that they must choose between being themselves and being liked. Their identity will emerge out of this conflict and the ways in which they choose to deal with it. Several characteristics contribute to their struggle.

Difference

Gifted children realize fairly early not only that they are different, but also that there is something vaguely unacceptable about this difference. Our society is ambivalent about difference, as well as intelligence, and children can easily develop the uncomfortable feeling that something is wrong with them. Most often, they do not know what it is or even why they are different; they only know that when they exercise their creativity or knowledge, they do not fit in.

They feel alone, wrong, even freakish, and ironically, they often feel inferior to those around them.

At the same time, especially if their environment provides enough stimulation, these children may experience the elation of the insights and awareness that giftedness makes possible. They can know the joy of discovering new ideas, new people with whom they can use their vocabularies fully, and new stimuli such as museums, music, or films that excite them.

Gifted children live with this paradox. They must learn, in the "down" times when they are feeling different and alone, to trust that the "up" times, when they can enjoy the benefits of their extra measure of perception, will come again. Some of them must learn to make a little "up" time last over a long "down" period. One friendship established at summer camp may be what carries a child through the next school year, and just one understanding and stimulating teacher may keep a child going through two or three years of indifferent or mediocre teachers.

> *Attending a high school that places more emphasis on sports than on academic achievement, Melissa finds her work with a statewide youth organization more stimulating than school. Although meetings occur only twice a year, the friendships she has made with other youth leaders, the creative energy she puts into planning conferences, and the experience of traveling to large cities around the state compensate for her feelings of not fitting in at school. Gradually she is learning to integrate the sense of being different and alone at school with the sense of inner delight and satisfaction that her giftedness brings in a different setting. Her identity includes both.*

Ambivalence about the Label

Middle elementary children, just becoming aware of the concept of giftedness, may be ambivalent about having the "gifted" label applied to them. If parents and teachers react positively and matter-of-factly to the idea of giftedness, children will probably do the same, accepting their abilities and learning to use them with enthusiasm. If anything in their environment causes them to be uncomfortable with the term, however, children's responses may range from what appears to be showing off to denying their gifts and the responsibilities that they imply.

> *Self-conscious about his lack of athletic ability, Derrick seeks approval by offering answers in class eagerly and frequently. However, the other children think he is boasting about how much he knows. Meanwhile, Tandi answers questions only when the teacher calls on her and even uses a doubtful tone of voice to give the impression that she knows no more than anyone else. Both children's responses indicate that they need help in accepting who they are. Establishment of a healthy identity depends on that acceptance.*

Overexcitabilities

Gifted children, especially the highly gifted, have extraordinarily high degrees of sensitivity and intensity. Kazimierz Dabrowski, a Polish psychiatrist, sheds light on this observation through his theory of positive disintegration—a personality theory that suggests that going through difficult and unsettling periods in our lives (disintegration) can be positive, preparing us for further growth and development as we re-integrate.

Positive disintegration is an emotional rather than an intellectual experience. In fact, Dabrowski's theory "places emotions in a central role, relegating intelligence to a secondary position of influence on personality development," according to Dr. Sal Mendaglio.[3] Speaking of the implications of the theory for gifted individuals, Dr. Michael Pyryt concurs: "The current emphasis on the cognitive domain in gifted education, in conjunction with neglect of the emotional domain, is viewed as misguided."[4]

In the 20 years since Michael Piechowski introduced Dabrowski's work to the field of gifted education, various aspects of his theory have been studied and adopted as fundamental to the growing awareness of the social and emotional implications of giftedness. The most important so far has been the concept of "overexcitabilities," a translation of a Polish word—and one that unfortunately has a negative ring in English—that literally means "superstimulatibility," or unusually strong neurological reactions to stimuli. Suggesting that the overexcitabilities should have been called "superexcitabilities" in English, Piechowski and Daniels point out that the term "means that life is experienced in a manner that is deeper, more vivid, and more acutely sensed," with a "more complex and more richly textured quality."[5] Dr. Linda Silverman suggests that it would be helpful to think of overexcitability as "an overabundance of energy or the capacity for exuberance and enhanced experience."[6]

Dabrowski's five overexcitabilities are psychomotor, sensual, intellectual, imaginational, and emotional. Offering snapshots of the positives and negatives that characterize each overexcitability, as well as coping strategies, Sharon Lind[7] states that psychomotor overexcitability, demonstrated by those who love physical activity, may appear to some to be hyperactivity, thus contributing to the possibility that gifted children may be mislabeled ADHD.[8] Sensual overexcitability brings a heightened pleasure in seeing, hearing, smelling, tasting, or touching things, as well as the potential of discomfort from too much sensory stimulation. Students who are intellectually overexcitable are intensely curious and often avid readers; they may appear impatient with others who cannot keep up with their ideas. Children who have imaginary playmates and love to hear stories rich in fantasy display imaginational overexcitability, which can also mean that they grow restless in classrooms where literal thinking is favored over imagination. Very young children may particularly demonstrate emotional overexcitability in their intense reactions, reaching beyond what is normal even for the "terrible twos." But as they grow older, these children are also capable of strong empathy and deep relationships.[9]

According to Piechowski, "It is unfortunate that the stronger these overexcitabilities are, the less peers and teachers welcome them, unless they, too, are gifted."[10] Any of these overexcitabilities can make a child stand out as different and can present a challenge to teachers, parents, and the child himself, who all must make an effort to understand and cope with this difference.

The concept of overexcitability sheds light on the observation that gifted people are often super-sensitive, sharply aware of their own and others' feelings. In fact, a heightened sensitivity may be the first trait of giftedness that parents see in a very young child.[11] These children are often intense, not only in their depth of feeling, but also in their commitment to an interest or a cause and in their manner of expressing that commitment. In the adult world, the sensitivity and intensity of the gifted usually meet some degree of tolerance, but other children are not always so understanding. Gifted children who exhibit emotional overexcitability need the support of an adult who takes Dabrowski's view that *the emotional extremes that these children experience are not a sign of neurosis, but an indication of potential for growth.*[12]

Awareness of Moral Issues

Gifted children follow current events with comprehension earlier than most children. At an early age, they become aware of adult concerns about war, the environment, racial and economic issues, and other social concerns. They may become deeply worried about the future of the world at a time when other children their age are unaware and uninterested—another difference between them and their classmates.

> *Nathan will never forget learning about the devastation caused by Hurricane Katrina. The five-year-old was watching television when the first news bulletin interrupted, and he followed the story avidly. It was the awakening of a political and humanitarian awareness that has become a major focus of interest for him.*

All of these characteristics of gifted youngsters—and the additional ones discussed elsewhere in this book—are aspects of the self that a high-potential child must learn to understand, accept, and balance as she develops a sense of identity.

Who They Will Become

The search for identity raises some complex issues for gifted people. Can they successfully explore all of the possibilities open to them? Will they accept and develop their ability or deny its existence and leave it unused? Will they use their leadership potential in positive ways? With a variety of choices open to them, how will they select a challenging and satisfying career? There are many ways in which gifted people confront these issues—some of them healthier and more productive than others.

Exploring Possibilities

Establishing an identity means more than merely discovering who we are. It also means creating who we will become through imagination, risk taking, and exploring available identities and choosing among them. Gifted youngsters may (and should) experiment with more identities than most children, displaying more imagination and less conventionality. Books offer possibilities that they might not otherwise encounter, permitting them to vicariously experience various roles and ways of living as they move through the process of creating a personal identity.

Developing Potential

In order to feel accepted and to fit in with their social group, some children deny their giftedness and avoid developing it. They may become restless adults, moving without a clear direction from one pursuit to another, and because they are not using their abilities, they are often dissatisfied with the limited opportunities available to them. We are happiest when we know that our talents are being stretched and used; we feel best about ourselves when we know that we are being useful. To reach that point, gifted children must develop the potential that lies within them.

> *Jabrae was identified as gifted in middle school. Although he loved to read and talked glibly about ideas, he never learned to focus his thoughts sufficiently to complete written assignments on time. After graduation, he held several restaurant jobs, intending to save money for*

college but delaying application because he feared that his lack of study skills would lead to failure. Within two years, he married a woman who met many of his emotional needs but did not share his intellectual interests. Soon, supporting a wife and children took precedence over his education. Jabrae might have become an excellent teacher—his original goal—but his lack of training now confines him to work that offers no security and does not require him to think. With less time for reading now and no one with whom to discuss his ideas, Jabrae is lonely and resentful. Early information about his ability and encouragement from others to use it well might have given Jabrae what he needed to pursue his early goals.

Some children feel that superior ability implies a responsibility. They see their gifts as something that they can develop and pass on through giving to others. These youngsters learn to rejoice in their abilities and to use them with humility and productivity.

Joy grew up in a well-to-do family and enjoyed an excellent education. After her marriage, there was no financial need for her to work. However, from her late elementary years, she knew that she wanted a career that would serve other people in some way. She stayed home with her young children, but she continued her education as a part-time student while gaining experience as a volunteer in several community organizations. Fifteen years later, she was ready to begin a career as a psychologist. Today she helps gifted girls make appropriate educational and vocational decisions.

Leading Others

Another issue facing bright, precocious children is their potential for leadership. Many of them are natural leaders, and for them, developing a sense of identity means finding ways to explore and use their leadership ability. In some, the talent for leadership is so strong that if it finds no positive outlets, it will express itself in negative ways.

These children need adults who can see past the negative expressions and offer guidance in the constructive use of leadership ability. Since books provide examples of both negative and positive leaders, book discussion is one way of providing this guidance.

> *Unchallenged by his high school courses, Ibrahim not only refuses to do his assignments but also loudly proclaims to other students his low opinion of the teachers, the curriculum, and various school requirements. Because Ibrahim's voice carries some weight in his small high school, other students are beginning to neglect their work, too. Ibrahim will all be happier if an adult can see what is happening and help him plan ways to redirect his leadership abilities.*

Choosing a Career

In exploring possible future roles for themselves, gifted students often discover that they can do so many things well that career choice is extremely difficult. Hence, they need to develop superior self-knowledge and excellent decision-making skills. Multi-talented young adults must face the fact that they will not have time to bring all of their strengths to full flower. Again, books can help, enabling children to explore various options without spending months or years on each, helping them to establish priorities and make both vocational and avocational choices.

Asynchrony

While dealing with these issues, gifted children may also face the enormous task of integrating various levels of their abilities. Different parts of themselves may develop at different rates, with academic interest and achievement sometimes far outstripping other areas, such as physical growth and social judgment. This disparity between rates of intellectual, emotional, and physical development is often called *asynchrony*,[13] an apt term for what happens with children whose various developmental schedules are not in tune with one another. In gifted children in particular, intellectual development can move rapidly, while social, emotional, and physical growth remain tied to chronological age.

Asynchrony is a factor that should be considered by the adults who make decisions concerning gifted children. It should be discussed when deciding whether or not a child should skip a grade level in school, for example. Similarly, a third-grade boy who joins an enrichment class of sixth graders in the middle school library to work on a research project may need to be allowed to make an audio recording of his report because his fine motor skills are not advanced enough to write about all he has learned. Asynchrony can cause surprise when the unusually tall, highly verbal 10-year-old does not behave like the 14-year-old that she appears to be. We must also consider asynchrony when we choose books for the second grader who is reading at the sixth-grade level.

If a child's intellectual growth has far surpassed emotional and social development, there may later come a necessary time of academic latency that allows social and emotional growth to catch up. This can happen during the high school years, after college, or any time in between. The educational path of such a person may be atypical, but appropriate *for him.*

> *Theo began kindergarten at four, was accelerated another year in high school, and entered college at 16. When he graduated from college at 20, he was sure of two things: he wanted to go to graduate school at some point, but he did not want to go to graduate school that fall. He spent two years working at various jobs, learning to be self-supporting while consolidating his career plans. Now in graduate school, he is studying for the first time with his agemates—still occasionally restless at the slow pace of coursework, but adapting to it with a new measure of maturity and self-understanding.*

Indeed, it may not be until the early twenties or later that the different aspects of a very complex person—the intellectual, emotional, social, and physical—begin to come together. It will help those living through this asynchrony if they and their parents recognize what is happening and know that the prognosis is good.

A Healthy Self-Image

Establishing a healthy identity means discovering and accepting who one is and creating the person that one will become. For gifted children, this includes acknowledging and using their abilities unself-consciously. On the one hand, they must integrate giftedness into their self-concept, and on the other, they must be able to see it, with humility, as a unique part of themselves that needs special challenges and nurturing. Only when they can do this have they fully accepted themselves as gifted individuals.

How does a gifted youngster reach this point? By understanding that she has several of the characteristics common to many gifted individuals, including some that are unpopular or misunderstood, such as being hypercritical, talking too much in class, or wanting more time alone than most people do; by accepting the positive and useful sides of those unpopular characteristics; by forgiving herself for having them; by bringing them under control to make good use of them; by recognizing the advantages of high abilities and learning to enjoy them; and by realizing that high intelligence is useless without training and self-discipline.

These attitudes cannot easily be taught by precept. Example is far superior, and examples can come from role models—gifted people whose lives are based on these understandings. Such role models can be real people that the child knows, such as parents, teachers, and friends, or they can be characters in books.

Being Alone

"Being alone" is an ambiguous term. It can mean being alone and liking it, being alone and feeling lonely, or being alone because one is different. A gifted child can experience all of these and can also develop conflicting emotions about being alone. The child's confusion is compounded by the reactions of other people to those who appear to be "loners." Human beings are social animals, suspicious of those who choose to be less social than the norm. Gifted children are aware of this, and their own feelings about being alone are colored by their assumptions of the feelings of others. Especially if their temperament tends toward introversion, they need understanding from adults around them that they must be alone part of the time.

Being Alone and Liking It

While gifted children appreciate the warmth of friendship as much as others, they also need time to develop their talents. Children—and adults—who are talented in specialized fields such as math, science, music, art, or athletics all spend unusual amounts of time alone. However, they do not suffer from being alone as much as others do; they know how to be alone and how to use time alone productively.[14]

Many of these individuals may prove to be close to the "introvert" end of the extrovert/introvert continuum. It has long been recognized that more gifted people tend toward introversion, needing more time alone, than does the general population. In a review of research, Williams states, "...in the gifted and talented population the majority appear to be introverts, while the general population contains from 25% to 35% introverts."[15] Characteristics of introversion include the following:

- ○ restoring depleted energy by being alone, while extroverts restore energy by being with people

- ○ forming deep and loyal relationships with a few best friends rather than needing many friends

- ○ being slow to respond to people and situations

- ○ thoughtfulness; needing time to reflect before speaking

- ○ preferring some of the time to read rather than to be with others

- ○ focusing on concepts and ideas

- ○ possessing an ability to work on complex problems and a willingness to work uninterrupted for long periods of time

Because most people are extroverts, introversion is often misunderstood and thought of as negative. To counteract this perception (and careful to point out that neither temperament is superior; they are just different), in one chapter of her book *The Introvert Advantage*,[16] Marti Laney explains how the brain chemistry of introverts differs from that of extroverts. All too briefly, it can be explained thus: messages are carried in our brains by neurotransmitters, each of which travels a different pathway, directing how much blood flows to brain centers. The neurotransmitter acetylcholine, which is associated with introversion, travels a longer and more complex pathway than does the neurotransmitter dopamine, which is linked to extroversion. Laney cites research indicating that, in introverts, acetylcholine carries more blood to the brain centers connected with inner experience, such as remembering, problem solving, and planning. In extroverts, dopamine takes more blood to areas of the brain related to sight, sound, taste, and touch that connect to external events. Accordingly, extroverts are more comfortable in situations that provide plenty of external stimuli, while introverts welcome quiet opportunities to reflect on internal experience.

Extroverts also have better access to the sympathetic (fight or flight) nervous system, and introverts to the parasympathetic (stop and examine) nervous system. There is some thought that the uneven balance in numbers between extroverts and introverts in the population may be due to survival needs: when a prehistoric tribe was attacked, the extroverts chose "fight" and rushed out to protect the group by direct confrontation, while a few introverts assessed the situation and hurried the children into the cave. The introverts were just as important to the survival of the group as the extroverts, but they were needed in fewer numbers.

True to its title, Laney's book emphasizes the positives of being introverted, and it offers suggestions to help introverted people appreciate and protect their gifts in a world in which they are in the minority. Because it is full of "Aha!" moments for those who will recognize traits of introversion in themselves, it is one of the adult nonfiction books annotated in Chapter 8.

For introverted students, the requirement that they act like extroverts for the entire school day exacts a toll. Kiersey and Bates suggest
that introverted children are often vulnerable in school, misunderstood and expected to change. To give them time to compensate,
parents and caregivers should respect their need for time alone after
school.[17]

> *In the question period after a parents' meeting on stress
> in gifted children, a mother expressed concern because
> her son resisted her attempts to sign him up for a full
> schedule of after-school programs. "Maybe he's an intro-
> vert," the speaker suggested. "Oh, no," the mother
> responded. "He gets along very well with people!" The
> speaker explained that many introverts do, only they
> need to do so for less time than extroverts. In fact, the
> speaker revealed, she herself was an introvert, and yet
> here she was, voluntarily speaking to a group. Once the
> mother realized that introversion is not a negative and
> certainly does not preclude getting along with people, she
> was ready to reconsider her son's need for alone time after
> school.*

Gifted children, and adults too, can use time alone productively;
in fact, they may well be far less productive if they do not have it.
Gathering large amounts of information, they require more time to
assimilate it; producing creative work, they require more incubation
time. However, the gifted child who enjoys being alone may secretly
believe that something is wrong with him. Parents should reassure
him and support the legitimate need for time alone, showing patience
with a child who spends hours apparently doing nothing, playing
with blocks, taking things apart, daydreaming seemingly without
purpose while chores remain undone. One such child later, as a college junior, worked on a medical research project at a major teaching
hospital, contributing his ability to "play" freely with computers as he
developed new ways to graph test results. He linked this ability to the
hours he had spent happily alone in a garage filled with treasures,
experimenting to learn how things worked—"useless" alone time

that fostered his current productivity. Studies of eminent adults have found that they typically had many hours of alone time as children.[18]

Gifted people who have developed a sense of inner-directedness and a protective attitude toward their own abilities may sense that time spent with other people can hold them back. Their characteristic intensity may keep them at their work for long periods of time, and time spent socializing can seem to them to be wasted. It may take years for them to recognize the value of relaxed time with other people, and they may always struggle for a satisfactory balance between time alone and time with others.

> *Ten-year-old Jesse came home from school every day to lose himself in books. For him, this was replenishment for his soul; for his mother, it was a source of concern. Usually she was silent, reflecting that after an hour or so of reading, Jesse was glad to go outside and play, and he was a welcome friend both at school and in his neighborhood. One afternoon, however, she ventured, "Jesse, you're always reading. Why don't you invite a friend over tomorrow?" Looking up in surprise from his book, Jesse said, "But Mom—some of my best friends are books!"*
>
> *Pondering his words later, Jesse's mother realized that Jesse was right. In books, he communed with authors whose interests and intensity matched his own—something he found in no child in the neighborhood. In coming home to read after school, Jesse was seeking his own balance.*

In *The Magic Bookshelf*,[19] Janie and Richard Jarvis relate the story of an elderly man who looks back over the interesting people he has known—and suddenly realizes that many of them were characters in books. These authors point out that while reading—a solitary activity—may seem lonely to non-readers, to avid readers, it is one of the pathways to an enriched life.

Being Alone and Feeling Unaccepted

Adults who watch a child spend time alone often fear that the child is lonely. However, gifted children who are busy with books, collections, music, or other favorite pursuits may not *feel* lonely. Instead, they may sense that they do not fit in with other children, and this is their response to the feeling of not belonging, which adults must monitor and try to guide. These children may feel different, isolated, and as though they *should* interact with other children. The following are some typical coping behaviors.

Fitting In

Gifted youngsters may respond to feelings of differentness by actively trying to fit in, and they do this by downplaying their abilities. Consequently, some children purposely produce mediocre work in school. By the time they complete sixth grade, this can become a pattern—one that becomes difficult to change as time goes on. Specifically, gifted girls are likely to lower their aspirations during the junior high years in ways that will profoundly affect their futures;[20] gifted boys may hide their academic ability in order to appear sufficiently masculine.[21]

Drawing Attention

Children who wish to belong to a peer group sometimes use another ploy: attracting attention to themselves. Capitalizing on their differences may be the only way they know to do this. For gifted children, this can mean showing off their knowledge or using sarcasm or condescension with other children—behavior that will most likely cause even more rejection.

> *Kirsten was a mature second grader with the highly critical nature that gifted children sometimes develop. Feeling insecure when she entered a new school, she adopted the role of class police officer, letting her classmates know when they did not measure up to her standards and too often informing the teacher of their failings. What began as her own fear of rejection led quickly enough to actual rebuff from her new classmates.*

> *A sympathetic teacher or other adult could help lead Kirsten toward better self-understanding, as well as helping her to enhance her social skills.*

Arrogance

In a few cases, a gifted child will display a sense of elitism or arrogance toward others who are not as able. Such an inappropriate response to a feeling of not belonging is more likely to occur in gifted children who do not understand giftedness. Self-acceptance must come before acceptance of others. If parents and teachers have not helped gifted children to understand themselves, the children are hampered in developing self-acceptance, and an *appearance* of arrogance may result—a defensive move by a child who is simply unaware and uncertain of how to relate to others.

Withdrawal

Some gifted children make no attempt to fit in but withdraw instead. They may spend a great deal of time reading, which causes concern for adults. (Negative aspects of reading too much are discussed in Chapter 3.) However, spending large amounts of time reading is not necessarily unhealthy for gifted youngsters. They may use this time as part of their identity search—reading for various role models, identifying with different characters, working out the basic question: Who am I? They may identify with undesirable characters some of the time, but usually this is only temporary.

Friendship Skills

Children who do not feel as though they are part of a group may need to develop better social skills. This can be especially difficult for those who experienced rejection from other children or from parents when they were young and who learned to protect themselves by getting along on their own. It is hard for these children to recognize that they do indeed need others and that they can take the first steps toward being a friend. School gifted programs that devote time to discussion of friendship skills can help, and parents can teach the concepts at home. The books listed under "Relationships with Others" in Chapter 8 of this book can help because they portray children learning how to be friends, or in the case of nonfiction, they directly teach about friendship.

Being Alone by Being Different

Being alone—that is, standing apart, being alone because one is different and quite deliberately being oneself—is something that almost all gifted children will have to accept at some time. They know that they are different, but they may not know, unless a trusted adult tells them, *why* they are different. As has been said earlier, knowledge of their giftedness and acceptance of their differences are very important steps in the search for identity.

It takes courage to be oneself—to be different and to like oneself despite the difference. This courage takes time to develop, and it must be done during that stage in life when conformity seems most important. Some gifted children need a great deal of support from parents, teachers, and other adults to move through this period successfully. Their independence and autonomous style must be incorporated into their identities, while at the same time, they must learn to get along with others. Fortunately, the importance of standing alone is a common theme in literature; it is easy to find books to promote discussion and guidance on this issue.

Relationships with Others

For all of us, one key to emotional well-being is to strike a balance between seeing ourselves as individuals and seeing ourselves as members of a society. While the latter can be harder for gifted people, they, as much as anyone, need the nurturing warmth of good relationships.

Gifted children often see things from unusual points of view that others cannot share, so others often misunderstand them. These children are even different from other gifted children: people at the upper ranges of intelligence differ from one another far more than people in the middle and lower ranges.

At the same time, friends are extremely important to most gifted children. Their eagerness to communicate with others shows itself very early. Consider the gifted toddler who stood up in his stroller, waved his arms, and crowed with delightful greeting whenever he saw another baby being pushed toward him—the very picture of emotional overexcitability. The response was usually a languid glance from the other child, yet until he outgrew his stroller, this toddler continued his enthusiastic greetings.

Parents often worry that their gifted child will have trouble fitting in socially, and they sometimes encourage educational decisions that hold the child back academically in order to favor social development. However, Pendarvis, Howley, and Howley noted long ago that there is:

> ...*no empirical evidence to support the belief that gifted children are socially incompetent. Rather, it seems that they are socially competent but that some gifted children, because of their preference for activities that engage their intellect, avoid social interaction with age-mates. They may prefer the company of older children or adults; or they may prefer solitary activities, such as reading. These preferences do not indicate emotional problems, nor do they appear to have a detrimental effect on gifted children's emotional well-being.*[22]

It seems, then, that parents should not worry but should accept their child's pattern of friendship, which may differ from adult expectations but may suit the child very well.

Finding Peers

Parents can play an important role in helping gifted children accomplish the two most important tasks that they face in building relationships with others: finding peers, and getting along with people of widely varying abilities. The special problem that gifted children have in finding friends is not that they are loners, but that they need at least a few friends who can function on their level and with whom they can speak as equals. As Kerr points out:

> *...whenever verbally gifted students find themselves in conversations with individuals of lower verbal ability, they may be constantly trimming their conversation to fit the group. Particularly tactful verbally gifted students may conscientiously avoid using long words and discussing topics about which their agemates are ignorant. However, years of attempting to relate to people of lesser verbal ability may transform the talkative and friendly gifted student into a sarcastic cynic.[23]*

Most of all, gifted children need a friend who can listen with understanding. Therefore, although they differ markedly from one another, their greatest social need is for friendships with other gifted children. Given the opportunity, gifted children often choose friends who match their intellectual age rather than their chronological age. Without such friendships, they may shrivel both emotionally and intellectually, but with them, they can thrive.

Getting along with others, then, means first finding appropriate others. The stratified grading arrangement in most schools makes it difficult for gifted children to find one another unless special arrangements are made by their parents or teachers. A gifted child may need to belong to several different groups—not necessarily of her own age—that will challenge her intellectually and introduce her to people with whom she can share her passionate interests.

This can be demanding and exhausting for parents. In order for one middle school student to join an adult astronomy group, his mother drove him to weekly meetings at a planetarium an hour away, arriving back home between one and two in the morning. Another family drove their daughter five hours each way every other week for two years to allow the child to play in a university youth symphony. These parents understood their children's need to share their interests with other youth, and they were willing to sacrifice time and energy to provide for that need.

Other Children

Getting along with others also means getting along with those who don't share one's abilities and interests, let alone understanding or respecting them. In classrooms where there are only one or two gifted students, a gifted child is likely to alienate his classmates because he can do schoolwork so easily.

A subtler cause of resentment may occur because of the intense interest that gifted children have in topics that do not interest their classmates. If they talk too long about their shell collections or use words that are too big, they can bore and alienate themselves from other students without understanding why. A lack of interest in seashells can quickly become a lack of interest in Tim, who talks about seashells all the time. And even before this happens, Tim may *feel* that it has happened—that the rejection of seashells is a rejection of him.

Gifted children are usually extremely sensitive, and remarks that most children toss off and forget can truly hurt them. They do not understand how lightly other children may make a cruel remark, and others have no idea how long and deeply the gifted child may brood over what is said. But the gifted child, if hurt, even if she was once as eager for friends as the baby in the stroller, begins to build a wall of defense, making it even harder to develop friendships.

Team sports are not interesting to some gifted children, and if they've been academically accelerated or skipped a grade, their physical coordination may not match that of their classmates. In most schools, a lukewarm attitude toward team sports or a lack of athletic ability can be another wedge between gifted children and their peers.

So gifted children can begin to feel rejected for a variety of reasons, and since giftedness does not necessarily include social maturity, these youngsters react in the same ways that most children do to feelings of rejection: they withdraw or act out. Either choice brings still further rejection, and a downward cycle begins.

To reverse this cycle, children must take several steps that require maturity, as well as adult guidance: they must develop empathy with those who are not as quick as they are, they must learn to cope with being misunderstood and teased, and they must recognize and modify the behavior that leads to rejection and teasing—all of this while retaining their own identities.

Parents and Teachers

Getting along with peers is the most obvious problem of getting along with others; however, gifted children can find themselves in other situations that may cause emotional problems, both at home and at school. These youngsters are vulnerable, and the attitudes that they perceive in significant adults can make a tremendous difference in their attitudes toward themselves and their giftedness.

Parents

Parents who accept their child's giftedness may be relieved to have the school confirm what they already suspected—especially if a suitable program is available and they have an opportunity to join other parents in support programs for the gifted students in the community.

Undeniably, parenting a gifted child places an extra strain on the parents' time, energy, and money. Whether or not parents have enough of these resources, their support can make all the difference. In some cases, memories of their own gifted childhoods can add richly to the support that they offer to their child. If a gifted child has difficulty in finding peers, his parents may be his best friends for a time. A child in such a family sees that giftedness is worthy of the effort needed to develop it, but there's a fine line between encouragement and pressure.

> *Raphael has studied piano for six years, and his teacher is pleased with his progress. When he enters ninth grade, however, homework, soccer, and the ski team will all demand more time, and he is considering dropping piano lessons. His parents are proud of his musical talent, which they believe is greater than his athletic ability, yet if they urge him to continue with piano, are they pressuring him to work beyond his endurance? Or are they encouraging him to develop a talent that could*

> *be a satisfying source of pleasure, relaxation, and artistic*
> *expression throughout his adulthood? To find an answer,*
> *they must make time for careful discussion with Raphael—*
> *discussion that includes listening to Raphael's ideas and*
> *reassurances to him of their support.*

By contrast, some parents want their child to be just like everyone else, and they try to ignore the evidence that the child is gifted. Such parents may refuse to place their child in a gifted program, preferring to believe that the school has made a mistake. Or parents may acknowledge signs of giftedness in their child but still refuse appropriate educational programs in the hope that avoiding a special program will help the child to be "normal." Either of these responses amounts to rejection of the child as she is and pressure or insistence that she be someone else. It can also mean failure to provide opportunities for enrichment or for college. The effect on the child's life can be devastating.

Giftedness may appear to some to be a "high-class problem"—a problem that any parent would be pleased to have—but parents of gifted children know that it is also exhausting, sometimes frightening, and always challenging. As awareness of giftedness grows, more books for parents are published. Many of them are referenced in this book.

Teachers

Gifted children can make themselves unpopular with teachers, especially with those who do not know about or are not sympathetic to the special characteristics and needs of the gifted. One grandmother still recalls with an inner cringe the scorn in her second-grade teacher's voice when she foolishly gave an answer from a few pages beyond the assigned reading. "You weren't supposed to read ahead!" the teacher accused. The child hadn't learned yet that in some classrooms, it is necessary to conceal such out-of-bounds curiosity.

Teachers whose energies are stretched as they try to meet the needs of a wide range of students may not always appreciate bright children who come up with many creative responses instead of the one "right" answer. Such students can go right to the heart of a lesson plan while the teacher slowly presents it to the rest of the class; these children's enthusiasm—or lack of tact—makes it hard for them to keep their insights to themselves. Consider the fifth grader who announced that the book the class had read was so simple that it would be easy to write a sequel. He then proceeded, on the spot, to outline a very plausible plot, making both the original and the sequel sound ridiculously trite. The teacher, who fortunately appreciated and respected this boy's giftedness and therefore was able to handle the situation well, laughed with the group and waited until everyone had enjoyed the spontaneous humor before going on to a productive discussion.

But even teachers who seek out and encourage gifted students find them frustrating at times. One excellent teacher told a gifted fourth grader's mother about a field trip they had taken. "He was at my elbow talking the whole day. I wanted to listen because everything he says is worth hearing, but I have to listen to the others, too!" she said with exasperation that the mother could well understand.

Many gifted children are analytic thinkers, highly critical of the status quo and only too willing to express an opinion about how things are being run. It is especially important for them to learn early how and when to question authority, as well as how important and effective politeness and respect can be. Parents' early efforts to teach these lessons to preschoolers will pay off when school starts. If both parents and teachers can enjoy giftedness yet also can understand—and gently modify—the negative traits that can go along with it, the child's self-acceptance and ability to get along with others, both adults and children, will be greatly enhanced.

Using Abilities

Psychologist Abraham Maslow's "hierarchy of needs"[24] is useful in conceptualizing steps that gifted children must take in order to grow into adults who make full use of their abilities. Maslow and his successors have arranged human needs into eight levels, from those so basic that life depends on them to those so advanced that only a few can feel and meet them. He makes the point that these needs

37

must be met in a certain order—that is, until the primary needs are met, we are not free to even sense the higher ones.

Of Maslow's four basic needs, the most fundamental are the physiological needs for nourishment—food and water—and bodily comforts. Safety and security needs come next. Only when we feel safe and secure can we experience the third level of needs, for belonging and love. When we are confident that we are accepted by others and welcome in our family and among friends, we are ready to sense the fourth basic need: esteem, first from others—initially we want others to respect us and to value the work we do—and then from ourselves. When we begin to gain confidence in our work and achieve mastery by our own standards, we have reached the highest goal of the basic needs: self-esteem.

Armed with a healthy self-esteem, we are able to move to the advanced needs—Maslow's "growth" needs that enable the individual to continue to develop mentally and emotionally. The fifth level in the hierarchy is the need to learn, to know and understand the world around us. The sixth focuses on aesthetics as we seek order and beauty in the world. The seventh and eighth levels, achieved by only a few, are for self-actualization (realizing one's potential) and finally for self-transcendence, helping others to reach their potential to improve the world.

How does Maslow's system illuminate the path that gifted children will take toward being able to make full use of their abilities? If we assume that the needs of the first two levels are met, we can start at the third level, belonging and love. Gifted children, as already mentioned, are especially prone to feelings of not belonging. After all, they're "different," and a sense of fitting in and being appreciated can be hard to come by. Developing self-esteem and finding appropriate opportunities to learn and to express aesthetic interest and talent can also be a problem.

If, despite obstacles, the needs at these levels are met, a gifted person may still have great difficulty with self-actualization—and yet some soar even to the eighth level, transcending themselves to help others reach their potential. As a gifted child matures, these issues have a profound impact on his ability to lead a satisfying life as an adult.

In reaching toward full use of their abilities, gifted students may find that even some of their own personal characteristics can paralyze them, making progress difficult. The following are some barriers that may hinder them.

Reluctance to Take Risks

To realize their full potential as adults, high-ability children must make decisions that enable them to develop that potential. Often, especially among young children, these children are not aware that they are making life-shaping decisions. But choices made at an early age, seemingly minor at the time, have a cumulative effect on how well-prepared a person will be to take advantage of opportunities in the college years and beyond.

> *As an eighth grader attending his first statewide church youth meeting, Nels felt out of place and wanted to leave early. A counselor spent an hour talking with him about his concerns and finally persuaded him to stay through the weekend. By the next day, Nels was comfortable enough to volunteer for a minor position in the organization.*
>
> *After a year of involvement at the state level, Nels was chosen to attend a national meeting, where he was selected to serve on the national council. Holding leadership positions at two annual meetings gave him the confidence and experience to win a scholarship for a summer program in Japan before his senior year in high school. This helped him gain a merit scholarship at a top-ranked university.*
>
> *Although much of this might have happened in any case, Nels still traces his rich experiences to that Saturday afternoon years ago when a counselor persuaded him to see the weekend through, and he still makes risk-taking decisions with that example in mind. His decisions have kept options open for him and have put him in a position to become a self-actualized adult.*

Whether or not to use all of one's potential becomes an issue early in the educational process. Gifted children often feel society's ambivalence toward those with high intellectual ability, and they may decide to understate their ability in order to just get along.[25] The second grader who read ahead was faced with a decision: would she read ahead again? The fifth grader who is aware that she answers too many questions in class and begins rationing how many she will answer per day is dealing with this issue, too, although she does not see it that way. The middle school student who lets his grades slide because fitting into a social group is more important than achieving academically is making decisions that will ultimately affect his potential for personal development. All of these children are making choices based on their reluctance to take the risk of social failure, giving little or no thought to the long-range consequences.

Perfectionism

Perfectionism, another common characteristic of gifted individuals, is yet another problem. While balanced perfectionism manifests itself as a healthy pursuit of excellence, when added to the intensity that also characterizes gifted students, perfectionism can become unbalanced and have a negative effect on children's lives. Perfectionists have unrealistically high standards for their performance and may feel worthless if they do not meet those standards. Since they equate flawless performance with self-worth, they may become unwilling to attempt a task that they're not certain they can perform well from the start. Their perfectionism thus puts them under severe stress.

To counteract perfectionism and learn to take risks, gifted children must see that failure is not disastrous. They must think of themselves not as perfect, but as experimenters.

> *Caitlin has always been a superb student, but now, in the eleventh grade, she has to work harder than she has in the past to maintain her A average. She spends extra hours on her homework, leaving little time for social activities. She's become tense and has frequent headaches. The debate coach has been looking forward to Caitlin's*

joining the team this year, but now Caitlin is reluctant;
she's never spoken in public and isn't sure how she'll do. If
she doesn't join the team, she'll be narrowing her experi-
ences, when she should be broadening her outlook and
options. If she joins, she probably will make some mis-
takes, and she can learn that life goes on after a defeat.
And having to manage her time more carefully will make
her establish priorities. She may also realize that she is
valuable to the team, even when she doesn't win.

As awareness has grown of the corrosive potential of perfectionism among gifted children, experts in the field of giftedness have
weighed in. Opinions vary slightly regarding definitions and causes,
but all offer valuable insights and suggestions.

One possible cause of perfectionism, according to Kerr,[26] is that
the child is unaware of her giftedness and so believes that her superior
performance is based entirely on her own efforts. Perfectionism may
also be due to an overemphasis by parents or schools on systems of
rewards or "points" for achievement rather than on doing well for the
pure pleasure of it.

To change perfectionism from a destructive paralysis to a positive
pursuit of excellence, Kerr suggests that students need to learn to set
priorities, recognizing that they cannot be perfect in all areas at once.
Parents and teachers can encourage these children to ask themselves
which is more important, the science report or the math test, or to
consider whether it would be better to take time for a long relaxing
walk rather than re-writing tomorrow's essay yet again. Davis[27] offers
helpful suggestions for parents, teachers, and counselors to help students find solutions to what he calls "neurotic" or "dysfunctional"
perfectionism.

Silverman[28] provides a detailed analysis of recent research, concluding
that perfectionism can be healthy. She encourages counselors, teachers,
and parents to help children "channel" their perfectionism. Among her
suggestions are that adults accept perfectionism as a natural component of giftedness, manage their own perfectionism, and (echoing

Kerr) help children set priorities and learn to choose the area(s) on which they will concentrate.

In *Freeing Our Families from Perfectionism*, Greenspon suggests that perfectionism, which he perceives as negative, is integrally related to family dynamics; overcoming it means change for each person in the family system, with benefits for everyone.[29] Greenspon has also written a book for children: *What to Do When Good Enough Isn't Good Enough: The Real Deal on Perfectionism: A Guide for Kids*, which is annotated in Chapter 8.

Adderholdt and Goldberg, authors of *Perfectionism: What's Bad about Being Too Good?*[30] which is also annotated in Chapter 8, speak directly to teenagers about how perfectionism works and ways to manage it. Among their many suggestions is to read for pleasure as a reward to oneself for work well done.

Lack of Motivation

Another problem related to the full use of ability for gifted and intellectually curious students is low motivation, or underachievement, which has several possible causes. One is lack of challenge in the curriculum. In many classrooms where teachers struggle with a wide range in ability levels among 25-30 children, some students are not appropriately challenged. For the gifted and the highly gifted, this is almost certainly the case unless some accommodation is in place for them.

A second and pervasive cause of low motivation among the gifted is the fear that their high intelligence will lead to rejection by peers. They can decide surprisingly early to hide their abilities in order to fit in, and some find that after several years of not performing, they have missed some important basic skills.[31] Suspecting and fearing that they are no longer able to perform at a high level, they resist trying. Underachievement then becomes a pattern that is hard to break. Adolescent girls are especially at risk if they believe that they must choose between academic achievement and popularity or intimacy.[32] Common issues for underachievement in gifted boys include social immaturity, emotional problems, antisocial behavior, and a low self-concept.[33]

There are other, far more complex reasons for insufficient motivation that are beyond the scope of this book, Teachers, parents, and
counselors may wish to consult other resources by educators and psychologists who focus more specifically on this issue.[34]

Multipotentiality

According to Kerr,[35] multipotentiality frequently shows up in elementary school, when students who perform well in several or all
school subjects have great difficulty, for example, choosing a report
topic from several options and then finishing the project because
their many interests lead them off-track. This pattern of excellence in
school subjects combined with difficulty in making choices and
following through continues through middle school. In senior high,
multipotential students may have problems with college and career
decisions, often displaying "high flat profiles" on aptitude and interest tests. These profiles lack the peaks and valleys of most students'
profiles, offering no areas of relative strength or weakness to guide
them in life decisions, and they lead adults to make the obvious but
unhelpful statement, "You can do anything you want to do!"

"Multipotentiality is most commonly a concern of students with
moderately high IQs (120-140), those who are academically
talented, and those who have two or more outstanding but very different abilities such as violin virtuosity and mathematics precocity,"
notes Kerr.[36] Choosing among areas that offer equal promise of different success experiences is surely painful, but one lifetime does not
provide time for excellence in several demanding fields of endeavor. If
these students resist narrowing and prioritizing their activities, they
jeopardize their chances of achieving significantly in any area. The
result can be poor career decision making and, ultimately, dissatisfac-
tion with career choice.

Low External Expectations

Gifted youngsters may fail to make full use of their abilities
because they are never given a chance to appreciate their own potential. A gifted student in a typical classroom can make A's without

much effort, and both the student and her parents may believe that the high grade means that she is not only fine but is doing as well as she can. In fact, the grade may mean only that the student has met the expectations set by that teacher or has performed at the top of what may be an average class. The teacher may not be aware that the student could accomplish much more. Thus, the student is deprived of opportunities to meet academic challenge and as a result fails to learn persistence and resiliency in the face of difficult tasks.

Lack of Appropriate Internal Expectations

Earning the best grade available does not necessarily equate with doing the best work that a gifted student is capable of doing, but what that "best" would be is never pointed out to some students. Since high grades and other measures of external expectations are not a reliable guide, it is desirable for gifted students at an early age to learn to assess their own potential and then to be the judge of whether or not it has been realized. This is a complex process requiring guidance from adults who recognize high ability, even if latent. With such guidance, students can learn to recognize the feeling—the joy—of doing well for its own sake.

Why is it important that gifted individuals use all of their resources? One obvious answer is that we need all the talent we have available to help us solve the world's problems. For the gifted student, it is more to the point to recognize that he will simply be happier and more satisfied—life will be much more interesting—if he learns to understand and manage his intensity and creativity. Little research has been done on the gifted adult, so we have no clear idea of the long-term impact of not making full use of one's abilities,[37] but Maslow's hierarchy points to the importance of being accepted, useful, valued, and free to use whatever talent one has.

How Books Can Help

Stories help us guide the social and emotional development of our gifted children when they touch the emotions. A skillful author can make us care about characters who have the same problems as those presented in this chapter. If a book can "hook" a child emotionally, she may be far more receptive to the ideas than if they are presented in a lecture by a concerned adult.

A child who is unwilling or unable to talk about things that are bothering him, or perhaps even to admit them to himself, can often identify with a character in a book ("*He's* bored in school, too!") strongly enough to experience an emotional release—a catharsis—when that character undergoes an emotional experience. He can also acquire some insights into his own situation. This process, often called bibliotherapy, is discussed in detail in Chapter 4.

Chapter 2

The Mind of the Child: Intellectual Development

The first edition of this book went to press in 1987, the year Diane Ravitch and Chester E. Finn, Jr. published *What Do Our 17-Year-Olds Know? A Report on the First National Assessment of History and Literature,*[1] one of the first calls to action regarding our nation's school system. Soon the rising awareness of crisis in our educational system generated a storm of studies and programs to reform and restructure the schools, resulting in major new developments such as mainstreaming, homeschooling, competency tests, and charter schools. In the early years of the 21st century, while concerns over terrorism and war overshadowed domestic issues, our nation's public schools continued to struggle with questions that had been raised more than 20 years earlier.

The world of gifted education has not been unaffected by these events. Any consideration of the intellectual needs of gifted and high-potential youngsters must be set within the context in which they currently live and go to school. What do these children need for optimum intellectual development? What obstacles face teachers and school administrations as they try to meet those needs? How can parents identify gaps and compensate for them at home? And what is the role of books and reading?

The Need for Intellectual Development

While concern for the *emotional* development of bright and gifted children is a relatively new addition to the educational scene, efforts to help them meet their *intellectual* potential have long been discussed, researched, and implemented. In many school districts, tests and inventories help determine IQs and learning characteristics of even very young gifted children.[2]

Some universities have developed programs to prepare teachers in gifted education. One of these, the Center for Gifted Education at the College of William and Mary, provides curricula in language arts, mathematics, science, and social studies for high-ability learners that can be used by parents and teachers of gifted students wherever they may be.[3] Other universities focus on providing students with special opportunities. For example, the Indiana Academy invites gifted Indiana students to spend their junior and senior years of high school on a small campus near Ball State University, where they can benefit from being with other bright teens and from the nearby university. In addition, there are several talent search programs that offer challenging summer programs for gifted students in grades 7-12. These include Northwestern University, Johns Hopkins University, Duke University, and the University of Iowa.

The programs above offer valuable resources for gifted children and the adults who teach them. However, the implementation of gifted education in local schools varies dramatically, leaving families frustrated in their search for the best schools for their children. As of 2005, only one state requires coursework in gifted education for regular classroom teachers, and less than half the states require that teachers working in specialized programs for the gifted and talented have graduate credits or a teaching certificate with an endorsement in gifted education. In 2007, 40% of the states in the U.S. did not require public schools to identify and serve gifted children.[4]

As our high-potential students attempt to find their place in the sun, they receive mixed messages from the world around them. Pointing to the impact of anti-intellectualism in American society, *National Excellence: A Case for Developing America's Talent*, a 1993 report on the education of gifted children in the United States, attests:

> *As a culture, we admire and reward the brilliant, creative mind after it has invented something practical or produced tangible results. Yet we are not inclined to support those who want to pursue an artistic or intellectual life, and we find ways of discouraging those who wish to do so.... [Responding to this discouragement,] students say they want to do well, but not exceptionally well, because it is more important to be accepted by the "in crowd" (which) is not the "brain crowd."*[5]

A little more than a decade later, a powerful book titled *Genius Denied: How to Stop Wasting Our Brightest Young Minds* by philanthropists Jan and Bob Davidson highlighted the same message.[6] In this book, Professor Tracy Cross, the Executive Director of the Indiana Academy, commented on the recent trends in education:

> *In essence, being passionate about academics holds no currency in schools that plan for the masses and put their focus on minimum-competency tests. What does hold value in such a setting? Compliance, complacency, a friendly, outgoing personality, and enthusiasm for working in groups are valued. Showing interest and participating in "in-the-moment," teacher-led activities, plus "going along," are often the lessons learned.*[7]

The path is not smooth for our gifted students—especially those whose interests are academic or intellectual. While they may find excellent educational offerings in their schools, these are certainly not universal. Their fellow students—and in some cases, their teachers—do not necessarily understand and welcome their gifts or their interests. And the manner in which their intellectual needs are addressed—or not—will have an impact on their current and future emotional development.

We must begin by recognizing that intellectual development is an emotional need for some intellectually gifted people, especially the highly gifted. In fact, psychologist Dr. James T. Webb asserts that "profoundly gifted children are ones for whom intellectual stimulation and/or creative expression are clearly emotional needs that may appear to be as intense as the physiological needs of hunger or thirst."[8] Dr. Linda Silverman concurs, stating that the neglect of appropriate educational opportunities for gifted children "affects their morale, motivation, social relationships, aspirations, sense of self-worth, and emotional development."[9] For these students, meeting intellectual needs is not a purely intellectual task; there is a driving force behind it that must not be denied. Adults who seek to help gifted children grow will be most effective if they acknowledge and reinforce this imperative to learn.

Imagine the frustration of an athlete who isn't allowed to run, jump, or swim. This gives some inkling of the frustration of a bright child denied the chance to challenge her mind. To have curiosity satisfied; to experience a wealth of diversity in ideas, places, and people; to explore all the world and find a place in it—all of this is a legitimate need for these youngsters. Ultimately, meeting that need will benefit all of us.

Intellectual Needs as Emotional Needs

A bright or gifted child has extraordinary abilities, each accompanied by needs—a need for the ability to be developed and used, and a need for the child possessing it to become creative and eventually able to produce something of value to himself or others. For unusually talented people, the point is not merely that where there is an ability, it is best to develop it. Rather, an intellectually gifted child will not be happy or complete, and certainly not self-fulfilled, until he is using his intellectual ability at a level approaching his full capacity. It is important that parents and teachers see intellectual development as a requirement for these children and not merely an interest, a flair, or a phase they will outgrow. One young artist explains, "I have a hard time *not* painting. I paint about 10 hours a day. Painting is my life." Another student says simply, "I read because I can't help it."[10] It is often harder work—less relaxing—for an intellectually gifted person to read lightweight material than to dig into a book that has some hefty new information to offer. Gifted adults who relax by learning to play a musical instrument or by reading in a foreign language are expressing the same drive for mental stimulation. These activities are not work for them; they are pathways to being fully alive.

Recognizing intellectual development as a need can help parents cope with the frustration that they may feel when a child reads or tinkers or practices an instrument for "too many" hours per day. It can also help teachers find patience when a child insists on working endlessly on a project or report, threatening to hold up the progress of the rest of the class.

Intellectual Overexcitability

A helpful way of thinking about this drive to understand comes from Kazimierz Dabrowski's intriguing ideas about developmental potential, which were introduced in Chapter 1, and his concept of intellectual overexcitability. These ideas can help adults appreciate not only the need for intellectual development, but also the strength of feeling behind it.

Piechowski, a student of Dabrowski, listed characteristics of intellectual overexcitability that may be familiar to those who deal with gifted youngsters: probing questions, problem solving, curiosity, concentration, capacity for sustained intellectual effort, voracious reading and starting on difficult books at a young age, a wide variety of interests, theoretical thinking (thinking about thinking, moral thinking, development of a hierarchy of values), independence of thought (often expressed in criticism), and processes of self-monitoring and self-evaluation.[11] All of these characteristics are part of the drive to learn, to know, and to understand.

Piechowski also states that intellectual overexcitability has more to do with "striving for understanding, probing the unknown, and love of truth than with learning per se and academic achievement."[12] More recently, he describes it as "an avidity for knowledge and the search for truth—expressed as discovery, questioning, and love of ideas and theoretical analysis."[13] It is this extra sense of urgency about *knowing* that underlies the need of some gifted children for intellectual development and that causes them to say, "I read because I can't help it."

Intellectual overexcitability, like the other overexcitabilities that Dabrowski lists, is not always understood or valued by those who may not discern how it contributes to the development of gifted individuals. Thus, gifted students quickly realize that it is often best to diminish their enthusiasm for learning. To counteract this dampening that may occur in a mixed-ability classroom, reading and book discussion with other gifted students can provide a welcome venue for expressing intellectual interests in a setting where these students can be accepted.

"Can you tell your readers how awful it feels when you have to go for two days without reading?" asked one young man when he learned that I was writing this book. A 19-year-old German student described to me why he was drawn toward a career in university teaching: "When I read about culture, then I am happy!" Both of these young men exhibit the unusual intellectual intensity that Piechowski describes.

Not everyone who has high intelligence also has a passionate interest in intellectual pursuits. For those who do, however, learning about the work of Dabrowski and Piechowski often brings reassurance, along with a shock of self-recognition.

The Child in Charge

Some bright children seem to lose touch with their drive to understand. Although as preschoolers they were exceptionally eager to learn, by the middle elementary grades, their intellectual curiosity appears to be dulled, and they are willing to settle for half-hearted efforts in school. "A lot of research shows that if gifted people aren't challenged, after a while they lose interest in challenging themselves," says Judith Shuey, who heads PEG, a high school/college program for gifted girls at Mary Baldwin College.[14]

Just as gifted children must achieve a sense of identity that incorporates their unusual abilities, so must they recognize early that the drive to understand is part of who they are.[15] At the preschool and primary levels, parents and teachers should help talented children know this about themselves: learning is a source of pleasure for them. The acknowledgement *"I enjoy learning"* should be integrated into their developing self-concepts.

Whatever steps adults take to satisfy the child's curiosity and enrich her experience, their underlying attitude that learning is important—not only for its own sake, but also *to the child*—is vital and must gradually be adopted by the child. Ultimately, the responsibility for keeping curiosity both satisfied and piqued must shift to the child as she makes decisions that enable her to continue learning. The knowledge that she *needs* to learn and that it is up to her to meet that need is part of her survival kit.

Characteristics and Needs

Many writers in the field of gifted education provide lists of intellectual characteristics of gifted children at all ages, and these behaviors are sometimes used in conjunction with scores on ability tests, such as the CogAT (Cognitive Abilities Test), to determine eligibility for school gifted programs. Lists of intellectual characteristics can also be used as a springboard for identifying the intellectual needs that they imply. The following compilation of three such lists[16] groups intellectual characteristics of gifted youngsters into three categories: verbal, thought-processing, and performance. Following each set of characteristics is a list of related intellectual needs, derived in part from Dr. Barbara Clark's examples of problems that may appear in work patterns or in getting along with others if the needs are not met.[17]

Verbal Characteristics and Needs

Gifted children in general:

○ have a large vocabulary and are able to use advanced terminology correctly

○ read early and may be self-taught; read enthusiastically and widely, often above grade level; select reading material purposefully and enjoy challenging books

○ understand language subtleties and use language for humor

○ write words and sentences early and produce superior creative writing (poetry, stories, plays)

○ display verbal ability in self-expression, choice of colorful and descriptive phrasing, and ease in learning a second language

To challenge and nurture verbal abilities, gifted students need to do the following:

○ use their full vocabulary and develop it further with intellectual peers

○ read books at an appropriate intellectual and emotional level

○ be introduced to books that represent a variety of literary conventions and styles and that use language gracefully

○ express ideas verbally and in depth by writing or speaking with others who challenge and thus refine their views and concepts

Thought-Processing Characteristics and Needs

Most gifted children display the following traits in thought processing:

○ enjoy experimenting and can generate original ideas and solutions

○ give evidence of divergent thinking, offering responses that are atypical rather than the convergent answers expected of most children and found in the teacher's answer book

○ accept open-ended situations and questions at an early age and do not require immediate solutions; can accept ambiguity

○ enjoy complexity and may try to create it—for example, by adding rules to games

- ○ have unusual power to process information, using logic, abstract thinking, and symbolic thought

- ○ show flexibility of thought and seek alternatives; are able to see all sides of an issue

- ○ synthesize well, seeing relationships that others miss; transfer past learning to new situations and draw generalizations

To develop thought-processing potential, gifted students need to do the following:

- ○ consider alternatives and possible consequences of choices in an accepting environment

- ○ be exposed to a great variety of vicarious experiences

- ○ test new ideas without required conclusions or products

- ○ discuss ideas with intellectual peers

- ○ be exposed to many ideas at different levels of challenge and complexity

- ○ take plenty of time for incubation of ideas

Performance Characteristics and Needs

In their performance, gifted children:

- ○ show great curiosity and unusual persistence in efforts to gain answers

- ○ possess a wide range of interests and information

- ○ comprehend new concepts rapidly at an advanced level; have little or no need for drill

- ○ display creativity and imagination; enjoy fantasies and science fiction; may have an imaginary playmate in their preschool years; can develop a variety of solutions to problems; generate original ideas

- ○ are persistent and goal-directed; have a long attention span and may want to spend more than the time allotted to complete a project

○ show unusual intensity regarding school projects, political or environmental issues, religion, world events, intellectual inquiry into an area of special interest, interpersonal relationships, and abstract values

To enhance performance characteristics, gifted students need to do the following:

○ have curiosity met with exposure to varying styles of life, values, and approaches to problems

○ be exposed to new information and new issues

○ be presented with material at their own rate of learning

○ develop skills in creative thinking and problem solving

○ pursue interests beyond the time desired by most students

○ learn skills for dealing with intensity by exploring ways in which others cope with it

Responding to the Needs

Unfortunately, the ideal conditions described above are not uniformly available to our bright and gifted children, and it is still true that many gifted children are not ever identified by the schools as gifted—particularly those who are nonconformist, rebellious, have learning disabilities, or who come from minority groups or from backgrounds of poverty.[18]

Teachers and parents of gifted children are usually dedicated, persistent advocates for these children. In recent years, we have seen a steady flow of new books from authors who approach giftedness from various viewpoints—note the wide range of topics discussed in books, articles, and Internet sites listed in the Reference section of this book, or that of a comprehensive work on gifted children such as *A Parent's Guide to Gifted Children.*[19] Leading textbooks in the field record the progress made over the last half century, including new research findings and innovative techniques. The gifted education movement continues to grow.

Based on these new resources, the rest of this chapter will highlight characteristics of an optimal learning environment for gifted children, obstacles that hinder efforts, how schools are currently responding, and how parents can fill in any gaps—including the role of books and reading.

Optimal Learning Environment

Children who are gifted show signs of their high ability very early. Preschool gifted children often talk early, may jabber incessantly, enjoy wordplay, may have long conversations with their dolls or play figures, may question parents about road signs until the parents realize that their child has learned to read, or may invent stories or songs.

Once these children start school, their abilities set them apart from their classmates. They learn differently—not only more and faster, but also, as Dr. Barbara Kerr points out, "in different modes and at greater depth."[20] Kerr asserts that "capable learners learn most effectively when appropriately challenged and tend to become bored and frustrated when the *pace* and *complexity* of material is below their ability"[21] (emphasis added).

In addition to appropriate pacing of complex material, gifted children need to be with others of their own ability level. Grouping gifted children together is controversial, but research indicates that it provides the optimum learning situation for them.[22]

These children also need teachers trained in gifted education and who are familiar with any of several systems for teaching thinking skills.[23] For example, in working with gifted students, a teacher using Bloom's Taxonomy would rely on the higher levels of thinking—that is, on analysis, synthesis, and evaluation, rather than primarily on knowledge, comprehension, and application.[24] An example of the use of Bloom's Taxonomy is found in Chapter 5.

Pace of learning, complexity of material, being with other bright learners, and instruction in thinking skills comprise four fundamental intellectual needs, and books and book discussion can meet these special needs in bright and gifted children. A reader can choose his own pace of reading, books are available at every degree of complexity, a discussion group can bring together learners of like ability (just two, a child and an adult, are enough), and the discussion questions can elicit higher levels of thinking.

Obstacles in the Way

Most educators want to do all they can to meet the educational needs of every student, and in many schools, there is awareness that this should include the special needs of gifted children. But sympathetic teachers and administrators often run into difficulties as they attempt to do this. Economic barriers and prevailing social influences are some of the obstacles.

Economic Barriers

Despite reports such as *National Excellence,*[25] which (with perhaps not enough fanfare) called the neglect of our most promising students a "quiet crisis," the federal government largely ignores gifted education, providing no requirements and almost no funding. Thus, the financial responsibility falls on state governments and school districts. In 2004, only 29 states funded gifted education at all, and their budgets for gifted programs ranged from "roughly $100 million a year to nothing"[26]—a startling indication of the disparity that families find as they seek an appropriate school for their gifted children. The economic crisis since that time has made the situation even more dire.

Since programs for mentally and physically handicapped youngsters are mandated by federal and state governments, they cannot be cut; however, gifted programs are open and vulnerable as one of the few ways that school districts can reduce costs. Parents and teachers have seen gifted programs trimmed or eliminated as state aid designated for them is frozen or dropped entirely.

Parents and educators may wish to know more about local and state policies and laws that affect gifted students. Questions could include whether your state mandates education for gifted students, the amount that the state budgets for gifted education, and whether there are schools for gifted students in your state. To learn about federal and state policies on education for the gifted, visit the website of the National Association for Gifted Children (www.nagc.org) or see the policy section of www.GeniusDenied.com, a website established by the Davidson Institute for Talent Development.

Parents who watch their gifted children move rapidly through their school years during a time of financial retrenchment occasionally resort to legal action as they attempt to force school systems to meet their children's special needs. Areas of potential litigation include early admission, provision of programs and appropriate curriculum, racial balance in gifted programs, gifted disabled students, transportation, and homeschooling. A report from Karnes and Marquardt, who have followed and recorded legal action and decisions, may be of interest.[27]

Social Influences

Alarming statistics revealing disturbing social trends in our children's lives and schooling are reported so relentlessly that we may become numb to them. Without question, children's potential for intellectual development is affected by divorce, poverty, malnutrition, a lack of health care, struggling single parents, frazzled parents in two-income families, and other social problems, including safety in schools. In her book, *Endangered Minds: Why Children Don't Think—And What We Can Do about It*,[28] Jane Healy looks behind these factors and expresses deep concern that the stresses and deprivations that our children experience—particularly the rapid pace of living and the reliance on instant sensory gratification—are actually changing their brains and their capacity for sustained analytical thought. Citing research into physical changes that occur in the brain as a result of learning, Healy suggests that our processing of language—an important part of the development of our ability to think—is at risk if appropriate language experiences are not available at the optimum moment in the brain's developmental schedule and then reinforced through practice. Among her concerns is the interplay between the developing brain and reading.

With this in mind, let's look at how two major contemporary forces, television and video games, affect our children's reading and thinking—and the implications for their intellectual growth.

Television

Without even considering the questionable *content* of many television programs, two compelling objections are immediately obvious to many experts: (1) watching television is passive, and (2) it steals time in which a child could be active. By contrast, reading is active, requiring the brain's involvement to interact with the words and to create our own mental images.

> *Reading triggers certain experiences in the brain that just don't happen if you don't read. I think our brains are designed to symbolize and represent information in the way that we call language. If we don't exercise it, we lose it. Television, even* Sesame Street, *is not very symbolic. It makes things very tangible and easy to understand, but reading is the kind of exercise that causes the brain to develop differently because it uses that symbolic capability.*[29]

> *To the extent that children commit time looking at TV, they're not spending time reading. When a child reads a novel, he has to self-create whole scenarios, he has to create images of who these people are, what their emotions are, what their tones of voice are, what the environment looks like, what the feeling of this environment is. These self-created scenarios are important, and television leaves no room for that creative process. I think brains are designed to meet cognitive challenges. It's just like muscles; if you don't exercise them, they wither. If you don't exercise brains, they wither.*[30]

Weakened reading and analytical skills present a serious problem on a national level. "The survival of our kind of democracy requires the...active mind that the print culture produces and that [the] television spectator habit does not," according to Librarian of Congress James H. Billington.[31]

Despite the intentions of well-meaning parents, children whose television time is limited when they are toddlers tend to watch more and more television as they grow older, and reading time decreases. Parents interested specifically in weaning children from television to books can begin with the suggestions in *The Magic Bookshelf.*[32]

Video Games

Video games demand more participation than television, but they, too, take time from physical activity and schoolwork. In addition, there are concerns about violence and isolation. However, not all video games are violent—among the most popular games at the time of this book's printing are Guitar Hero and Rock Band, which involve a group of gamers playing guitars and drums. The Wii, also hugely popular, uses a motion sensor that allows for games like golf and bowling. For many teens, video games are a focal point for socializing; a recent report states that most teens who game are not isolated but instead play with other people who are playing in the room with them.[33]

A gifted high school junior whom I interviewed provided a more reassuring view. He is doing well in school, plays guitar, and writes music. He has a close group of friends, and unlike most teens, he continues with as much leisure reading as when he was younger—which was a lot. And he has played video games since he was seven. Here is his story:

> *Although he spends considerable time each day on the Internet, Chris doesn't have as much time for games as he did in middle school. Instead, he reads online, researching topics of interest through Wikipedia and Google Scholar (http://scholar.google.com). He reads so much online that it seems strange to him that "reading books is seen as the best way to gain knowledge." In addition, he watches television programs, follows political events, and plays card games, all during his online time. He continues to read books in his leisure time, and he believes that his friends— who are also gamers—read about as much as he does.*

In Chris's opinion, children should not begin playing video games too early—he is glad that his parents insisted he wait until he was seven. He points out that the complexity of video games has rapidly increased, and current games require more mental activity than earlier games did. "Teens [unlike younger children] can <u>do</u> things with games; a steadily increasing number of games allow you to create content within the game. Kids playing with friends can change the rules, explore within the game and expand it. Generally, younger kids play them more linearly, but older ones can deliberately break the rules of the game and watch the results to see how the game responds."

Asked for his opinion about a statement that teen gamers often confront aggressive gaming behavior in others, Chris agreed: "Generally, if any gamer detects anyone creating a negative environment within a game that he loves, he will attempt to stop it.... [H]ateful behavior of any kind, whether by someone in the room with you or someone you're interacting with online, is almost always actively discouraged."[34]

My conversations with Chris gave me new insight into the role of video games for him and his cohorts. It also made me think about reading in a new way. For more than 500 years, the surest path to life-long learning was reading books and newspapers. Some people (like myself) still carry the subliminal assumption that a habit of reading printed material is required for those who would be well-informed; it therefore follows that those who do not read print must be ill-informed. Obviously, that is changing. The Internet is a lifelong source of information for readers around the world. Although Chris still waits eagerly for the latest book in his favorite fantasy series, his major sources of information are on the Internet: newspaper, news and educational sites, and Google and Wikipedia.

Here is another story:

> *To counteract the potential negative effects of TV and video games on the school performance of their sons, writer Daniel Akst and his wife initiated changes in their home. Telling their sons that they know the boys can do well in school and that they as parents expect them to, they make it clear that the boys' education is the family's top priority. The parents do not help with homework, but they do ensure that it is done on time and without distractions, and while the children are young, the parents look over their homework every day. "Computer time is limited; there's no gaming system and, during the school week, virtually no television. Extracurricular reading is constantly encouraged," notes Akst. It's not all serious; the family finds time for fun together, and the boys have learned that, in addition to carefully chosen movies, "acing exams is lots of fun for kids, too, and once they got going, my guys wanted to keep it up."[85]*

The key to confronting the potential negative influence of television or video games seems to involve several factors, including:

- O how much time the child spends with television or video games
- O the content and quality of the shows she watches or the games she plays—including the presence or absence of violence
- O whether the reading habit has already become well established
- O whether the child's activities incorporate a balance that includes mental, physical, and social activities unrelated to television or video games

One of the mental activities that a child should engage in is reading a good book. Reading seems so simple that it can easily be taken for granted. In fact, we may need to worry less about illiteracy than about *aliteracy*—citizens who know how to read at a functional level but who do not choose to read, thereby avoiding the mental demands of reading and losing the benefits of the mental exercise, as well as the information that can be learned. This trend begins in our middle schools,[36] and gifted students as well as average ones are at risk.

Schools Respond

Education is a creature of trends, in part resulting from our efforts to teach many different kinds of learners in public schools. Since no one approach reaches all students, educators continually revise teaching methods. A long look at the history of education in the United States, such as the one offered by Ravitch,[37] reveals that revision is often accomplished by returning to older methods, once rejected but now seen in new light. Educational reform can be seen as a pendulum, swinging from one theory to an opposing theory, and then when it has gone too far, moving back again.

An example of the effect of this sway in educational trends on gifted education is the response to the 1983 report of the National Commission on Excellence in Education, *A Nation at Risk*, which resulted in efforts not merely to reform but also to restructure the public school system in this country. Echoes of this restructuring include a swing of the pendulum away from ability grouping (sometimes thought of as tracking), which is arguably the most effective classroom strategy for gifted children, toward others that not only do not work as well, but in some instances are seen as harmful. According to Colangelo and Davis, "Detracking is one recent damaging reform movement; cooperative learning is the other."[38] Both are described below, along with two other possible approaches: acceleration and differentiation.[39]

The descriptions that follow are by no means complete—we are getting rather far afield from books and reading at this point—but are offered here to give a picture of the lay of the land and to point educators and parents toward resources that cover each topic in more depth.

Ability Grouping

Ability grouping is a century-old mainstay of gifted education—a strategy that meets the very real need of gifted children to learn with others of like ability. It brings gifted students together and enables teachers to provide specific instruction aimed at their level, as in homogeneous reading or math groups in a heterogeneous elementary school classroom.

Unfortunately, ability grouping is too often perceived as tracking, the term originally used for the European system of testing students at an early age to determine whether or not they would follow a college-bound curriculum. In the mid-1980s, an opposing "detracking" movement gained momentum in the United States, often resulting in the elimination of special classes for the gifted and, sometimes, of the entire gifted program.

To answer charges that ability grouping harms students of average ability, Kerr cites research concluding that "ability grouping has minimal effects, either positive or negative, on the achievement of average or below-average students. Substantial evidence shows, however, that ability grouping has a positive effect on the achievement of gifted students."[40] James Kulik concurs, noting that with ability grouping, the *achievement* of low-ability students is not harmed, but instead the *self-concept* of average and below-average students tends to rise, since ability grouping results in more opportunity for them to shine. Further, he states that in ability grouping, "the gains [in achievement] associated with advanced and accelerated classes are especially large."[41]

Cooperative Learning

Often used to replace gifted programs, cooperative learning places children in small, short-term groups which include students of all ability levels. The group is responsible for the learning of all its members. Thus, the top learner in each group typically leads the others, without the opportunity for expanded learning of his own. This practice can exploit gifted children when it deprives them of appropriate curriculum and time with intellectual peers.

Research indicates that cooperative learning in heterogeneous groups is not academically beneficial to gifted and talented students.[42] If used excessively, it may be resented by gifted students, who prefer to work individually and to be responsible for their own learning.[43] Proponents suggest that gifted students benefit by learning to work with less able students, but "from the gifted students' point of view, it teaches that they are being asked to do the work of the teacher; that the lesson will be at a non-challenging level for them; and that a high level of knowledge and skill are not valued in this classroom."[44]

It is not surprising, then, that when detracking results in the loss of ability grouping in favor of cooperative learning, the outcome is strongly disliked by gifted students and is of serious concern to leaders in gifted education.

Acceleration

Like ability grouping, acceleration is a time-honored strategy that often meets resistance in the current cultural climate. But for some children, it is the best answer, according to the authors of *A Nation Deceived*, who analyzed more than 100 years of research and concluded that it is the most effective way to maximize gifted children's learning.[45] Acceleration is usually thought of as skipping one or more grades, and for some students, this can be exactly the right step. However, many players must be involved in the discussion to make an acceleration successful, including the child, the parents, the receiving teacher, and the principal.

There are more ways to accelerate than we can list here, but some of the most popular include early admission to kindergarten, compacting the curriculum, whole-grade acceleration (grade skipping), single-subject acceleration (or subject skipping, in which, for example, a child moves from the second-grade classroom to the fourth-grade one for math), and early admission to junior or senior high school, or to college. Some children, especially the highly gifted, may use of several of these options during their school years.

Acceleration is not for everyone, and the decision to accelerate should be made carefully. To determine whether a child is a suitable candidate for grade skipping, consider the child's intellectual ability (a tested IQ of at least 130 is recommended), large and small motor skills, current achievement levels in reading and arithmetic, and social and emotional maturity, among other factors.[46] A helpful tool for gauging readiness is the *Iowa Acceleration Scale*,[47] which is designed to help a child's parents and teachers gather information about factors that research has shown to be important in decisions regarding early entrance or whole-grade acceleration. It also lists circumstances in which acceleration should *not* be used.

Differentiation

One widespread approach to meeting the needs of gifted children in a regular classroom is through differentiation of both curriculum and instruction. This means that in a mixed-ability class, the teacher plans and organizes different content, materials, and methods of instruction for the different types and levels of learners in the class.[48] Ideally, this allows the gifted students in the class to work at their own level of ability.

Deborah Ruf views differentiation somewhat differently, suggesting that students in the same class "might study the same topic at the same time with the same basal textbook and materials, but the extensions, enrichment, and practice assignments are modified according to each child's needs."[49] She then offers a caveat: this version of differentiation is limiting for highly gifted children, since the same textbook and materials would not challenge them.

Unfortunately, research shows that "very little differentiation of instruction occurs for gifted children unless the teacher is experienced, has training in the techniques, and has support from others such as administrators or other teachers."[50] Finding value in the idea of differentiation while promoting more focus on the different needs of high-ability learners, the National Association for Gifted Children strongly encourages schools to provide differentiation for gifted students.

Parents as Advocates

Successful parent advocates prepare by gathering much more information than we've had room for here from books such as *Helping Gifted Children Soar,*[51] *Re-Forming Gifted Education,*[52] and *Academic Advocacy for Gifted Children.*[53] These books provide invaluable insights to help parents learn what they need to know about their child, both as a unique individual and as a gifted learner; about the teaching strategies most likely to help the child blossom; and about how the local school can provide appropriately for their child and others like her. With this background, they can begin to inquire politely—but persistently—about their school's provisions for students of high ability, remembering that some decisions about programming for gifted students require administrative approval and that individual teachers may be limited in what they can do. In short, parents should gather all the information they can and then work from there.

Parents Respond

Remember that for gifted children, intellectual needs carry double weight—they are emotional needs, too—and parents are on the front lines in the struggle to meet both types of needs. Fortunately, in recent years, parents have become much more active in monitoring their children's school experience. They support the schools' good efforts for all children and ask for more for their own children when more is needed. Sometimes the mere fact that parents are asking questions helps the schools to move forward.

But sometimes parents seek other options. In a book that combines her background as both a neurologist and a middle school classroom teacher, Dr. Judy Willis[54] describes her decision to send her gifted daughter to private school. Quoting research showing that public school teachers are almost twice as likely as other parents to choose private schooling for their middle school-age children,[55] Willis explains why she joined them. Through parental "due diligence," she learned that because of pressure to improve test scores to meet requirements of the 2001 No Child Left Behind legislation, the gifted program in her daughter's public school suffered from reduced funding and no longer offered the challenge and enrichment that her daughter needed.

Whether they are considering public (including charter) or private schooling for their gifted children, parents should actively seek these three pieces of information:

○ a description of the kind of educational program that is best for their child

○ how much of the desired program the child is receiving in school

○ what they can do at school or at home to compensate for any missing elements

Even though they may advocate for suitable programs at school, in the end, parents must compensate at home for what schools do not provide. They can do so through becoming informed; through enrichment; in some cases, through homeschooling; and through reading to and with their child.

Becoming Informed

If you are a parent reading this book, you have already begun to respond. You may be familiar with the growing collection of books on every possible aspect of giftedness, or you may want to follow through by reading many of the books referenced here. One of the most comprehensive books for parents is *A Parent's Guide to Gifted Children*,[56] which addresses both emotional and intellectual development, as well as a wide range of issues encountered in parenting gifted children. Many other helpful books on a wide variety of topics related to giftedness are listed at www.us.mensa.org/Content/AML/NavigationMenu/Programs/Gifted Children/BookList/Gifted_Children_s_Bo.htm.

Enrichment

Chances are excellent that you as a parent are already responding to your child's need for intellectual challenge every day. You answer questions as patiently as you can, or you look up answers with your child in a book or on the Internet (see Chapter 5, and ask a librarian's help to learn Internet search methods that will take you beyond Wikipedia and Google). You enjoy learning with your child, working with him at his "cutting edge" until his knowledge surpasses yours. You take him to the library, find movies you can enjoy together, and watch television with him so you can talk about the program. You plan family vacations and trips to museums and concerts and plays with your child in mind. You introduce him to the outdoors with hikes and camping trips, if that is an interest, and you find summer enrichment classes or music or art lessons that he will enjoy.

Our older son told us, years after the fact, that for a few years in elementary school, he tacitly understood that learning did not happen at school—but it did happen at after-school programs at the Nature Center and through the books that he found in the school and public libraries. Like my husband and me, you may not know what you are now doing that your child will always remember. The enrichment that you provide should be seen not as a series of optional extracurricular activities, but as an essential component of his education. You may well be better than the school at pitching to your child's intellectual level. Trust your intuitive response to your child, and stay involved.

Homeschooling

Parents decide to homeschool for a variety of reasons, one of which is to meet a gifted child's schooling needs when the school does not. This is particularly true of parents of highly gifted children, whose unique needs may not be met in even a strong school gifted program.

Although it is not an easy path to follow, when homeschooling is offered to enthusiastic learners by parents who are skilled at teaching and who have access to rich community resources, it can be a very successful alternative.[57] In fact, the average scores of homeschooled students on standardized tests range from the 65th to the 80th percentile—15 to 30 points above the norm.[58] College admissions officers now receive so many applications from homeschooled students that they have established criteria by which to judge their nontraditional resumes.

A good place to start when considering this educational option is the book *Creative Home Schooling: A Resource Guide for Smart Families.*[59] If you do decide to join the ranks of homeschooling parents, you will find the list of books in Chapter 8 in this book helpful as well.

Reading Aloud

When their children learn to read, parents should give some family reading time over to hearing the children read aloud—but they should also continue reading aloud to their children. Regrettably, most parents stop this practice by the time youngsters are eight or nine.

Research shows that soon after parents stop reading aloud, their children's television time begins to increase. In contrast, parents who continue reading to and with their children will have "found" time to introduce them to literature that the children might not find on their own, such as classic children's stories, folklore, poetry, and mythology. Children will happily listen to adults read not only more advanced literature than they can read themselves, but also books they can read but would not necessarily choose. Children's literature consultant Jody Fickes Shapiro writes in a column for parents, "By continuing to read aloud daily, you can remain active in the development of your children's intellectual and spiritual lives. Select books that challenge and entertain, expand awareness of the world, generate thoughtful discussion, and whet the appetite to read more."[60]

Slower-paced books of real quality lend themselves to reading aloud. *Old Ramon,* by Jack Schaefer, is one of these; it is not initially an exciting book, and children who want adventure will not choose to read it themselves; however, a fifth grade class that included many gifted boys sat silently listening day after day, coming to love the book and identify with the boy, and sad to have the story end.

The story hour at home remains important for the warmth provided by the luxury of reading in a frenetic world, and it can answer a crucial need: unhurried, quiet time for reflection. One mother, a busy physician, took turns reading the entire *Harry Potter* series aloud with her gifted daughter, valuing the shared experience enough to make time for it. Another mother said that she read to her eight- and

10-year-old daughters each morning at breakfast before leaving for her work as a middle school English teacher. How much would have been missed if they had stopped when the children learned to read!

The longer parents keep up the tradition of story hour, the better, both for the quality of family life and for the intellectual development of their children. Booklists of literature for reading aloud (and suggestions for choosing books especially for this purpose) include the *Books Kids Will Sit Still For* series[61] and *The Read-Aloud Handbook*.[62]

In addition to reading a wide variety of literature, parents looking for ways to compensate for gaps in the school program can use read-aloud time to branch out to nonfiction. A good place to begin is with a visit to the children's section of the public library, where the librarian can learn of the child's current interests and help with an initial set of books to check out. With parental encouragement and the librarian's help, the possibilities are endless.[63]

How Books Can Help

Many bright and gifted people suppress awareness of their need to learn. Teaching children to use books is one way of demonstrating that learning is important and that books can be a significant part of their lives. When teachers go to the trouble of establishing book discussion groups, or when parents take the time to read what their children are reading and talk to them about it, it becomes clear that these significant adults value and encourage reading. If reading and book discussions are happy and successful experiences, children learn to love books.

A glance back over the list of intellectual characteristics and needs found earlier in this chapter should confirm that reading and book discussion are ideal ways to respond to the characteristics and meet the related needs of gifted children. Especially where programs designed for gifted children are unavailable, a vigorous use of books can be a real contribution to children's growth. Few activities are as available, as inexpensive, and as richly rewarding. No wonder some of their best friends are books!

Part Two

The Process

Chapter 3

Reading Guidance

One of the changes that my husband and I noticed when our younger son departed for college, in addition to how long it now takes the dishwasher to fill up and how seldom the trash has to be taken out, was the loss of the sense of urgency about each day that we had felt when we had children in residence. Almost always now, whatever doesn't get done today really can be put off until tomorrow.

With growing children, this is not so. Especially in the early years, each day is important, and if the needs at a given stage are not met at that time, the child cannot conveniently make up for the loss later on. The child's changing developmental requirements march on, regardless of parents' commitment, energy, patience, presence, income, and whatever else makes the difference between good and inadequate parenting. Thus the sense of urgency; the need, the readiness, is *now*, and the attentive parent senses the demand for an immediate response.

This principle extends to children's reading. Each stage of childhood lasts a breathlessly short time, and so also does the period of peak response to the literature appropriate to that stage.

As adults, we feel a certain leisure about our reading, assuming that two or five years from now we can read a given book and expect much the same emotional and intellectual response as if we read it this week. Not so with children. They can, of course, read Mother Goose rhymes much later, but after the age of four or five, the emotional response to the rhythms and the intellectual response to the wordplay are dulled. They can read fairy tales even as adults, but after the early elementary years, the intense interest—the magic—is gone, and with it the power of the tales to enrich the growing imagination of the child. There are far too many excellent books available for the upper elementary and middle school reader to have time to read them all. No wonder the thoughtful school librarian feels a sense of urgency, trying to expose children to the best of the wealth before they are too old—that is, before they are 11 or 12!

Using books with bright and curious children requires knowledge of the needs of these youngsters (Part One), the processes of fostering development, presented here in Part Two, and the books available to them (Part Three). We begin with reading guidance— how to help children seek out the best books *for them* among the wide range of literature available.

Fundamentals of Reading Guidance

Reading guidance is often summarized as offering "the right book for the right child at the right time." It means being aware of what a child is reading, in terms of quality, content, and age-appropriateness, and being ready to offer suggestions for further reading that will move that child along with good literature at each stage of development.

By noticing what children choose to read, we can see when their preferences in literature change—from nursery rhymes to a wide range of adult fiction and nonfiction. While this change in their interests occurs naturally, it does not follow that a maturing of their literary taste is just as natural. The steps from grocery store picture books to insightful fiction and accurate, challenging nonfiction almost always require guidance.

Practicing reading guidance means watching a child read through the *Hardy Boys* series and being ready at the right time with a suggestion that he might also enjoy Alfred Hitchcock's short stories, and a few years later a Leon Garfield novel and then Edgar Allan Poe—all filled with suspense but moving up the ladder of age appropriateness and sophistication. Or it may mean noticing that a third grader who has re-read Laura Ingalls Wilder a number of times is ready to be introduced to Louise Erdrich's *Birchbark House* series and *Caddie Woodlawn*, and then later to the historical fiction of Elizabeth George Speare, Avi, and Scott O'Dell. Later still, she may enjoy *Johnny Tremain* or *Across Five Aprils* and eventually Willa Cather's novels of the American West. In addition, she could be encouraged to branch out horizontally, with biography or with fiction about the history of other countries, perhaps beginning around fourth grade with the work of Gloria Whelan.

Parents are in the best position to offer such long-range reading guidance. Teachers usually see only one year, and elementary school librarians perhaps six or seven years of a child's development, so they must work harder early in their relationship with a child to learn what she has enjoyed reading. This book will provide the background information needed to suggest books that will interest and delight the child and keep her coming back for more good literature.

Reading guidance involves stretching a child's mind and spirit—always trying to suggest a book that meets him where he is in the hope that when he has read it, he will have grown a little. Those who guide reading do not reject escape literature, but they want the child to learn to use it appropriately. This means that the child must learn to recognize when he wants to read something easy and when he wants to be challenged—and then be able to find each type at the right moment.

Adult influence on the *priority* that a child places on reading is limited primarily to about four years, roughly from second grade to fifth. Our influence on the *quality* of children's reading lasts perhaps two more years—through the important middle school years (longer for those who continue leisure reading). Thus, time is precious indeed, and there isn't very much of it to introduce them to the wealth of children's literature. These are crucial years to stimulate imaginative thinking, to ensure that they will know some of the classics when they enter college, and to help them establish a pattern of reading that will last a lifetime. It is a time for subtle intervention, for suggestions, for sharing and passing on the enjoyment of reading. It is no time for well-intentioned adults to watch passively as mediocre reading habits unfold and stabilize.

Reading guidance takes many forms. It can be as informal as the casual mention of a title or an author that a parent has enjoyed or the "floor work" that librarians do—talking with students as they browse the shelves. Or it can be more formal—a book talk carefully planned by a librarian or a teacher, or a list of books from which students are required to select five to read each semester for an English class. Reading guidance can also be subtly woven into the fabric of family life:

> *Although she is now a grandmother of teenagers, Ginny has warm memories of summers spent reading when she was a child and adolescent. Her own mother had always enjoyed reading, and she was ready each year with suggestions of books that Ginny might enjoy over the summer. They were books she might otherwise have missed, like* Cry, the Beloved Country; Too Late the Phalarope; My Name is Aram; Madame Curie; Wind, Sand, and Stars; *and* A Death in the Family. *Some were in her mother's library; she found others in the public library at her mother's suggestion. She has less time now, but reading is still a source of immense pleasure for Ginny, in part a result of her mother's gentle reading guidance years ago. Reading is a passion that she hopes to pass along to her grandchildren—a gift from their great-grandmother.*

A warm relationship between the guiding adult and the student is important for the success of reading guidance, as is the genuine love of the adult for books and the natural wish to share this pleasure with children. If these are present, then an adult can establish a reading guidance relationship with students even without a formal program. Any adult who listens to a student talk about books that she is reading and is ready with suggestions for more good reading at appropriate times is offering reading guidance.

Reading Patterns: What to Expect

As they grow from preschoolers to high school seniors, from non-readers to independent and voluntary readers and perhaps even to mature readers, children's reading patterns evolve in predictable ways— beginning with the basic observation that regardless of age, gender, or interests, children prefer to read stories about characters just a few years older than themselves. This section will provide a brief overview of interest in leisure reading as an activity, as well as usual preferences for topics and types of literature, from preschool to college.

We can learn about groups of children from research,[1] but of course, the best way to learn what an individual child likes to read is to ask. Although a direct question may not elicit clear information—a bit of probing may be necessary—you might ask: What does the child do with leisure time? What are his favorite television programs? What was the last good book he read?

A child cannot be interested in literature that she hasn't been introduced to yet, so the questioner must learn not only what she has enjoyed, but also what kinds of books she has in her background. A third grader may not have a complete answer to questions about what she likes to read. The ninth grader will, and if she has been introduced to a variety of good books and has had perceptive reading guidance, her answer will include good adult literature.

Gender Differences

Her brother's answers may differ. As children grow older, the reading interests of boys and girls diverge as one would expect, with girls more responsive to books about relationships and boys liking books with facts. Thus, girls often prefer fiction, while boys tend to prefer nonfiction, although boys are more flexible—more willing to try fiction than girls are to try nonfiction. Reading studies have long shown this divergence—although a recent Canadian study shows that in grades 1-6, both check out more fiction than nonfiction.[2]

Despite this divergence, reading studies have often disregarded nonfiction and looked for preferences among types of fiction for both boys and girls. Today there is a new focus on nonfiction with a more positive label: information books. Apparently in response to Michael Gurian's books about boys,[3] in recent years, awareness has grown regarding differences in boys' and girls' brains. As a result, teachers and librarians are re-thinking the reading material that they recommend for boys, with more emphasis on how-to manuals and information books, along with sports and adventure stories.[4] This new emphasis is reflected throughout the rest of this chapter.

Preschool

In the preschool years, children gain language skills more easily than they ever will again. It is a critical period for parents to provide rich language experiences for their children by talking directly to them and reading aloud. This is especially so for unusually bright and curious children, who respond eagerly to the stimulation and the exposure to new ideas that reading aloud can provide.

It appears that even before birth, babies listen to voices. This is the beginning of language acquisition, which continues immediately after birth as parents talk to babies while they care for them, and it is reinforced in even very young infants when someone reads aloud to them.[5] Nothing in a preschooler's life can quite match the warmth of being held and read to, and if the one who is reading loves not only the child but also the literature and the experience of sharing it, so much richer are both reader and child.

Given the child's short attention span at this age, it is best if there can be several brief "story hours" a day, which may fit more easily into the parents' schedule. Those who need encouragement to find time to read aloud will find *Babies Need Books* an eloquent and persuasive statement of the pleasures of reading aloud—and being read to.[6] Parents who make the effort to plan read-aloud time provide their children with pre-reading skills, information, and opportunities for intellectual and emotional growth.

Pre-Reading Skills

Children who are read to as preschoolers enter school better prepared for learning to read. With solid language skills as a base, they are equipped to do well in any area that depends on language, and what area does not? Quite apart from the pleasures of children's literature, savvy parents may read to their preschoolers specifically to build language and pre-reading skills. Books such as *Reading Begins at Home*[7] and *Straight Talk about Reading*[8] offer suggestions for pre-reading activities.

Information

In addition, parents may read to their preschoolers simply to enrich their children's store of knowledge. An ever-increasing supply of information books for young children makes this an easy project, and one that is sure to interest the parents as well as the child. In the process, the child learns that books are an infinitely varied source of fascinating information.

Intellectual Response

Good nonfiction for preschoolers offers text as a starting point for interaction: children asking questions, parents answering, and vice versa. Parents should feel free to depart from the text and talk about details on each page. What makes this machine go? Let's draw a picture of what is *not* on the page. Gail Gibbons' book *Farming* provides an example: a parent or teacher might ask, "How does the hay arrive through the door in the haymow, on the second floor of the barn?" and then suggest, "Draw the outside view, with the elevator."

Emotional Response

Reading is not only an intellectual response to information, but also an emotional response to the art of literature. Reading to a preschool youngster, several times a day if possible, demonstrates that reading is a source of pleasure. By sitting with a child, cuddling, enjoying a good story and lovely illustrations, talking about the pictures and characters, and imagining what would happen if this child were in the story or had the same choices to make, adults lay the foundations for a lifetime of reading for pleasure and information. The openness to the emotional response begins here, in a loving environment, when children's imagination is most accessible and flexible. Children who miss books at this age will never be able to make up entirely for the loss because never again will they be so receptive.

Library Story Hour

In addition to loving adults who enjoy reading to them at home, preschoolers can attend a library story hour, where they can experience literature with other children. The children's librarian knows the range of children's literature and understands how to make it live. Skilled librarians use music, puppets, and storytelling as well as reading aloud, and they involve the children as participants, making the literature an immediate experience.[9]

Reading Interests

Young preschoolers enjoy stories with simple plots about everyday experiences and about "things that go," such as trucks, trains, and cars. They like stories with talking animals or toys, or with characters their own age. Older preschoolers are ready to begin hearing tales from folklore, like "The Three Billy Goats Gruff," "The Little Red Hen," and "The Gingerbread Boy," and they are eager listeners to anyone who will read from the rich trove of nonfiction available for them.

Teaching Preschoolers to Read

Some gifted children of this age teach themselves to read, often to the alarm of parents who have been told not to push. Clever preschoolers can learn simply from being read to and asking questions about letters and words on signs. As many parents have learned, there is not much a parent can do to prevent an inquisitive child from teaching herself to read if she is ready.

The harder question is whether parents should actively teach their children to read. This is one of the unresolved issues in education: teaching preschoolers to read is frowned upon by some educators and encouraged by others.[10] The parent of a gifted child may reason that knowing how to read could keep the child occupied in school while the teacher works with slower learners, preventing the disruptive behavior that may accompany boredom. Certainly, it is difficult to withhold information from a child who clamors for it.

> *A mother who had taught her children to read when they were three and four later asked her son, by then in college, how he had felt about his reading lessons at the time. His surprising answer was that it was confidence-building for him, not because he would start school already reading, but because the time she spent teaching him was proof that "I was worth being taught to read." For him, learning to read was a rite of passage, a welcome into the circle of his reading family.*

To be certain they are not pushing, parents should identify what it is that motivates them to teach their children to read. Are they hoping to meet the child's need, or is a secret need of their own being met? One clue to parental need is this: Have they imagined telling a friend or relative that Jennifer is now reading? The brief pleasure of that conversation is surely not worth risking the possibility of turning reading into a chore for Jennifer. If they decide to go ahead, they should monitor their behavior. Lessons should be very brief, and if there is any hint of impatience or stridency in their voices or in the child's, they should stop.[11]

Joy is the only really good criterion for judging the value of pre-school reading lessons at home. Is there joy in it for the child and the parents? If not, it would be better not to bother. Continue to enjoy reading aloud, carry on with weekly trips to the library, and wait for nature to take its course.

Early Elementary (Grades K-2)

These are the years when most children learn to read—that is, they learn the techniques of decoding, or interpreting the words on a page. As they gain reading skills in the classroom, they eagerly come to the school library. First or second graders swarm over the shelves of easy-to-read books. They select a wide range of books, some of which they can read themselves, but most of which they will have to find an adult to read. Whatever the library's limit on books per child, they will come to the circulation desk with that number or more.

As they become independent readers, they become more selective. They learn to use the "five finger test," reading a page and putting one finger down for each word they do not know. If by the end of the page fewer than five fingers are down, the book is probably close enough to their reading level for comfort. They begin to recognize authors' names and may want to read all of the *Encyclopedia Brown* books or everything written by Beverly Cleary.

Gifted children and those most enthusiastic about reading often become independent readers earlier than most. When they do, they should have free access to books at their reading level in the school library. If library policy limits access to the collection by grade level, the policy should bend as soon as students are ready for more challenging books. It was a proud day when a child in such a school came home to announce, "I can read chapter books now!" He was finally— and appropriately—allowed to walk past the picture books to where the chapter books were kept, although not every child in his class had achieved this level of reading expertise.

As they become independent readers, primary children choose realistic animal and nature stories, as well as adventure and mystery. They continue to enjoy folklore of increasing complexity, and they love fairy tales.

The enthusiasm for the library story hour of children in kindergarten through second grade is undiminished, and as important as it is for parents to continue to read aloud at home, it is also important for teachers to find time to read aloud daily to the class. One primary teacher greets the children as they return from their library time and selects one book that has been checked out for immediate reading aloud to the entire class. Then, all of the children have quiet time to look at and read their library books. Children in this class look forward to library hour as one of the most important times of the week.

Upper Elementary (Grades 3-5)

For those who will predictably become lifelong readers, a surge in reading begins at about fourth grade and carries through into middle school.[12] Most children's leisure reading is done between fourth and sixth or seventh grade, and these few years are vital in forming the reading patterns that will continue into adulthood. If at this time they have access to good books, time to read, and an enthusiastic adult to guide them, gifted children in particular have an excellent chance of joining that fortunate group of adults whose lives are immeasurably enriched by the pleasure they find in reading.

By third or fourth grade, readers have usually identified their favorite authors and ask for their books in the library. Some young readers become interested in fantasy and science fiction at this age, often introduced to it through C. S. Lewis's *Narnia* series or the *Harry Potter* books, while a few begin to show an interest in biographies or historical fiction.

By the fifth grade, the reading habit is becoming well fixed. Among information books, boys are interested in sports, space, and science, while girls choose to read about horses, cats, crafts, and friends. While both enjoy humor and books about animals, boys like to read about sharks, snakes, and dinosaurs, while girls read about pets, deer, and bears.

At this late elementary stage, children begin to read contemporary realistic fiction, including books that depict young people coping with difficulties such as physical or mental disability, divorce, drugs, and death, as well as with the typical questions and concerns of growing up—finding friends, moving through puberty, and developing a sense of one's own identity.

Children may begin to lose interest in reading as a leisure activity toward the end of the upper elementary years. Some youngsters become deeply involved in computers, video games, or sports and do not want to spend time reading. In addition, gifted students may resent being forced to read material not of their own choice. They want "interesting" and "exciting" reading, and their opinion of what is interesting and exciting often does not coincide with assigned reading material.

One classroom answer to this resistance is a reading curriculum that departs from the textbook and emphasizes reading from a collection of trade books so that students can choose. The freedom to choose their reading, even if within a group of books pre-selected by an adult, adds greatly to children's motivation to read. At home, parents can encourage reading with frequent trips to the library or bookstore and by reading the same books and talking about them with their children.

For children who are drawn from reading to computers or sports, it's a good idea to suggest books about these topics so that reading can complement their areas of major interest rather than compete with them. And it is still important, difficult as it may be, for teachers to find time in the school day to read aloud and for the students to read silently.

Middle School (Grades 6-8)

What happens to young adolescents at this age in other aspects of their lives occurs in their reading lives, too—they are leaving childhood and the literature appropriate to it. They move gradually to the young adult (YA) section in bookstores and libraries, perhaps looking for genre fiction and reading only romance or only fantasy.[13]

At this age, boys generally are less flexible than girls in their reading choices. They will read about female characters as long as the plot provides suspenseful action in an outdoor setting. Girls prefer internal action focused on what a character thinks and feels, not just on what she does, and they are willing to experiment with a wider range of reading.[14]

Gifted students are more likely than others to continue reading avidly. One study designed specifically to determine leisure reading interests of gifted students at this age—a classic among early reading interest studies—reports that the gifted students read more than twice as much as the students in the control group, choosing more science fiction and fantasy, fewer problem novels, and a wider range of historical fiction than students in the comparison group.[15] Of the students in the study, only the gifted showed the pattern of moving toward reading adult fiction, with this shift beginning to occur at the end of the eighth grade.

As middle school gifted students come to grips with their differences from others, reading begins to serve social and psychological needs as well as academic needs. Although they are able now to read adult literature, they may need to read about people their own age. Barbara Baskin points out that as reading interests mature, advanced readers may select books on the same topics that average readers choose, but with more sophisticated treatment, and they may also seek not only novels, but also drama, poetry, biography, and autobiography.[16]

As they begin the transition to adult literature, young people need reading guidance more than at any other time. Perhaps surprisingly, gifted students are no more skilled than others at selecting excellent literature without adult help. Girls are likely to discover the more simplistic, sentimentalized romantic adult novels, while boys tend toward sensationalized, violent adventure. Without direction, they may never find the superb adult literature that can fill their present need for romance and adventure while also developing their taste for good literature. If they don't learn the difference between sentimental or sensational novels and good literature at this age, chances are slim that they will eventually develop into mature readers. Adults guiding them can use both the fiction and nonfiction that is available for this age group.

Fiction for Gifted Middle Grade Students

This is a transitional age, and the literature that these students enjoy reflects this. Early middle school youngsters may appropriately read a combination of children's and young adult literature, while mature, older middle schoolers may be reaching from YA into adult novels for leisure reading. But YA novels may be overlooked in the English curriculum (they will be found in the school library) for a surprising reason: many teachers have little knowledge of this fast-growing body of literature.[17]

Young adult literature is written for and about young adults (around ages 13-20), frequently by authors who also write for the adult market.[18] It has been an important genre for decades, but college students preparing to teach English study the classics of the English language and may never have a course in YA literature. Therefore, English classes for gifted middle school and high school students may emphasize literary classics in which the protagonists may be in their teen years, but the issues are not those of teens today.

Several educators have promoted offering YA novels to middle school students to encourage them to develop into lifelong readers, and introducing classics later on. Carlsen, Rakow, and Samuels are three who have made this suggestion.[19] Middle school teacher Rakow presses for the use of young adult literature to help gifted students understand the typical experiences of adolescents; in her opinion, discouraging young adult literature for this group is failing to provide appropriate guidance. Carlsen puts it succinctly: "Accelerating the intelligent child by giving him or her adult classics of literature will not increase enjoyment of reading."[20]

The classics should not be ignored entirely, of course, but neither should they be overdone with young students. Especially in the middle school years, mixing just a few classics with several young adult novels is advisable, leaving heavier use of classic literature for the later senior high years.

Nonfiction

Nonfiction is far more important to middle school readers than teachers have recognized, according to Carter and Abrahamson.[21] Not only do young readers choose to read nonfiction for pleasure, but they need plenty of experience with it to prepare for standardized tests, which require skill in interpreting expository prose. These authors show that the range of nonfiction topics that middle school students choose is as diverse as the range for adults, and there is a wealth of nonfiction books available to them. As with fiction, the problem with nonfiction is one of choosing the best among the abundance that is available. Chapter 6 offers suggestions for guidance.

In seeking suitable literature for middle school students, parents who homeschool their children would do well to read the articles cited above: Baskin on gifted readers, Samuels on young adult novels, and Carter and Abrahamson on nonfiction for middle school youngsters. And for all adults looking for appropriate reading for teenagers, Anita Silvey's *500 Great Books for Teens*[22] is highly recommended.

Senior High (Grades 9-12)

During the senior high years, students read from the YA section and then blend into adult reading. By ninth grade, boys read more science fiction, fantasy, sports, war, and spy stories than girls, but both girls and boys read crime and detective stories—such escapist reading may help them deal with the angst of this time in their lives.[23] Senior high students prefer protagonists who are making the same transition they face—from adolescence to adulthood. They are not interested in books with middle-aged characters, but they do enjoy stories about the elderly, who face some of the same problems they do—a changing peer group and adjustment to physical and mental changes.

A 2007 report of a study of the reading interests of gifted girls reflects changes wrought by the women's movement: the girls interviewed rejected romance stories and much preferred books with strong female characters. In some cases, they chose science fiction and fantasy precisely because the women characters in these books are more independent than those in contemporary fiction. They also liked characters who modeled career choices that interested them. Furthermore, this study showed that the girls benefited simply from being part of a group that discussed books—something that did not happen when they were with their other classmates.[24]

Adolescents glean suggestions for books to read from parents and friends, as well as by following favorite authors and from book covers and movie-related titles. As they grow older, their interests will become so individualized that general statements no longer apply. Some of them will have strong interests in philosophical issues as they attempt to formulate their own opinions and value systems. Anyone hoping to guide or influence their reading will have to know them as

individuals and their reading background, as well as special considerations which are discussed in Chapter 4 under "Goals of Bibliotherapy at Different Grades."

Reading Lists for College-Bound Students[25] is a book highly recommended for intellectually curious high school students who want to
read more of the classics on their own. The authors have gathered
lists from more than 100 colleges of classics that the colleges would
like their first-year students to have read before they arrive on
campus. Reading these books ahead of time is usually not required,
but it does provide a background to give new students a head start on
college assignments, as well as an extra measure of self-confidence in
their own reading background.

Gifted students may want to use *Reading Lists for College-Bound
Students* to plan their summer reading throughout high school and to
begin their college search. The book provides information about
each college, introduces each book list with comments about reading
requirements on that campus, and for some colleges, includes essay
questions from the application that draw on the applicant's response
to literature. In addition, the book offers help in creating a planned
reading program. Rather than assume that anyone would try to read
all of the books on any college's list, the authors provide suggestions
for creating a personal reading list. One chapter lists the 10 most recommended authors and the 100 most recommended works, and
there is a section on keeping a reading diary. Finally, the book provides titles related to majors in a variety of subjects, such as science,
political science, business, the fine arts, and others. The list for those
planning to take Advanced Placement English is a good pre-college
reading list in itself.

For the most fortunate, the reading experience at this age is one
of long, leisurely discovery, as described by the novelist John Updike:
"...certain kinds of novels, especially 19th-century novels, should be
read in adolescence, on those dreamily endless solitary afternoons
that in later life become so uselessly short and full of appointments,
or they will never be read at all."[26]

Special Characteristics of Gifted Readers

Alison, a nine-year-old growing up in a Midwestern university town, exemplifies the characteristics of a gifted reader.

Alison read before she entered kindergarten, and according to school and home records, she read at least 73 books in the third grade, including Little Women. *She has also read* Charlotte's Web, Anne of Green Gables, Peter Pan, Heidi, *and* Alice's Adventures in Wonderland, *most of them recommended to her by her mother or a teacher.*

Alison looks for books by her favorite authors: Patricia MacLachlan, Patricia Reilly Giff, and L. M. Montgomery. When she discovered the Babysitters Club *series, she read several in a row, then immediately re-read* Charlotte's Web.

At school, she reads constantly, even during math and spelling tests.

Everyone in Alison's family reads, including all of her grandparents and her great-grandmother, who uses talking books for the blind. Alison still enjoys having bedtime stories read to her, and she sometimes reads a bedtime story to her younger brother. She "appears to belong to that group of people for whom reading is as natural and necessary as breathing." [27]

Only a few studies, including those mentioned under the age groupings above, consider the points at which gifted readers differ from the average. As a whole, they report that many gifted children are like Alison, in that they read *earlier, better, and more* than most children. [28] Gifted youngsters read a greater variety, and they may be more adventurous in exploring different types of literature, but in general, their reading interests closely parallel those of other children their age (although the specific books they choose may vary). At some points in their elementary years, they read three or four times as many books as most children, and some continue to do a great deal of reading after the time when children's reading typically tapers off.

A summary of reading patterns of gifted youngsters indicates the importance of guiding their reading early and consistently:

○ They may teach themselves to read before they start school.

○ Whether or not they are reading in kindergarten, they are probably independent readers by second grade at the latest.

○ By third grade, they may have identified their current favorite authors.

○ By fifth grade, the habit of reading is well established, if it is going to be.

○ By sixth grade, their reading may diminish if they are among the many gifted youngsters who become involved in sports, computers, or video games.

○ By eighth grade, extracurricular reading may well have disappeared for some, although it may reappear later.

○ Others spend extraordinary amounts of time reading but need guidance to identify good literature.

○ Capable of reading sophisticated literature, they have the potential to gain a great deal from the best books if they are directed to them.

For the adult who works with such children, reading guidance is especially rewarding because these children are likely to respond with great enthusiasm and develop a close relationship with the adult who talks about books with them.

Avid Readers and Resistant Readers

As readers, gifted children fall into two groups: those who pick up a book in their free time, and those who find something else to do. Members of the first group seem to have copious reading as a daily goal, and when tasks must come first, they feel distracted and annoyed. Those in the second group usually *can* read quite adequately (unless there is a learning disability); they simply do not choose to read *much*.

Avid Readers

Voracious in the pursuit of books, avid readers often keep several going at once.

> *For a period of several years, Kevin could be traced through the house by the open books spread face down on the floor of each room he had left. He exemplifies those who learn early how to use the local library and the school library, becoming personal friends of the librarians who in turn are delighted with such enthusiastic patrons.*

Such children may read with amazing speed and comprehension, or they may pore over a passage, savoring the beauty of words. They know how to skim and when to study. These are often the early readers, teaching themselves before they start school or being taught by parents who respond to their interest.

In working with avid gifted readers, there are three potential problems: the impulse of some children to read books that are emotionally too advanced for them; the challenge of finding books at the right level, both emotionally and intellectually; and the child who reads too much.

Reading beyond Emotional Readiness

It is important to remember that "read" in the early stages can mean something closer to "decode"—children can understand the words, pronounce most of them, and glean meaning from the sentences and paragraphs. They may be able to read a book of a hundred or more pages and summarize the story at a time when most of their classmates are still reading early readers with controlled vocabularies. But even gifted and avid young readers are not always emotionally ready to *comprehend* what they can decode—to understand the symbolism or grasp everything that the author says about human relationships.

Some children push themselves, or are pushed by their perception of the pride that others take in their reading, to read whatever they can decode before they have developed the emotional readiness to comprehend. Then they may avoid reading a book later, when they are emotionally ready for it, because they have already read it. They do not realize that it would be an entirely different book for them at the right time.

> *Seven-year-old Yun-Fei is reading at the sixth-grade level. Therefore, she can read* The Witch of Blackbird Pond. *While she can follow the storyline and answer fact questions about the plot, Yun-Fei is not ready to understand why the old Quaker woman who lives at the pond is feared as a witch, nor can she appreciate the courage shown by Nat and Kit in befriending her.*

Children like Yun-Fei, especially those who know how proud their parents are of their reading ability, need guidance to help them find appropriate reading. In some cases, it seems that more than anything else, they need permission not to stretch too far—permission to enjoy the books that are appropriate for their level of emotional development.

Finding the Right Books

The resulting problem for the guiding adult is to know what books to suggest. It is without doubt a challenge to find a book for a second grader who reads at the sixth-grade level. In general, it seems best to match fiction with the child's emotional level, while guiding him toward nonfiction at his reading level. Good sources for recommendations of intellectually challenging books are *Books for the Gifted Child*[29] and Chapter 8 of this book, as well as websites dedicated to gifted children.[30]

Reading Too Much

Constant and prolific reading can be a sign of trouble. Occasionally, it signals that reading has become a safe haven from fear—for example, the need of a gifted child to fill time that she really would prefer to spend playing with neighborhood children, if only she knew how to be accepted. It is best to respond to this situation positively. The child should not be told that she is reading too much or playing with others too little, but she should subtly and persistently be led to increase time with other children to achieve a better balance. It's quite likely that this child sees herself as a "reader" and that "I am a reader" is a positive part of her self-concept. Anything that makes her feel guilty about the time she spends reading may convince her that reading is somehow wrong; she may also begin to believe that she herself is not quite acceptable as the reader she is. Therefore, no connection should be made between time spent with other children and time spent reading. Each should be valued independently.

How much is too much time spent reading? That varies with the child. One who tends toward introversion may spend more time alone than adults consider appropriate (especially if they are extroverts), but the child needs this quiet time to replenish depleted energy; though adults may not understand how this could be, he enjoys it. Parents and teachers should base their evaluation on how much time the child spends with other children, how content he seems to be with himself, and how happily he spends time alone. If reading is an escape because interpersonal skills are lacking or because of depression or fear, then some intervention—perhaps professional—should be considered.

However, in our socially-oriented society, it is quite possible that adults are overly zealous to see children relate to others. If a child relates well with other children when she does play with them and seems happy with herself in general, then it probably should not be of great concern if she spends less time with other children than adults think necessary.

Resistant Readers

Some highly intelligent and able children simply choose not to spend their leisure time reading. They may be quite capable of reading to gain information, and they certainly have the potential for success in college and career, but they aren't people who enjoy literature as an art form. In the long run, this is no more alarming than the fact that some children never learn to enjoy music or dance or theater or to participate in sports or cooking. No matter how much we want our children to be well-rounded, they retain the right to develop their own interests. All we can do is to expose them to the world around them and accept them as they are—without unduly imposing our values upon them as we watch them make their choices.

Nevertheless, in the short run, it is to the child's advantage to read—both to hone the skill and for the vast amount of information that he can gain. Therefore, adults should avoid the tendency to view the middle-grade child as a non-reader—and thus also allow him to see himself in this way. It may help them understand what is going on if adults recognize that the roots for a child's resistance to reading may have been established long ago in the preschool years, especially if an older sibling has pre-empted the reading role.

Consider the plight of the two- or three-year-old second child growing up in a reading family. We know that children growing up in homes where reading is valued are more likely to be good readers themselves than those in homes where little reading is done. But for this child whose parents and older sibling are all readers, there is a negative side: everyone in her world takes pleasure from an activity not yet available to her, inevitably ignoring her in the process. Frequent read-aloud sessions can only partially atone for this, and if the older child reads when the second child wants to play with him—as he will if he is an avid reader—it seems natural that she will resent reading to some degree. She learns to capitalize on what she *can* do, and so may begin her self-image as one who *does* rather than one who reads. Regardless of this child's ability to read by the time she is a third grader, the "doer" identity will have had a significant head start over the "reader" identity, and the reader may never catch up.

> *Jessica's parents and her older brother, Michael, had open books in every room. She was included in the reading orgy, with plenty of read-aloud time and trips to the library. But if she wanted Michael to play with her, his invariable response was, "Jessica, I'm READing." When*

she wanted her mother's attention, it was "When I'm through with this chapter," and Dad's response was an absent-minded, "That's nice, dear," as he turned a page.

So Jessica began to draw, then turned to clay, and as a teenager, to beads. While her family read, she sat among them working with tiny crystals and wires. Her gifted-ness found its outlet in the handiwork of her fingers as she created beautiful, intricate designs for necklaces and earrings. At 20, she has already sold her work at local art fairs and planned a career in jewelry design. While she enjoys reading, she spends leisure time with beads, not books.

Jessica's story illustrates that gifted non-readers can be productive and happy. Nonetheless, because reading is such a critical skill for success in school, it is important that adults in reading families not give up on their young children as potential readers, particularly during the peak reading period in the elementary grades.

At School

Because some bright children who do not choose to read in leisure time are conscientious about completing assignments, under-standing teachers include full books in the curriculum, as well as fragments of literature, in order to encourage the student to read. Parents may simply ask the teacher to do what they cannot do at home—assign a book.

The assignment may be all the incentive necessary, and it need not add to the teacher's burden. A simple notebook for recording titles of books read may be enough to keep students going if the teacher has no time for reading logs or elaborate book-reporting pro-cedures. The book assignments should be free choice from a list of recommended titles for quality control. Suggestions for the list can come from the school librarian, from Chapter 8 in this book, from *Books for the Gifted Child*,[31] or from relevant websites.[32]

There are many ways for a teacher, with the help of the school librarian, to bring children's literature into the classroom. But when there are too many children and not enough time to meet the pressing curriculum requirements in every subject, literature may seem like a luxury. In classrooms like these, it is especially important that reading be assigned to competent but resistant readers.

At Home

Parents can also gently build reading time into their children's schedule. One common practice is to set bedtime a half-hour earlier than necessary, with optional reading time. In a variation on this theme, when one boy's interest in reading began to decline, his mother noted that, unlike TV, bedtime reading had no lights-out rule. It was a successful ploy. Many more suggestions for working with resistant readers can be found in *The Magic Bookshelf*.[33]

If parents are aware of their child's reading—by occasionally reading one of his books, talking with him about it, asking his opinion, and listening well—the child will benefit in several ways. He will begin to think of himself not only as a reader, but as one who can respond to books and make judgments about them—judgments that others value. Parents usually find themselves truly enjoying children's books, giving the child something of importance to share with them. Most important, books can become a bridge for more real communication than would otherwise occur. The elementary years are the ideal time to build these bridges of trust and sharing—they will be needed in the adolescent years!

Finally, parents and teachers can help keep a gifted child from prematurely deciding that she does not enjoy reading simply by continuing to read aloud, taking turns with her as she gains skill and interest.

Older Resistant Readers

As these children reach middle school, they may yet begin to enjoy reading, even if not as much as avid readers do. It will help if reading continues to be assigned. When these youngsters understand that a background in literature is part of a good education, some highly motivated and curious students, avid readers or not, will read from lists of classics or suggested pre-college reading during the summers simply to gain the background that they understand is important. Some will turn to reading even later—Jessica's mother reports that Jessica (the bead-working artist mentioned earlier) is now, as a young adult, reading Dostoevsky.

Some children will never be avid readers, and those of us whose business or interest it is to push books will do better if we accept that gracefully. These children can grow into happy, productive adults anyway, and there is nothing to be gained if they feel guilty about their lack of interest in reading. If the goal is simply to experience joy in the literature that we have been able to introduce, and if we achieve that, we must be satisfied that it is enough.

Mature Readers

Gifted and intellectually curious children have an opportunity to develop into what is known as a "mature reader," and many adult readers of this book may recognize themselves in the description that follows.

Mature readers consider reading an integral part of life not something they do only to relax or to escape or if there is nothing good on television, but something they plan for each day; they feel uneasy and restless if the day develops so that they have no time for it. Some busy parents, for example, stay up late at night to read their daily quota once the house is quiet, tacitly acknowledging that balance in their lives is more dependent on reading time than on sleep.

The time spent reading each day may be very brief, especially for individuals who lead active family and professional lives; however, these individuals often choose their reading material carefully with a long-range goal in mind, if only vaguely so. Their reading will reflect a pursuit of personal needs or interests, and the material they read will be chosen for its appropriateness to that pursuit.

Mature readers read about a variety of subjects, but with particular depth and perception in one or more interest areas. The gender gap has closed by now, and individual interests predominate. Seen as a tool for individual growth, their reading is generally purposeful, not random or accidental. They read not just for the characterization and storyline of a novel or the information gained from well-chosen non-fiction, but also for the aesthetic pleasure found in language presented as the art form it can be. Mature readers may read slowly, savoring sentence structure and descriptive passages, or they may devour several books simultaneously. While not everything they read is written on a high level, much of it is, and their competence in the skill of reading is superior at all levels.

Among mature readers, differing patterns emerge, reflecting personalities and life stages. One 16-year-old who was about to begin his freshman year in college showed his idiosyncratic taste in his summer reading list. Not following any of the college-bound lists, he pursued reading that he had not had time to complete in his shortened high school career. He read *The Idiot*; *1984*; *Jude the Obscure*; *Tom Jones*; *Tales of the Mabinogi*; *The Journey through Wales* and *The Description of Wales*, by Gerald of Wales; *Macbeth*; and Bulfinch's *The Age of Chivalry* and *The Legends of Charlemagne*.

A different style of mature reading belongs to a young man in medical school. Seeking a balance to his daily diet of science and memorization of facts, he pursues music avocationally. Without a musical instrument available at present, he has begun a planned program of reading and listening—reading about the structure in Bach's music, for example, and then listening to it with an informed ear. He also consults an art history text, adding "his" composers to the time line in the book to aid in placing them chronologically in his mind. Once a resistant reader, this young man now uses reading systematically as a tool to enrich his intellectual life.

Another example is of a mature reader in his mid-forties who gave up an academic career in order to have time for outdoor activities he loved, particularly fly fishing. He and his wife belonged to a book club in their small town for more than 10 years. His reading interests encompassed modern fiction, nonfiction, and poetry. Books that he said were particularly meaningful to him included Moon's *Blue Highways*, Freud's *Future of an Illusion*, Kerouac's *On the Road*, *The Sportswriter* by Richard Ford, Joseph Campbell's *The Power of Myth*; *This Boy's Life* (which is annotated in Chapter 8); and *The Last*

Lion, the second volume of Manchester's biography of Winston Churchill.

The list reveals the breadth and depth of interests of a thoughtful, open-minded adult—characteristic not only of this fly fisherman, but also of the friends with whom he and his wife met to discuss the books they read. The unexpected existence and longevity of the group in this small northern Michigan town testifies to the value of reading in an enriched adult life—as well as a possible future for students who list books among their best friends and who may worry that their love of books sets them apart. In the tiny town near the river, a common love of books brought friends together.

The concept of mature reading as an adult can be useful in guiding the careers of multi-talented teens. Gifted students heading toward college and career must make a choice among interests, giving one priority as a vocation and the others as avocations. It can be easier to give up the full-time pursuit of a favorite interest if one understands that he can continue to follow it through reading. In fact, a student may make a career choice partly on the basis of which other interests are most accessible through a program of planned and deliberate reading.

The possibility of becoming a mature reader should be introduced in high school so that students can consider how to make use of it in their lives. It will be helpful if they realize that mature reading is an acceptable and enjoyable life pattern. With this reassurance, dedicated readers who have reached the age when few of their peers still enjoy leisure reading can avoid any concern about their own continuing interest in books.

Chapter 4

Emotional Development through Books

On the surface, it often appears that most eager learners have everything going for them and that they can handle any difficulties they encounter on their own. They themselves help to perpetuate this myth—they are quick to perceive what is expected of them and to produce it so that even alert adults may not be aware of these children's specific problems and vulnerabilities. However, as we know from Chapter 1, gifted children—different, sensitive, and demanding much of themselves—are emotionally vulnerable.

Books, and conversations about them with understanding adults, can become catalysts for helping children recognize and talk about some of the experiences, both joyful and painful, that are part of growing up different—whether that difference is due to giftedness or to unusual intellectual or artistic interests. Such discussions offer adults a low-key method of helping children become aware of the feelings that they may encounter as a result of their differences. Discussing experiences and reactions of the characters in books can also lead children to a new understanding of experiences that they have already faced.

Books in which characters struggle with some of the same problems that the reader has experienced can give assurance that someone else has had similar difficulty, and the reader can solve the problems vicariously with the character. If a trusted adult reads the same book and then discusses it with the child, an intimate problem can be discussed at third-person distance. And if it is a group discussion, the child can benefit from the experiences of other children in the group. Individual or group discussion can lead to fresh insights that will help the child cope with difficult situations in her own life. This process is especially suited to gifted children because so many are enthusiastic readers and enjoy discussing what they read.

For parents and teachers, the rewards are in the reading, in the discussion, and most of all in the response from the children. At the end of a discussion series, one student said in her evaluation, "I learned that being gifted is important." Her statement needed further clarification, but she had taken a step toward accepting her talent as part of her identity.

The many gifted children who have not been formally identified have the same emotional needs as those who have been, and they too can benefit from discussions that will help them to establish an identity, recognize their need for alone time, learn to get along with others, develop their full potential, and take responsibility for their drive to understand. This chapter offers both theoretical and practical information on using books to enhance the emotional development of children who are different from the norm by reason of giftedness or intense interests through the form of bibliotherapy.

Bibliotherapy

Webster's Third New International Dictionary defines bibliotherapy as "the use of selected reading materials as therapeutic adjuvants in medicine and in psychiatry; also, guidance in the solution of personal problems through directed reading." Among those who use bibliotherapy, one of the classic definitions is: "A process of dynamic interaction between the personality of the reader and literature—interaction which may be utilized for personality assessment, adjustment, and growth."[1]

Webster's reference to medicine has a long and honorable history. Libraries in the ancient world bore inscriptions such as "Medicine for the Mind" in Alexandria and "The Healing Place of the Soul" in Thebes. In America, the use of bibliotherapy goes back at least to Dr. Benjamin Rush, who recommended the reading of books as part of a treatment regimen for hospital patients in the early part of the 19th century.

The two definitions in Webster's refer to the two major types of bibliotherapy: clinical and developmental. Doll and Doll[2] recommend a cooperative effort between librarians and mental health professionals for clinical bibliotherapy, while suggesting that teachers, counselors, and parents who have the appropriate qualifications and are motivated to do so are quite capable of leading discussions in developmental bibliotherapy without the assistance of mental health workers. The distinction is an important one. The type of bibliotherapy proposed here is developmental, with referral to mental health professionals when emotional issues are more profound. This section is designed to help readers understand the differences. They can perhaps best be described by contrasting them.

Clinical bibliotherapy occurs when people who have emotional or behavioral problems meet to discuss recommended books in a clinical setting such as a drug treatment center. With a trained mental health professional serving as facilitator, they hold a discussion or counseling session designed to address their problems in the hope of bringing about changes in attitudes and behavior. Clinical bibliotherapy could also take place in a school, with a school psychologist working in a team approach with the librarian.[3]

In developmental bibliotherapy (the most commonly used type), ordinary people who are facing a normal life stage or transitional period meet in community settings such as schools or libraries to discuss books related to the issues that concern them. In a school setting, groups facilitated by a teacher, librarian, school counselor, or school social worker are designed to help students resolve normal developmental issues of adjustment and growth—again, through changes in attitude and/or behavior resulting from reading and discussion. In bibliotherapy for gifted students, it is recognized that normal developmental issues of adjustment and growth are complicated by specific characteristics and feelings common to gifted children.

Developmental Bibliotherapy

Developmental bibliotherapy is used preventively, attempting to anticipate and meet needs before they become problems. The goal is to help people move through life's predictable stages by providing information about what to expect and examples of how other people have dealt with the same developmental challenges.

Several psychologists have created lists of developmental tasks that everyone must meet. In an article about bibliotherapy in public libraries, Lack summarizes Zaccaria's compilation of such lists:[4]

Life Stage	Developmental Task
Infancy	Achieving a sense of trust
Middle childhood	Achieving a sense of initiative
Late childhood	Achieving a sense of industry
Adolescence	Developing a sense of identity
Early adulthood	Achieving a sense of intimacy
Middle adulthood	Achieving a sense of generativity
Late adulthood	Achieving a sense of ego integrity

Those who are interested in the development of gifted children will see immediately how important the tasks are for middle childhood, late childhood, and adolescence. A sense of initiative, industry, and identity are essential to enable gifted youngsters to avoid underachievement and develop their abilities to their own full satisfaction. Yet for some gifted children, the response of others to their giftedness makes it especially difficult for them to move through these developmental stages with complete success. Here are some examples.

> *Todd showed a sense of initiative when he asked his fourth-grade teacher for harder math problems. Busy with 32 other students and unable to believe that Todd wanted to work harder, she brushed aside his request.*

When her class studied ancient Egypt, Sasha became so interested that she persuaded her family to travel to a nearby city one weekend to visit the museum, delaying the completion of her report. Her parents encouraged Sasha's sense of industry; the teacher, who would not accept a late report, discouraged it.

Yeung knew that he was unusually bright, but because his parents wanted him to be "just normal, like everyone else," he had difficulty accepting his own ability. It was a junior high teacher, patiently working with Yeung as he built a project for a science fair, who enabled him to enjoy his talent and develop a sense of identity that incorporated his intelligence.

The stories of Todd, Sasha, and Yeung exemplify the impact of adults' responses to gifted children's attempts to establish a sense of initiative, industry, and identity. The reactions of others can encourage or thwart the healthy growth of these children. Developmental bibliotherapy can help make the difference. Through it, teachers, librarians, counselors, and parents can help gifted youngsters recognize and articulate their feelings and prepare them for the particular spins that being gifted puts on normal developmental tasks.

Therefore, in this book, bibliotherapy is seen specifically as a way of helping gifted and talented children understand and cope with growing up different in a world that is geared to the average. It can be used to help them anticipate difficulties, as well as give them a basis for self-understanding when they feel alone and misunderstood or when they are reluctant to use their abilities because it is not popular to be smart. Through bibliotherapy, adults can encourage gifted children to build a strong self-concept so that they can develop their full potential in spite of the inevitable pull toward the peer group and so that they will resist pressures—both from inside and outside—toward perfectionism. Developmental bibliotherapy can be part of a planned effort to help them meet their childhood and adolescent tasks.

Studies of Bibliotherapy

Bibliotherapy is based on the belief that our lives can be changed by what we read, particularly if there is an opportunity to discuss what we read with others. Although difficult to document, this belief persists, perhaps because of the inner certainty of those who love books; we may feel that we do not need scientific proof of what we so surely know. Many of us can relate to having identified so strongly with a character that we made him or her a part of ourselves or adopted his or her attitude toward a situation, and we have all been comforted by knowing that an author has perfectly described our innermost feelings. Additionally, developments in the practice of psychology have shown that group discussion can be a therapeutic process.

Research results confirming this intuitive evaluation of the effectiveness of bibliotherapy would be welcome, but studies thus far yield ambiguous results. The libraries in Thebes and Alexandria notwithstanding, bibliotherapy as we explore it in this book is a relatively young discipline. While there is yet little research to confirm the theories behind it, there is a steady flow of articles by educators and mental health workers describing how they have used bibliotherapy successfully with various populations.[5]

In the 1970s, reading research focused on whether reading had the power to change attitudes. Schrank and Engles reviewed the research studies of that period and reported that, while the effectiveness of bibliotherapy in some other areas was not supported, "research in this category suggests an overwhelming Yes to the question of whether bibliotherapy is effective."[6]

It is difficult, however, to point to research findings that verify or refute the effectiveness of bibliotherapy with bright and gifted children. The reasons for this, however, may have more to do with the mechanics of research than with the topic under investigation.

First, inconsistencies in definition and method weaken the collective impact of findings. In an article reviewing earlier studies, Tillman[7] reveals the difficulties of using them to make definitive statements about the effectiveness of bibliotherapy. For example, some studies have gathered information simply through a checklist that asks students how reading has affected them. In others, the effect of reading on attitudes was studied by administering a pre-test, a reading, and a post-test.

Second, in some research, the bibliotherapeutic process does not include discussion of the book or of students' reactions to it, although other studies do include discussion as a part of biblio-therapy. If the definition of bibliotherapy includes a follow-up discussion of the reading, as it does here, then research must attempt to assess the entire process.

Third, many studies reflect the work of counselors and other mental health practitioners who typically use bibliotherapy as an adjunct to therapy—that is, who are using it clinically. This research has concentrated on self-help books rather than on fiction, so the effectiveness of fiction remains unvalidated.[8]

Fourth, research investigating the use of bibliotherapy with gifted children is rare, in part because of the failure of researchers to recognize that gifted children have unique problems that might be addressed through bibliotherapy.[9]

And finally, the impact of a book varies significantly from one reader to another, determined by an overwhelming number of variables. Attempts to measure and quantify the effect of art on personality will always be thwarted to some degree by the elusiveness of the concepts involved.

Therefore, current studies can point toward but not confirm the effectiveness of using carefully selected books and well-planned dis-cussion to help gifted students cope with their giftedness. At present, only the experience of educators and children supports the assertion that bibliotherapy is valuable for gifted students. Children probably say it best when they affirm, time after time, that they would want to be in a discussion group again and that it is definitely worth the time it takes from their regular schedule—typical responses when they are asked to evaluate the experience at the end of a discussion series. In addition, textbooks on gifted education increasingly include a sec-tion on bibliotherapy, affirming that experts in the field believe that connecting gifted children with books and giving them a chance to talk about their responses makes intuitive sense.

Since the research we do have indicates that the process has potential, continued and expanded use of developmental bibliotherapy with gifted youngsters should be encouraged. From the knowledge now available, adults who work with books and gifted youngsters can do so with assurance that they are using a recommended method of guiding gifted children. They must, though, proceed with caution, with respect for the infinite variability of human nature, and in the knowledge that they are practicing an art and not a science.

Qualifications for Bibliotherapists

Do parents, teachers, or librarians who lack special training have the expertise to lead a bibliotherapeutic discussion? If it is developmental bibliotherapy, the consensus is that they do. One factor that clearly differentiates developmental from clinical bibliotherapy is that developmental bibliotherapy does not require a trained mental health professional, and clinical bibliotherapy does.[10] After all, for teachers, librarians, and parents, it is very natural to listen to children talk about their feelings and reactions. Bernstein asserts that bibliotherapy does not necessarily require training in psychotherapy but "can be and is safely undertaken by those with less sophisticated expertise in human nature: teachers, librarians, doctors, lawyers, parents, and others."[11]

Here, we take the view that many parents, teachers, and librarians are already practicing bibliotherapy in various degrees, perhaps without knowing it and almost always without formal training. The information provided in this chapter is offered in the belief that the more these discussion leaders can learn about what they are doing, the more effective they will be.

For discussion leaders who would like additional background, *Bibliotherapy: The Interactive Process: A Handbook*[12] is an excellent resource, offering a thorough and thoughtful explanation of the process. While it emphasizes clinical work, it also provides a good basis for developmental bibliotherapy. Those who are interested in doing bibliotherapy probably already have some of the qualifications listed by the authors:

○ maturity: self-awareness, self-acceptance, tolerance of others

○ integrity: respect for self and others that enables the therapist to avoid exploitation of emotions

○ responsibility: an attitude of responsiveness, as well as a willingness to guide group participants through potentially difficult discussions

○ adaptability: the ability to adjust plans to meet the needs of the group at the moment and to allow participants their own interpretations

In addition to these inherent characteristics, the authors point out that bibliotherapists must acquire and develop therapeutic attitudes, such as:

○ empathy: the ability to understand another person's feelings without actually experiencing them

○ respect: the recognition of the value of another person's feelings and of his or her inherent worth and uniqueness

○ genuineness: sincerity, spontaneity, openness; awareness and acceptance of one's own inner experiences

To use developmental bibliotherapy with gifted children, leaders should also know and enjoy children's literature, understand child development in general and that of gifted children in particular, have the trust of the children with whom they are working, and know something about counseling and discussion techniques.

The Bibliotherapeutic Process

Present theories about what happens in bibliotherapy date back to 1949, when educator Carolyn Shrodes studied the relationship between bibliotherapy and psychotherapy for her doctoral dissertation. Shrodes identified three phases of the bibliotherapeutic process, corresponding to phases of psychotherapy. These form the basis of subsequent concepts of bibliotherapy.

The three stages of bibliotherapy are identification, catharsis, and insight. A fourth phase, less often mentioned but especially interesting for work with gifted children, is universalization,[13] the recognition that our difficulties and sense of difference are not ours alone.

Identification

Bibliotherapy depends on the dynamics set up among the reader, the literature, and the discussion. It begins with *identification*, the process by which the reader identifies with a character in the book, recognizing something of himself in—and so coming to care what happens to—that character. Mollie Hunter, author of *The Mermaid Summer* (which is listed in this book under "Recommended Books from Earlier Editions"), describes identification with the understanding and skill of a fine writer:

> *Even the most superficial reader will follow the incident by identifying with the character concerned in it; and so, willy-nilly, there comes a point when reader and character are involved in the same emotions.... The reader...glimpse[s] a reflection of himself in another young person caught in a situation that demands the enunciation of some value, the setting of some standard. Temporarily at least, he will have had a sense of participating in the decision taken, and the process of thought set unconsciously in train may yet surface in his mind.... [T]he reader will still be essentially free to formulate his own eventual philosophy; but [he will have been shown] something of what may be implied by the choices occurring in those adolescent years.*[14]

It may sound improbable that identification with a fictional character can be such a powerful experience, but book characters are real people to most children, and these children continue to see the characters as real people, even under the close scrutiny of discussion.[15]

At the same time, the child's awareness of the distancing effect of literature provides a sense of safety. Lerner and Mahlendorf point out that:

*...it is for the reason of emotional safety by proper dis-
tancing that literary works can do more than merely
instruct us.... They...make us more sensitive to [our]
feelings and ourselves. In this way, we gain an emotional
awareness that transforms us and gives us the motivation to change ourselves.*[16]

Catharsis

Catharsis occurs as the reader follows the character through a difficult situation to a successful resolution. Spache defines catharsis as:

*...[the] sharing of motivations, conflicts, and emotions of
a book character. Defined in psychological terms, catharsis is an active release of emotions, experienced either
first-hand or vicariously. Catharsis goes beyond the simple
intellectual recognition of commonalities as in identification.... It involves empathetic emotional reactions
similar to those that the reader imagines were felt by the
book character. Or, in another sense, the reader relives,
insofar as his own emotional experiences permit, the feelings he attributes to a character in a story.*[17]

I recall a quiet summer morning years ago when I was working
contentedly in the kitchen, the children still in bed upstairs, when
from my younger son's room came the sudden heart-stopping sound
of deep sobbing. He had been awake for some time, reading *Julie of
the Wolves*, and had reached the cruel and emotionally painful climactic point in Julie's conflict between two cultures. Anyone who
knows that book will recognize that he was experiencing catharsis. It
is not a bad thing, after all, to be able to cry over a book.

Insight

Insight is the reader's application of the character's situation to
her own life. If identification and catharsis have occurred while reading the book, insight may occur during discussion or even later, as the
reader reflects on the story. She may transfer her understanding of the
character's personality and motivations to herself, increasing self-

understanding and bringing her own options into sharper focus. Thus, insight can lead to changed attitudes, which can then lead to changed behavior.

However, insight does not necessarily lead to immediate action. The discussion leader may not even know whether insight has occurred, but assumptions can be made. What insights might have resulted from my son's reading of *Julie of the Wolves* years ago? A confirmation of his sensitivity to cruelty and his tender-heartedness toward animals; a reluctant recognition, perhaps, that true endings are not always happy ones; and the newfound confidence that he could accept this fact with sadness—a growing experience for a 10-year-old.

Universalization

Universalization is behind James Delisle's description of "John" in an article recommending bibliotherapy as one means of preventing suicide among gifted young people. Delisle affirms that John:

> *...probably does not realize that thousands of other persons throughout the centuries have wrestled with the same types of issues that he now confronts.... More than anything else—anyone else—what John now needs is someone to tell him that it is OK to be confused, anxious, and ambivalent. This person may be a teacher, a counselor, Holden Caulfield from* Catcher in the Rye, *or the protagonist in* Zen and the Art of Motorcycle Maintenance. *To gifted students like John, getting the answers to timeworn philosophical issues is less important than merely being told that his questions are legitimate.*[18]

This process, of course, does not take place with every reader or with every book. A discussion leader can help to bring it about, though, by asking questions that focus first on identification with one or several characters (and on the universality of the experience, if that is appropriate); then on the critical situation, the way the story character handled it, and the feelings stirred in the reader in response; and finally on ways in which all of this relates to the reader's own life.

A demonstration of this process will be found in the sample questions given later in this chapter.

It should also be noted that these steps do not necessarily fit neatly into a half-hour discussion session. Many readers continue to mull over books long after they have finished them. If there is not a good response to one of the deeper questions during the discussion, a seed that will lead to thought later on may nevertheless have been planted. Bibliotherapy discussion leaders, like parents and teachers, will know only a small portion of the impact that they have on children's lives.

Caution with Bibliotherapy

As with any helping relationship, bibliotherapists must exercise caution—always aware of the possibility that deeper problems may be present, while also remembering that developmental bibliotherapy is meant to help prevent problems, not to cure them. Anyone who encourages children to discuss their feelings should know when to refer a child to a mental health professional. Children may exhibit any of several warning signals that the bibliotherapist should discuss with the child's parents or a psychologist.

There may be underlying problems if a gifted child or his parents appear to be denying giftedness. If the child shows unusual reluctance to be placed in the gifted category, or if the parents are unable or unwilling to allow the child to participate in enrichment activities, there is some cause for concern. Comments from the child may indicate prejudicial treatment at home in the form of parental attitudes disclosed in statements like, "If you're so smart, why can't you remember to take out the trash?"

A problem may also be indicated if a child seems incapable of relating to the purpose of the book discussion group or unable to relate meaningfully to at least some of the other children in the group.

Jamal made it clear that he didn't want any part of a book discussion group; he slumped in his chair and glowered at the floor except when spoken to directly. He talked as little as possible, contributing one comment that revealed very low self-esteem. After three sessions, he stopped attending, and after the discussion leader called his mother for a conference, the mother made arrangements for individual sessions for him—a much more appropriate arrangement in this instance than group discussion.

Responses can indicate much more than low self-esteem. There is reason to be concerned about students whose responses reveal excessive anger, aggression, anxiety, depression, fear, preoccupation with sexuality, inability to have empathy for others, little or no social life, or inordinately high or perfectionist standards for themselves. School performance that is far below ability level or a lack of investment in achievement in any area—even those in which the child possesses high ability—are further signals of underlying problems that might be helped by clinical therapy.

Anna had been invited to join a bibliotherapy discussion group because her test scores indicated that she was gifted. Her academic performance had never measured up to her potential, and teachers hoped the group would bring about changes in her behavior. Although the other students in the group were her friends, Anna did not join in the discussion. It was clear by the second session that she had transferred her attitude toward schoolwork to the group; she would not read the books—not because she was too busy, but because she had decided not to participate. Recognizing that the bibliotherapy group was not appropriate for Anna, the leader referred her to the school counselor.

Of course, a leader must be concerned about a student who gives evidence of physical or psychological abuse or neglect, who shows signs of drug or alcohol abuse, or who is carrying a weapon. She may be alerted in discussion, for example, by a student who strongly defends the right of individuals to use drugs.

A bibliotherapist must also be aware of the possibility of serious depression or even potential suicide in students. Indications of depression include insomnia or other sleep disturbances, lack of interest in life or in any number of activities that formerly were motivating and exciting, emotional outbursts, noticeable weight gain or loss, and changes in clothing and dress standards. Direct mention of suicide and a strong defense of suicide as a desirable choice are clear danger signs.

These warning signals do not occur often, but a bibliotherapist should be aware of them and realize that he is in a unique position to help. Concern about suicide or suicidal thoughts should always be reported to school authorities and to the child's parents. A discussion leader's best contribution to some children may well be a referral to psychological help. Schools typically have clear policies to follow when teachers or other school personnel suspect any of the concerns listed. Parents seeking a referral can consult a school counselor for advice.

In addition to watching for signs of emotional problems, discussion leaders should be careful to control the depth of the discussion. It is not necessary that everything be explicitly said; participants can be trusted to take and use what they can. If a discussion at greater depth seems potentially beneficial, a teacher or librarian could ask the school guidance counselor or psychologist to serve as co-leader. In developmental bibliotherapy, without a mental health profes sional present, discussion leaders should not invite self-disclosures that would make participants feel exposed or embarrassed.

Literature for Bibliotherapy

For developmental bibliotherapy, the focus is on fiction, but nonfiction should not be overlooked.

Nonfiction

In the first two chapters of this book, we recognized intellectual challenge as both an intellectual need and an emotional need of gifted children. For this reason, providing challenging material is a main concern for teachers and parents of gifted children, and non-fiction books are a major source of such material. In addition, many young people strongly prefer nonfiction; for them it may be the wiser starting point. With children who may be reluctant to discuss feelings, a conversation about a "fact book" with an adult who shares the child's enthusiasm for the subject may help to build an important relationship—not quite the same goal as for a bibliotherapeutic discussion, but a very worthy outcome.

Nonfiction is included in the information about books in Chapters 6 and 7; in this book, more space is given to nonfiction titles in Chapter 8 than has been the case for previous editions.

Biography

The form of nonfiction most frequently recommended for bibliotherapy is biography. Biographies of eminent women can provide role models for girls; gifted girls who are not personally acquainted with women in high-level careers may be inspired by these women's life stories, possibly without need for discussion.[19] Boys can benefit from biographies of men who have overcome difficulties and achieved not only success, but deeper self-understanding as a result of their struggles.[20]

According to Dr. Tracy Cross, reading biography:

> ...raises awareness that many highly accomplished people also struggled with some of the same issues the student faces. This realization tends to reduce feelings of isolation while at the same time providing ideas for dealing with the difficulties gifted people encounter. [In reading biography, a student] creates his or her own understanding of the issues he or she faces. This is a vastly different experience from having one's parent discuss issues with you.[21]

Moreover, biography—the story of a life—can be written as fiction or nonfiction, or a blend of the two. More information on types of biography is found in Chapter 7.

Other Nonfiction

Reading to and with a child who much prefers nonfiction may be a challenge to an adult whose major interest is fiction. However, there is an unlimited world of fascinating information, often creatively presented, for the adult to discover in the nonfiction section of a library. By following the child's lead, perhaps with the help of a librarian or a good independent bookseller, adult and child will start on a rewarding journey as one book—and one topic—leads to another and another.

But some fact books are better—more accurate and better written for children—than others. The nonfiction sections in Chapters 6 and 7 explain how to choose the best nonfiction books, especially for gifted children.

Fiction

Robert Coles, the psychiatrist who wrote *Children in Crisis* with such insight of children's responses to traumatic situations, draws on his teaching experience at Harvard for another book: *The Call of Stories: Teaching and the Moral Imagination.*[22] In seminars on "Literature and Medicine" and "A Literature of Social Reflection," Coles encourages medical, law, and business students to explore how a thoughtful reading of fine novels, poems, and plays can affect their lives. The stories he tells of the emotional impact of fiction on the developing values and goals of college students provide inspiration—an excellent starting point for anyone selecting books for a bibliotherapeutic discussion.

A child's response to fiction typically begins at the emotional level. For this reason, fiction is ideal for developmental bibliotherapy, especially when reading is accompanied by an opportunity to discuss the book with someone else who has read it. Hearing the comments of others enables the child to see that their responses are similar to hers—that she is not alone in her feelings. This demonstrates to the child that she is not so different.

Using fiction for bibliotherapy, then, is not simply a matter of handing a child a book about a problem that he is facing himself. A story is not a pill that will cure if administered at the proper time; it is a starting point. To be most effective, the reading must be followed by discussion with a concerned adult who has also read the book. This statement cannot be made too strongly: *The adult must read the book, too*, and be prepared with his or her own response to the literature and with a few key questions to promote discussion.

The delightful surprise in store for adults unfamiliar with current children's literature is its high quality. There is no need to settle for the mediocre; there is plenty of both the good and the excellent, and good literature is not boring, no matter what the age of the reader.

Nevertheless, a warning: with the rising concern over the number of social problems facing today's children, we have seen an increase in didactic fiction—stories designed to teach a lesson. At first glance, these books may seem ideal for bibliotherapy. However, fiction written for bibliotherapeutic purposes usually fails as literature—it is too earnest, and since discerning readers see through it quickly, it cannot bear the weight of serious discussion. To speak authentically to the emotions and to reflect truly the human condition, fiction chosen for bibliotherapy must exemplify literature as the art form it was meant to be.

Logistics: Organizing Discussion Groups at School

When teachers or librarians use book discussion with high-ability students, they are most likely to do so with a group, although they may occasionally hold informal talks with individual students. This next section provides detailed information on selecting children to join discussion groups, on choosing books for groups to read, and on setting a place and time for book discussion at school.

Before a leader can sit down with a group of youngsters, all of whom have read the same book and are eager to discuss it, there is much work to be done. Setting up a group means bringing appropriate children and appropriate books together, in sufficient numbers of each, at a time and place that will suit everyone's needs. The advance planning will vary considerably, depending on such factors as how the school identifies gifted students, the academic structure of the program for them (if any), the flexibility in the schedule, and how important the faculty and administration feel it is to deal with the emotional needs of gifted youngsters.

The Children

It is easier to hold effective discussions if the children involved are close in age. Students from two grade levels can meet together, but a wider age range makes it difficult to choose literature that will appeal to everyone.

Children should also be relatively close in ability level. As with academic programs for the gifted, a book discussion group that combines students in the moderately gifted range with those who are highly gifted will probably fail to meet the needs of the highly gifted members; it would be better to have a separate group for them if possible.

Remembering that highly gifted people differ from one another more than do people in the average range of ability, the leader for this group should keep the individual characteristics of each reader in mind while selecting books. For the same reason, discussion should be specifically planned for the individual students rather than for the group in general. In addition, at least some of the books chosen for them should offer examples of highly gifted people.

With any discussion group for gifted or intellectually able children, the leader should know how much the children understand about their selection for the group. If the term "gifted" is used, the comfort level of the students will depend largely on how the use of the term is handled within their school. It may be a good idea in the first session to discuss how members will describe the group for children who are not included. The leader can help the children avoid hurting others without downplaying their own abilities: "We're going to read books and talk about them. It's a group for good readers who like to read a lot. We're going to learn ways to think about a book after you've read it and how to discuss the ideas in the book."

The leader should consider whether the self-concept and personal strength of each potential member is sufficient to allow participation in the group without inappropriate self-revelation or hypersensitivity. If the leader knows that a child has a specific problem that may be discussed and that it is so close to the surface that the student will be unable to think or speak about it objectively, then for the protection of the child, an individual discussion is preferable to a group experience.

> *Stacie's parents have recently divorced, and her mother has asked Stacie's school counselor to include her in a support group for children of divorced parents. In talking with Stacie, however, the counselor has learned that she is not yet ready to discuss her experience in a group of peers. Rather than participate in a group discussion of* A Girl Called Al, *a book dealing with the emotional aftermath of divorce, Stacie should be given the option of meeting individually with the counselor for a time.*

Unexpected self-revelation may well occur during group discussion, and the leader can deal with it at that time through reassurance, redirection of the topic, or by offering to talk about it after the meeting. It is better if selection of group members can minimize its occurrence. Members of a book discussion group designed to help them cope with developmental issues of giftedness should be children not currently in crisis. A group for children in crisis should be planned and led differently, with a counselor as leader or co-leader.

A group size of six to eight children is optimum. With more than eight, there may be some who will remain silent because the group is large enough for them to do so. With fewer than six, the group can become ineffective if even two members are absent or have not read the book.

Should group membership be optional for those eligible to join? If it is, there will be better potential for good discussion. The key is each student's interest in the topic and in participating. Those who do not wish to join now may wish to do so later.

The Books

In some contexts, bibliotherapy is practiced with little regard for the quality of the literature chosen. The only requirement is that the subject of the literature be appropriate to the goals of the discussion. For a couple of reasons, this cannot be the case in bibliotherapy with especially bright students.

First and most practically, inferior literature will not lend itself to discussions that will touch and challenge gifted students. They may not recognize the technical differences between good and bad literature, but they will certainly recognize (and mention with notable lack of grace) when a book is "*bor-ing.*" Discussion about books perceived as boring is bound to be boring itself, for any age group.

Second, it is a disservice to skilled and enthusiastic readers to encourage them to spend their time on less than the best. Of course they will experiment with escape literature from time to time, but they can learn to recognize it, and they can learn how to find good literature when they want it. Parents and teachers who are guiding them in the larger sense of helping them develop their potential must have the courage to differentiate the inferior from the good, and they must take the time to find the best for them.

To find good literature, use as many sources of book lists as possible. Parents and teachers should have access to such sources as *Booklist* and *School Library Journal*, which contain book reviews and recommendations. Librarians use such selection aids in considering which books to buy. Journals about parenting and educating gifted children often have book review sections. Newsletters of local associations for parents of gifted children may include suggestions of good books. And there are websites, such as www.hoagiesgifted.org/hot_topics.htm and www.hoagiesgifted.org/shopping_guide.htm# kidsbooks.

Browse through the education section of bookstores; there are always books to help adults encourage children to read. For discussion purposes, however, look for publications that focus on books themselves rather than on the process of reading or on reading readiness. There is a partial list of these at the end of Chapter 6.

Develop the habit of reading reviews of children's books, keeping in mind the criteria listed in Chapter 6 for books that meet emotional needs while challenging the intellect. Good ideas can also come from other educators and sometimes from children. As discussion leaders gain experience with excellent literature, they will recognize trusted authors and good writing, so they can browse effectively. Before long, by reading just a page or two, they can sense whether a book is likely to justify their time to pre-read it for use with the children they have in mind.

After gathering lists of suggested titles, leaders should preview the books and select titles to recommend to students. It is best to suggest several titles, giving book talks to generate interest, and have the students vote on which one the group will read. Because several copies will be needed, cost considerations may limit the choices to paperbacks.

If students must provide their books, they may wish to buy their own copies to build personal libraries, or they can borrow from local libraries. Perhaps the public library will have multiple copies. And single copies of almost any title can be located through interlibrary loan at public libraries. However, the most efficient way of making sure that each student has a copy of the book under discussion is for the school to provide them. Schools may have classroom sets of some titles. Multiple copies of the titles selected may fit into the library budget, or perhaps the school or gifted parent association would be willing to help with the purchase. The books can be kept in the school library for use by discussion groups in future years and can be made available to other students in the meantime.

Place and Time

Privacy is important when choosing a place for the discussion group. A special room or corner of the school library would be best if the library is empty at the time. A corner in the classroom is not a good place to discuss feelings that the participants would not want all classmates to hear.

The difficulty in scheduling a time will depend on whether children are coming to the group from more than one class and on what degree of priority the school gives to the book discussion group. It is generally not a good idea to schedule programming for gifted students at a time that requires them to miss recess, physical education, or lunch—which would take them away from social opportunities and emphasize their differences. In one school, however, these were the only options. The principal's suggestion that the students vote on the time they preferred was a happy one for all concerned.

For children in grades 3-5, a series of four sessions may be adequate, spaced one week apart. Middle school students may need more time to read their books; biweekly sessions might be better for them. For high school students, book discussions could be held once a month throughout the school year. Each session should last just 15 or 20 minutes in the early elementary grades, up to a full class period for senior high students.

Book discussion groups can also be offered as part of summer enrichment programs. Sessions may be spread over a period of two to three weeks, with two or three meetings a week, since children typically have more time to read in the summer. These groups can incorporate students from different schools, granting them an anonymity that may make it easier to talk.

In planning the dates for the group to meet, remember that it may be four to six weeks after books are ordered before they arrive.

Logistics: Organizing Discussions at Home

Parents may want to discuss books with their children for a number of reasons: to supplement the reading program at school, because they are homeschooling, or simply for pleasure. In addition to the suggestions offered below, consider forming a group of parents and children to read and talk together.

In an effort to continue into the school year the long, relaxed conversations that she enjoyed with her children during vacations, Shireen Dodson formed a mother-daughter book club in 1995 when her daughter, Morgan, was nine years old. In *The Mother-Daughter Book Club*,[23] Dodson describes their experience and offers suggestions for starting a club, along with reading lists and discussion guides. The subtitle is enticing: *How Ten Busy Mothers and Daughters Came Together to Talk, Laugh and Learn through Their Love of Reading*. What a wonderful way to make early adolescence not only survivable, but a time for bonding!

When parents discuss books with their children at home, the question of which children to involve is not an issue. Still, as with teachers and librarians planning a discussion group at school, parents must solve the problems of locating good books and finding a suitable place and time for discussion. In addition, they need to consider different ways to motivate their child to participate, and they must use slightly different techniques in talking with an individual instead of a group.

Finding Good Books

The bibliography in Chapter 8 is designed to help parents and teachers find books that are well-written, challenging (as they must be to hold the interest of discriminating readers), and suitable as discussion-starters. In addition, parents can use the suggestions listed for teachers earlier in this chapter. The children's department of the public library carries resources like *School Library Journal, Booklist,* and others. While your child browses for books, you can learn how to gain access to these materials, building a helpful relationship with the children's librarian at the same time.

Suitable Place and Time

Where and when are good opportunities for you to read and talk about books with your children? In a more leisurely era, I might have suggested firmly establishing a family book discussion at the same time every week. Some modern families may be able to manage this, and I applaud them, but I acknowledge that for most, hectic schedules require imaginative solutions.

Busy working parents can make use of snippets of time throughout the day. If books are a priority, they will be in the car, carried into the dentist's waiting room, or tucked into a backpack or handbag to be pulled out while waiting for a ride or a rider. Conversations about books can take place in the car, over dishes, after the homework is done, or while taking a walk.

One family's tradition of book talk time, available to each child after the lights go out, provides a satisfying place and time to talk about books. Another family might designate a routine chore, such as a Saturday run to the recycling center, for book talk time. For homeschooling families, book talk can be part of the school day. Once the importance of finding time to read and talk about books is established, every member of the family can get into the act of finding time to do it—and meeting the challenge tells children how important it really is.

Motivation

With an avid reader, a parent may only need to mention that he or she would like to read a book that the child is reading; then, when both have finished the book, they can talk about it whenever there are 15 or 20 uninterrupted minutes. After a pattern of discussing books is established, the parent can reciprocate by recommending a book to the child, and they will be on their way.

With a resistant reader, parents may have to be more assertive. It will help if reading time has been built into the daily schedule from the early years, and it will certainly help if the parents are readers. Some parents find that they can strike a deal with their child: the child will read what the parent recommends, and in turn, the parent will read what the child recommends—at least some of the time.

Discussion with an Individual Child

What a parent does in bibliotherapy will be much the same as what a teacher or librarian does, except he or she will usually be talking with one child instead of a group. The parent can use the same procedures for planning and leading a discussion that are listed later in this chapter for use with a group, modifying them to suit the home situation and the child.

The discussion itself will be slightly different from one with a group. If one child is doing all of the responding, then he is likely to become more involved in the discussion than he would if he could leave some of the work to others. On the other hand, he will miss the reinforcement of ideas from peers; the parent may need to compensate for this by bringing up the points of view that other children might mention if they were there.

Just as scheduling is likely to be less structured at home than at school, so discussions at home tend to be more relaxed. Parents should capitalize on the advantages of this difference rather than worrying about following a plan too closely.

Because home is less structured than school, parents may accomplish less in a given amount of time, but they have the advantage of being able to continue over a period of several years. In addition, they will bring such a wealth of family experience to the conversations that in the long run, they may well be able to accomplish far more. Imagine the following scenario:

> *The Browne family began reading to their children in the nursery, and both Mark and Brie started reading early. When they were three and four, Dad would push back his chair from the dining table in the evening and say, "I feel a little Pooh coming on," and they would pile into his lap for a chapter or two of* Winnie-the-Pooh. *The family read aloud on vacations and camping trips, and it was a natural step to begin talking about the books that the children were reading.*
>
> *Usually, Mother had read the books they read, and when she asked Brie what she thought of* The Wolfling, *the discussion expanded to include Dad's and Mark's thoughts on why higher education is important for someone like Robbie Trent—as well as for Mark and Brie. Brie's excitement over* Anno's Medieval World *led to a family discussion that helped Mark understand superstition and scientific thought in a new light—an understanding that he tucked away for further attention as he pondered budding career ideas. When Brie showed evidence of feeling uncomfortably different and out of place in her new middle school, Mother reminded her of Jess in* A Bridge to Terabithia, *who did not fit in his family or school but who did have one friend and one teacher who understood. Over the years, their shared love of books led to productive conversations and mutual understanding for the entire family.*

Planning for Discussion

After the logistics are settled, whether working informally with a child at home or setting up a series at school, planning is necessary before discussing a book with a child. Prior to a book discussion, the leader must choose a book, read it, prepare discussion questions, and motivate the children to read the book.

Choosing the Book

For help in finding books to discuss, parents can consult Chapter 6, which is devoted to selecting appropriate literature for gifted students and eager readers. Briefly, we can follow the suggestions of Robinson: look for situations that evoke emotions, circumstances that offer alternatives, and characters with whom the reader can identify.[24] For a good discussion to ensue, the book must deal with a range of human emotions, not just the fear or excitement engendered by adventure stories. When characters are faced with alternatives, readers are led to consider the options, too—a focal point for discussion. And for bibliotherapy to be effective, at least one character must be someone with whom the reader can identify.

Reading the Book

After the discussion leader chooses the book, the next step is to read it. For those not familiar with children's literature, this may at first sound like a tedious task, but good children's literature will hold adults' interest, too. In fact, a book that does *not* hold the leader's interest should be reconsidered before being recommended for gifted students. One way to test for good writing is to read a passage aloud. If the tongue feels stiff and stumbles over the words, the book simply may not be well written. Look for books that glide along, flowing from word to word and from thought to thought when read aloud. But above all, read the book!

The leader must then plan discussion questions related to the book; this will be easiest if she thinks about them as she is reading. She must also keep in mind the child or children with whom the book will be discussed and the purpose in discussing it with them. She can use as a bookmark a three-by-five card or slip of paper on which she can jot down page numbers and key phrases that strike her as potential discussion material. When she goes back later to write questions, she will have an overview of the themes in the book that will be useful for discussion.

It is a good idea to allow a day or two after finishing a book to let it "settle in" before writing questions. During this incubation period, the leader will be subconsciously working on the book, and when she does sit down to write, the questions that come will be a distillation, probably of better quality and drawn more from the true heart of the book than if she had begun to write immediately. What she is doing in that dormant period is allowing the book to sift down into deeper levels of her own understanding so that her responses will contain some measure of wisdom, as well as intellectual analysis. Some people find that certain "pump-priming" activities, such as walking, drawing, or playing a musical instrument, are helpful during this period.

Adults may find that their immediate response to a book is that it can't possibly be used with gifted children. When they sit down with pencil and paper, they may still think that the book has nothing to offer. But if they go on with the physical act of writing, beginning with a summary of the plot, the potential of the book begins to unfold, and usually questions will occur as quickly as one can write them down. Sometimes, of course, this does not happen; the book truly is unsuitable for this purpose. In this case, it is worth taking the time to clarify exactly why it is unsuitable. This bit of discipline helps in the ongoing definition of what the leader *is* looking for in books to use for bibliotherapy with gifted students.

Preparing the Questions

Bibliotherapy differs from intellectually-oriented book discussion in that it is based on the readers' emotional responses to the book rather than on questions of literary analysis such as plot, character development, writing quality, and style. Chapter 5 focuses on discussion for intellectual understanding. Here, we will consider ways of evoking and exploring emotional responses.

For either type of response, the leader must know the difference between fact questions and interpretive ones and must use each intentionally. Fact questions are those to which the answer can be found in the book; the leader knows what answer he wants when he asks the question, and he will use the answer to judge how well the student has read the book. Interpretive questions are those whose answers are open to interpretation. They are "honest" questions, in that the leader does not know the answer—that is, he does not know what the student thinks. Having had time to think about it, the leader may know what his own answer is, but the student may well give an equally valid different answer. Interpretive questions are appropriate when the leader: (1) assumes that the youngster has read the book, and (2) is interested in the student's response.

It is best to begin a discussion with a few fact questions to ascertain the general level of understanding and response to the book. These introductory questions also provide a warm-up period—a chance for readers to recall the impact of the book and the emotional awareness called for by the interpretive questions.

The annotations of the books listed in Chapter 8 include a few suggested interpretive questions for each book. Here is a list of general interpretive questions that can be adapted to specific books:

1. What is the central character's biggest problem?

2. How do you think he/she feels when…?

3. What strengths does he/she have that help him/her cope?

4. How has someone you know handled the same situation?

5. What would you have done?

6. If you were his/her best friend, what advice would you give?

7. How would that help the situation?

8. What effect do the people in the book have on one another?

For writing interpretive questions, the stages of bibliotherapy—identification, catharsis, and insight—are more easily understood as actions: recognizing, feeling, and thinking. In planning bibliotherapy sessions, structure the questions so that they lead students from one mental activity to the next.

For example, here are discussion questions for Constance C. Greene's *A Girl Called Al*, which can be used with gifted third, fourth, and fifth graders. The questions progress from encouraging identification with Al to generating insight into the reader's own life.

Identification (*Recognizing*)	Describe Al, and now describe the narrator, who is never named in the book.
	Whom are you most like: Al or the narrator? Why? (Al is a leader; the narrator is a follower.)
	In what ways does Al have extra trouble because she is bright?
	How are things easier for her because she is bright?
Catharsis (*Feeling*)	How do you know that Al is lonely, even though she never says so?
	What happens in the book to help Al overcome her loneliness?
	What effect does Mr. Richards have on Al? Do you know anyone who is as important to you or to someone else as Mr. Richards is to Al? What effect will his death have on Al? On what do you base your answer?
	How does Al feel when Mr. Richards dies? How do you know? Do you know anyone who has trouble showing feelings as Al does?
Insight (*Thinking*)	When do you hide your real feelings? What are the advantages of doing so? Why is it hard to show real feelings? Why does showing real feelings make people feel less lonely?

The above questions pursue just one of the themes in the book: loneliness. An equally productive theme is Al's defiant nonconformity.

To follow that theme, a discussion leader might use the same identification questions and then continue with these:

Catharsis *(Feeling)*	Why has Al chosen to be a nonconformist? How do you think she feels about it?
	Think of nonconformists you know, or even of yourself, if you are one. What feelings (good or bad) do you think compel people to be nonconformists?
	How do you imagine nonconformists feel about themselves generally?
Insight *(Thinking)*	When do you choose not to conform? Why? What are different ways to be a nonconformist?
	When is nonconformity destructive? When is it productive?

These questions assume identification with Al more than with the narrator. If a child in the group is more likely to identify with the narrator, the leader may want to develop different questions, perhaps with the purpose of encouraging understanding of what the follower brings to a leader/follower relationship or of developing empathy for nonconformists from the point of view of those who find it easier to conform.

For a 30-minute discussion with upper elementary children, a list of 20 questions is more than enough. Each interpretive question can carry the entire discussion, if it catches the imagination of the students. Having more questions than needed gives flexibility, preparing the leader to go in any of several directions when student interests become apparent. And for beginning discussion leaders, it builds confidence to know that there is more than enough material to fill the time.

The questions listed above and in Chapter 8 are only suggestions to get started. As leaders gain experience, they will want to use their own insights and questions.

As students gain experience, they also will be able to generate their own questions. When they can do this, they are learning enough of bibliotherapy to be able to use it independently, and it can become a skill that they will be able to use even in adulthood. In *Reading to Heal,*

Jacqueline Stanley introduces the principles of bibliotherapy for independent adult use.[25] Although she does not use the term "developmental," her book encourages the reading of thoughtfully-selected books to help adults face typical challenges of daily living, like the developmental bibliotherapy discussed here for children.

Motivating the Children

Of course, book discussion can't proceed until the student has read the book. This may be no problem at all, or it may be a matter of some difficulty, depending on the level of interest that the student already has in reading and on how the whole idea is presented.

It is clearly better to pique students' interest in the book itself, as well as in the discussion of it, than to present reading and discussing as a way of "working on gifted people's problems." (This motivation may come up later as a natural result of conversation and will be more authentic as a result. Or such problems may never be mentioned directly but left unspoken, to be addressed by the child's internal processing.) The best aid in motivating children to read specific books is the leader's enthusiasm and her ability to convey it.

For the teacher or librarian planning a discussion series at school with a group of children, motivation is done according to good teaching practices. The leader gathers the group for an initial meeting and outlines her plans: duration of series, meeting time and place, how many books are to be read, how the discussions will fit into their reading program, their responsibility to read the books on time and be prepared for discussion, etc.

Agreeing to participate in the group should constitute agreement to read the books on schedule. This may be a problem in a few cases, and the leader should know ahead of time how he will deal with those who have not finished a book on time. May they participate or not? One solution is to allow participation but to try to change the parameters of the group to prevent recurrences. Allowing more time between sessions may help; so may providing more classroom reading time, as well as counting the reading done for this group toward required book reports. In practice, however, finishing books on schedule is usually not a problem because students quickly learn that it is more fun—and much more appreciated by others in the group— when they participate.

When the group parameters are settled, it is time to present the first book to be read. This can be done in a brief book talk, in which the leader:

○ hints at the plot or conflict in the book: "In *Jacob Have I Loved*, Louise's abilities are unrecognized, and all of the family's meager resources go for voice lessons for her musically gifted twin, Caroline."

○ mentions ways in which the conflict might relate to students' own experiences: "Louise grows up believing that her family loves Caroline more than they love her."

○ tells enough about the characters to initiate the readers' identification with them: "Louise is hard-working and resourceful but not much interested in schoolwork or in her own future until circumstances force her to make a decision."

○ tells why he likes the book enough to think that they would like to read it, too: "I like this book, especially because I like each of the characters—even Caroline—by the end of the book."

Any difficulties in the book might be mentioned as well: the structure of Konigsburg's *Father's Arcane Daughter* (on the "Recommended Books from Earlier Editions" list at the end of this book) may be discouraging to some readers unless it is pointed out that the book has flashbacks that will become clearer as they read. *Across Five Aprils* will start slowly for some; the leader might pass along the judgment of one sixth grader that the book does not get interesting until page 64!

Leading the Discussion

Whether leading a group or talking about a book with a single child, there are certain techniques that will help to make the book discussion as meaningful as possible:

○ Confidentiality is important. Group members should understand that what is said in the group should not be repeated elsewhere. Confidentiality will be difficult for some children to maintain. Therefore, it is important to help children avoid giving information that they will later regret. Children may not yet have a firm sense of how much personal revelation is appropriate. If they begin to reveal too much, leaders can use the "capping" technique, especially in a group; be alert to those times when a child may be saying too much, and divert attention to another question and another child, effectively "capping" the overflow of emotion and self-revelation. (The leader may speak to the child later, giving her a chance to continue the discussion individually.)

○ Encourage children to share ways that they have found useful for coping with common problems. Some of the more mature children may have adopted attitudes that enable them to transcend difficulties, at least part of the time, and it can be helpful for others to hear about these.

○ Let the conversation flow where the group or the child wants to take it. The leader may understandably be eager to get to his prize question—the one that for him gets to the heart of the book or the problem; however, if he forces the discussion in that direction, his wonderful question may fall flat. This is not to say that he should allow the discussion to wander away from the book; rather, if the children select another theme that they are more ready and able to discuss, the leader should be prepared to follow their interest.

○ Outline good discussion techniques with the children before beginning, and remind them of these when necessary. Some rules to establish are that everyone must have a chance to talk, that only one person will talk at a time, and that there are no right or wrong answers.

○ Remember that the leader's role should be not too intrusive. She is not there to be sure that they understand her interpretation of the book, but to moderate and to facilitate their own understanding.

○ Help the children focus by highlighting the motivations of the characters, the problems in the book, and the solutions presented. Ask the children to suggest other possible solutions, and discuss the likely consequences of them.

At first, it is only natural that the leader will be concerned about pacing. With experience, though, he can relax about time and become more involved in the discussion himself, giving real answers to the children's comments and validating their emotional responses. In a 30-minute session with upper elementary school children, it is enough if only the middle 20 minutes are spent on interpretive questions. The leader can close with a review of the major points that have been brought out or ask the group to do this, then introduce the book to be read for the next meeting.

Follow-Up Activities

Finally, to encourage students to spend more reflective time after the discussion, activities such as journaling, role-playing, or independent music or art projects may be helpful.[26] Especially for students who tend toward introversion, such opportunities help to integrate new ideas gleaned in the discussion with their own thoughts about the book.

Goals of Bibliotherapy at Different Grades

How a child feels about being different because of giftedness or unusual intellectual curiosity is determined partly by the child's age and partly by the degree to which adults have openly discussed differences in ability. In turn, the child's level of awareness will determine the nature of the book discussion.

Preschool and Early Grades

A conversation about books with preschoolers or early elementary children will be just that: a conversation, not a discussion in the sense of a series of questions and answers. Accordingly, in most instances, this book does not suggest discussion questions for this age group in Chapter 8 but merely lists concepts found in the book that would be useful as the focus of a conversation.

Young children not yet able to empathize with the feelings of others or to understand the consequences of actions need adult guidance to glean as much as possible from what they read. Parents and teachers can question to learn their level of understanding and gently explain concepts that they may have missed. In particular, adults cannot expect a young child to discern a subtle lesson from a book if it goes unstated. The applicability of a story to their own lives must be clearly expressed by the guiding adult.

Reasonable goals with children this age are to introduce concepts, label feelings, and develop frames of reference so that when an event in the child's life recalls a story read together, the concepts can be reinforced. This process establishes the importance of books as windows into various life experiences, builds foundations for years of discussion based on books, validates the child's feelings, and assures the child that talking about feelings is not only permissible, it is also a positive way to release emotions.

For early elementary children, a combination of conversation and deliberate questioning can be used. Watch for signs of fatigue or restlessness, and be prepared to stop as soon as they appear. This is still a preparation time for true give-and-take discussion; the emphasis should be on the warm relationship between adult and child, with books as the catalyst for occasional conversation but not yet the focal point.

Upper Elementary

It is in the later elementary years, grades 3-5, that gifted programming typically begins. Many children hear the term "gifted" applied to them for the first time at this age; however, they may not know what it means or how they are expected to react.

When children are invited to join a gifted program, there is usually a larger group of children who are also very bright who did not meet the criteria established by the school. They, too, need to understand their potential, and they should have special attention at this time.

It makes sense at this stage to discuss giftedness, talent, and appropriate aspirations with both groups. Since these are also the peak reading years, it is a particularly good time to begin book discussion groups, with a realistic goal of helping children become aware of the word "gifted" and gain some understanding of what it means. Looking inward, they may not yet be comfortable applying the term to themselves, but they can recognize some of the problems that gifted children in books have and how they cope. Looking outward, they can also begin to recognize the importance of empathy and respect for all people who are different, in whatever way.

On the other hand, students can talk about differences related to giftedness without using the term. In a program designed but not labeled for gifted students, fourth graders who had read *Mrs. Frisby and the Rats of NIMH* talked about why other rats edged away from the super-intelligent ones who had escaped from NIMH. The students agreed that they, too, had felt others pull away from them, and they discussed how they responded to that: by trying to be more like other people. Later, when they evaluated the series, one gain that they mentioned was "learning not to edge away until you know a person better."

As children of this age develop social awareness, they become more adept at interpreting the literature they read. Still, they need the guidance of adults who are able to perceive the gaps in their understanding and tactfully expand their level of comprehension. For example, an adult can help significantly by pointing out the needs or motivations of characters in a story. With such guidance, children can begin to make connections to their own needs and motivations, and perhaps to make conscious changes in their attitudes or behavior as a result of the insight gained from reading and discussion.

Middle School

Social needs are paramount for middle school students. The major contribution of a book discussion group may lie in simply bringing bright and intellectually-oriented students together, allowing them to belong to a group of peers. These students need to be able to blend with their social group while retaining their own identity, which includes their high ability level. One goal will be to remind them from time to time of this part of their identity so that awareness of it will be available to them to build on when they emerge from this period. Books with characters who have the same abilities or interests (whether labeled gifted or not) can help to keep them aware of their potential.

Some gifted adolescents in middle school and senior high become poignantly and cynically aware that adults have failed to realize the potentials that life has to offer. They may begin to question the meaning of life, and given the intensity that characterizes gifted youngsters, they may carry this questioning to the point of existential depression. Leaders should be prepared to refer a student showing serious mental health problems to a school psychologist or other health professional.

Adolescents are becoming mature and independent enough to need less adult guidance—some of the time. Parents and teachers talking about books with them must be perceptive enough to know when to add their own insight and when to accept a child's interpretations without comment. They can also offer alternative interpretations of the literature to help students realize that the unique experience they bring to a book can lead to a valid conclusion, even if others do not agree. Adults should help students clarify personal attitudinal or behavioral goals that they develop as a result of their reading, and they can follow up with subsequent discussions to help adolescents stay on track.

Senior High

During the senior high years, students become increasingly concerned about the decisions that they must make for the future. High-potential students of this age are working on college and career choices, very often struggling with the issues raised by their multipotentiality and the reluctant realization that they must choose from among several abilities and interests. It is important now that they recognize that their abilities are different from the norm, become comfortable with them, and acknowledge some of the responsibilities that their talent may imply.

A major goal of book discussion with senior high students is to help them consider these issues. The books chosen will be a mix of young adult and adult literature—as reflected in the senior high section of Chapter 8, which includes YA and adult titles in nearly equal numbers. Since these students want literature that deals in depth with the moral and ethical decisions that they are making, their reading list will include some of the classics—books whose characters struggle with eternal issues and which are written in language that has stood the test of time. However, classics should be chosen with care to ensure that modern teenage readers can identify with the characters.

Another goal is to encourage teens to continue to use bibliotherapy independently. If they analyze the process of bibliotherapy as they experience it or afterward, they can duplicate it with literature that they choose to meet their individual interests and needs throughout their lives.

Young adults are eager to define what they want to read and what it means to them. Discussion leaders at this stage serve as listeners and facilitators rather than the more directive leaders who guide discussion for younger children. Still, to enhance the possibility that bibliotherapy will have a long-range impact on attitudes and behaviors, leaders should find ways to follow up by staying in touch with student participants.

An Author's View

When Stephanie Tolan, author of *Welcome to the Ark* and other books for young adults, was asked what she would say to potential bibliotherapists, she answered that discussion leaders should realize that the purpose of writing literature is not to prescribe solutions to problems. The author is trying to create a world that is real and true, not to teach. Discussion, she said, should be open-ended, helping the child to see why things work out as they do in *this* book. The author is not saying that this is what *should* happen, only that this is one way it *could* happen. It is not the only answer.[27]

If we look from an author's point of view, we understand that during the writing, stories are organic, developing in their own ways, and that other ways are possible. There is always the question "What if…?" Realizing this will help to derive the widest possible meanings from the story and the most flexibility in relating a book to a child's own life.

In books in which characters make life-shaping decisions, such as *Shadow of a Bull* and *Jacob Have I Loved*, the possibility of other options is especially clear. Each reader can respond to these books by making the decisions for herself, adding components from her life that the author did not include in the book. Thus, the book continues to live in the reader, informing her future decisions. With healthy development, children as they grow create lives that are real and true, even though they differ from the world that the author creates.

Bibliotherapy: An Affirmation of Strengths

To most people, giftedness doesn't sound like a source of trouble at all. Those of us who call attention to potential difficulties for persons whose very label implies that they have been blessed could be accused of making up problems where there may not be any and generally holding too gloomy a view of the lives of unusually bright children. It may appear that we have forgotten that they have strengths and joys as well as vulnerabilities and loneliness.

Not so. It is important, however, that we recognize that those whose high ability and intellectual or artistic interests distinguish them from the norm have a particular set of challenges. With that recognition accepted, we can emphasize their strengths and abilities. Bibliotherapy can be used to affirm and develop those capabilities. The fact that it is a vehicle for discussing problems should not cloud the fact that it is also a tool for calling upon the strengths of gifted children and young people. Bibliotherapy is a process uniquely designed to do just that, as Hynes and Hynes-Berry point out:

> *The emphasis on strengths plays a fundamental role in the bibliotherapeutic process. In the first place, the initiative for each step of the process lies with the*

participant. The facilitator can guide, but it is the individual participant who must recognize, examine, juxtapose, and integrate the feeling-responses and the understandings.... Moreover, progression from the first to the final step calls increasingly on the individual's strengths... including (1) some ability to analyze issues, (2) sufficient honesty to look at the inner self, (3) enough objectivity to view a feeling or behavior pattern from another perspective, and, finally, (4) adequate self-confidence and hope to feel that change is possible and that one is personally capable of making such a change.

Another way of making the same point is to say again that bibliotherapy is a process of self-actualization. Moreover, we consider the self-actualizing process to be one that not only enhances existing strengths but also corrects discrepancies.[28]

For gifted and talented children at home or at school, in groups or as individuals, bibliotherapy is a way of building on the strengths of their reading abilities, their analytical skills, and their heightened sensitivity. It uses and enhances their ability to see relationships, draw conclusions, synthesize, and evaluate. And it can give direction, focus, and purpose to their introspective self-awareness. It is a positive, forward thrust toward the full use of the strengths that these children possess—and, eventually, toward self-actualization and transcendence.

Chapter 5

Intellectual Development through Books

Since teachers are trained to teach reading and to introduce students to books and literature, teachers reading this book are no doubt already well-versed in the information gathered here. Accordingly, this chapter is addressed primarily to parents—first, to familiarize them with what is happening in schools, and second, to help them support and supplement that work at home.

The chapter begins by exploring how reading and discussing books, whether at school or at home, can meet the intellectual needs of gifted children (outlined in Chapter 2). Following that is a section on new developments in school reading programs, then on steps for leading groups in an intellectually-oriented book discussion. There are suggestions for parents who wish to supplement the school programs at home, and the chapter concludes with information for parents who want to be certain that their children are learning how to seek information independently.

What Books Can Do for Intellectual Development

The needs listed in Chapter 2 suggest that for optimum intellectual development, highly able children should have opportunities to do the following:

○ learn to think effectively
○ encounter a variety of people and ideas
○ benefit from individual pacing of learning experiences
○ talk with intellectual peers

Reading and book discussions can accomplish all of these goals. Simply reading well-chosen books challenges us to think, enables us to experience a wider range of people and ideas than we encounter in our daily lives, and permits us to move at our own pace among books of our choice, and a discussion group for gifted children provides an opportunity to talk with intellectual peers. Furthermore, a group discussion increases the chance that we will think *effectively*, exposes us to even more people and ideas, and expands our avenues of response to the reading.

If books are chosen for high-potential students with their age and interests in mind (using the criteria for intellectually challenging books which are listed in Chapter 6), a program of reading and book discussion—though it may lack the glamour of more expensive programs—can be remarkably effective in developing intellectual ability.

Thinking Effectively

Many bright children are able to move easily (not to say lazily) through the elementary grades without learning to make effective use of their intellectual abilities. They can listen with half an ear and pick up enough to stay up with the class. If this pattern continues too long, they develop neither study skills nor thinking skills.

> *Daniel was a very bright child in elementary school, and he shone in high school, graduating near the top of his class. No one was surprised when he was accepted at one of the most academically demanding and prestigious universities in the northeast. However, although he is*

the same serious, purposeful student, he is not doing well there. He knows why: he has not learned to think analytically or to examine his assumptions. In grade school and high school, his answers were correct so often that few listened critically to what he was saying. Now, in a class of many other outstanding students, his lack of study and thinking skills is hampering his progress. His intellectual ability is not diminished, but he has not learned to use it effectively.

Expressing Ideas Freely

Children who are eager to talk about their ideas are stimulated by opportunities to talk in more depth than is possible in usual classroom discussions or casual conversations. Using their vocabularies without restraint and sharpening their thinking in talks with knowledgeable others who can spot flaws and helpfully point to discrepancies in their reasoning, they are encouraged to develop their verbal abilities.

Young people who have unusual ability to think critically, evaluate, and reason out unusual solutions to complicated situations should be able to voice opinions and ideas in an environment that respects divergent thinking, where their different approaches will be encouraged and heard rather than ignored or openly rejected by others.

> *During the Vietnam era, a fourth-grade class discussed sending bandages and soap to the people of South Vietnam. One student, Jeff, suggested that probably the same staple commodities were needed in North Vietnam. Could the class send packages to both? This was so serious a departure from the norm that Jeff's father (not his mother, although she normally interacted with the school and would not have had to take time off work) was called in to discuss the situation—and presumably to handle it with appropriate severity. Jeff's story is an example of why a sensitive child with a global perspective needs a safe environment in which to express his divergent opinions.*

The sense of safety is terribly important to children whose intellectual abilities drive them to express thoughts which others may think are strange. Such safety is, in fact, essential to their further intellectual growth.

Various situations presented in books can provide safe focal points for in-depth discussions. Children can follow up on ideas that a good book has generated, feeling safe enough to express even half-formed ideas without fear of ridicule. With an understanding adult or in a group with other insightful children, they can feel free to exchange views without toning down their vocabularies. These opportunities for regular dialogue with intellectual peers and bright adult friends are enriching and valuable.

Precise Thinking

Too often, careless use of language and the lazy thinking that it permits are accepted both in school and at home. Children must be free to speak the way their peers do, but adults can do children a great service by creating a milieu in which, some of the time, they can practice the exact expression of incisive, critical thought. In the process, they will be learning to think with improved precision. Just as they should learn the difference between good and escape literature, they should learn the difference between casual conversation and productive discussion of ideas so that they can use each when appropriate.

In individual or small group discussions, the leader has opportunities to probe for exact statements, demanding penetrating thinking that produces greater understanding. This kind of questioning can be used in any context, but books provide an especially productive opportunity for it.

> *In a discussion of Sperry's* Call It Courage, *the leader asked, "Why is someone in the book alone or lonely?" When the response was a retelling of the events of Mafatu's childhood, she said, "You are telling the whole plot. I only asked why someone in the book is alone or lonely." Nine-year-old Andy immediately answered, "Mafatu was lonely because he was afraid of the sea and*

everyone else was courageous," eliminating all extraneous information and zeroing in on exactly what the question asked.

Higher Levels of Thinking

To develop their ability to analyze, synthesize, and evaluate (the higher levels of thinking in Bloom's Taxonomy, which is discussed in more detail later in this chapter), students should work with these processes, identifying each level of thinking as they use it. Open-ended book discussions conducted in an atmosphere that promotes respect for individual opinions can be rich training ground for higher levels of thinking.

For example, the leader might talk to the students about analysis, synthesis, and evaluation. As he asks about the books, he labels each question so that the students, in answering, know that they are analyzing, synthesizing, or evaluating. For the last meeting in the series, he may ask the students to bring three questions for discussion, one of each kind. The books provide the focus, and the discussion group provides the opportunity for the students to clarify the meaning of each process and learn to use those processes independently.

Encountering a Variety of People and Ideas

When trying to describe the constant need of gifted children for new information, parents and teachers often find themselves using metaphors for food. "I've never known a student so thirsty for knowledge." "She is so hungry to learn." "He is a voracious reader." These are not just clichés; they express how eager gifted students seem to observant adults. Indeed, knowledge, information, and new ideas are nourishment for gifted minds, and (perhaps unconsciously) they sense that they are in danger of intellectual starvation without them. Book discussions can expose these receptive readers to a broad spectrum of information, to alternative ways of doing things, and to different kinds of people.

Information

Children who absorb information rapidly and well and then clamor for more should have access to many more subjects and concerns than typically are covered in the standard curriculum. The extensive range of nonfiction available through school libraries makes this need easy to meet.

However, fiction is useful in this regard, too. Literature introduces children to times and places they will never see and to lives they will not live. It can expand their awareness of a variety of human concerns, styles, emotions, and ways of relating to others. And it can do this in a way that makes them care, opening doors to topics ranging from the conflict of cultures when French, English, and American Indians met in the Upper Great Lakes in the early 19th century (*The Loon Feather*), to the struggle for equality for African-Americans in the post-Reconstruction era (*Words By Heart*), to the horrors of the Holocaust (*The Book Thief*)—subjects that might not seem real if read about only in history books or newspapers.

Alternative Ways of Doing Things

Many bright children enjoy a capacity for thought processing that includes the ability to think in alternatives, to sense consequences, and to make generalizations. To turn these abilities into skills, they must play with a variety of ideas, including some that may not be familiar to most people in their schools and neighborhoods. Opportunities to experiment with these ideas in exploratory conversations build both ability and confidence.

For example, during the reading of *The Arm of the Starfish*, a group of eighth graders might be directed to stop reading at designated points and write down whether Adam should side with Dr. O'Keefe or with Kali and her father, along with reasons for and probable results of their decisions. These students will then have the makings of a discussion that enables them to test their judgment and decision-making skills against the outcome of the book, as well as against the ideas of their peers.

Books are laboratories for bright students—proving grounds where they can reason out solutions to complex problems, examine the consequences of their decisions, and then try something else. Good fiction reflects life truly, and as in life, the outcome of the story can depend on one small decision or a series of events beyond one's control. There are always turning points that lead to the question "What if…?" Book discussions that consider "what if" invite the expression of divergent thought.

By suggesting books that approach an issue from several angles, adults can introduce new ways of looking at that issue, helping students toward a broader point of view. Gifted children respond readily to this expansion of vision; through their broader awareness of human potential, they will learn what is possible for themselves.

Different Kinds of People

A less obvious reason why gifted children need to be exposed to a variety of people is that they can be highly critical, even intolerant, of people (including themselves) who do not measure up to their standards. They need to be aware that there are different abilities and talents and different ways of solving problems. Exposure to a variety of people can help them develop tolerance, empathy, understanding, and acceptance of human traits, including weaknesses in others and perhaps also in themselves.

Literature not only provides an infinity of characters who exhibit human weaknesses and learn somehow to accept them, it introduces these characters in ways that make children care about them as they learn to accept human weakness and to celebrate human strength.

Individual Pacing

When they encourage voluntary reading and discussion, teachers introduce flexibility to the standard classroom format, meeting individual needs by allowing for accelerated thinking, slower processing, and willingness to delay closure—all common learning characteristics of high-ability, high-potential learners.

Accelerated Thinking

When a child's thinking processes are faster than normal, the pace of a typical mixed-ability classroom discussion can be agonizing.

It is a welcome relief for pent-up frustration and boredom if, for at least part of the time, those who learn more rapidly are allowed and encouraged to acquire knowledge at their own rate.

Reading is wonderful for this—it is a thoroughly self-paced activity. Skimming and re-reading by turns, readers can move at whatever pace they choose. A reading program increases the amount of self-paced learning available to quicker students as soon as they become independent readers.

These youngsters should be able not only to learn at their own rate, but also to talk, at least part of the time, with others who process at an accelerated pace. Book discussions provide this opportunity. For some gifted children, it may be the only such opportunity available during this period of their lives.

> *When Aaron began sixth grade at a new school, he found the pace of instruction too slow and the other children reluctant to accept him. He took refuge in the school library, where the librarian soon learned that he loved to read, and what's more, he was eager to listen to her suggestions. She recommended books such as* Anthem *to Aaron, and he began asking questions about the books when he returned them. Throughout the year, this give and take of books and talk allowed Aaron to learn at his own accelerated rate, despite the repetitive pace in the classroom.*

Slower Processing

Though they are quick learners, gifted people are capable of comprehensive synthesis and can benefit from a rather long incubation period to integrate new ideas. Some gifted children process information more slowly and deeply—and thoroughly—than others. Those who tend toward introversion are especially likely to be more reflective and to take extra time to reach a conclusion or decision.

Reading and book discussion, if properly arranged, can accommodate this slower processing better than the typical routine of classroom assignments. If an adult discusses the concepts of incubation and slower processing time with these students, they can gain useful knowledge about their own work patterns and learn to provide incubation time for themselves. For example, some students may realize that they will have more to offer to the discussion if they plan to finish a book a day or two before meeting to discuss it.

> *Maia is in the gifted program, but she isn't sure she belongs there. While most of her classmates are racing to be first with the right answer, she is quietly going over information in her mind, connecting new ideas with already acquired knowledge. For book discussions, how-ever, she plans time to think about the book. As a result, she is ready to speak with the rest, and her well-formed opinions are respected by the group. When the teacher mentions that Maia makes good use of incubation time, she begins to understand and appreciate the advantages of her slower processing.*

Delayed Closure

Earlier than most, gifted children often show the ability to delay closure—to accept a situation for which there is no immediate solu-tion. Therefore, questions with single, final answers are not always appropriate for them. They are more likely to want to wait until all of the information is in, to spend time looking at all sides of a question. To develop this ability, they should be allowed to pursue their ideas and integrate new ones into their thinking without being forced to make final decisions or judgments immediately. They need open-ended discussion and open-ended situations to discuss.

In a book discussion, final judgments are never necessary; in fact, one result of a good book discussion will be the new insights that it evokes. The discussion of a book may be only the beginning of a child's interaction with it. In fact, some children's literature inten-tionally provides open-ended situations; such books do not come to final conclusions, prompting the reader to consider a variety of possible endings.

Talking with Peers

We all need friends we can talk to comfortably as equals. It can be difficult for unusually bright children or for those with artistic or intellectual interests to find such friends—even harder than for gifted adults—and it is impossible to measure what a positive effect such a friend can have in their lives.

> *During the summer between seventh and eighth grades, Ben spent two weeks on a college campus at a summer program for gifted teenagers. He had never before been exposed to so many people with exciting ideas and the eagerness to talk about them. When the program ended, his parents and younger brother picked him up and took him out for dinner and then to a nearby campground to begin a family vacation. Ben was so stimulated by the campus experience that he talked about it nonstop through dinner and while they set up camp. He woke up the next morning still talking; it was late that afternoon before it was completely out of his system. Ben had discovered something momentous: there are other people like him. A new confidence began to replace Ben's long-standing sense of isolation.*

One reason that the summer experience had such an impact on Ben is that it included older students. When children's comprehension is advanced beyond that of their contemporaries, they need contact with intellectual peers, regardless of age. It is essential for them to be able to talk with people who challenge and stimulate them and who respect their ideas, at least part of the time. Adults who talk about books with young people like Ben can provide intellectual challenge during the awkward years before high school or college, where they can finally find agemates who match their intellectual ability.

Intellectual peers offer other benefits. For one, equally-intelligent friends usually can be counted on to see through glibness and to question shaky assertions—lazy discussion techniques so easily developed by highly verbal and socially charming youngsters who benefit when their opinions are challenged in a well-managed discussion group. Also, most gifted and bright young people are socially aware, sensitive and concerned with values and ideals at a surprisingly early age. They need to know others who can help them put these concerns into perspective so that they can develop a positive focus rather than becoming negative or cynical.

Parents, teachers, and librarians can suggest books that deal with social concerns and depict committed people taking positive action. Discussion about these books may help students see serious issues from a problem-solving point of view rather than from one of hopelessness. Such perspective-building is especially important for sensitive, concerned adolescents.

What Schools Are Doing with Books and Reading: A Primer for Parents

"Serious reading, serious teaching of reading, and inculcation of a love of reading are the proper goals of education." This is a fair summary, according to at least one reviewer, of the argument presented by Jacques Barzun in his book *Begin Here: The Forgotten Conditions of Teaching and Learning.*[1] Whether or not Barzun's goals are a national educational priority, methods of reading instruction continually undergo changes. A relevant example of the pendulum used to describe educational trends is the debate labeled the "reading wars."

The century-old question continues: Should children learning to read be taught phonics, a tool for decoding words? Or should they be taught to recognize whole words without analyzing the parts? Early in the 20th century, children learned phonics; in the 1930s and 1940s, the Dick and Jane readers used the whole word, "look-say" method. In mid-century, the pendulum swung back toward phonics with the publication of *Why Johnny Can't Read,*[2] in which the author cited the neglect of phonics as the cause of lower literacy rates.

Comparing the merits of phonics and look-say in the 1960s, Jeanne Chall concluded that neither method, used alone, suffices.[3] She found that presenting phonics in the early years, as children begin to read, provides a basis for later understanding of the meaning of language. In response to her findings, by the end of that decade, most textbooks for the early grades included phonics. However, the pendulum swung again. Throughout the 1980s and 1990s, the whole word method was back in the form of the "whole language" movement, which has gradually merged to form a blend.[4]

Whole Language and Phonics

The whole language method—sometimes called a literature-based curriculum—assumes that if children experience plenty of listening, speaking, and writing, along with opportunities to read real literature, they will learn to read without specific instructions in discrete reading skills.

In a whole language classroom, children learn to read by using not textbooks (basal readers), but trade books (the children's books that are found in bookstores), and a classroom should have plenty of them—at least five for each child in the class.[5] Ideally, each day includes times when the teacher reads good literature aloud, times when the children read good books silently, and times when daily oral discussions of the reading occur in groups or one-to-one with the teacher. Librarians and others interested in reading have hailed the move to real literature as a long-awaited positive step.

Whole language instruction alone, however, neglects the use of phonics. In 1996, after years of whole language instruction (and no phonics), California students' reading scores were among the lowest in the nation. In 1997, California revised its reading curriculum to include both phonics and literature.[6] Since California's huge purchasing power has significant influence over curriculum and textbooks nationwide, at the turn of the century, the pendulum was in motion again.

The "reading wars" demonstrate one disadvantage of going to the extreme with any one method of instruction. Research indicates that about one-third of children learn to read regardless of the method used, as long as they have some sort of organized instruction. These children do well with a literature-based approach. Some of the remaining children learn to read more easily if they have instruction about spelling and sounds. But one-quarter of children *cannot* learn to read without this instruction.[7] These children learn differently, but they are not necessarily of lower intelligence. Some of them may even be gifted.

Given this clear example of differences in the ways people learn, the need to include both phonics and whole language approaches in a reading curriculum is evident. With the thought that children should have exposure to phonics in the early years and then an emphasis on real literature later, in the last few years, "balanced reading" has been introduced as educators develop curricula that incorporate both.[8] But even this compromise has not been without controversy.[9]

In 2008, James Kim reviewed the research and concluded that "a broad consensus about effective reading instruction has evolved slowly over four decades."[10] He cites the 2000 National Reading Panel (NRP) report, which recommended using phonics to decode new words, guided oral reading activities to develop fluency, and multiple strategies to improve reading comprehension. The NRP report in turn influenced Reading First, a part the No Child Left Behind Act. Reading First requires the use of the "five pillars" of reading instruction: phonemic awareness, phonics, fluency, vocabulary, and comprehension. Kim comments: "As Peggy McCardle and Vinita Chhabra noted in their 2005 Kappan article, the five pillars of scientifically based reading instruction should replace the 'artificial dichotomy' between phonics and whole language."[11] Kim concludes his article with a call for more rapid application of the findings of research and more opportunities for classroom teachers to participate in setting policy.

Recently, whole language instruction has taken a worrisome turn: in some schools, teachers are no longer be able to create their own plans for combining phonics and whole language, but instead are required to follow prescribed, scripted programs.[12] These scripted programs serve to prepare all children for the tests required by the No Child Left Behind Act, but they limit children's options in choosing what they will read. In the reading wars, the solutions may change, but the difficulties continue.

Teaching to the Test

In the first decade of the 21st century, the focus in education shifted to the requirements of the No Child Left Behind Act, a federal mandate passed in 2001, early in the George W. Bush administration. Under this Act, unless all students in a school meet a minimum standard, the school faces sanctions and a loss of funding, and teachers may be penalized or dismissed.

Quickly, the emphasis in many classrooms turned to preparing students to meet minimum standards, as determined by the standardized tests required by No Child Left Behind. Often, the result is that the needs of the lowest one-third of the class set the pace of learning. In some schools, teachers feel compelled to teach to the test—often forsaking time for the inquiry, exploration, and creativity that many children need—while students learn the importance of supplying the one right answer for the test. The question of how well students think and learn takes a back seat to how well they perform on specific tests.[13]

Parents of gifted children must inform themselves about the impact of No Child Left Behind on the reading program offered in their child's public schools so that they can identify any losses the child may be experiencing and determine how they can compensate.

Reading Programs for Gifted Students

In an article on reading programs for gifted students, Reis and Renzulli write:

> *The frustration faced by a precocious reader entering kindergarten or first grade may be impossible for most adults to understand. When a six-year-old who loves to read and is accustomed to reading several books a day encounters the typical basal reading system, the beginning of the end of a love affair with reading may result. As Brown and Rogan have stated, "For primary level gifted children who have already begun to read, modification toward the mean represents a serious regression."[14]*

While the authors point out that early reading and giftedness are not synonymous, they suggest that early readers need an appropriate reading program, whether or not they are identified as gifted. One example of this is a well-developed model reading program for children in grades 1-12 directed by Dr. Joyce VanTassel-Baska at the Center for Gifted Education at the College of William and Mary.[15]

Flack suggests that in an appropriate reading curriculum, gifted students learn to read widely, critically, and creatively.[16] A comprehensive reading program exposes gifted youngsters to a wide range of the best authors currently writing for young people. To read critically, they learn discrimination, developing and using criteria for judging the quality of what they read. In reading creatively, they integrate the new reading with what they already know, and they make use of the blend in their own way, going beyond what they read to find their own voice in writing a response.

A reading program for gifted students should also include learning about authors and illustrators. Flack points out that students can use the Internet to investigate where authors get their ideas, how authors and illustrators collaborate, and how the life experiences of creative people inform their work. One very helpful website, written to and for children but also useful for adults, is The Children's Literature Web Guide from the University of Calgary, found at www.ucalgary.ca/~dkbrown.

In another treatment of the elements that distinguish a reading program specifically designed for gifted students and precocious readers, Dole and Adams propose the following list:[17]

○ independent research projects
○ opportunities to pursue these projects over a long period of time
○ development of research skills
○ self-selected reading experiences
○ guided study of literary genres
○ involvement with the Great Books Program

To the last item, I would add "or other structured book discussions," for which several models follow.

Discussing Books at School

When I was in high school, one English teacher invited about six of us to form a small reading group. This group was an experiment in my school—it may have been a one-time project related to the teacher's doctoral program; I do not know whether it was considered a success. We met for just a few months, and although I remember nothing specific from the discussions, it stands out in my high school experience because in that group, students truly were a part of excellence as we tried to match the thinking of great authors with our own best thinking. That sense of touching excellence is the basis for my conviction that book discussion groups have value, even when they may not seem as successful as the leader would like.

Pulling a group of gifted students together for a book discussion can present logistical problems. Where ability grouping is not currently in favor, it may also present policy problems. Teachers, counselors, and librarians who attempt it and administrators who must approve it will want to know that it is worth the effort.

And it is, according to conclusions reached by Clark.[18] After charting intellectual characteristics of gifted children, the needs that those characteristics imply, and possible related problems, she offers organizational patterns and strategies for them. She emphasizes that gifted students need educational programs that offer:

- small group discussion
- flexibility
- respect for ideas
- time for reflection
- opportunity to compare communication and decision-making processes with academic peers

Students discussing literature in small groups are meeting all of the above requirements. This should be good news to parents, teachers, and administrators who are concerned about efficient use of valuable school time and about meeting the needs of all students. In schools using literature circles, a group for gifted children may fit relatively easily into the existing system.

Logistics

Arrangements for an intellectually-oriented discussion group differ only slightly from those offered in Chapter 4 for bibliotherapy groups. For a full discussion, please see the section "Logistics: Organizing Discussion Groups at School" in that chapter. In this section, only the differences are mentioned.

The Children

Although these discussions are more cognitive than emotional, the selection of children for the group should be based on their emotional development as well as on reading ability. For younger children accelerated into older reading groups, it is especially important that their emotional level be weighed against the material to be read.

The Books

The leader of an intellectually-oriented discussion group can choose from an array of books, including nonfiction, limited only by the desire to present books of the highest quality and intellectual challenge. The usual requirements for finding appropriate books apply: knowing children's literature and what makes a book especially appealing to gifted children, examining reviews, and pre-reading all books before recommending them.

Place and Time

While privacy may not seem as important as in a bibliotherapy group, quiet is necessary. The discussion should be in a place where students feel free to become thoroughly involved and to voice opinions with passion. Finding a time to meet presents the same challenges for both types of groups, and the same possible solutions are recommended.

The discussion can incorporate drama, art, music, guest speakers, and projects. The leader may develop lesson plans to introduce the children to criteria for good literature so that they can move toward making their own informed judgments about books.

Discussion Techniques

In bibliotherapy, discussion is based on the reader's emotional response to the *story*. Questions, designed to clarify that response, often focus on the inner lives of the characters: Why do they act as they do? What personal characteristics lead to success or failure? What are their relationships to others in the story? What are their feelings? Their attitudes? How and why do these change?

An intellectual discussion, by contrast, aims to develop the reader's understanding of the *literature*. While the leader may ask all of the questions given above, he may also inquire into the motives of the author: Why did she decide to have this or that happen? What response did she hope to elicit from readers? How did she plan to accomplish her aims?

An example of this contrast in discussion techniques is exemplified in the following two questions for *A Bridge to Terabithia*:

1. Why did Jess and Leslie spend so much time in Terabithia? (*character's motive*)

2. Why did Paterson have Jess and Leslie spend so much time in Terabithia? (*author's motive*)

In forming an answer to these two questions, we can almost feel an interior shift in focus take place. To answer the first, we try to feel our way into the minds and hearts of Jess and Leslie, while the second question moves us some distance from the story, which allows us to stand outside of it and look at it analytically—to consider the author's carefully planned use of symbolism.

Another line of questioning in an intellectual discussion, evaluating the author's techniques and skill, helps to avoid limiting the discussion to the plot. Are the characters believable? How does the setting contribute to the development of the plot? To the mood? How effective is the author's use of language? In answering these questions, we gain an understanding of literature as an art form that has specific methods that, if employed well, convey much more than the mere progression of words on the page can do.

Children's Responses

For those who have not led a discussion group, this section outlines how children of different ages may be expected to respond. The
stages of children's ability to perceive theme in a story can be understood in light of Piaget's study of the gradual development of children's
ability to symbolize events.[19]

Preschool and early elementary children—up to about the age of
six—are in the pre-operational stage of development, characterized by
egocentric and magical thinking. Visual perception is all; a child at this
stage believes that a taller glass has more water in it, even if she has
watched the water poured from a shorter, fatter glass. The focus on self,
magical thinking, and reliance on appearances affects the child's experience of a book and her conversation about it. Very young children
can understand the meaning of a story but cannot put it in their own
words, while most five-year-olds can give a brief narrative.

Children from around ages seven to 11, in the concrete operational stage, begin to use logic to explain events. Discussion leaders
will find these children able to summarize a story and can use to
advantage their strong interest in understanding and analyzing experience and relationships.

Adolescents, at the formal operational stage, are able to think
more abstractly and hypothetically, to organize facts and events by
manipulating symbols in their minds. Capable of viewing problems
from several different vantage points, they can resolve conflicts
through mental effort alone. Young adolescents are able to analyze
the structure of a plot or the motives of the characters in a book.
Older students can make generalizations as they consider the theme
or author's point of view. Not everyone, even among adults, func-
tions at the formal operational level; however, it appears that most
gifted people do.[20]

Thus, children see different themes in books than adults do, and
they respond to them differently—a point for discussion leaders to
remember. Furthermore, the construction of meaning is individual,
based on the background and experience of the reader, accounting
for differences in responses to reading. A factually inaccurate answer,
however, should be addressed. Lehr suggests doing so not with a

correction, but with another question—"Does that seem right?" "Are you sure?"—to encourage the child to reexamine his response.[21]

Questions

Rather than fact questions, which have known answers, gifted children should be asked interpretive questions that require creative responses. Questions should be open-ended, and the teacher or leader should welcome unexpected, divergent answers or digressions that extend the topic.[22]

Leaders should plan questions to serve specific purposes, asserts VanTassel-Baska.[23] She suggests the following:

- ○ factual questions to determine the students' comprehension

- ○ interpretive questions to develop a deeper understanding

- ○ divergent questions to encourage the reader to think outside the story

- ○ evaluative questions to challenge the student to make judgments about the story

VanTassel-Baska's question types may be easily used if the leader thinks in terms of the following opening words:

- ○ factual: What happened?

- ○ interpretive: Why did it happen?

- ○ divergent: What if something else had happened?

- ○ evaluative: What did you think about what happened? Why do you think so?

These openings provide only a skeletal framework to start the leader's thinking. A good discussion leader will build a structure based on them to suit the story at hand.

Questioning

Techniques of questioning include observing *wait time*—the length of time that the teacher waits for a student to answer before calling on someone else—after a question and also after a response. This pause for reflection causes anxiety for leaders but encourages more achievement for students. It also allows for the fact that while we value quick responses, we know that some gifted people process slowly. Castiglione says that the average wait time is 0.2-0.9 seconds; if a discussion leader increases that time to three seconds, major changes occur in the quality of the discussion.[24] Others recommend 10 to 20 seconds after a higher-level thinking question.

Castiglione suggests asking divergent questions to increase participation in the discussion. If a child's answer is unclear, he recommends that the leader not say, "Your answer is unclear," but rather, "I'm not sure what you mean," so that the burden of responsibility is on the adult, not the child.[25]

Another questioning technique is "think-pair-share." After asking a question, the leader allows two minutes of individual thinking time and two minutes for students to discuss it with a partner before beginning group discussion.

Other techniques of successful discussion leaders include asking follow-up questions, requiring students to defend their responses against other points of view, inviting one student to summarize the response of another, asking participants to describe how they arrived at an answer, and letting students develop their own questions.

What follows next is a summary of a structured approach to discussion that is well-known to teachers, described here primarily for the benefit of parents.

Bloom's Taxonomy

In Benjamin Bloom's *Taxonomy of Educational Objectives*,[26] the higher levels of thinking are analysis, synthesis, and evaluation. One way to approach book discussion with gifted children is to focus on questions that call forth these kinds of thought.

Analyzing a book involves questioning some of the author's decisions. Why did he choose that form, setting, or organization? Are there inconsistencies or inaccuracies? How does he make the characters seem like real people? Analysis questions might begin with phrases such as the following:

○ What are the parts of…?
○ Which steps are important in the process of…?

- ○ If…, then….
- ○ The difference between…and…is….
- ○ The solution would be to….
- ○ What is the relationship between…and…?
- ○ How would you have…?

Synthesis means connecting elements from a book to each other or to knowledge that the students have already acquired to create a new way of looking at the issues. Some examples of synthesis questions are:

- ○ Can you retell this story from the point of view of…?
- ○ How is a character from this book like…in…?
- ○ Can you write a similar story that would…?
- ○ Change…so that….
- ○ Develop an original plan for….
- ○ Good background music for this story would be….

Evaluating a book or a decision of a character in a book requires making a judgment based on established criteria. The criteria can be developed in group discussion before the children are asked evaluative questions. Such questions could include:

- ○ Which characters are best developed?
- ○ Which character would you like to be?
- ○ Which of these stories is the most believable?
- ○ Rank these books on the basis of quality of language.
- ○ Which situation required the most courage?

Junior Great Books

A program that offers training in both forming questions and in the techniques of leading a discussion is Junior Great Books. Although it was not originally developed for gifted students, it is often used as the first offering when a school initiates services for high-potential youngsters. Inexpensive and highly regarded, Junior Great Books is easily accepted as a program that will challenge gifted youngsters.

Please note, however, that Junior Great Books is a *reading* program and cannot be considered a complete program for gifted children, who of course are endowed with abilities in other areas as well. But it does develop a seriousness of purpose in reading and offers a structured discussion format that makes it an excellent introduction to intellectual book discussion.[27]

Other Models

Creative teachers may develop their own methods of leading discussions based on preferred elements from Bloom's Taxonomy, Junior Great Books, and other formats, such as reading workshops and literature circles.

Literature circles are a way to promote reading and discussion in small groups, which may include journaling and extension projects.[28] They could easily be adapted for gifted children by:

○ creating groups based on ability, especially for students with high verbal ability

○ selecting a wide range of appropriately challenging literature

○ pacing the group at an appropriate rate

The significance of ability grouping was discussed in Chapter 2. The selection of challenging literature will be discussed in Chapter 6. The third adaptation, pacing, is especially important, since avid readers frequently read a book (or more) per day in the middle grades. Literature circles usually spend several weeks on one book and require that group members not read ahead—a swift way to kill interest for avid gifted readers, who find this stipulation impossibly restrictive. When the above adaptations can be made, the early practice in discussion techniques offered in literature circles is invaluable for bright and eager readers.

Authors' Comments

Laudable though it may be to read books and discuss them, the sudden widespread use of this procedure has led to some concerns that books are being "used," in a negative sense, so zealously that we are overlooking the fragile nature of the art of literature. Authors, of course, are particularly sensitive to this, and some of them have written quiet protests that deserve our attention.

The poet Lee Bennett Hopkins raises objections to the use of discussion guides so extensive that they overwhelm the poetic experience. Describing a teaching guide for the poem "City" by Langston Hughes, he concludes, "In the time—the meaningless time—students might spend doing all this, they could relish an entire volume of poetry, coming away with so much more…!"[29] Some poems, like some books (see Bauer's suggestions below) are best pondered over as a whole rather than analyzed.

In an open letter to teachers, author Marion Dane Bauer offers several points arising from letters received from students as class assignments:[30]

○ Books selected for children should be appropriate for their emotional age. "There is a difference between the ability to absorb facts and the readiness to deal with issues."

○ Not all books are meant for group discussion. Some need to be a private experience, a kind of personal letter between author and reader.

○ A book is more than a summary of its plot.

○ Books should not be used to teach lessons. "Fiction is about questions, not answers."

Bauer's last point, especially, should be taken to heart, not only out of respect for literature, but also because it is with an openness to questions and questioning that we can offer the most benefit to sensitive, intelligent children through book discussion.

Discussing Books at Home

Although a group discussion is often not possible at home, parents can meet many of the same needs through a loosely structured plan for family reading and conversation. Moreover, by providing a favorable environment at home, they can offer a haven to their children—a place where the children can know that they are safe to express their thoughts, ideas, and opinions without risk of censure. As parents, you can offer the psychological security that schools cannot guarantee.

For parents who want to provide enrichment for highly able children at home, reading is surely the form of enrichment closest at hand—and, with the use of the public library, the least costly. By adding discussion to the reading, you can use books not only for the pleasure which is their primary reason for being, but also to respond to your gifted children's intellectual needs and as a focus for thoughtful family conversation.

When you encourage reading and promote book discussions at home, you are doing your part to meet the intellectual needs discussed in the first section of this chapter. Your unique contribution can supplement a school reading program or compensate for your child's loss if the school does not provide an appropriate reading program.

Especially if you homeschool, you will surely want to go beyond just assigning reading to discussing the books with your child as an alternative to worksheets and as preparation for your child's writing assignments. A number of specific and helpful options are offered in *Creative Home Schooling: A Resource Guide for Smart Families.*[31]

Thinking Effectively

At home, your child should feel free to use the full range of her growing vocabulary, trying out new connotations as she tests the full meaning of words she has read. If she makes a mistake in pronunciation (common for children who pick up new words by reading, as well as by hearing them), you can correct her gently.

Allow divergent thinking, recognizing that children need to try out ideas by talking about them. In this trying-out period, children may sound more convinced than they really are, and your role is to listen calmly, ask thoughtful questions, and offer your own opinions as something that the child might want to consider.

Provide enough time to consider ideas in depth. By asking follow-up questions ("What do you mean by that?") and identifying meaningless slang expressions when your child uses them, you can help him think carefully and use language more precisely. By asking questions that require analysis, synthesis, and evaluation, you can challenge your child to think more deeply.

Encountering a Variety of People and Ideas

When you routinely take your child to the library and help her select books, you have an opportunity to expose her to new worlds of people and ideas. You can suggest books that open up new topics and points of view. When discussing these books, guide her to think of alternatives and to predict and examine the consequences.

If your child is hypercritical of others, as some gifted children may be, make a special effort to find books that promote sympathy for people in difficult situations. Librarians are always glad to make suggestions.

Individual Pacing

Simply by helping your child find books that interest and challenge him, you are individualizing his reading. You will find suggestions and criteria for choosing books in Chapters 3, 6, 7, and 8 of this book.

Introduce your child to the idea of an incubation period, and help her learn to recognize her own patterns of processing information. This self-knowledge will be useful in scheduling book discussions at home and can be transferred to the scheduling of school assignments and social relationships.

By allowing open-ended discussion and not expecting a conclusive answer, you can give your child experience in considering diverse approaches to problems. Your acceptance will confirm the value of different responses and encourage individuality.

Talking with Intellectual Peers

In a discussion of a book that both participants have read, the importance of the age differences between them tends to diminish. If you have a genuine desire to know what your child thinks rather than an overriding need to give your own opinion, then you and your child are starting the discussion as peers.

Parents who lack time for or interest in book discussion may find a relative or friend who can act as reading partner for their children. Although this means the loss of family interaction, it could be a mutually enriching relationship and a very satisfactory solution.

In a book discussion, whether group or individual, there is always a triad: the leader, the child(ren), and the author. As gifted children grow older, they will find authors who can play the role of intellectual peers. Thus, when you foster book discussion at home, you are setting the stage for continually introducing your child to potential peers.

If book discussions are offered at school, you can reinforce them at home with your unique knowledge of your children. If they are not offered at school, then home may be the only place where intellectually curious children have the advantages of reading and talking about books.

Discussing Books with Your Children

The first step, if you are unsure of how to begin talking about books with your children, is to read the section earlier in this chapter called "Discussion Techniques" carefully, and perhaps look into some of the references listed at the end of this chapter. Many questioning techniques, as well as the programs mentioned, can be adapted from group to individual discussion.

With this information in your background, you are ready to begin. The following tips provide a good starting point:[32]

- ○ Make available as many books as your child wants.

- ○ Ask your teen to recommend books that he would like you to read.

- ○ Read the recommended books, and focus your thoughts on the main characters.

- ○ Discuss the books with your child.

- ○ Encourage the exchange of ideas and opinions without being judgmental.

- ○ Find a special family time to talk about books, and encourage each family member (even the youngest) to join.

In addition to asking your child for book recommendations, you may wish to suggest books for her to read. You can arrange with your child to trade book recommendations so that both parents and child have an opportunity to ask the other to read a favorite book.

To prepare for a discussion, plan ahead, thinking about your conversation as you read the book. You will probably find the plot and the characters to be the best sources of questions, although you may want to go beyond these to questions about the setting or the author's writing style.

Plot Think about the points of *conflict* and *decision*. How did they affect the outcome of the story? What would have happened if…? Would that have been better or worse than…?

Characters Consider their *motivation*. Why did…do as he/she did? What would you have done? How did relationships among the characters affect their choices?

Setting In some books, the setting is enough of a factor to warrant discussion. How does the environment (social, political, natural, or family) affect the plot? (*Decisions*) How does it affect the characters? (*Motivation*)

Writing Style Pay attention to the author's choice of words, symbolism, and figurative language—imagery, metaphors, similes. Note elements of style that you relish, and mark sentences that you find especially apt or beautiful.

Have two or three questions in mind as you begin talking with your child. Be certain that they are real questions. Having thought about them, you may have your answers ready, but that doesn't make them the right answers. You must truly want to know *what your child thinks* about the question in order to have a real discussion. The less you talk and the more you listen, the more you will learn about your child. Listen to him first, and only share your thoughts later.

If your child is not in a school reading program that includes the use of a reading log, you may want to encourage her to begin one at home. Different from a mere list of books that she has read, the reading log is a record of the date of entry and the book read, followed by the child's responses or reactions to the book. She can write her thoughts and questions about the characters, plot, ideas, symbols, theme, or any other aspect of the story after each reading session, not waiting until she has finished the entire book. Also appropriate are comments about what she does or doesn't like or doesn't understand, as well as personal experiences that relate to the story. What she should *not* write—because it is not really helpful—is a simple summary of the plot.

Whether your child shares her journal or parts of it in discussion with you should be her choice. In any case, the thinking and analysis that have gone into the reading log should become evident in your discussions.

Using the Library

The school library may be called a "library media center" or some other term conveying the fact that libraries now offer much more than books—but here we will call it simply the library. Just as a K-12 education should prepare students to continue learning after graduation, school library programs should prepare children to use public libraries throughout their lives.

Since good school library services are not available everywhere, parents should know how to evaluate library staffing, resources, and programming. This section is designed to help parents examine the school library services available to their child. If they find them less than ideal, it may be possible to find a nearby public library with more resources and a helpful staff.

Staffing

At least at the secondary level, state accreditation standards often require that the school library be staffed by professionally-trained librarians—members of the faculty who hold a master's degree from a graduate school of library or information science. Where accreditation standards do not apply, the library may be staffed by library aides. These assistants are often called librarians; you may have to ask the principal to learn whether your child's school library is staffed by a professional.

Elementary libraries, especially, often lack adequate staffing. A single professional librarian may oversee the libraries in several elementary schools, supervising the library assistants who are there when children visit the library. These assistants may receive in-service training from the professional librarian; they are typically deeply committed to children and books, and they make children welcome in the library, conducting a story time and helping them find and check out books.

A professional school librarian, in addition to these services, develops a library curriculum and teaches students how to use all of the library's resources. He or she works with teachers, helping to develop curriculum in any subject and ordering materials that support it. And as a member of the faculty, he or she is able to speak in support of the library's services and needs at faculty meetings.

If your children attend a school without a professional librarian, learn how much the students are being taught about library skills, and ask for help at the public library if necessary. Redouble your efforts to learn about children's literature, and encourage your children to read good fiction. If possible, become a library volunteer, support the library assistant, and work for the hiring of more professional librarians in your community's schools.

Resources

Libraries hold print resources (fiction, nonfiction, and reference books; magazines; and newspapers) and audio-visual media (films, audio recordings, CDs, DVDs, and audiobooks), plus computers and the Internet. Here, we will focus on books, computers, and the Internet.

Most school libraries are equipped with computers, but how they are used—and the skills that students are taught in using them—varies widely from one school to another. Your child's library books may be checked out on a computerized circulation system, with the only terminal in the library kept at the desk and inaccessible by students. Or your child may be able to use a computer to search the library's online public access catalog (OPAC). In more sophisticated libraries, children will also learn to use computers to consult online encyclopedias and to search for magazine or newspaper articles through a variety of databases.

Information-Gathering Skills

The school library should have a curriculum—a grade-by-grade plan for teaching library and research skills. When a professional librarian is available to work with teachers on curriculum planning and then to guide students, she has a major advantage—the opportunity to teach library and research skills *at the right time*, when the student needs the resources of the library to proceed with a study for which a skilled teacher has already sparked interest. Then, the library materials are important tools and the librarian a valued resource while the focus is on the information that the student wants.

The next section should be helpful for parents assessing their child's school library; it could also serve as an outline of a library skills and research curriculum for homeschooling parents. The process of learning to do research via print material is described for each age level. Because children learn to use the Internet at various ages depending on accessibility, a discussion of issues related to research on the Internet follows in a separate section.

Books: What Children Need to Know and When

The ideal time to teach children how to find books in the library is during the elementary and middle school years, when they regard the library system as both a code they can break and an exciting challenge. Secondary school instruction in library use should be reinforcement and enhancement of skills gained earlier.

Lower Elementary Grades

In the early years, children should learn the basics: what resources are in the library and how to find them. Primary children begin by learning that fiction books are arranged alphabetically by the author's last name—they can make the connection between the label on the shelf and the letter on the spine of the book. Soon they differentiate between fiction and nonfiction, and they learn where these sections are in the library. They are taught to identify information on the title page (title, author, and illustrator)—preparation for the bibliographies that they will be asked to include with reports as they grow older.

Using the online public access catalog—or the card catalog in schools that still have one—children learn to locate information about a book, whether they know the author, the title, the subject, or a keyword. They learn how to decode the call number, and then, knowing that nonfiction is in order numerically by subject, they can search the shelves for both nonfiction and fiction.

Learning basic research skills, children learn how to use long encyclopedia articles (in print or online) effectively, as well as how to use an index, a key to the information in nonfiction books.

Upper Elementary Grades

Older students need more sophisticated techniques for gaining access to information. For example, they need instruction in the use of indexes to find information hidden in magazines. Some libraries still have the print version of *Readers' Guide* (a listing of articles in periodicals); others may have access to the same information in various online databases. Encyclopedias provide key words and phrases, as well as outlines that help organize information from several sources.

Middle School and Senior High

If the basics of library use—the location of materials and the means of access to information, whether print or electronic—are taught in the elementary years, older students can focus on using more sophisticated reference sources, branching out from encyclopedias to specialized references for art, biography, science and technology, education, and the humanities. They also learn good bibliographic form, writing correct and complete bibliographic references to books, encyclopedias, magazine articles, and Internet sites. If they have not already done so, they should begin to use the public library as well as the school library. Becoming comfortable in more than one library will help in the transition to a college library.

Helping Your Child Use the Public Library

Your child's elementary years are a good time for him to establish a working relationship with the public library. Yet some public librarians report that because teens are so busy with sports and after-school work, a few parents have begun doing their research for them, coming to the library to swoop all of the books on the designated topic off the shelves and take them home. These parents may have forgotten that high school teachers assign research papers to help students learn the *process* of research so that in college it will be automatic. Over-helpful parents sabotage the learning of this process. There is a better way to help your teen use the public library. Here are some tips:

○ Help your student go prepared to the library for research. Be certain that she can clearly articulate the assignment for herself and to the librarian. If she cannot, have her ask the teacher or classmates to clarify the assignment before she makes the trip to the library.

○ If possible, your student should take with her a written assignment sheet. Experienced public librarians have probably seen the same assignment in previous years. They can help interpret it.

○ Because most public libraries have converted the card catalog to computers, students must be able to type and spell accurately. Ensure that your teen can spell any unfamiliar key words in her assignment, including author names, titles, and subjects.

○ The computer catalog is not infallible. It includes mistakes and always needs to be updated, just as the old card catalogs did. Students should be comfortable in asking for help if the catalog does not yield what they need.

○ If your student lacks library research skills, investigate what the public library offers. Many offer classes for school, Scout, or homeschooling groups. Some offer classes in computer use and research. If no classes are available, perhaps you can make arrangements for a librarian to work individually with your child until she can use the library independently.

Research on the Internet

Because students may spend more time using the Internet than their teachers or their parents do, they need guidance from school or public librarians to learn to use it effectively. Parents should determine whether students are learning good Internet research practices and then supplement where necessary.

By the middle school years, many students are using the Internet to do research for school projects. There is much for them to learn in order to use it well, but the basic point is this: beginning now and continuing through senior high school, students should know the difference between *search engines* (such as Google and Yahoo) and *databases*, and they should gain increasingly sophisticated skills in using each. This is important for gathering valid information, not only for high school and college research assignments, but also for any research that they do on the Internet for the rest of their lives. The main issue is determining the reliability of the website and of the information that they are accessing.

Search Engines

Young students doing their homework online are probably at home, where it is tempting to write an entire report using only a search engine such as Google. Using keywords, they locate websites that offer information on a vast range of topics, and they select whatever looks useful for the report at hand.

Children must understand, however, that this information can be submitted by anyone who can put up a website. Because the information is unmonitored, it must be carefully evaluated by the user—and students need guidance to judge the value of the information that they find. Colhoun recommends that to question effectively and make sound judgments about articles found through search engines, researchers should:[33]

- ○ examine the qualifications of the author by looking for evidence of training or experience

- ○ infer any biases that may be present by noticing the suffix of the site's address (sites ending in ".com" may be selling something;

those ending in ".org" may wish to influence their viewers' thinking)

○ observe how often the site is updated (Is the information too old for the topic?)

○ determine whether the information is properly documented and verifiable

Obviously, this places a lot of responsibility on the user, and the information may simply not be available on a search engine site. Colhoun quotes Jacqueline Hess regarding teaching students to use the Internet for research: "You have to teach how to identify source bias and balance that with other sources—teach how information fits in a larger context.... The art of logical reasoning—once a staple in educational training—will have to be taught again."[34]

Databases

Internet users who rely exclusively on search engines may believe that they are accessing all of the information that is out there on the Web. But databases hold an "Invisible Web" of information that search engines do not reach. This information-rich Invisible Web puts the researcher in touch with a vast and growing body of knowledge that Google does not find.

The Invisible Web replaces—and greatly expands—print indexes of magazines and scholarly journals. The *Readers' Guide*, a listing of articles in periodicals, is a database in print. Online databases cover more magazines and journals in more fields of inquiry, and they provide more current information than any print version can. They also contain links to the full text of articles from about 1980 on—some from professional, peer-reviewed journals, and all from documented sources. In short, databases provide all of the reassurance that Colhoun recommends in the checklist above. Accessing databases requires some training and practice, but that is much easier than confirming the validity of each posting on a search engine.

Databases are sold by subscriptions too costly for most individuals to buy, so libraries buy subscriptions for their patrons to use. Patrons can go online at the library, and libraries may also provide remote access—that is, the students served by a school library or the cardholders of a public library can use the library's subscription to access databases from home.

As an example, I offer my own experience with Michigan eLibrary, or MeL. The State of Michigan has designated tax money to enable the Library of Michigan to provide all Michigan residents with free access to online full-text articles from tens of thousands of magazines, journals, and newspapers, as well as full-text books which are made available to public libraries throughout the state—and through them to the homes of library patrons. To log on to MeL, I can go to my local public library, or I can log on from home. I need only my Michigan driver's license or my library card.

Then I can click on "MeL Databases" for a list of 46 databases, including several created for students. For example, a Michigan student can access SIRS Discoverer Deluxe, a database of articles for children in grades K-9, in a library or from home. To sample it, I typed "chlorophyll" in the search box, and a list of 65 items popped up from six newspapers, 19 magazines, 27 reference sources, and one website. They included full-text articles, with reading levels indicated. Some offered related activities and suggestions for teachers. Another database, SIRS Renaissance, provides full-text articles for high school and college students in a number of areas. MeL offers much more than this to the residents of Michigan; it is a truly remarkable resource. If you do not know what similar access might be available in your state, ask a librarian.

Because the Internet has forever changed the process of doing research for school projects, an important mark of a good school library is the quality of instruction that students receive in using databases for their school research projects. Today's students have at their fingertips an unimaginable wealth of information, and it will only grow. The challenge is not so much to find information as it is to know how to find and identify the most valuable and trustworthy information.

Part Three

The Books

Chapter 6

Choosing Books
that Challenge

Nearly everywhere children go, they can easily pick up inexpensive books. While many of these are excellent, books of poor quality—but with enticing covers—are everywhere. How can we help children learn to make good choices?

Selecting books for children and helping them select their own reading requires thought and effort. Yet parents who carefully monitor their children's television may pay no attention to what the children are reading; they simply may not know what is good and what is not. (Monitoring reading, incidentally, is much more fun than monitoring television, because there are many more alternatives to bad books than there are to bad television programs.)

For teachers and librarians, too, a perennial issue is the quality of children's reading. Some say, "It doesn't matter what they read, just so they're reading." But if we apply this attitude to children who have the potential to become serious readers acquainted with books of substance and literary value, then we do our children a disservice.

Those who guide the development of children have the responsibility and the pleasure of supplying them with the most meaningful material available. Part of the pleasure is that there is a wealth of good children's literature. But what is it that makes certain books especially appropriate for *gifted* children?

Like the children themselves, the books they cherish have a special spark. This spark has been analyzed and codified so that it is possible to list the characteristics that make some books particularly good choices—not exclusively for children of high potential, but especially for them.

This chapter brings together ways to identify books that not only are good literature, but also appeal to gifted readers. Some of the titles used as examples have been removed from the annotated bibliography in this edition to make room for newer books, but they are listed under "Recommended Books from Earlier Editions" at the back of the book.

For Emotional Development

Finding literature that speaks to the emotional world of the bright or intellectually curious child requires knowledge of that world, reflected in the categories in Chapters 1 and 2 of this book (establishing an identity, being alone, forming and maintaining relationships with others, using one's ability, and the drive to understand); also helpful is the Index of Categories, a guide to emotional themes in the books annotated in Chapter 8. Secondly, it requires a wide-ranging knowledge of books that depict that world.

Meeting these two requirements takes time and sensitivity, but it can be done. Children's author Katherine Paterson relates that she declined an invitation to serve on a panel on using books with troubled children because she wants a reader to "come to a book from his own experience and take from the book what he can and will. I don't want anyone telling a child what he should get out of one of my books." But she attended the panel discussion and was pleased to hear:

> ...*three highly competent, obviously compassionate people tell about the healing power of the imagination. They never diagnosed a child and then prescribed a particular book. They read widely themselves and had available in their offices many books. "When I get to know a child,"*

one of them said, "I also know four or five books that I think he might like and that might mean something to him.[1]

To build toward this kind of intuitive response, most of us must begin with concrete criteria. Here are some components of the spark that gives a book emotional appeal for gifted readers:

1. The characters are coping with one or more of the same problems that the readers are facing, such as establishing an identity—learning how to be human in their own particular way. In *Call It Courage*, Mafatu leaves his home island in order to overcome his fear of the ocean. When he returns, he knows without being told that he has earned his place among his people.

   Readers may be learning to find friends, as in *Jennifer, Hecate, Macbeth, William McKinley and Me, Elizabeth*, in which Jennifer displays her own rather unusual method of making a friend when she needs one. Or readers may be learning to keep friends, as are Millicent and Emily in *Millicent Min, Girl Genius*, who discover that there are times when it is best to tell secrets.

   Or the issue for the reader may be choices about commitment to schoolwork, to practice time, or to one's own talent—a theme which is especially well-developed in stories set in a time when school conflicted with farm labor, as in *Across Five Aprils* and *The Wolfling*.

2. The characters stand alone or in a small group for their convictions. In *The Cat Ate My Gymsuit*, Marcy takes a stand against an administrative decision at school and then finds herself, for the first time, part of a group, as students who agree with her speak out.

3. The characters may be different from their peers and might be learning to cope with this difference—which could be an interest, a family situation, a handicap, or anything that sets

a person apart. For Joshua Taylor in *A Time to Fly Free*, the difference is his extreme sensitivity to his classmates' cruelty toward living creatures. Through the understanding and support of his parents, he is able to work with an older man who helps Josh learn to use his sensitivity and to temper it with realism.

4. The characters may be learning to accept someone else who ~~others~~ is different, as in *Summer of the Swans*. This is the story of a sister's affection for a mentally handicapped younger brother—affection not always shared or understood by neighborhood children.

5. Adult characters should be present and supportive in at least some of the books. Some contemporary literature for adolescents depicts adults who are weak or absent, giving the young people more control over their own lives. They still need adult concern, however, and it is comfortingly present in books such as *Caddie Woodlawn*, *Anne of Green Gables*, and Lois Lowry's books about Anastasia Krupnik and her family.

6. Some characters should be gifted adults who lead produc- *children or gifted adults* tive and enjoyable lives and who in general function well as gifted people in the adult world. The O'Keefes in Madeleine L'Engle's books are vivid examples of this.

combine

7. Some of the child characters should clearly be gifted themselves so that the reader can say, "He's like me! I feel that way, too! Maybe I'm not the only one who thinks this way!" Several books in the annotated bibliography meet this criterion. Young readers can see themselves in stories told as myths, too, like Jane Yolen's *The Boy Who Had Wings*; these children can then discuss the nature of their own "wings."

combine

8. Giftedness need not necessarily be labeled, but may be implicit—that is, clearly present in one of the characters but not mentioned by anyone. It goes without saying, for example, that Meg in *At the Sign of the Star* and *A True and*

Faithful Narrative would have been assigned to a gifted class if here had been one in 17ᵗʰ-century London.

9. Characters should be people to whom readers can relate: open-minded and questioning, with a passion for learning everything, such as Nathaniel in Latham's *Carry On, Mr. Bowditch*; or idealistic and intense, with a devotion to a cause, such as Raisha in *My Name is Not Angelica*, Scott O'Dell's novel based on a slave revolt in 1733.

10. Some books for gifted readers should depict characters struggling with issues of personal or moral courage, personal values, and moral and ethical choices. In *The Witch of Blackbird Pond*, Kit Tyler, newly arrived from Barbados, befriends an old woman who is thought by the people of her village to be a witch. Evident in the story are Kit's courage and also the greater moral struggle of her Puritan uncle.

11. Some books should have humor of a high level—spontaneously arising from a situation, springing from a character's way of looking at the world, or based on intelligent use of language. An example is *A Day No Pigs Would Die*. The humorous use of language by the character Rob is unconscious, but author Robert Newton Peck clearly knew what he was doing. Picture books, too, can provide sophisticated humor, as in *Not a Stick*, in which humor is based on the interaction between a clueless adult and a long-suffering child who finally and definitively brings the discussion to an end with cleverness rather than a confrontation.

Of course, no one book can be expected to meet every item on this checklist, but a collection can. The goal is to keep the criteria in mind while gathering as many books as eager readers have time to read. With the list as a guide, and with experience and exposure to a number of excellent books, it is possible for adults to develop an instinctive sense for books that will catch and hold readers' interest and give them something to think about long after the books have been read.

For Intellectual Development

For optimal intellectual development, very bright children must learn to acknowledge and satisfy their need to know. Books that will help them achieve this goal must both whet and satisfy their curiosity, as well as be intellectually challenging. What makes a book intellectually challenging? The specific criteria for picture books are different from those for older children's books, but the underlying idea is the same: the pictures, the words, and the themes must expand the child's world, encourage further exploration, and enrich the mind and spirit with artistic integrity.

Picture Books

Writing about requirements for successful picture books, Rosemary Wells begins with feelings:

> *First of all, a good picture book must ring with emotional content, so that children care about what's going on. William Steig's* Amos and Boris *and* Sylvester and the Magic Pebble *never fail to overwhelm a reader with both worry and love.... What is in them is in all of us: guilt, fear, devotion. As a writer you have little time and few pages to achieve this. The characters in a children's book must reach into the heart of the reader on page one.*[2]

Moving on to more practical criteria, Wells says that picture books must be short.

> *A picture book is in trouble if it's longer than eight double-spaced typewritten pages. It's also in trouble if it's bland, or if the tone is false and hysterical. It must never be cute or it will insult children. It's in trouble if it uses television characters, or if it's written by anybody with a degree in child psychology.*[3]

This last comment can be read as a warning against picture books written by any author, regardless of educational background, whose intent is to teach or "improve" children through the writing.

Picture books are a unique blend of visual art and language. Looking for the best among them means assessing the illustrations, the text, and the fit between the two. Furthermore, even picture books can be intellectually challenging, demanding that readers use higher-level thinking skills. Mockett and Welton[4] stress the importance of books that promote creative and divergent thinking and provide humor and wordplay. At first, these expectations may seem unrealistically high for a picture book, but the best of them have much to offer, and a rich assortment will contain all of these elements. Picture books for gifted children should have the following characteristics:

1. Illustrations should be vibrant and original rather than stereotyped. This is what Wells means when she says that a picture book is in trouble if it uses television characters—and she might have added animated movie characters, as well. For an example of excellent work, see the illustrations by Marcia Brown for Cendrars' *Shadow*—artwork that evokes in color and shape the sense of awe and mystery that is conveyed by the words of the poem.

2. Illustrations should not merely accompany the storyline but should complement and enhance it. Good examples are the books by Maurice Sendak, in which the expressions on the characters' faces tell the story from their own points of view. In Lyon's *Who Came Down That Road?*, the illustrations show the faded presence of ancient life as the boy's questions and the mother's answers take the story backward through time.

3. Details of the illustrations should be so fascinating that a child can look repeatedly and always find more: a surprise or a bit of humor, a private joke between the illustrator and the attentive child. Books by Richard Scarry and Mitsumasa Anno are prime examples.

4. Some books should be provided that offer abstract illustrations which, while recognizable, still require mental exercise to be understood. Tana Hoban's *Shadows and Reflections* invites children to study each picture to see what is really there.

5. Illustrations should not supply all of the details or information so that some imaginative effort on the part of the child is needed to complete the picture. Ljunkvist's *Follow the Line* is an example of artwork that *is* the story, requiring the child to interact intellectually with the visual image on the page.

6. Books should introduce new and fascinating words—satisfying to the tongue as the child learns to say them—mixed in plentiful measure among the familiar words. Cuteness and condescension are neither necessary nor welcome; what is needed is respect for the child as an intelligent, learning person. Authors of good children's books about dinosaurs, for example, make the correct assumption that four-year-olds can pronounce *Ichthyosaurus* and *Tyrannosaurus Rex*.

7. Authors who obviously take delight in the use of language—whose books demonstrate a playful, joyful sense of fun with words—appeal to gifted children. Dr. Seuss books encourage children to experiment with words, making them up as necessary and bending them slightly to create a rhyme.

   Some picture books offer play with languages other than English. The texts of *Abuela* and *Siesta* include Spanish, tantalizing an English-speaking child with the possibility of learning bits of another language. *Who's In Rabbit's House?* and other African folktales are told with the soothing repetition of sounds typical of speech.

8. Books should depict characters, whether animal or human, who display real emotions, feelings, and relationships that children will recognize. In *Alexander and the Terrible, Horrible, No Good, Very Bad Day*, for example, Alexander displays frustration, anger, and finally resignation toward the kind of day he is having—a day in which ordinary, everyday

disasters happen to him all day long, as they sometimes do to everyone.

9. Plots that are not completely predictable allow for conjecturing and discussion between adults and children as the book is read. *Free Fall* is an example—a visual presentation of a dream, leaving readers to interpret a storyline to suit the pictures.

10. Even picture books can raise moral questions, helping young children who are already concerned, for example, about the environment. These books can too easily be cloying and "preachy," but if well done, they can offer reassurance that a child is not alone in her concerns. In *Hey! Get Off Our Train*, Burningham provides a vehicle for discussion of environmental concerns—a topic that worries many gifted children before most of their agemates are aware of it.

11. Stories, pictures, and characters that are outside of the daily experience of children can help to expand their awareness. *Anno's Journey*, the story of a journey through medieval Europe, supported by illustrations that are filled with detail and interest, presents not only other countries, but also another time.

Books for Older Children

"Language," says Barbara Baskin, "is the single most important component...in selecting engaging and stimulating material for gifted students."[5] She argues that gifted children should have higher-level books, including books at the adult level in some cases, as well as longer and more complex books than teachers would select for most readers.

In addition, Baskin contends that theme is more important than plot, since important themes present the larger picture that intellectually able readers are eager to assimilate. She suggests that appropriate motifs for these students include philosophical, moral, and social issues, as well as the nature of heroism, boundaries, and relationships.

Baskin also recommends aspects of literary structure that create challenges for the reader, including time manipulations, parallel plots, ideas pulled together from several disciplines, and metaphor.

All of these criteria are considered when books for older readers are judged according to their language, style, plot, and setting. In each area, books appropriate for gifted readers are complex rather than simple, rich and varied rather than predictable, and open-ended and thought-provoking rather than neatly contained.

Look for the following characteristics in books that provide intellectual stimulation for gifted readers.

Language

1. Language should be on a high level, making strong demands on the reader's vocabulary. Hermann Hesse's *Demian*, first published in 1925 in Europe, assumes an extremely well-educated reader and rewards good readers with a rich and unrestricted vocabulary.

2. As with illustrations in a picture book, language in a book for older readers should reflect and enhance the plot. In Garfield and Blishen's retelling of Greek myths, *The God Beneath the Sea*, the level of language serves to ennoble the text. In *The Phantom Tollbooth*, humorous, pun-filled language is part of the message of the book: that language itself is a source of delight and challenge. In both cases, the language accomplishes more than presenting the story; it becomes an essential part of the reading experience.

3. Books that contain pronunciation guides are helpful for gifted readers (though they are rare, and a pleasant surprise when found), since so many avid readers know words only from reading and therefore mispronounce them. One excellent teacher of gifted high school students calls this "The Calley-ope (*calliope*) Syndrome."

4. Look for masterfully-chosen descriptive words that stimulate strong visual imagery. For example, in *A String in the*

Harp, Bond's descriptions encourage the reader to picture the modern Wales that Peter knows in daily life—and later, to superimpose onto that picture the Wales of Taliesin's time, which Peter envisions.

5. As with picture books, books for gifted readers should be written by authors who delight in language and who skillfully express nuances of thought and feeling. Joyce Carol Thomas's *Marked by Fire* is notable for the way in which language—prose and poetry—evokes place and mood, moving the story along on an emotional level.

6. Language patterns and vocabularies from other times and places, used without apology or explanation, encourage the reader to glean meaning from context. Examples abound: Garfield's *Smith*, which evokes 18th-century England; Mayne's *Earthfasts*, employing the language of remote corners of modern Wales; Ayn Rand's *Anthem*, with an imagined language of the future; and Auel's *The Clan of the Cave Bear*, which supposes a language system from the past.

Style

7. Books for gifted readers can display the full complement of literary devices that enrich the fabric of literature, and therefore the readers (whether they recognize these devices by name or not): metaphor, simile, paradox, symbol, and allusion. Poetry does this by nature; one example in prose is *The Bat-Poet* by Randall Jarrell.

Plot

8. In book selection, as in curriculum, it is helpful to remember Maurice Freehill's insight that gifted children are "challenged by the unfinished and the misunderstood."[6] Some of the books they read should present problems that are unresolved, even at the end of the story. Such plots cause readers to look at a situation from different perspectives, see possible conclusions, and ponder what desirable or likely options are

available. At the end of *Izzy, Willy-Nilly,* for example, we know that Izzy is forever changed—but we are left to conjecture about how the changes in her will affect her relationships with friends and family.

9. Good readers should be developing the ability to hold different levels of meaning in their minds simultaneously, and some of the books that they read should give them experience in doing so. For example, *The Village by the Sea* requires the reader to look below the storyline to understand the universal human motives that are being played out as the characters reveal themselves and the plot unfolds.

10. The structure of a plot can put the mind to work. Flashbacks, narration that shifts from one person to another, or the use of a journal format can all challenge and reward the careful reader. A good example is Konigsburg's *Father's Arcane Daughter,* in which each chapter is introduced by a dialogue between unidentified characters, adding to the mystery while simultaneously supplying clues for the surprise ending. More complex and demanding is the structure of Vonnegut's *Slaughterhouse-Five,* which presents a fluid view of time through Billy Pilgrim.

Setting

11. The settings of some books allow children to experience vicariously lifestyles that are not their own. An example is the vivid description of traditional living patterns on Mafatu's Pacific island in *Call It Courage.* Children growing up in small towns or rural areas can learn something of great art museums and of life in New York City by reading *From the Mixed-up Files of Mrs. Basil E. Frankweiler,* or they can see a darker view of New York street life in *Slake's Limbo.*

One quick way of finding books that are intellectually demanding is to look for books from England or in translation from a foreign language, because authors of children's books in other countries generally assume more background and education on the part of the reader than many American children's authors do. Such books will probably contain some colloquial terms unfamiliar to American readers, but the meaning of most can be determined from the context, and they add both to the challenge of the book and to its power to expand the reader's knowledge of other cultures.

Bloom's[7] terminology (described in Chapter 5) helps to form a neat statement of the characteristics of books that offer intellectual challenge to gifted students: such books invite *analysis* of characters and events; *synthesis* of ideas from the book under discussion and from anywhere else in the reader's experience; and *evaluation* of the relationships, actions, consequences, alternatives, and possibilities found in the book and in the reader's interpretation of it.

Again, it is obvious that no book will contain *all* of the characteristics listed for intellectually stimulating reading. However, if adults keep the characteristics in mind while they read reviews and browse the shelves of young people's literature, they will gradually be able to gather a collection that includes these criteria in abundance—a collection that will be invaluable for the gifted children and youths who have access to it.

Suggested Book Lists

In addition to the annotated bibliography of Chapter 8 in this book, several other selection guides are available for parents and teachers looking for books to recommend.

Hauser, Paula & Gail A. Nelson. *Books for the Gifted Child* (Vol. 2). Bowker, 1988.

Hearne, Betsy Gould. *Choosing Books for Children: A Commonsense Guide* (3rd ed.). University of Illinois Press, 1999.

Weber, Olga S. *Good Reading: A Guide for Serious Readers* (23rd ed.). Libraries Unlimited, 1989. (For senior high and older students.)

Parents looking for magazines to interest gifted children may wish to consider *Calliope* (world history), *Cobblestone* (U.S. history), and *Odyssey* (science)—all for ages 9-14.

Chapter 7

All the Wealth:
Kinds of Literature

"Literature is the dominant art," says one of our sons, who holds a doctoral degree in comparative literature. In order to know music, sculpture, or painting, he points out, we have to know literature. Through most of history, composers have assumed that listeners have read classic literature, but a writer does not normally assume that his readers have heard a certain body of music. As far back as Homer, makers of literature were recognized as artists, but 2,300 years later, sculptors were still considered stonecutters. In his lifetime, Michelangelo was recognized as a great craftsman, not an artist.

Historically, painters, sculptors, and musicians sought inspiration in literary themes to legitimize their work as art. Even now, the modern critic of other arts uses the history of literature as a frame of reference, while a literary critic—perhaps mistakenly— finds the history of his own field sufficient.[1]

If our children are to be truly educated and culturally literate, they must have a rich background in literature. They won't acquire all they need before the age of 18, but if we enthusiastically introduce them to all kinds of literature, they'll have a chance to become discriminating, mature readers who continue reading literature for pleasure throughout their lives. This chapter is designed to remind parents and teachers of the wealth of good books available to children.

The comfortable phrase "curling up with a good book" brings to mind the prospect of spending an evening with a thick novel—a romance or a mystery, perhaps a historical novel, but certainly fiction. Although we tend to think of fiction first, the field of literature is more complex than that.

Within fiction there are several different types; there are also various categories of nonfiction. All of these are available to the child who wants to curl up with a good book—but only if she knows about them.

Here are four points to remember in using books to guide and enrich bright children:

○ Some children, especially as they grow older, resist reading fiction.

○ A lack of interest in this genre does not mean that they must stop reading. There are many kinds of literature; *fiction, nonfiction, biography, traditional literature, fantasy and science fiction*, and *poetry* are all discussed in this chapter.

○ Gifted and talented youngsters, like other children, must be introduced to the best in literature. They will not automatically find it on their own.

○ The different types of literature vary in their power to meet emotional and intellectual needs for gifted children, and their effect varies from one child to another. It is important that children be introduced to all kinds of literature, with enough exposure so that each child can decide which is most valuable for him or her.

Fiction will fall naturally into the hands of good readers in elementary school, but unless a planned effort is made to introduce children to other types of literature, especially traditional literature and poetry, children may miss them altogether. Middle school and senior high students need guidance, too, to become aware of the wealth of literature as they develop into adult readers. Any kind of literature can be an important part of education—it can be a key to histories, arts, and cultures, particularly for these youngsters who are more likely to draw information from many sources and integrate it in new ways.

Guiding the reading of intellectually curious children, therefore, includes making them aware of the varieties of literature and helping them learn which kinds have the most appeal for them. The resulting knowledge of books and of one's own preferences is part of what makes a mature reader.

Table: K-6 Literature Curriculum*

	Picture Books	Poetry	Traditional	Nonfiction	Fiction
Kindergarten	x	x	Folktales, Fairy Tales	x	Picture Books
First Grade	x	x	Folktales, Fairy Tales	x	Picture Books, Story Books
Second Grade	x	x	Folktales, Fairy Tales	x	Realistic, Fantasy
Third Grade	x	x	Folktales, Fairy Tales, Fables	x Biography	Realistic, Fantasy
Fourth Grade		x	Folktales, Legends	x Biography	Realistic, Fantasy, High Fantasy
Fifth Grade		x	Legends, Myths	x Biography	Realistic, Fantasy, High Fantasy, Historical
Sixth Grade		x	Myths, Epics	x Biography	Realistic, Fantasy, High Fantasy, Historical, Science Fiction
	These are read aloud when classes come to the library.			These are introduced in the library through excerpts or book talks.	

Each genre is presented at the grade levels indicated by an x or by the name of a type of literature.

In elementary schools, the logical person to coordinate the introduction of literature through the grades is the librarian. Not every elementary school, however, boasts a professional who has time to plan and implement a program for introducing various types of literature to children at the appropriate grade levels. For teachers in such schools, the table on the previous page outlines a sample literature curriculum. Parents whose children have no school librarian will find that the children's staff at a nearby public library can suggest good books in each literary category.

Fiction

Fiction (called "realistic fiction" when fantasy is considered as a separate category) is the broadest body of literature, the earliest found by children exploring on their own, and the most easily judged by the traits given in the previous chapter. Since authors write about what they know, and since many authors were gifted children, the characters in juvenile fiction are often gifted. However, rarely is the giftedness pointed out; it is simply there to be recognized by child readers who see something of themselves in the story.

Types of Fiction

Realistic fiction can be divided into a number of subtypes, including adventure, animal stories, mystery, sports stories, humor, romance, and historical fiction. Most of these can be thought of as one group, although historical fiction deserves special consideration.

How well each type suits the emotional or intellectual needs of especially talented children depends largely on the author's point of view and on how well the books are written. Each kind, but some more than others, can be treated in ways that offer intellectual challenge or provide insights into emotional development.

Recognizing Good Fiction

In order to continue to appeal to new generations of young readers, fiction must speak to their universal concerns, help them explore themselves through the characters in the books, and introduce them to life in other places and times. It does this by dealing honestly with the material and with its readers.

Honesty and accuracy are the two most important criteria for children's fiction. Settings must be described so that the reader can imagine them. Plots must relate something that could plausibly happen. Above all, characters must react with understandable emotions and behavior; their speech must be true to their ages and experience and to the environment established for them in the story.

Beyond that, for fiction that has enough depth to engage the imagination of sensitive readers, something should happen *within* the characters during the course of the book. Even fiction for young children offers this; *Evan's Corner*, for example, is not just a story about a boy who needs a little privacy and is allowed to turn a corner of a room into his own space. It is also about Evan's getting everything he thought he wanted and then *realizing* (the internal event) that it is not enough. He wants to share it, too.

Especially in books for young children, watch for the comforting rhythm of language. Modern classics in literature for preschoolers provide good examples: *Good Night Moon, Millions of Cats, Blueberries for Sal*. In these books, parallel events are expressed in parallel language patterns, smooth and almost (but not quite) predictable. Literature of lower quality—such as that designed to sell in connection with a movie—lacks this polish, often written instead in short, choppy sentences that do not flow.

Historical Fiction

Writers of historical fiction must walk a line between over-burdening the plot with too much historical detail and using so little historical background that the book amounts to a modern novel placed in a historical setting. The best writers base their books on serious research and then weave realistic details into the narrative to lend authenticity to plot and characterization.

For alert and questioning readers, historical fiction should show not only the culture and daily life of the period, but it should also deal with some of the political and personal issues encountered by people of that era. An example is Esther Forbes's *Johnny Tremain*, in which Johnny, initially concerned with his burned hand, is gradually caught up in the political and military turmoil around him as the Revolutionary War begins.

Finding Good Fiction

Young children find a "good book" mostly by watching what their friends are reading. They may also get recommendations from the school librarian or get ideas from what their teacher reads aloud. However, unless someone guides them to good books, their progress is haphazard at best.

Those who want to recommend good literature to children can follow a more systematic procedure. See the resources listed at the end of Chapter 6 and under "Books about Children's Literature" at the end of this chapter. On their local library's website, patrons may be able to see reviews from *Booklist* or *School Library Journal* for books in the library's holdings.

A rich source of information is the librarian's own reference collection. Here are reference books and periodicals that list children's books by categories, often providing annotations or reviews for each. For most of these, inclusion equals recommendation—that is, these periodicals list only books that by some established standard merit recommendation. The public is usually welcome to use these references, though they probably cannot be checked out of the library. The list at the end of this chapter includes some of the most useful sources.

Nonfiction

It may surprise some to know that at the end of a library story hour for primary-grade children, when the children are free to find a book to check out, they are more likely to swarm to the nonfiction shelves than to picture books. No matter how attentively they have just listened to fiction or folklore, they appear to be hungry for fact as they explore on their own. It may be that as non-readers, they feel that they can gather more information from the pictures of a fact book than they can from those in a picture book whose story they do not know.

Whatever the reason, it is obvious that even at that early age, information books are important to children, and this continues to be true as they grow older. With the development of teaching methods that require students to search for information beyond their textbooks, the number and quality of nonfiction books for young people have increased dramatically in recent years. Gifted students in particular benefit from exploring the views of different authors in books that offer more information at a more challenging reading level than graded textbooks can.

For readers of any age, nonfiction written for children is a good introduction to a new field. For a report on any topic only vaguely familiar to them—examples might be continental drift, the human brain, astronomy, or economics—older students can begin with books written for younger children to gain a quick overview of basic concepts, essential vocabulary, and an organizational framework. All of this will help them make better use of information they find later in more advanced books and articles.

Recognizing Good Nonfiction

It is not easy to write good nonfiction. Lacking a plot to maintain interest, the author must write with both a lucid style and a clear purpose. The author's attitude toward his audience and his reason for choosing to write about his topic for young people help determine the success of his book, providing a framework that may be nearly invisible but nevertheless gives shape to the contents.

The physical appearance of the book, the size and format, and aesthetic qualities such as the appeal of illustrations and the print type all add to the book's ability to attract and hold readers.

Beyond these essential considerations are the characteristics of good nonfiction: accuracy, readability, structure, and for especially bright readers, open-endedness and the potential for both stimulating and satisfying their curiosity.

Accuracy

Accuracy is absolutely essential in nonfiction. The copyright date should be recent, especially if the book is in a field that is changing rapidly. The dust jacket or endpapers may provide biographical material on the author, indicating his or her level of expertise. If possible, check the accuracy of a section of text that covers an area of knowledge that is familiar to you, or ask an expert to check it. Try to determine whether the author is writing from a biased point of view, keeping in mind that young children in particular are vulnerable—they are likely to believe what they read simply because it is in print.

Look for accuracy in the graphic material, also. For illustrations in science books, a clear and precise line with correct labeling is needed. Photographs may be best for some social studies books, but they should be updated when the books are revised. Graphs and charts must be clear and current.

Readability

Since the appeal in nonfiction is to the intellect rather than emotions, the author must be skilled in techniques that hold the reader's interest. Readability—the way in which the material is presented—is of paramount importance. Like a good teacher introducing a new subject by referring to what the children already know, the author of a good nonfiction book will begin with an image or a setting that is familiar, then take the readers into new territory. A book for primary children on building barns, for example, might demonstrate stress factors with illustrations showing structures made of building blocks.

Nonfiction requires clear writing, logically and sequentially presented. In addition, writing for children requires some special techniques. Because young children cannot yet think in abstractions, abstract concepts should be supported by concrete images, either in illustrations or by giving clear examples. A written description of the structure of a bridge, for instance, should be accompanied by a drawing, preferably with the parts labeled. And general statements must be followed by specific examples. Repetition is also important—authors should repeat key words throughout the book and provide a summary at the end. The vocabulary should be accurate, reflecting the terms used by workers in the field discussed in the book. A glossary in books about specialized topics is always welcome. The writing style should flow comfortably, drawing the reader along.

Readability can be enhanced by the organization of the book. Maps, charts, graphs, drawings, and photographs increase readability and should be placed near the text they illustrate. An index helps readers find their way around the book. Even young readers seeking information should use some books that include bibliographies so that they can learn where they can read more, and so that they can become familiar with the researcher's practice of documenting sources of information.

Often, an assumed reading level is indicated either on the book or by its placement in a library or bookstore. However, gifted children with a strong interest in a topic will read beyond their grade level or even their measured reading level to learn as much as they can from a book that might otherwise be considered too advanced for them. They should, of course, have the freedom to select books for older readers, along with those that are at a comfortable reading level.

Structure

Information is often presented in chronological order, like a narrative. However, students are sufficiently familiar with narrative from their reading of fiction; nonfiction can challenge with different structure. Good nonfiction authors use various presentations: organizing their materials in lists, comparing and contrasting, using cause and effect, enumerating, providing cumulative evidence, challenging with problems to which solutions have been or must be found, offering a question/answer format, and arranging information from simple to complex. These organizational patterns require different types of thinking, more like the kinds of thinking that adults do in their daily lives.[2]

Open-Endedness

Finally, nonfiction for gifted readers should be open-ended. This may sound like a contradiction in terms for a fact book, but consider: Is the author clear about which statements are accepted facts and which are still unproven hypotheses? Does she use an interdisciplinary approach, indicating points at which this subject leads into other, related topics? Is there some mention of ethical questions raised by new knowledge in the field?

Much of what most teachers and parents memorized as children—about astronomy, genetics, bioengineering—has been modified by newer discoveries. With their ability to delay closure, gifted children are receptive to uncertainty and challenged by the unknown. They should be informed of the unanswered questions and methods used in current research, and they should be stimulated to examine the field more deeply themselves. Challenging nonfiction gives satisfactory answers to some questions, but it also raises more questions, inviting readers to continue the search for information at a new level.

Nonfiction and Gifted Readers

Intellectually curious youngsters can and should learn to select nonfiction well so that they can pursue their own interests through reading. It is helpful to discuss with them the characteristics of good nonfiction books so that they can make judgments for themselves.

Sometimes gifted children run into barriers as they look for new books that match their interests. Adults who can't believe that their children can read far beyond their age level may be reluctant to allow them to use expensive books.

> *Andreas discovered at the age of eight that the library in his K-12 school had purchased a new astronomical atlas for the high school students. More than anything, Andreas wanted to take that atlas home, even though he could hardly carry it. In addition to the question of a third grader's reliability with a costly new book, the librarian had to consider that it was a reference book and could circulate only overnight. However, she knew Andreas and understood his passion for science, so arrangements were made. For months, Andreas came to the library every Friday afternoon and checked the book out for the weekend, always returning it early Monday morning in perfect condition in spite of the winter weather. This young boy certainly gained more from the atlas than the seniors for whom it had been ordered.*

When librarians are not acquainted with children such as Andreas, parents or teachers may have to run interference, explaining why a child may need and merit special consideration. They may also help by coaching the child in how to respond effectively to restricting rules.

Finding Good Nonfiction

Even armed with a list of characteristics to help select the best, a reader approaching the nonfiction section of a school or public library is likely to be overwhelmed by the sheer volume of material. You may wish to make a list of recommended books, using reviews or booklists as references, before turning to the public catalog.

Reviews of nonfiction may be difficult to uncover because reviewing children's nonfiction is especially demanding—reviewers must be knowledgeable about the topic of the book, as well as about good children's writing. Reviews of newly-published books appear in periodicals first; it is usually at least a year before they appear in book form. The periodical *Booklist* divides reviews of books for young people into several sections, placing reviews of nonfiction books first in each case. In addition, journals for teachers often list a few new books for students among the book reviews. And newsletters for parents of children enrolled in gifted programs sometimes offer recommendations for good reading.

Finding a review of a book that sounds ideal is only the first step toward placing it in the child's hands. With so much nonfiction available—some of it highly specialized—it is unreasonable to expect bookstores and libraries to stock enough for the varied needs of curious, avid readers—underscoring the value of reviews, which prepare you to make specific requests when ordering. Once you know what you want, you can order most titles through interlibrary loan, through your local bookstore, or online.

Reference books suggested at the end of this chapter provide lists of recommended books. Some have nonfiction sections; others are entirely about nonfiction books.

Biography

Biography often becomes a favorite with young people who prefer more difficult reading. Life stories of individuals who realized their high potential can offer intellectually and emotionally rewarding reading for gifted adults, and by the same token, it's important that bright children have a good introduction to this genre. Like other forms of nonfiction, biography is often assigned as part of a study unit, so most children are aware of it as a separate kind of literature by the time they are in the upper elementary grades. For gifted children in a regular classroom, biography is an excellent tool for extending the regular curriculum.

Types of Biographies

Biographies can be classified on a continuum, with nonfiction at one end and fiction at the other. At the nonfiction end, *definitive* (or *authentic*) *biography* relies on historical evidence, containing nothing that cannot be documented. *Fictionalized biography*, in the middle, is a blend—the author conducts extensive research and then invents dialogue or events based on the historical record. At the other end of the continuum, *biographical fiction* is frankly fiction with a historical person as the main character.

The characteristic that most reliably establishes where a given biography rests on the continuum is dialogue. In definitive biography, dialogue is rare and occurs only when there is a written record of the discussion. For the most part, the characters "speak" only through their letters.

In fictionalized biography, the author is free to blend fact and fiction by creating scenes in which an imagined conversation furthers or dramatizes the historical account. For a cataloging class in library school, a professor described fictionalized biography with this example: "If there is a line like, 'After the last guest had left, Victoria dismissed the servants, retired to the royal suite, closed the door, turned to Albert, and said, "…",' then you know you have a fictionalized biography."

In biographical fiction, conversation flows as freely as in any other kind of fiction, even between bit players for whose very existence there is no historical record.

The type of biography that children enjoy depends in large part on their age. For young children whose sense of history is not developed, biographies are stories that familiarize them with names such as Abraham Lincoln, Jane Addams, or Martin Luther King, Jr. Older children enjoy both biographical fiction and fictionalized biography, and talented senior high students with specific interests may be encouraged to read some of the recent definitive biographies, such as Scott A. Berg's *Lindbergh* or David McCullough's *John Adams*.

Recognizing Good Biography

At one time, biography was a weak link in children's literature. Much of it was didactic—written to teach a lesson—as young readers could clearly see. However, there have been three significant changes: more biographies about women and members of minority groups have appeared, the subjects are presented as real human beings rather than impossible paragons, and authors model good scholarship for their readers through the biographies that they write by including references listing their sources.[3] An excellent example of all of these developments is Albert Marrin's *Sitting Bull and His World*, one of the books recommended in Chapter 8.

Because it runs the gamut from nonfiction to fiction, biography can be judged by some of the criteria used for each. As nonfiction, it must be accurate, readable, and objective. Even in biographical fiction, however, historical details should be authentic, as they should be in any good historical fiction. A readable biography must bring a historical person to life, presenting characters as real people with human problems and responses. Small, intimate details make the biographee seem like a contemporary friend. Where there is dialogue, it should flow as naturally as it does in a novel.

All nonfiction writers should approach their subjects with objectivity, but it is more difficult to be objective when the subject is a person. Objectivity requires authors to maintain a balance between admiration of and criticism for the person whose life they are describing. Objective authors leave readers free to draw their own conclusions based on the facts; they do not suppress relevant but negative aspects of the principal character's life and place in history. That said, biography for children should show restraint and sensitivity in discussing character weaknesses, particularly when they are unrelated to the person's historical importance.

Finding Biographies

In libraries, biographies are usually shelved together in the nonfiction section at the point in which the number 921 would occur in the Dewey Decimal system. However, the call "number" is often a B followed by the last name of the biographee, so the books appear in alphabetical order by the person whose life they tell, not by the author.

The biography section of a library may be astonishingly large in proportion to the rest of the nonfiction. To find the best, check the sections on biography in the sources suggested at the end of this chapter.

Biography in Bibliotherapy with Gifted Students

While biography is recommended for all students, it can be used for gifted students with specific purposes in mind for them. One is to demonstrate that many trials and failures often precede success. The biographies of scientists in deKruif's *The Microbe Hunters*, for example, provide evidence of the hours of preparation and even drudgery that must pay for the moment of discovery—and it is obvious that deKruif's scientists paid the price gladly, with lasting enthusiasm for their work. It is not difficult to imagine that this book might be informative, perhaps even inspiring reading for a gifted child who resists routine work.

Another purpose is to show the role of personal characteristics in achievement—characteristics that could be either evident or latent in the gifted child reading the book. *Carry On, Mr. Bowditch* is a good example, illustrating how Nathaniel Bowditch's inner drive, his energetic curiosity, and his thoroughness in inquiry helped him achieve far more than usual for those with scant opportunity for a formal education.

In searching for appropriate biographies for gifted readers, consider the following questions about the people in the books: What is revealed about their motivation, moral imperative, intellectual curiosity, and/or impulse to inquiry? What advantages did their high intelligence bring to them, and what problems? How did they turn their talents to their own advantage in coping with the problems? What evidence is there, if any, that they recognized their gifts and consciously made use of them? What role did a sense of commitment, mission, or responsibility play in their achievements?

A third use of biographies with gifted adolescents is to provide them with examples of gifted people who experienced the feelings of isolation and loneliness that readers can recognize. Gifted young people, especially those with a strong sense of their own high potential, are likely to be able to identify with the aspirations and struggles of gifted adults like Marie Curie, who, studying alone in a Paris apartment, was so cold that one night she piled everything she could, including a chair, on top of her bed for warmth. Some gifted teenagers can understand that to Marie, the cold and the loneliness were incidental nuisances compared to the privilege of studying science at the Sorbonne. Rather than feeling overwhelmed, these adolescents can use such people as models without necessarily expecting themselves to achieve to the same degree.

Biography can be one of the most intellectually demanding forms of literature, but it can also be among the most inspiring. On both counts, it should be part of the reading program for gifted young people.

Traditional Literature

The literatures that have been passed from generation to generation since the beginning of human culture include folk and fairy tales, fables, myths, legends, and epics. This rich heritage, once oral, is now collected in many written versions, available to children in greater variety and from more different cultures than ever before. It is a vital part of the background of anyone who hopes to be truly educated.

Most children will not find traditional literature on their own. When they swarm to the nonfiction shelves after the story hour, it is to science, technology, and craft books, not to the mythology or folklore sections (which are classified as nonfiction, strange as it may seem, because they are a way to learn about the cultures from which they come). Rare is the child who spontaneously asks where to find fairy tales or King Arthur stories, although they enjoy these stories when they hear them.

Traditional literature, therefore, must be actively introduced or most children will grow up without adequate knowledge of it. Presenting it effectively requires knowledge of the ages when children are most likely to respond to the different types.

Introducing Traditional Literature at the Best Time

Traditional literature ranges from the simplest folktale cherished by preschoolers to complex epics that form the basis of classic adult literature. Teachers and librarians who guide children's reading know at what age children are ready to respond to each type. For those who are just beginning with children's literature, a brief outline follows.

Folktales

The first traditional literature that children hear, at three and four years old, is folklore—tales of the wisdom and foolishness of common people. Preschoolers love simple cumulative tales like "The Three Little Pigs," "The Gingerbread Boy," and "The Little Red Hen."

Fairy tales such as "Cinderella," told with variations in different cultures around the world, come next, appealing to children from about five to eight years old. Although the Grimm tales are the most familiar, there are many others in collections from different countries. Any concerns that adults may have about violence in fairy tales can be allayed by reviewing the wide variety available—and remembering Bettelheim's view that, in their eagerness to see justice served and with their black-and-white view of the world, children are not nearly as alarmed by the violence as are adults.[4]

Legends and Tall Tales

Fourth and fifth graders are ready for legends—stories of larger-than-life figures whose historical existence is shadowy but whose deeds, exaggerated for dramatic effect, have lived in story. The first legends that children encounter may be those of England's Robin Hood and King Arthur; another example is Kate Seredy's *The White Stag*, based on Atilla and the founding of Hungary. Out of the pioneer experience in the United States came the Jack tales[5] from the Appalachians (such as *Jack and the Beanstalk*) and stories of men like Mike Fink, Davey Crockett, and Paul Bunyan. The trademark American humor of these stories helped European newcomers cope as they struggled with the challenges that greeted them in exploring and settling the land in the 18th and 19th centuries.

Mythology

By the fifth and sixth grades, as students study early cultures, they should be introduced not only to the histories of those cultures, but also to their religions, which we now call mythology. In particular, a knowledge of the Greek, Roman, and Norse myths will go far toward making young people feel at home with European and American art, literature, and history.

When we say "myths" in general conversation, we mean "untruths" more often than we mean the stories that human beings have used through most of history to express ultimate truths and values. The psychoanalyst Rollo May regrets our failure in recent years to take myths seriously as givers of meaning. "Western society has all but lost its myths," he states, and "many of the problems of our society, including cults and drug addiction, can be traced to the lack of myths."[6] Perhaps the loss is not only our knowledge of myths, but also our capacity to think mythologically—to use symbol and metaphor to make or discover meaning in our lives.

Epics

Blending the human and the divine as men and women interact with gods and goddesses, epics are stories of danger and heroism. Often, they form an essential part of the origins of a group's national identity. For middle school youngsters, there are excellent versions of epics, including Rosemary Sutcliff's *Beowulf: Dragonslayer* and retellings of the *Iliad* and the *Odyssey* by Sutcliff and others.

As American society diversifies, we are becoming familiar with more than the Greek and Roman myths. Folktales reveal the values and wisdom of a culture, and they appeal to children regardless of their origin.[7] Norse mythology, Celtic legend, African tales, and Eastern European stories hold the cultural heritage of many children, some of it from so long ago that it is nearly forgotten. Books can keep it alive. Middle Eastern and Asian traditional literatures represent the heritage of a growing number of children in American schools. Knowledge of these stories and others that appear in similar versions from different parts of the world helps children understand their common humanity. In encouraging students to think of themselves as citizens of the world rather than having a provincial outlook, traditional literature is a valuable tool.

Recognizing Good Traditional Literature

Imagine, of all that is written today, what will have survived 500 or 1,000 years from now. Even with many details lost, that distillation will provide a better picture of the essence of our time than any of us could perceive by browsing in a library today or glancing through the daily newspapers. It will have become traditional literature.

By definition, traditional literature is the best of the ancient stories—those that have survived. In many tellings over the years, folk and fairy tales have been shaped and polished. Fortunately, in the 19th and 20th centuries, scholars gathered many of them from storytellers who were still part of the oral tradition and put them into print. Myths and epics represent the highest literary achievements of the cultures that produced them. In a sense, the term "good traditional literature" is redundant.

But this does not mean that every book on the shelves is a masterpiece. How do you choose, especially for gifted children? It is best to look not for one specific story or genre over another, but for *versions* written in rich, demanding language and which are perceptive in delving into human character, as well as into relationships among people and between human beings and their fate or their gods. The way to judge is to read as widely as possible.

Look first at the quality of the language. These tales, after all, represent the beginnings of our literary heritage, and the language should both respect and reflect the long history of refining that the stories have undergone. Modern versions do not always serve them well; some of the wonder that they stirred in their listeners centuries ago should linger in the present telling. Rosemary Sutcliff achieves this in her version of the Beowulf story; so does Padraic Colum in his compilation of stories of the heroes who lived before the Trojan War, *The Golden Fleece.*

Illustrations, too, should convey a sense of the simple and eternal truths with which the stories are concerned. Banality and cuteness are too often found in children's collections of fairy tales, but a little searching will yield books whose illustrations shine with integrity and grace. Examples of artists who illustrate traditional literature well are Kate Greenaway and Arthur Rackham.

Finding Good Traditional Literature

Information about fine versions of traditional literature can be found in textbooks and reference books on children's literature—see the listings at the end of this chapter.

Libraries usually carry much larger collections of traditional stories than bookstores do, and they include valuable books that are now out of print. In the nonfiction section of the children's collection, folk and fairy tales are found in Dewey Decimal number 398. Mythology may be shelved with religion in the 200s, since it was the religious literature of its culture, and epics in the 800s, with the literature arranged by country of origin. Each library may interpret the Dewey system slightly differently, however, and your library may be cataloged by the Library of Congress system instead of Dewey; as always, ask for help if necessary.

Many, many versions of the different tales are available. What follows are a few examples that will appeal to good readers.

African
Bryan, Ashley, reteller. *Ashley Bryan's African Tales, Uh-Huh*. Atheneum, 1998. Ages 8-12.

American
Caduto, Michael J. & Joseph Bruchac. *Keepers of the Earth: Native American Stories and Environmental Activities for Children*. Fulcrum, 1997. Ages 4-8.

Chase, Richard. *The Jack Tales*. Sandpiper, 2003. Ages 9-12.

Sanfield, Steve. *The Adventures of High John the Conqueror*. August House, 1989. Ages 9-12.

Taylor, C. J. *How We Saw the World*. [Native American]. Tundra, 1999. Ages 8+.

Wood, Nancy. (Ed.). *The Serpent's Tongue: Prose, Poetry and Art of the New Mexico Pueblos*. Dutton, 1999. Ages 9+.

Arabic
Alderson, Brian, reteller. *The Arabian Nights*. Illustrated by Michael Foreman. HarperCollins, 1995. Ages 9-12.

Celtic
McBratney, Sam. *Celtic Myths*. Hodder & Stoughton, 2004. Ages 9-12.

English
Hodges, Margaret, reteller. *Merlin and the Making of the King*. Illustrated by Trina Schart Hyman. Holiday House, 2004. Ages 9-12.

Pyle, Howard. *The Merry Adventures of Robin Hood*. Book Jungle, 2008. Ages 9-12.

Sutcliff, Rosemary. *Beowulf: Dragonslayer*. Red Fox, 2001. Ages 10-13.

Far East
Courlander, Harold. *The Tiger's Whisker and Other Tales and Legends from Asia and the Pacific*. Harcourt, 1995. Ages 9-12.

Yep, Laurence. *The Rainbow People*. Harper & Row, 1989. Ages 9-12.

Greek and Roman

Aliki, reteller. *The Gods and Goddesses of Olympus.* HarperCollins, 1994. Ages 4-8.

Colum, Padraic. *The Golden Fleece.* Macmillan, 1983. Ages 9-12.

Coolidge, Olivia. *Greek Myths.* Houghton Mifflin, 1949. Ages 9-12.

Sutcliff, Rosemary. *Black Ships before Troy: The Story of the Iliad.* Delacorte, 1993. Ages 11-14.

Sutcliff, Rosemary. *The Wanderings of Odysseus: The Story of the Odyssey.* Delacorte, 1996. Ages 10-13.

Norse

Philip, Neil. *Odin's Family: Myths of the Vikings.* Scholastic, 1996. Ages 9-12.

Picard, Barbara Leonie. *Tales of the Norse Gods.* Illustrated by Rosamund Fowler. Oxford University Press, 2001. Ages 9-12.

World

Mayo, Margaret, reteller. *Magical Tales from Many Lands.* Illustrated by Jane Ray. Dutton, 1993. Ages 8-11.

McCaughrean, Geraldine. *The Golden Hoard: Myths and Legends of the World.* Illustrated by Bee Willey. McElderry, 1996. Ages 8-12.

The above list is a mere beginning. There are many more collections and individual stories on library shelves—evidence of the stature of traditional literature in the human story. For some, it is the literary form most likely to move the spirit in the same mysterious way that art and music can do. Elizabeth Cook expressed this in *The Ordinary and the Fabulous*:

> *There is another door that can be opened by reading legends and fairy tales, and for some children, at the present time, there may be no other key to it. Religio, in one Latin sense of the word, implies a sense of the strange, the numinous, the totally Other, of what lies quite beyond human personality and cannot be found in any human relationships. This kind of "religion" is an indestructible part of the experience of many human*

*minds, even though the temper of a secular society does
not encourage it.... It may very well be in reading about
a vision of the flashing-eyed Athene or the rosy-fingered
Aphrodite that children first find a satisfying formulation
of those queer prickings of delight, excitement and terror
that they feel when they first walk by moonlight, or when
it snows in May, or when, like the young Wordsworth,
they have to touch a wall to make sure that it is really
there. Magic is not the same as mysticism, but it may lead
towards it; it is mystery "told to the children."*[8]

Fantasy and Science Fiction

For our older son's ninth birthday, I went shopping, as usual, for
a book. Browsing through the children's section of a favorite bookstore, I came upon a title that was then new to me: *The Book of Three.*
Something about that title, something about the very feel of the book
in my hand, told me that this was the book for my son at this time.

The book was my son's introduction to fantasy, and he could not
have had a better one. The story was based on Lloyd Alexander's
extensive knowledge of Welsh legend—part of his unknown heritage, and mine. Later, after much more reading of fantasy, then
medieval and modern literature, my son spent a summer studying
Welsh at the University of Aberystwyth; his personal library now
includes several titles in Welsh. *The Book of Three* may have reached
him at the right moment to catch his imagination and give it
focus—with a lasting influence on his life.

Fantasy and science fiction can do this for some children. They discover it at just the age when they are entering their own personal quests
for identity and beginning consciously to establish their personal values.
The quest and the attempt (sometimes failed) to live up to lofty ideals
are hallmarks of high fantasy. To judge from the devotion with which
many young people read fantasy, it must be exactly what they need in
the late elementary and middle school years.

With the popularity of the *Harry Potter* series, the audience for
fantasy has grown; it now includes adult readers who enthusiastically

continue looking for fantasy long after their school years. At the same time, science fiction has lost readership and become an offshoot of fantasy rather than an equally popular genre. Another thriving field is "dystopia"—books about dysfunctional, often post-disaster societies.

Still another *Harry Potter* legacy is magic, with more books being written in which some of the characters—but not all—have magical powers. An example is *Sorcery and Cecelia or The Enchanted Chocolate Pot*, set in England in 1817—a humorous and sophisticated story for verbally adept young adult readers.[9]

Fantasy, Science Fiction, and Gifted Readers

Gifted readers are likely to read more fantasy and science fiction than average students; some children go through a stage lasting for several years, from the late elementary grades through middle school, during which they read fantasy and science fiction almost exclusively. The interest in fantasy may concern adults who hope that children will read more "serious" literature. But a period of strong interest in fantasy should not be seen merely as a stage to be endured. Lynch-Brown and Tomlinson observed, "Modern fantasy has appeal for people with nonliteral minds, for people who go beyond the letter of a story to its spirit."[10] Indeed, we are learning that the productive use of knowledge can be enhanced by the ability to be imaginative.

Undoubtedly, creativity is a product of integrating imagination and knowledge. Thus, it is important that children have the chance to continue to be imaginative as they progress through the grades—as they spend more and more time gaining factual knowledge in school. Fantasy and science fiction provide just such an opportunity.

Introducing Fantasy and Science Fiction at the Best Time

For young children who have had a rich background in traditional literature in their preschool years, the introduction of fantasy may be barely noticeable, but for adults who guide their reading, it is helpful to mark the inexact line between folklore and modern fantasy.

One way to clarify the difference is authorship. Traditional literature—true folklore—began as oral tradition and has no known author. The Grimm brothers did not write their tales; they collected them from those who were still telling them in the oral tradition. Hans Christian Andersen, on the other hand, created his stories, which incorporate many elements of folklore but are modern fantasy. Many authors since, such as MacDonald, Tolkien, Lewis, Alexander, Cooper, and Le Guin, whose works are mentioned below, have done the same, building a rich body of modern imaginative literature.

Fantasy

Elements of traditional literature linger in modern fantasy. Familiar characteristics of folklore and fairy tales blend over into fantasy in books like A. A. Milne's *Winnie-the-Pooh*, in which animals talk, and P. L. Travers' *Mary Poppins*, in which the source of magic is not fairies but Mary Poppins herself. Children can move in easy stages from these early fantasies to modern fairy tales, fantasy based on time warps, high fantasy, and science fiction. With care, they can read excellent literature every step of the way.

For early elementary school children, animal characters continue to appear in classic fantasies like *The Wind in the Willows* and *Charlotte's Web*, echoing the talking animals of folklore. In George MacDonald's late 19th-century story *At the Back of the North Wind*, the North Wind is a lady remarkably like a fairy godmother. Some fantasies written for this age group, like Mary Norton's *The Borrowers*, feature characters who are miniature people, reminiscent of the elves and dwarfs of folklore.

The element of the time warp appears in Lucy M. Boston's *The Children of Green Knowe* and its sequels, and in Philippa Pearce's *Tom's Midnight Garden*. In these books, a contemporary child meets and plays or struggles with a child or children from the past.

There is much more fantasy for middle and upper elementary children than can be mentioned here. A few titles will suggest the scope: talking animals appear in Kipling's *Jungle Books*, Lawson's *Rabbit Hill*, O'Brien's *Mrs. Frisby and the Rats of NIMH* (which might also be classified as science fiction), Jacques' *Redwall* series, and Adams' *Watership Down*, which young gifted children enjoy hearing read aloud. Children of this age also read the *Harry Potter* series independently. These books are very different from each other and represent a wide range in reading level, but they all appeal to children of this age, and they are all fantasies.

For older readers, another author worth knowing is Robin McKinley, whose retelling for older readers of *The Beauty and the Beast*, called simply *Beauty*, is completely credible and compelling. An enthusiastic readership has welcomed the British author Matthew Skelton's first novel, *Endymion Spring,* which alternates between 15th-century Mainz, Germany and contemporary Oxford, England and blends myth, magic, and mystery.

High Fantasy

It is in high fantasy that the protagonists are usually involved in a quest, drawn into it by forces beyond their control. They go willingly, but there is often some sacrifice involved and much learning; they grow up in the process of the quest. The theme is often no less than the epic and never-ending struggle between good and evil, the relationship between human beings and the gods, with ordinary human beings risking all, often alone, in their attempts to perform seemingly impossible tasks and live up to high ideals. Authors of high fantasy typically spin out their tales in a series of books instead of a single volume because the theme is so large and the plot so involved.

High fantasy is frequently based on mythology and legend—in particular Germanic and Norse mythology, the Welsh *Mabinogion*, and the Arthurian legends (which are also Welsh in origin). This background gives it a mythical quality that heightens the effect of the quest theme and strengthens the potential for nobility and a kind of grandeur, even when humor is also present.

Both grandeur and humor are certainly present in a classic example of high fantasy (and among the first to be introduced, in the upper elementary years): Lloyd Alexander's *Prydain* series—five titles, beginning with *The Book of Three*. Although he tells his stories with a light touch, Alexander's purposes are serious. To achieve them, he departs from Lady Charlotte Guest's edition of the *Mabinogion*, which is the basis for this series. When Eilonwy declares her independence, she breaks from the Celtic legend, and Alexander's story becomes an American fantasy protesting the monarchy.[11]

Children in the late elementary grades may also discover Ursula Le Guin's *Earthsea* series, as well as the *Dragon* books of Anne McCaffrey.

Middle school readers enjoy Susan Cooper's series, which begins with *Over Sea, Under Stone*. They have probably already found Tolkien's *The Hobbit*, and some may attempt the trilogy which follows, *The Lord of the Rings*, although it is more difficult. McKinley's *The Blue Sword* and its prequel, *The Hero and the Crown*, for readers of middle school age and older, are also in the tradition of high fantasy.

Science Fiction

The line between fantasy and science fiction is blurred. One way to distinguish them is to remember that fantasy could not happen in the future because it includes imaginary creatures (and often magic), while science fiction tells what conceivably could happen based on current scientific knowledge. A further distinction may also be that fantasy is concerned with the development of the internal, intrapersonal world, and science fiction with that of the external, interpersonal world.

Science fiction includes an emphasis on technological expertise, and it comments on what future societies might be like based on present predictions regarding factors such as the environment, population density, and the likelihood of catastrophic war. Or, as Rosenberg puts it, science fiction is "speculative about the potential uses of science and speculative about the potential future of mankind on this world and within the universe."[12]

Interestingly, children's science fiction often differs from that written for adults; in many science fiction novels for children, the view of technology is strongly negative, and the path to a better future lies in returning to a pre-technological age.[13] Science fiction is not often written for very young children because the content is so complex. It isn't until the upper elementary grades that students may begin reading William Sleator's *House of Stairs*; John Christopher's trilogy, *The White Mountains*; and Madeleine L'Engle's *A Wrinkle in Time* and its sequels.

By middle school, students are reading single-book fantasies like Natalie Babbitt's *Tuck Everlasting*, and many are also beginning to read adult science fiction. Frank Herbert's *Dune* series, Michael Crichton's *Andromeda Strain* and *Jurassic Park*, Ray Bradbury's *Fahrenheit 451*, and many of Madeleine L'Engle's books are titles that middle and senior high students enjoy.

Intensified concern for the quality of life often prompts senior high gifted students more than others to become interested in reading utopian literature and also dystopian books, which are not about ideal societies but about society gone wrong. Aldous Huxley's *Brave New World* and George Orwell's *Animal Farm* and *1984* are examples of good literature in this category.

Recognizing Good Fantasy and Science Fiction

Good fantasy and science fiction are judged much like good fiction of other types. Plot, setting, literary style, and convincing characters are just as important here as elsewhere. The criteria for literature that meets emotional and intellectual needs listed in Chapter 6 apply here, too.

Science fiction lends itself to one particular flaw: it often relies too much on adventure and provides too little in characterization or plot complexity. Plenty of action is an initial draw, but good science fiction also has characters who are real enough to grow—that is, something changes within them—and a plot that retains interest. Action alone quickly becomes boring to discriminating older readers.

One additional criterion of good fantasy and science fiction is that it must be believable—which may sound paradoxical. However, readers must be drawn into whatever world the author has created, and they must believe in it; the created world must be consistent within itself. In addition, the theme—the underlying thread that reveals the author's attitude toward the intrapersonal or the interpersonal world—must ring true.

Finding Good Fantasy and Science Fiction

There are excellent, prolific authors in both fields, and one way to find good fantasy or science fiction is to look for books by the authors named above; however, we have certainly not mentioned all of the authors worth knowing. To learn more, consult the booklists suggested at the end of this chapter. Not all of these references list fantasy and science fiction separately, so you may need to search in the fiction section of the reference book.

Usually, fantasy and science fiction are shelved with fiction on library shelves, but some libraries shelve them in a special section or place stickers on the book spines with symbols identifying specific types of fiction.

Traditional Literature, Fantasy, and Gifted Children

If I have overemphasized traditional literature and fantasy in this chapter, it is because I believe that the first is neglected and the other unfairly maligned, and that together they offer a vital mixture for the balanced development of gifted children.

Mythology and high fantasy in particular validate children's inner drive to cherish high ideals, to make commitments that cannot be justified on rational grounds, and to find meaning outside of oneself. In our contemporary world, it may be only in literature that some adolescents can find such affirmation. For especially bright and talented children, with their emerging sense of the potential in themselves and the accompanying confusion about how or whether to reveal it and use it, every possible source of affirmation must be recognized and encouraged.

Poetry

It is not difficult to introduce poetry to children, and the rewards are great, but it does require a special approach. No matter how effectively they encourage children to explore other forms of literature, many people lose their enthusiasm when they consider introducing poetry. The result is that children also may grow up feeling vaguely uneasy with poetry, not understanding it and not knowing how to approach it.

This is a regrettable loss. For the very young child who is experimenting with sound and language, the rhythm and nonsense syllables of nursery rhymes provide invaluable enrichment. Nursery rhymes may sound light and frivolous to adults, but they appeal to young children at a critical point, as the youngsters master one of the most important tasks of early childhood: the acquisition of language.

The elastic mind of a child of four or five shows an agility for learning foreign languages that the more rigid mind of the adult has lost. Parents who grow impatient with the repetition of Mother Goose rhymes need to understand that their child's language ability is greater than their own, and her fascination with the sounds reflects her intelligence as she works at learning language.

In addition, poetry is one way to encourage intuition and imagery while the child also learns to think more scientifically and literally. Music is another way, but children will be exposed to music in at least some forms, whether or not adults make a conscious effort to introduce it. Unless someone deliberately shares poetry throughout the elementary years, though, most children will be left with a nursery school level of awareness of it—as serious a handicap, perhaps, as it would be to enter middle school with "Three Blind Mice" as their highest musical attainment.

Many children are offered nursery rhymes when they are preschoolers. From then on, however, their exposure to poetry may be limited to a few poems in elementary school reading texts or those taught as part of secondary school literature courses. Children need more guidance than this if they are to learn to love poetry—more guidance, in fact, than other forms of literature require. They will surely discover books by Beverly Cleary, for example, in the second or third grade simply because Cleary is part of the culture of children of that age, but they are not likely to discover each new step in poetry for themselves.

Preparing to Introduce Poetry

For poetry, more than for any other form of literature, adults must love it themselves—or learn to love it—in order to give it to children. Teachers know that they have to make an effort to find time in the day for poetry if it is important to them. It may be up to parents to keep poetry alive in their children if teachers cannot.

How can you as a teacher or parent achieve this if poetry has not previously been part of your own life? You can go to the public or school library for books of poetry for children and for books about children's literature. If children's poetry has never held much appeal for you, it is a good idea to begin with the chapters on poetry in the books on children's literature, which are probably in the reference section of the library's children's department.

More background reading may help. *Climb into the Bell Tower,*[14] by the poet Myra Cohn Livingston, is a collection of writings and speeches spanning her career, from 1967 to 1986. Admittedly based on her personal point of view, this book nevertheless offers helpful touchstones for evaluating children's poetry. For example, Livingston summarizes the contributions of several well-known poets: William Blake leading the way from the older didactic poetry (verses designed to teach moral lessons) by insisting on the need for "joy, dreaming, and play," Lewis Carroll and Edward Lear adding nonsense and wordplay, Robert Louis Stevenson focusing on a child's everyday experiences, and Shel Silverstein reviving didactic poetry but using humor so skillfully that readers may not realize that he is teaching as well as providing entertainment.

Livingston makes a distinction between *comprehending* and *apprehending* poetry. Comprehension, she says, is complete understanding, while apprehension is "the almost unconscious awareness of what is rumbling beneath the words, the intuitive understanding…. I tend to view literature and art in terms of apprehension, and I suspect children do too."[15]

And Livingston speaks of image and symbol. Image is necessary, but it is not enough. "[T]o pretend that poetry is sugar-coated rhythm and rhyme and image is to rob [children] of the ability to deal with more serious aspects of life that they will surely meet, in ways we do not even suspect."[16] To convey adequately the more serious, darker side of life, poetry must transcend image and offer symbol; it must lead from a picture to a universal response that the reader can remember and adapt when in need. Symbol offers:

...the opportunity to respond beyond stereotype, beyond despair, with new insights and meaningful action. Symbol helps us learn that change is possible, that action is possible, and that each of us has the creativity to effect that change and action in a unique way.... Symbols...sustain and strengthen us when times are out of joint.[17]

After reading and reflecting on such background material, adults can examine poetry anthologies, both traditional and modern. Begin a pattern of reading a poem or two aloud at story time, along with the prose. You could start with just two collections: Untermeyer's *A Golden Treasury of Poetry* and Harrison and Stuart-Clark's *The New Oxford Treasury of Children's Poems*. Inevitably you will develop favorites, and so will the children. When you find yourself or the children reciting lines spontaneously at appropriate moments, you will know that poetry is alive in your home or classroom.

Introducing Poetry

Poetry requires a unique approach. With other kinds of literature, teachers introduce examples to children as soon as they can read well enough to decode the language, and the children generally continue independently to find other examples if they are interested. However, until early adolescence, poetry is more accessible to children if they can hear it rather than read it silently, and they will need adult suggestions of poetry that will appeal to them. Adults need to be more active in finding poetry to present, and they must plan for time to read it aloud.

The teaching of poetry should begin with plenty of reading aloud until children have effortlessly learned a few poems by heart. Gradually, discussion can then begin about the power of poetry. Rhythm, for instance, can be felt by the children when they are encouraged to sway with the lines of Stevenson's "The Swing," and they can hear how the words of David McCord's "The Pickety Fence" reproduce the staccato sound of a stick being pulled along the top of a picket fence.

Generally, it is thought that the best way to teach poetry to young students is to draw on their imagination, reading a poem aloud and then inviting children to respond to it through another medium, such as movement or drawing. Analysis—discussing elements of poetry like meter and imagery—is usually considered best left for secondary students. Textbooks in children's literature books often suggest creative ways to introduce poetry.

Parents and teachers need to know what kinds of poetry will hold the interest of children of different ages. From Mother Goose rhymes in the preschool years, children in the primary grades grow to love humor and nonsense verses that play on words. Middle elementary children begin to enjoy ballads and other narrative poetry, and they prefer modern children's poems with ordinary, everyday language and content to traditional poetry. At all ages, humorous poetry is a great favorite—Paul Janeczko and Shel Silverstein are always welcome. In order to explore the potential for emotional depth in poetry, some lyric poetry should be presented as well to older students. Literature courses for senior high students should introduce them to a variety of poets and types of poetry, including modern poets like Maya Angelou, Billy Collins, or Ted Kooser, whose allusions are more familiar to contemporary readers than the references found in the poems of historical writers.[18] Currently, a creative new form of poetry is emerging—novels written in free verse, such as *Out of the Dust*, a story of the Dust Bowl told in verse by Karen Hesse.

Recognizing Good Poetry

As the title of one book of children's poetry tells us, "It doesn't always have to rhyme." Poetry is not necessarily about rhyme; it *is* about rhythm, though, and words, and the concise, even startling expression of thoughts and feelings.

Poetry's rhythm appeals to young children—they clap their hands or bend their bodies to the beat of the lines. They should experience a variety of poetic meters and poetry with lines of varying length.

Words used in good poetry are vivid, evoking strong, clear images, like the opening line of Irene Rutherford McLeod's "Lone Dog":

I'm a lean dog, a keen dog, a wild dog, and lone.

They are also imaginative, perhaps made up for the occasion or used in a new context, like e. e. cummings' words "Just-spring" and "mud-luscious" for his poem "In Just-." For young children, Dr. Seuss books offer imaginative and creative uses of words.

Children, especially highly verbal children, respond well to poetry with unfamiliar words. There is no need to worry about a controlled vocabulary—the rhythm and the content of the poem carry the listener along.

The expression of thoughts and feelings—the humor, the narrative, the moods expressed in lyric poetry—should use subject matter of interest to children: animals, friends, heroes, and the stuff of their everyday lives.

Children prefer poetry that rhymes; limericks are a favorite. They respond to a strong rhythmic beat, and they love humor, but they should also learn to go beyond humor to other types of poetic expression. *A Kick in the Head: An Everyday Guide to Poetic Forms* combines examples of nearly 30 types of poems; written and defined by Paul Janeczko with humorous illustrations by Chris Raschka, it is an excellent way to introduce children of all ages to poetry.

There is a difference between poetry and verse. Verse usually rhymes, as does some poetry, and both typically have meter. But poetry incorporates other, more sophisticated poetic elements as well, such as onomatopoeia, wordplay, alliteration, and literary techniques used in prose: imagery, metaphor, symbolism. Verse, like poorly written prose, *tells* too much ("John was sad.") Poetry, like good fiction, *shows* an image ("John walked slowly, his hands in his pockets and his head down") and leaves the reader to interpret as he will. Verse explains all; poetry leaves something out for the reader to add—to *apprehend*, using Myra Cohn Livingston's word.

What is considered acceptable content for children's poetry, especially for adolescents, has undergone a change in recent years, along with the change in fiction for young people. Contemporary poets write about the harsh realities of modern life; hence, modern poetry provides a vehicle of expression for the outraged idealism that is one characteristic of gifted children and adolescents. Such poetry assures gifted students that others share their moral concerns, and it can prompt discussions that allow them to voice their own feelings.

Finding Good Poetry

In the library, poetry is shelved in the Dewey Decimal 800s, the literature section; the 800s are subdivided by country so that American poetry is 811, British poetry is 821, and so on. As with other types of literature, recommended books of poetry are listed in the booklists mentioned at the end of this chapter.

Many excellent anthologies and books by individual poets are available for children. Only a few are listed here:

Clinton, Catherine (Ed.). *I, Too, Sing America: Three Centuries of African American Poetry.* Houghton Mifflin, 1998. Ages 12-14.

Collins, Billy. *Picnic, Lightning.* University of Pittsburgh Press, 1998. Ages 13+.

Gordon, Ruth, compiler. *Peeling the Onion: An Anthology of Poems.* Harper, 1993. Ages 12-14.

Harrison, Michael & Christopher Stuart-Clark, compilers. *The New Oxford Treasury of Children's Poems.* Oxford University Press, 1997. Ages 4-8.

Hesse, Karen. *Out of the Dust.* Scholastic, 1997. Ages 12-14.

Janeczko, Paul. B. *A Kick in the Head: An Everyday Guide to Poetic Forms.* Illustrated by Chris Raschka. Candlewick, 2005. Ages 4-12.

Keillor, Garrison, compiler. *Good Poems for Hard Times.* Penguin, 2005. Ages 13+.

Kooser, Ted. *Delights and Shadows.* Copper Canyon Press, 2004. Ages 13+.

Myers, Walter Dean. *Harlem.* Scholastic, 1997. Ages 4-8.

Nye, Naomi Shihab. *19 Varieties of Gazelle: Poems of the Middle East.* Greenwillow, 2002. Ages 12-14.

Untermeyer, Louis, compiler. *A Golden Treasury of Poetry.* Golden Books, 1998 (1975). Ages 4-8.

Willard, Nancy (Ed.). *Step Lightly: Poems for the Journey.* Harcourt Brace, 1998. Ages 9-12.

Books about Children's Literature

The preceding is only the briefest introduction to the wealth of literature for children. As with the literature itself, there is plenty to read about children's literature.

Textbooks in Children's Literature

For teachers who wish to refresh their memories of their children's literature course, for parents who homeschool or who have never studied children's literature, and for the many people who assist children in school libraries without the benefit of professional training, textbooks written for college courses in children's literature provide excellent background reading.

Textbooks offer much more information than this chapter has provided on the various kinds of literature, including plot summaries of hundreds of books, as well as critical commentary. Many of them suggest activities for introducing literature to children in the classroom. Creative parents can adapt the ideas to home use.

Look for texts in the school or public library or in the library of a college or university that trains teachers. Parents may wish to select a favorite for purchase, since these are guides to refer to again and again over a period of years. The following texts provide a good introduction:

Lynch-Brown, Carol & Carol M. Tomlinson. *Essentials of Children's Literature* (6th ed.). Allyn & Bacon, 2007. After brief background material on children's literature, the authors introduce each category (picture books, traditional literature, modern fantasy, etc.) with several pages of general information, followed by suggested titles.

Nilsen, Alleen P. & Kenneth L. Donelson. *Literature for Today's Young Adults* (8th ed.). Longman, 2008. This text focuses on literature for young people between the ages of 12 and 20.

Norton, Donna E. & Saundra E. Norton. *Through the Eyes of a Child: An Introduction to Children's Literature* (7th ed.). Prentice-Hall, 2006. Including criteria for evaluating and selecting books using the principles of child development, this text provides strategies for involving children in literature, as well as comprehensive lists of books for children.

Silvey, Anita. *500 Great Books for Teens.* Houghton Mifflin, 2006. For teachers—and parents and grandparents looking for book ideas—Silvey provides brief information about a wide range of genres and topics, including graphic novels, historical fiction, humor, mysteries, plays, poetry, politics, sports, and more. Within each grouping, she lists recommended books with helpful annotations, and she suggests an appropriate age level: 12-14 or 14-18.

Reference Books for Children's Literature

Here, at last, is the promised list of reference books for children's literature. In these books, you will find titles and annotations for books recommended for specific reading levels and on specific topics. Librarians use these reference sources to select books for library purchase, so you may have to ask for access to them and will probably have to use them in the library. But if you want to find a recommended book on coin collecting for an eight-year-old, a biography on Beethoven for an 11-year-old, or appropriate science fiction for a 13-year-old, here is the place to look.

The following are for children in preschool through middle school:

Barr, Catherine & John T. Gillespie. *Best Books for Children: Preschool through Grade 6* (8th ed.). Libraries Unlimited, 2006. This listing of books, most of which have been recommended in at least two respected sources of reviews of children's literature, covers fiction and nonfiction for elementary students. Biographies are especially easy to find here, with a separate section and an index.

Cianciolo, Patricia Jean. *Informational Picture Books for Children.* American Library Association, 2000. For preschool through middle school children, the author has included 250 outstanding picture books evaluated for their skillful combination of text and illustrations. The selections cover a variety of subjects, including the natural world, the physical world, and peoples and cultures.

Gillespie, John T. & Catherine Barr. *Best Books for Middle School and Junior High Readers: Grades 6-9.* Libraries Unlimited, 2004. Covering fiction and nonfiction, this reference provides plot summaries for more than 14,000 books, most of which have been recommended in at least two sources. Reading level and citations of reviews are included; award-winning and series titles are also noted. This reference can be used for advanced students in grades five and six.

Kobrin, Beverly. *Eyeopeners II: Children's Books to Answer Children's Questions about the World around Them.* Scholastic, 1995. Kobrin's list is enthusiastically and entirely devoted to nonfiction.

McClure, Amy & Janice Kristo (Eds.). *Adventuring with Books: A Booklist for Pre-K-Grade 6* (13th ed.). National Council of Teachers of English, 2002. A list of both fiction and nonfiction, this book gives annotations without reviews. Although it is published by the NCTE, it covers more than English or the humanities, with sections on social studies, biographies, the sciences, the arts, and recreational activities.

Books for high schoolers can be found in the following:

Carter, Betty & Holly Koelling. *Best Books for Young Adults.* American Library Association, 2007. This book offer lists of the best young adult books chosen by young adult librarians from 1966-1999, with a one-sentence plot synopsis for each.

Estell, Doug, Michele L. Satchwell, & Patricia S. Wright. *Reading Lists for College-Bound Students* (3rd ed.). Peterson's, 2000. For more than 110 colleges, *Reading Lists* provides suggested reading compiled from faculty members, websites, and catalogs—not (in most cases) required reading, but books that the faculty would like new students to have read by the time they arrive on campus. There are also reading lists related to subject areas, such as business, political science, and history. These lists make very interesting reading for college-bound high school students who want an idea of what's in store for them.

Gillespie, John T. & Catherine Barr. *Best Books for High School Readers: Grades 9-12.* Libraries Unlimited, 2004. This is the third in the "Best Books" series, which was created "to furnish authoritative, reliable, and comprehensive bibliographies" for readers from preschool through grade 12. This volume reflects a wide range of reading levels; more than a third of the entries are adult books. Grade levels given for each title indicate that some of the books listed here would be appropriate for grades five and up.

And finally, to locate fantasy for all ages:

Lynn, R. N. *Fantasy Literature for Children and Young Adults: An Annotated Bibliography* (5th ed.). Bowker, 2005. With an easy-to-use index, this resource annotates thousands of fantasy novels and story collections for readers in grades three to 12, and it provides information on the genre of fantasy.

Book Awards

Another approach to good books is to follow the many awards given annually to authors of children's and young adult literature. The Caldecott and Newbery medal winners and honor books are well-known, but there are many others, such as the Coretta Scott King award, honoring African-American authors and illustrators, and the Michael L. Printz Award for Excellence in Young Adult Literature. Dr. Susannah Richards has written helpful descriptions of several awards that will be of particular interest to parents and teachers of gifted youngsters.[19]

Book Lists on the Web

Book suggestions are also available on the Web. One recommended site is www.homeschooldiner.com/subjects/language_arts/literature/reading_lists.html. In addition, Richards has compiled an excellent and more comprehensive list of additional resources:[20]

○ American Library Association:
  ● www.ala.org
  ● www.ala.org/alsc
  ● www.ala.org/yalsa

○ Book Adventure: www.bookadventure.org

○ Carol Otis Hurst: www.carolhurst.com

○ The Bulletin for the Center of Children's Books:
www.lis.uiuc.edu/puboff/bccb

○ Children's Book Council: www.cbcbooks.org

○ Children's Literature Web Guide: www.ucalgary.ca/~dkbrown

○ Hoagies' Gifted Information Page: www.hoagiesgifted.com

○ International Reading Association: www.reading.org

○ National Council of Teachers of English: www.ncte.org

○ Notable Social Studies Trade Book for Young People:
www.socialstudies.org/resources/notable

○ Outstanding Books for the College Bound:
www.ala.org/ala/yalsa/booklistsawards/outstandingbooks/
outstandingbooks.htm

○ Outstanding Science Trade Books for Children:
www.nsta.org/publications/ostb

○ Planet Esme: www.planetesme.com

Chapter 8

Annotated Bibliography

This bibliography is arranged according to grade level:

- ○ Preschool:
    For the Very Young
    Two and Three Years Old
    Four Years Old
- ○ Early Elementary: Kindergarten to Grade 2
- ○ Upper Elementary: Grades 3-5
- ○ Middle School: Grades 6-8
- ○ Senior High: Grades 9-12

Under each grade level grouping, books are arranged in alphabetical order by the authors' last names. Each listing is followed by an annotation that includes a brief plot summary, a few comments about the potential value of the book, and in most cases, discussion aids. For preschoolers and children in the early grades, discussion aids are often merely suggested themes that an adult will want to have in mind when talking casually about the book. For older children, specific questions are suggested to stimulate the thinking of discussion leaders. These questions are offered only as a starting point. Each leader will learn to develop questions based on her interpretation of the book and her knowledge of the children who will be discussing it.

Some of the suggested questions are fact questions, but in every case, these are followed by the core or interpretive questions to be asked after children have warmed to the discussion with introductory questions. In planning a discussion, the leader can choose or develop other core questions that look promising and then lead into them with appropriate introductory questions.

Categories

Giftedness, talent, and high intellectual ability are not necessarily explicit or even represented in every book annotated in this chapter, but every book offers potential for discussion based on the *characteristics* of intellectually and artistically talented children and/or on the *issues* that they face. The categories listed below—which are based on these characteristics and issues—will be familiar to those who have read the first two chapters of this book. Following are brief explanations of how books were chosen to represent each of these categories.

Achievement	plots that question whether or not a bright child or young adult will achieve
Aloneness	books that can help youngsters explore feelings of isolation, recognize that there may be good reasons for experiencing aloneness, and understand that alone time is necessary and can be productive
Arrogance	characters who display arrogance because they do not fit in or because they do not fully understand a situation
Creativity	characters whose creative impulses set them apart
Developing imagination	books that stimulate thinking, observing, and questioning, keeping children in touch with the joy and power of using their imaginations
Differentness	stories dealing with people who are different because of traits such as ability, insight, and

	sensitivity, because of a life experience, or because of a physical or psychological characteristic that sets them apart
Drive to understand	the most wide-ranging category, listing books that will challenge children intellectually and present them with new ideas. In some cases, no questions are suggested, since discussion topics should be chosen to suit the child's interest. Questions may also be curriculum-driven.
Identity	characters who learn to accept talent as a positive attribute and work toward a strong self-concept. Gifted children often feel different and "wrong;" these books can help them become comfortable with and even celebrate their abilities.
Intensity	characters who are unusually focused on an interest, ability, or cause with a single-mindedness not shared by most children their age
Introversion	people who prefer to spend much of their time alone and who use that time creatively
Moral concerns	personal or community issues that require difficult decisions
Perfectionism	examples of what happens when a character puts too much emphasis on a perfect product
Relationships with others	books that facilitate discussion of interdependence, empathy, and respect for others, or that promote an understanding of friendships and how they are formed
Resilience	stories in which characters learn to tolerate frustration, adapt to situations that require them to change, overcome maladaptive patterns, and/or set goals—in short, stories that show characters recovering from setbacks

Sensitivity   characters who are intensely aware, introspective, unusually alert to the hurts of others, and/or particularly sensitive to being hurt themselves

Using ability   books that raise questions about the responsibility that gifted people have for their own talents, about decision making, and about the rewards that can follow the best use of those talents

The "Index of Categories," which follows the bibliography, is a guide to the books that are annotated in this chapter. Characteristics and issues change with age, and each index entry will be found only in the appropriate grade level groups.

Most index entries are matched by questions in the bibliography, but in some cases, the index entry acts as a reference to a related category. For example, questions suggested for aloneness may be easily adapted to a discussion of introversion, so while a book may be listed under both headings, questions might be found in the annotation under only one of the two. Again, this bibliography is intended only to indicate possibilities, with parents and teachers developing their own approaches based on suggestions given here.

Many books published in the last five years are included, but there are also a number of older titles—because children's books don't have to be new to be better. The reading life of an adult may span decades, so most adult books enjoy a period of popularity and then fade as interest turns elsewhere. But a new generation of young readers comes along about every few years, keeping much-loved older books in print as long as children find them meaningful. And older books often provide challenging reading, with longer, complex sentences, wider-ranging vocabulary, and a glimpse of values and patterns of thought from an earlier time.

All of the books listed here were in print in 2009. At the end of this volume, you will find "Recommended Books from Earlier Editions," a list of books culled from the 1994 and 2002 editions of *Some of My Best Friends Are Books* or from *Guiding Gifted Readers* (1988). Some of these titles are currently not readily available, but they are still valuable. If a book you seek is out of print, I hope you will be able to find it at your library, through interlibrary loan, or with the help of an online book search service.

Finally, the decision regarding whether a book is fit for eight-year-olds or 10-year-olds is always somewhat arbitrary. The books are listed here under grade levels recommended in nationally recognized sources, but many of them can be enjoyed by children older and younger than the ages given. To find a book for a particular child or group, begin with the appropriate grade level and make adjustments as necessary, keeping emotional maturity in mind, as well as reading level.

In some cases, picture books provide a quick introduction to a personal or moral issue—they are useful as discussion starters with middle school or even senior high students. The "Index of Books for All Ages" at the end of the "Index of Categories" identifies books suggested for this purpose.

Preschool

The preschool years, those of greatest intellectual growth in human development, cover a wide maturational span. Consequently, books for infants are decidedly different from books for four-year-olds. Accordingly, this preschool bibliography is divided into three sections: "For the Very Young," "Two and Three Years Old," and "Four Years Old."

Books are listed at the age when they first appeal to children who have been read to enough so that they relate easily to books. A title recommended here for three-year-olds might better be held until later for a child who does not have this experience of being read to. Likewise, a book suggested for twos and threes may continue to hold interest for years and may still be appropriate for fours and fives. The best measure of a book's appropriateness for any child is that child's response to it.

For the Very Young

Books for infants and toddlers come in specialized sizes and shapes. Most are chunky "board books," three to five inches square and an inch thick, with pages made of heavy cardboard. Board books are so popular that classic titles are now being re-issued in this baby-proof format. Since most children are about two years old before they can reliably turn paper pages one at a time, the new material is a boon to parents who want to read to their children in the first two years.

The very first books read to babies should have only one object, or very few of them, on each page, with a solid-color background. Books that are visually "too busy" make it difficult for a child to focus on the object that matches the text. Illustrations are often photographs, since their realism helps children relate the picture to three-dimensional objects in their surroundings, but these, too, should be kept simple.

Reading aloud to very young children is best done by parents who are highly attuned to their child—sensitive to and accepting of her unique responses—and so do not approach reading with preconceived ideas of how she "should" react to a book. The child may be fascinated for the first three pages and then lose interest. A book that is a favorite one week may be supplanted next week by another. One particular picture may hold the child's interest, while the rest of the book is ignored. All of this signals the child's readiness to learn according to her own schedule. Parents who enjoy observing the child's interest without trying to manipulate it will be most successful at reading to the very young.

Some people wonder how much children grasp from books before they can talk, but consider this true story:

> *When 18-month-old Chris had an upset stomach, his mother was directed to feed him only fluids for one day. The toddler grew hungry, and as usual, he communicated this fact to his mother by standing in the kitchen and pointing up to the spot on the counter where he knew bananas were kept, although he could not see them from his position on the floor. Always before, this had produced at least part of a banana, but today, inexplicably, his mother said no. He tried pointing and chattering repeatedly; she was kind but adamant. Surely, he reasoned,*

she must not understand, but he knew how to explain.
He strode purposefully into the living room, searched
through his books until he found the right one, turned
the pages to the picture of a banana, and marched back
into the kitchen, pointing to the banana in the book and
then to the counter.

Dr. Deborah Ruf has documented many similar examples showing the reading comprehension of youngsters at very early ages.[1] Here
is a small sample of books for children like Chris. Parents are urged to
browse in the preschool section of a good bookstore for a better idea
of all that is available to them.

Baggott, Stella. *Baby's Very First Colors Book*. Usborne, 2009.
　　With one picture and the name of one color on each page, this is
truly a "very first" book. Some pictures use more than one color, and
some pictures show shadings of the color named (the toy bear is light
brown, with dark brown facial features)—if these are pointed out,
the child will learn to differentiate light and dark in colors. A board
book with a comfortable soft cover, this one is likely to be an early
favorite.

Bridwell, Norman. *Clifford's Bathtime*. Scholastic, 2003.
　　Clifford the puppy does not want a bath, but he enjoys it when
he gets one anyway. He climbs onto the floating soap, and when he
falls off, the rubber duck rescues him. The humor is not missed by
one-year-olds, as parents can tell by the giggling when Clifford falls
off the soap.
　　There are many other Clifford books, some for older children.

Brown, Margaret Wise. *Goodnight, Moon*. Illustrated by Clement
Hurd. HarperCollins, 2005.
　　This is a classic sleepytime book, with illustrations growing softer
and dimmer as the little rabbit, tucked into bed, says goodnight to
the beloved objects in his room. A favorite for generations, it is now
available as a board book.

Calver, Susan. *My First Things that Go.* DK Publishing, 2007.

For children ready to see details and a more complex page layout—and to build vocabulary—this book presents clear photographs of all kinds of "things that go"—from roller skates to cars and trucks to watercraft (small, medium, and very large) and airplanes and spaceships. A section on specialized vehicles includes farm machinery, emergency equipment, and trains. At the end, the child is challenged to match four of the vehicles with appropriate gear for operating them.

Carle, Eric. *The Very Busy Spider.* Grosset & Dunlap, 2006.

For the older children in this age group who can listen to narrative, Eric Carle's books are delightful. In *The Very Busy Spider,* he describes a spider spinning her web. She is interrupted by a horse who invites her for a ride, followed by many other animals, all encouraging her to join them in their daily round. Always, the response is the same: the spider does not answer; she is very busy spinning her web. At last, when a rooster asks if she wants to catch a fly, her web is complete, and she promptly does exactly what the rooster suggests. When the owl asks who built the beautiful web, the spider does not answer. It has been a very busy day, and she has fallen asleep.

As we watch the silver strand develop into a web, the child can feel it, raised on the page. The growing web and the comforting repetition of the refrain, along with illustrations that capture the essence of each animal, make this book a favorite.

Dyer, Jane (Compiler and illustrator). *Animal Crackers: A Delectable Collection of Pictures, Poems, and Lullabies for the Very Young.* Little Brown, 1996.

Dyer has collected poems that range from Mother Goose to modern children's poetry for this beautifully illustrated anthology, which features poetry for children who do not yet know letters, numbers, lullabies, rhyme, or rhythm. They will be introduced in a most delightful way to all of these things through this book—an excellent choice for a baby gift, to be available when the child is ready.

Eastman, P. D. *Are You My Mother?* Random House, 1998.

A young bird who has lost track of his mother asks various unlikely creatures if they are his mother until his mother predictably returns.

The mother of a curious and active one-year-old says that this is the first "plot" book her son sat through, and it is a good bedtime book at this age.

Hill, Eric. *Where's Spot?* Puffin, 2003.

Spot's mother looks for her puppy all over the house—in the grandfather clock, in the piano, in the closet. She finds an unexpected creature in each location, but no Spot, until the turtle under the rug suggests she try the basket.

Not a board book, this flap book has moveable tabs that the child lifts to discover the hidden animals—something some children enjoy doing by the age of eight or nine months. Other Spot books are available; he is a favorite puppy among children this age.

Hoban, Tana. *Black on White.* HarperFestival, 1993.

This board book offers pictures of various shapes—a fork, a spoon, an elephant, glasses, keys—in stark black outlined against a white background. A companion book is *White on Black* (1993). Both books are designed for infants, who are thought to see the high contrast of black and white before they discern colors.

Hoban, Tana. *Colors Everywhere.* HarperCollins, 1995.

Not for infants, but for one-year-olds who are ready to distinguish objects and colors, this book is a feast of both. On each page, a clear and brilliant photograph is accompanied by a side panel showing a rainbow of the colors in the picture, banded in sizes to show their proportion in the photograph. There are animals, birds, fish, flowers, and people, as well as familiar objects like plastic dishes, and some that may be new to the child, such as a ride at an amusement park. The end pages gather all of the photographs together in a collage for more discussion. Suitable for many ages, *Colors Everywhere* can be used with very young children to label objects, identify colors, and match pictures from the body of the book with those on the end pages.

Page, Liza. *Opposites*. Illustrated by Ana Maratin Larranaga. Innovative-kids, 2008.

The page with the picture of the bunny has just one word: "soft." On the opposing page, we see a turtle with a rock pile and just one word: "hard." "Short" is a dachshund; "tall" is a giraffe. So go the text and pictures in this board book, ingeniously designed with a rippled opening edge so that little fingers can easily turn the pages. Very young children can learn about opposites, animals, and colors from adults showing them this book, and they can then go back to it on their own—which they surely will.

Priddy, Roger. *Animals*. St. Martin's Press, 2004.

This beginning animal book is suggested for "Ages 0+," and certainly it will appeal to curious children well before their first birthday. Each page shows one animal with one word: the name of that animal. Clear photographs against plain, often colorful backgrounds help very young children to distinguish the subject from its background. Extending beyond familiar barnyard animals, the book includes a penguin, a butterfly, a macaw, and forest creatures.

Ross, Katharine. *The Little Quiet Book*. Illustrated by Jean Hirashima. Random House, 2002.

This small board book with pleasing illustrations tells us that "quiet" is a spider, the fireplace, and a chipmunk, among other examples. In the companion book, *The Little Noisy Book* (2002), "noisy" is a hammer, a brook, wet sneakers, and so on. Each book presents both familiar and new sources of quiet or sound.

Seuss, Dr. *The Foot Book*. Random House, 1996.

A good beginning Seuss book, this one shows one foot and then two feet in various positions, with the rhyming text so typical of Dr. Seuss.

Shaw, Charles G. *It Looked Like Spilt Milk*. HarperFestival, 1992.

In white silhouettes on a blue background, we see shapes that look like a tree, a squirrel, or spilt milk. They turn out to be—a cloud. A good stimulus for imaginative looking, this is now available as a board book.

Two and Three Years Old

Children of two and three, with their rapidly growing skills of comprehension, are attentive read-aloud companions. They are ready to follow a simple plot, and they enjoy humor in text and illustrations. After hearing a story outlined while viewing a wordless picture book, they can tell it themselves. They enjoy the rhythms of more complex language, and they linger over pictures as they strive for understanding. By now, reading aloud and trips to the library should be an established part of family life, and the child's home library should be growing.

Barton, Byron. *Bones, Bones, Dinosaur Bones*. HarperFestival, 1990.

With simple text, bold colors, and clean lines, Barton presents an introduction to the work of paleontologists, showing the youngest dinosaur buffs that after bones are found, they are dug up, packed in trucks, transported to a museum, and reassembled. Demonstrating serious respect for the intelligence of his readers, the author includes illustrations of eight dinosaurs, labeling them and (adults reading the book aloud will be glad to know) providing a pronunciation guide. This book may well clear up a mystery for beginning dinosaur fans, bringing science and a level of credibility to a subject that has been overwhelmed by cartoons in recent years.

Benjamin, A. H. *It Could Have Been Worse*. Illustrated by Tim Warnes. Scholastic, 2000.

Mouse is having problems getting home from visiting his cousin in town. He loses his balance, he falls into a hole, he sits on a thistle—but unknown to him, each misadventure results in a lucky escape from danger. It could have been much worse, as the reader knows from the humorous pictures of the stalking cat, the bird of prey, the snake in the grass, and other threats—and as his mother tells him when he arrives home safely. After enjoying this book, a family may adopt "It could have been worse" as a motto that helps them put difficulties into perspective for some time to come.

Brett, Jan. *The Hat.* Putnam, 1997.

The Scandinavian winter is coming, so Lisa hangs her woolen clothes on the line to air. When a sock falls from the line and a curious hedgehog pokes his nose inside, the sock—now serving as a hat—sticks to his prickles. Other animals laugh at Hedgie, but he answers by listing every advantage he can think of in wearing clothes. Taking this to heart, the other animals don Lisa's other clothes as the wind blows them off the line. Meanwhile, in border pictures, we see Lisa in the house, engaged in her daily activities until she realizes that she has lost a sock; then she must go in search of her hats, scarves, and mittens as well. The illustrations of Lisa's farm home and the winter landscape are lovely and full of conversation starters—a good introduction to another country.

Brown, Margaret Wise. *The Runaway Bunny.* Illustrated by Clement Hurd. HarperCollins, 2005.

In this conversation between a bunny and his mother, the bunny suggests that he might run away, and his mother gently tells him what she would do to find him if he did. Clearly no action of this little bunny will separate him from his mother and her love for him.

Emmet, Jonathan. *Bringing Down the Moon.* Illustrated by Vanessa Cabban. Candlewick, 2001.

Mole thinks the moon is so beautiful that he wants to bring it down to earth. Rabbit warns him that it is not as close as it looks, but Mole is undeterred. He tries jumping, he tries a stick, he tries throwing rocks. Nothing works, but each attempt disturbs another animal, and each one tells him it is not as close as it looks. Finally he sees the moon's reflection in a puddle, but when he reaches to touch it, the reflection breaks up. Mole fears that he has ruined the moon, but the other animals explain that he could not have done that. This time Mole agrees with them: indeed, the moon is not as close as it looks.

Fleming, Denise. *In the Small, Small Pond.* Henry Holt, 2007.
  Colorful images made by pouring colored cotton pulp through hand-cut stencils illustrate the variety of life in even a small pond. The few words on each page are rhymed, fascinating, and memorable, telling of the activities of each of the creatures: "Sweep, swoop, swallows scoop." The changing colors tell us that the seasons are passing, until the tadpoles we met at the outset are frogs burrowing into the mud for the winter.

Fleming, Denise. *Time to Sleep.* Henry Holt, 2001.
  When Bear decides that it's time to find a spot to hibernate, she first tells Snail that winter is coming. Snail tells Skunk, and so on, until the news has spread full circle back to Bear, who by now is sound asleep in her den. From frost on the grass to bright leaves to shorter days, each animal recognizes another sign of fall as they all trundle off to sleep. The text has the comfort of a repetitive pattern, and the illustrations are vibrant and imaginative.

Gag, Wanda. *Millions of Cats.* Puffin, 2006.
  The very old man sets off to find a cat for the very old woman, and when he cannot choose among the millions of cats, he takes them all home. The very old woman protests that so many cats will eat them out of house and home, so the very old man asks the cats to decide which is the prettiest. After the ensuing struggle, only one homely kitten is left. Under the tender loving care of the old couple, it grows healthy and plump—the prettiest cat of all.
  This perennial favorite was first published in 1928, which may explain why, when the cats quarrel and disappear, the very old woman concludes, "I think they must have eaten each other all up," adults may or may not wish to be inventive as they read aloud. The well-loved story is still recommended for the comforting repetition and the refrain, "Hundreds of cats, thousands of cats, millions and billions and trillions of cats."

Gibbons, Gail. *Farming*. Holiday House, 1990.

The illustrations in this book take us through a year on a farm, outlining the seasonal changes and the outdoor and indoor chores for everyone. This traditional family farm supports both livestock—chickens, pigs, sheep, horses, cows, and even a beehive—and crops, including a garden, an orchard, a cornfield, hay to mow and store in the hayloft, and a sugar bush.

Parents will probably read the book through once and then abandon the text, using the illustrations as a springboard for conversation, adding all they know, as well as asking and answering questions based on the pictures. Attentive three-year-olds will want to stay with each page until it is thoroughly understood before moving on. Gibbons' books inspire questions that will drive even parents of three-year-olds to reference books for the answers.

Henkes, Kevin. *Oh!* Illustrated by Laura Dronzek. HarperCollins, 1999.

On a snowy morning, all of the creatures want to play. In succession, we see the squirrel, the rabbit, the dog, and two children, all playing in the snow in their own way. Then, in a double-page spread, "Oh!"—everyone is is shown at once. They play again in the afternoon until, at the end of a perfect bright winter day, everyone goes home. The soft textures of the illustrations echo the softness of fresh snow in this very appealing evocation of winter. This is a calming, quiet book—good for naptime.

Hest, Amy. *In the Rain with Baby Duck*. Illustrated by Jill Barton. Candlewick, 1999.

Baby Duck does *not* like rainy days, so today she is in a bad mood. Mr. and Mrs. Duck lead the way through the rain for Pancake Sunday at Grampa's, waddling and shimmying along, enjoying the rain as ducks should. Baby Duck pouts and dawdles, grumbling the whole time: "Wet face," "Mud, mud, mud." But while her parents cannot understand a duck who doesn't like rain, her Grampa can. In the attic, he finds a beautiful umbrella and matching boots, and he explains to Baby Duck that a long time ago, her mother had been a baby duck that did not like rain. Then Grampa takes Baby Duck, with boots and umbrella, for a walk in the rain. They waddle, they shimmy, they hop in puddles—and Baby Duck sings a happy song.

Although Baby Duck acts exactly like a two-year-old, older children, too, will ask for this book again and again. They will recognize the mood swing from pouty and grumpy to happy and singing, and they will perhaps acknowledge that a little understanding and a new attitude can change a day from miserable to happy. The story is one that can be recalled in similar situations long after it's read, and the appealing illustrations will draw the reader into Baby Duck's affection-filled world.

Hoban, Tana. *Construction Zone.* HarperCollins, 1997.

Photographs of workers using machinery at construction sites fill the pages of this book, wordless except for naming the equipment. The last double-page spread shows small pictures of each machine and provides fairly complex information on how it works—which may lead to questions that adults need to explain further. This would be a good choice to read and discuss before and after watching the action at a building site with a child. The pictures offer plenty of opportunity to point to and label the various parts of, for example, a backhoe—and in this case, to compare and contrast the rubber-tired and the crawler backhoes.

Huneck, Stephen. *Sally Goes to the Beach.* Abrams, 2000.

Sally is a black lab who knows, when she sees the suitcase, that she is going on vacation with her human, who appears only as an arm or a leg here and there throughout the book. The point of view and the commentary are entirely Sally's, and her droll sense of humor is matched by the pictures. "After dinner we do the dishes," Sally says, as we see her licking a plate held out to her by a human hand. The illustrations are stunning woodcut prints, created by a multi-step method described in an artist's note. Adding realism, the book is dedicated to Huneck's black lab, Sally.

Hutchins, Pat. *Rosie's Walk*. Aladdin, 1983.

"Rosie the hen went for a walk…and got back in time for dinner." The text is deliberately commonplace; the real story is told in the illustrations. The child watches in suspense as the fox nearly catches Rosie over and over again, landing in positions of ever greater indignity as the story goes on. The fact that Rosie is blissfully unaware of the fox gives the child the opportunity to be in on a secret.

Although this is not a wordless book, it offers the advantages of one by encouraging children to "read" the pictures and tell the story in their own words, and to laugh at the understated humor of it all.

Krauss, Ruth. *The Carrot Seed*. Illustrated by Crockett Johnson. HarperCollins, 2004.

A little boy plants a carrot seed, and despite everyone's warnings that the seed won't grow, he weeds and waters faithfully. The reward for his labors is one very large carrot.

Kuskin, Karla. *James and the Rain*. Illustrated by Reg Cartwright. Simon & Schuster, 1995.

It's going to rain all day, but James is undaunted. Gathering his yellow raincoat, rubber boots, and a large umbrella, he sets out. On his journey, he meets a succession of animals: one cow, two ducks, and so on to 10 cats. At each encounter, he asks the words of Kuskin's poem:

"What do you do in the rain?" said James.

"Do you have any excellent rainy day games?"

As it turns out, all of the animals love the rain, and they demonstrate the various ways in which they embrace a rainy day. Then, the growing entourage strolls on to the next meeting. In the end, the cats reveal that they enjoy the rain best from in front of a roaring fire. In the final picture, James and all of the animals are gathered in a cozy room, asleep in front of the fire.

The dramatic illustrations and bold colors, as well as the rhythm of Kuskin's poetry, carry the story for a young listener. Meanwhile, that listener is absorbing Kuskin's imaginative language—including several words made up to fit the occasion, with meanings either readily plain to the child or given Kuskin's definition in the poem. Both verbally and artistically, this book will enrich the child's world.

Lowrey, Janette Sebring. *The Poky Little Puppy.* Illustrated by Gustaf Tenggren. Golden, 2007.

Five puppies dig a hole under the fence and go exploring the wide, wide world beyond it. Only four arrive at the top of the hill, and when they look for the poky puppy, they discover that he is sniffing the rice pudding that their mother is making for dessert. Home they tumble, but their mother, who is displeased about the hole under the fence, sends them to bed without supper. But the poky little puppy, when he arrives home late, gets rice pudding. The theme repeats twice more, but the third time, the poky puppy misses his dessert. The next morning, the sign over the hole under the fence seems convincing enough to provide a satisfying end to the story.

A favorite among the Golden Books, this classic offers more challenge than some newer books for twos and threes. The repetitive pattern is longer than is now typical, and each time through, there are subtle changes that move the storyline along. The poky little puppy and his siblings offer a satisfying reading experience for children who are ready to point to objects as they count.

Martin, Bill. *Panda Bear, Panda Bear, What Do You See?* Illustrated by Eric Carle. Holt, 2007.

With the same lilting rhythm as their classic *Brown Bear, Brown Bear, What Do You See?*, Martin and Carle present a book featuring rare (in fact, endangered) creatures. In addition to the panda, we see Carle's illustrations of a water buffalo, spider monkey, sea turtle, macaroni penguin, whooping crane, black panther, and others. Whether or not a child is ready to learn about disappearing species, the names and illustrations will delight, while stretching her awareness of the variety of life on earth.

Milich, Zoran. *City Signs.* Kids Can Press, 2008.

The only words in this book are the signs that children see in a city (or a town), vividly displayed on the objects they name: "Taxi,"

"School Bus," "Railroad Crossing," "Park," and so forth. For pre-schoolers who read signs from their perch in the back seat as a parent drives them around town, *City Signs* is an ideal extension of what they are learning on their own. If they wonder what "Horse" or "Litter" means, the colorful photographs will provide a clue, with concepts becoming more sophisticated toward the end of the book: "Used Cars," "Construction," "Road Closed." The last page is one that they will surely recognize—"Stop."

Miller, Margaret. *Guess Who?* HarperCollins, 1994.

Who goes to school? Seagulls? Puppies? Umpires? No-o-o— (turn the page) CHILDREN! Miller illustrates a series of questions with improbable answers, followed by the one that the child guesses all along, with vivid photographs. *Guess Who?* is an intensely interactive book combining the ridiculous with the predictable, told with a delicious suspense. Parents and children who share this book will inevitably end up laughing with the child's delight at getting the right answer yet again. All the while that the child is guessing the right answer, he is also learning to identify the photographs of the wrong answers—juggler, potter, crab, hot-air balloon, veterinarian, parrot, violinist—so this happy book is also a picture dictionary for young children.

Opie, Iona (Ed.). *My Very First Mother Goose*. Illustrated by Rosemary Wells. Candlewick, 1996.

In choosing some 68 rhymes for this new collection, Opie, a co-editor of *The Oxford Dictionary of Nursery Rhymes*, seems to have intentionally sought the most comforting of the genre, leaving those depicting violence and mayhem for the scholars. Rosemary Wells apparently agreed; her illustrations feature rabbits, cats, mice, pigs, and bears whose droll expressions add warmth, humor, and original insight into the well-known plots. For example, is it possible that Humpty Dumpty's fall was in fact caused by a small rabbit who did not want to eat his coddled egg?

Although newer Mother Goose collections are available, my very knowledgeable bookseller says that this is still the one she prefers to recommend. An ideal marriage of text and illustrations, it will entertain readers of all ages, as another generation of parents teach their children to love language—beginning with the polished rhythms of Mother Goose.

Piper, Watty. *The Little Engine that Could.* Illustrated by George & Doris Hauman. Philomel, 2005.

On her way over a mountain carrying good things for the girls and boys on the other side, a little engine stops, unable to go farther. Several large, proud engines refuse to help, but finally the Little Blue Engine says she is willing to try, although she has never been over the mountain. With the classic line, "I think I can, I think I can, I think I can...I thought I could, I thought I could, I thought I could," she succeeds.

Some children carry with them into adulthood the lesson about perseverance so gently taught in this book.

Rosenthal, Amy Krouse. *Little Pea.* Illustrated by Jen Corace. Chronicle, 2005.

Little Pea enjoys such familiar activities as play with his friends and bedtime stories about when Mama Pea was little—but he does not like dinnertime, when the fare is always the same: candy. His parents insist that he must eat five pieces of candy in order to have dessert. Over five pages, and with appropriate expressions of dislike, Little Pea downs five pieces of candy and is delighted with his reward—dessert is spinach. The twist on a familiar dinnertime routine will not be lost on youngsters with a lively sense of humor.

Scarry, Richard. *Richard Scarry's Best First Word Book Ever.* Random, 1979.

Each page of Scarry's book is filled with pictures for discussion, with labels to promote vocabulary building. A very slight storyline carries the Cat family through a day that allows Scarry to touch on colors, counting, letters, and shapes, as well as everyday events such as housework, school, shopping, trips to the doctor's office and to a farm, and more. The book presents a wide range of information for discussion and plenty of detail for sharp eyes to search out, with an adult asking questions to guide the search. Children can then spend time alone with the book, looking for more.

Swift, Hildegarde H. *The Little Red Lighthouse and the Great Gray Bridge.* Illustrated by Lynd Ward. Voyager, 2003.

This restored edition tells the classic story: every night, the little red lighthouse on the Hudson River sends out a beam of light to warn boats about the rocks, and when there is fog, the man who turns on the light every night also sets a bell to ring a warning. The lighthouse keeps boats safe, and it is very, very proud of its work—until a huge bridge is built, making the lighthouse feel very small indeed. When a great light first shines from the top of the bridge, the lighthouse sadly believes that it is no longer needed.

One foggy night, the man does not come, and without the bell from the lighthouse, a tugboat crashes on the rocks. The bridge calls down, saying that its light shines for airplanes; the little red lighthouse is still needed for the ships on the river. But the lighthouse cannot turn on its light or its bell alone. Finally the man appears, delayed because some boys had stolen his keys. The lighthouse knows now that it is still needed, and while it knows it is small, it is still very, very proud.

The real little red lighthouse on the Hudson River closed when the George Washington Bridge opened in 1932. In part because of this book, first published in 1942, it was restored as a focal point in a park. Beyond the history, however, the story is a gem for its spare, memorable phrasing—"Each to his own place, little brother," the bridge calls down to the lighthouse. Meanwhile, the personification of the lighthouse invites small children—who enjoy books about small things—to identify with it. Thus they are ready to absorb the lighthouse's lesson that it is still important, even after it learns that it is small in comparison to the bridge, and to appreciate the gentle statement of the universal need to be needed.

Waddell, Martin. *Owl Babies*. Illustrated by Patrick Benson. Candle-wick, 2002.

Sarah and Percy and Bill respond differently when they wake up in their nest and find their Owl Mother gone. As they wait for her return, Sarah is reassuring and Percy is reassured. But Bill, the littlest, repeats the refrain, so basic to a child's experience: "I want my Mommy." When she returns and says, "You knew I'd be back," Sarah and Percy agree; they knew it. Bill says simply, "I love my Mommy."

With its simple message that Mommy will come back, *Owl Babies* can be a very important book for children entering daycare. Young children identify with Bill, even speaking his line for him each time and jumping up and down when the little owls bounce up and down on their branch at Mother Owl's return. This book offers a way to remind children that Mommies sometimes have to leave—Mother Owl is searching for food for her babies—and provides comfort to a growing young mind.

Four Years Old

An eager, expansive four-year-old of high ability probably already experiences some sense of being different from his playmates. Books can increase his understanding that he is an individual with differ-ences to be enjoyed and celebrated, help him gain skills in getting along with other children, encourage his lively imagination, and add to his rapidly growing knowledge base. Such books can build his con-fidence and pleasure as he begins to learn about himself. Because he is ready to conceptualize some self-understanding and social skills, the following annotations include pointers—and in some cases, sug-gested questions—for casual conversations about issues that may concern the bright four-year-old.

Albert, Burton. *Where Does the Trail Lead?* Illustrated by Brian Pinkney. Aladdin, 2008.

A book to ponder through the winter, remembering the warmth and scents of summer, this is a gentle story of an inquisitive boy who has the self-confidence to be off on his own, exploring the trail from the family's summer cabin to the sea. He encounters tide-pools, blueberries, an abandoned railroad track, a ghost-town of shanties, and much else, all depicted in scratchboard illustrations with sweeping lines, just right for sand and sea. At the end of the day, he is welcomed by his family, cooking fresh-caught fish around the campfire in the twilight, at the edge of the sea.

Aloneness; Developing imagination. A quiet, introspective book, *Where Does the Trail Lead?* encourages daydreaming and exploration, as well as more careful observation on hikes along real trails.

Andreae, Giles. *Giraffes Can't Dance.* Illustrated by Guy Parker-Rees. Orchard, 2001.

"Every year in Africa they hold the Jungle Dance," but Gerald's long thin legs are no good for dancing, and the other animals laugh. As he slinks toward home, a cricket stops him: "Sometimes when you're different, you just need a different song." The cricket encourages Gerald to hear the sounds of the jungle, and as Gerald listens, his body begins to move to the music of the grass and the breeze. Now the other animals cheer, and Gerald concludes, "We all can dance when we find music that we love."

The lively illustrations and the sometimes bumpy rhythms carry this story along. It is frankly didactic, but it teaches a lesson that many children can use at an age when it is important to begin learning it—and with a beat that will help them remember the lines.

Developing imagination; Differentness; Identity.

Anno, Mitsumasa. *Anno's Counting Book.* HarperFestival, 1992.

This wordless book begins with a snowy landscape for zero. The "one" page shows one adult, one child, one tree, one building; then, on subsequent pages, two of each, and so on, progressing to 12. In the meantime, the seasons change, the clock tower shows the time for each number, a tower of blocks increases by tens, and the trees, buildings, and people offer enough variety for many discussions with much observing, identifying, and counting to be done along the way.

Drive to understand. There is always something more to see in Anno's illustrations, and children will enjoy looking with an adult and then alone.

Appelt, Kathi. *Where, Where Is Swamp Bear?* Illustrated by Megan Halsey. HarperCollins, 2002.

In the river basins of Louisiana, Granpere and Pierre go fishing. Along the way to and through the swamp, Pierre asks all about the elusive swamp bear, hoping to see one. As Granpere patiently answers Pierre's questions, observant readers will note that on each page, hidden in the foliage or under tree roots or even floating underwater, a gently smiling bear follows the pair through their day. And in addition to the bear, other swamp creatures fill the pages. The text is gently rhymed, so it is a pleasure to read aloud, and the illustrations, softly colored and lovely at first glance, are very informative on closer inspection. A note at the end gives more information on the Louisiana black bear, an endangered subspecies of the North American black bear—including a link to Teddy Roosevelt and teddy bears.

Developing imagination; Drive to understand.

Burningham, John. *Hey! Get Off Our Train.* Crown, 1999.

A boy and his stuffed dog go to sleep after a day of playing with a toy train. In a dream sequence, they go for a train ride through the night, stopping for such diversions as playing ghosts in the fog and going for a swim. Each time they return to the train, a new animal has climbed aboard. The boy challenges each with "Hey! Get off our train," but each pleads for sanctuary—the elephants are being killed for their tusks, the seals find less food in polluted waters, etc. Each ends the plea with "and soon there will be none of us left"—so of course, all are allowed to join the group on the train. When the boy's mother wakes him for school, she tells him that the house is full of animals—all have come home with him.

Drive to understand; Moral concerns. Burningham's book is included in this list because environmental issues are among the moral concerns that gifted youngsters may worry about more deeply and earlier than most children. The train metaphor may help children conceptualize the problem. No solutions are offered here, but discussion about what the child and her family can do to help the environment is a logical follow-up and will reassure the child that there is something she can do.

Charlip, Remy & Lilian Moore. *Hooray for Me!* Illustrated by Vera B. Williams. Tricycle, 2007.

Here is a joyful picture book celebrating the individual. The section on relationships with others can lead to conversation about how the child fits into his family and his neighborhood. The section on identifying with things that the child does ("I'm my dog's walker") is good for expanding from the book into the child's own life. Wise use of this book can enhance the child's self-concept. Personalize the book, talking about your own family, your own neighborhood, and your child's place in them.

Identity; Relationships with others.

Demi. *The Empty Pot.* Henry Holt, 2007.

Ping lives in China, and even in a land where everyone loves flowers, he is known for his skill in growing things. One day, to choose a successor, the Emperor gives every child, including Ping, a seed. In a year, the children are to return with the plants from their seeds, and the new Emperor will be chosen based on the results. Ping plants his seed hopefully and cares for it tenderly, watering and transplanting and providing the best soil, but he fails—nothing grows. He must return to the Emperor with an empty pot. The Emperor is delighted with Ping's honesty, and the story finishes with a surprise ending.

Demi's delicate illustrations evoke old China and suit the folkloric quality of the story—a memorable introduction to another time and place for a discerning child.

Identity; Moral concerns; Perfectionism; Resilience. In talking about the book, mention that Ping is not only honest but also courageous, willing to admit failure. In this, he is encouraged by his father, who assures him that he has done his best. Our best is enough, if honestly done, even when we seem to fail.

George, Lindsay Barrett. *Inside Mouse, Outside Mouse.* HarperCollins, 2006.

On facing pages, two mice live parallel lives, one in a house and one outside. The inside mouse travels from his home in the clock through the house, past the cat and the dog, to a window, while the outside mouse leaves his home in a tree and moves through the yard, past a rabbit and a bird, to the outside sill of the same window. There, each mouse looks into the other's world.

These are not cartoon mice but beautifully rendered animals that fit into their different—but also somewhat similar—environments. The book is about comparing and contrasting the surroundings of each mouse, in elegantly realistic illustrations. George provides plenty of visual details to discover and discuss, and there is challenge for the child in observing the two worlds at the same time.

Developing imagination; Drive to understand.

Gilman, Phoebe. *Something from Nothing.* Scholastic, 1993.

Joseph's grandfather is a creative, thrifty tailor who makes a wonderful blanket for his new grandson. As Joseph grows, the blanket becomes worn, and Mother suggests throwing it out. "Grandpa can fix it," says Joseph, and Grandpa finds "just enough material" to make something smaller from the good cloth that remains. This pattern is repeated until the last fragment of blanket is only large enough to cover a button. When the button is lost, Joseph, now a schoolboy, finds just enough material to make something else—a wonderful story!

Basing her story on a traditional Jewish folktale, Gilman offers three parallel stories. Each double-page spread shows, on the left, a cutaway view of a two-story building in the Jewish quarter of a city somewhere in Eastern Europe. On the top floor lives Joseph's family, his father's cobbler shop curtained off from the living space. On the ground floor, his grandparents live and work. Below the floor, a family of mice carry on busy lives that reflect the activities of the people above them. The right-hand pages are filled with active street scenes, with horse-drawn wagons and vendors displaying their wares. Each page offers much to discuss.

The love in the faces of all of Joseph's family adds immensely to the appeal of this book. The text is repetitive and reassuring, with the well-worn polish of a traditional tale.

Developing imagination; Resilience. The illustrations offer so much to see that an attentive four-year-old becomes completely engrossed, even following the shift from physical to intellectual object when there is just enough material left to make a story.

Guy, Ginger Foglesong. *Siesta.* Illustrated by Rene King Moreno. Greenwillow, 2005.

"Ven, osito. Come, little bear," begins this book as an older sister invites a younger brother to play outside. Together they gather all they will need: backpack, jacket, flute—each item a different color, each named in Spanish and English. One child asks "Algo mas?" Anything else?" on the left page, and the other answers on the right page, adding to vocabulary—especially the names of colors. Finally the children go outside with their supplies, create a "carpa – tent" with a "manta – blanket" and take a siesta. This is a lovely way to introduce an English-speaking child to Spanish, or vice versa.

Drive to understand.

Handford, Martin. *Where's Waldo?* Candlewick, 1997.

Waldo hikes to a variety of interesting places—a museum, a fair, the seashore, a railway station—each place illustrated in a double spread, teeming with people and miniature stories. The reader is invited to find Waldo at each location, and Waldo's postcards invite us to find other people and events on each page, too. At the end, however triumphant we may feel about our success in finding Waldo, we face one last challenge: Waldo says that on his travels, he has lost his camping gear, one item at a time. Can we find the items?

Developing imagination; Drive to understand. This is a re-issued special edition of an old favorite. Like other classics illustrated by Peter Spier, Richard Scarry, and Mitsumasa Anno, this one is filled with detail, encouraging careful observation and story telling. Adults and children will find new interest with each viewing.

Heine, Helme. *Friends.* Aladdin, 1997.

First published in Germany, this picture book shows three friends— a mouse, a rooster, and a pig—as they spend a day together, defining friendship as they share their adventures. "Good friends always stick together," "Good friends always decide things together,"—even, at the end of the day, "Sometimes good friends can't be together." There is humor in the illustrations, and a touch of European landscape.

Relationships with others. Each of the friends' definitions of friendship can be explored, with examples from the child's experience as a test of validity.

Hutchins, Pat. *Shrinking Mouse.* Greenwillow, 1997.

Four friends—Fox, Rabbit, Squirrel, and Mouse—watch with concern as Owl flies off to a distant forest, shrinking as he goes. Will he disappear? One after another, they follow to bring him back, each one shrinking in turn, while those remaining watch in growing distress and then follow. Yet when they reach the forest, all are the proper size! They turn to see that the wood they had left is now too small, and hesitantly they return to find that when they arrive, it is just the right size. Some of them begin to understand the principle of spatial perspective that is at work here, and the child will learn, too, and chuckle with understanding.

Drive to understand. Looking at the pictures and hearing the friends talk about what they see, the child can learn what perspective is and transfer that awareness to other books and landscapes.

Relationships with others. Each of the friends is concerned about the others, and each tries to help, regardless of their worry. Mouse, who suddenly understands what is happening, gladly comforts the others, and we can guess that he will explain in a friendly way.

Hutchins, Pat. *Titch.* Aladdin, 1993.

Titch has an older sister and a bigger brother, and they have larger bicycles, noisier musical instruments, and higher-flying kites than Titch does. But more exciting than Pete's large spade and Mary's fat flowerpot is Titch's tiny seed, which "grew and grew and grew." The lesson is clear: potential counts more than size, and young children who are constantly trying to keep up will be reminded of their own potential by this simple story.

Identity. What else grows besides seeds into plants? What will *you* be like when you get bigger?

Relationships with others. How can big children help little children? Is there anyone smaller than you whom you can help by being kind?

LaRochelle, David. *The End.* Illustrated by Richard Egielski. Scholastic, 2007.

The End begins at the end of the story and works backward, each page explaining the cause for the event on the preceding page, until we reach the beginning of the story at the end of the book. The spoof continues, with the publication information and then the title page appearing last. Then we can review the story from back to front by focusing on the illustrations instead of on the words, with the pictures filling out the storyline with exaggeration and humor.

This very clever conceptualization of a simple story will keep young minds wondering and returning to it again and again, finding more enlightening details with each re-reading.

Developing imagination.

Leaf, Munro. *The Story of Ferdinand.* Puffin, 2007 (with CD).

Ferdinand is a peaceful bull who enjoys sitting under his favorite cork tree and smelling the flowers while the other bulls cavort and butt their heads together. But on the day that five men come seeking the biggest, fiercest bull in all of Spain to fight in bullfights in Madrid, Ferdinand has just sat on a bee, and he is not sitting quietly. The five men think that they have found their bull, but in the bullring, Ferdinand is himself again—far more interested in smelling the flowers that the ladies throw into the ring than in giving the toreador a contest. He is soon returned to his quiet life under the cork tree.

Ferdinand is serenely and successfully himself, uninterested in what others think he should be. Such contentment is admirable—he is different in ways that harm no one, after all—and can be a model for children who want to be like others in ways that may not be suitable for them.

Differentness; Identity. Do you know people who are different but seem to be happy, anyway? How does Ferdinand help you understand them better?

Ljungkvist, Laura. *Follow the Line.* Viking, 2006.
A single black line begins on the title page and continues through the book, weaving and looping past counting questions around an early morning cityscape, (faces, cars, signs…) to the ocean (ships, sea creatures…) and the sky, into a forest and then a village and finally to a little house where people are sleeping. Everywhere are objects to find, observe, count, and then look again—there may be more.
Drive to understand. This is a book for building vocabulary and expanding awareness, as well as for counting—an excellent choice for an adult and child reading together.

Luciani, Brigitte. *How Will We Get to the Beach?* Illustrated by Eve Tharlet. North-South Books, 2003.
Roxanne wants to go to the beach, and she wants to take five things with her: her baby, a ball, a book, a turtle, and an umbrella. But her car won't start. She considers alternate forms of transportation, but with each possibility, something cannot go with them—and here the book asks, "What was it?" To respond, a younger child can look at the picture and see which is missing, while an older child can be asked to reason—for example, which item is least likely to go in the kayak? The simple words make it easy to remember the five items that Roxanne wants to take, and the pictures add humor as well as details: Where is the ladybug on *this* page?
Developing imagination.

Marzollo, Jean. *Sun Song.* Illustrated by Laura Regan. HarperTrophy, 1997.
Cued by Marzollo's gentle poem, Regan has created illustrations that follow the sun's light through a single day, shining on the spots of a newborn fawn, warming the rocks at the water hole, calling the sheep, waking a boy and his puppy, gloriously illuminating tulips and lilacs, painting the evening sky, and slipping away toward night. The

poem offers new words to stretch a child's listening vocabulary, and the illustrations are luminous and evocative.

Developing imagination. These illustrations can be a springboard to help the child see, for example, the colors in a sunset.

Drive to understand. After reading *Sun Song,* a teacher or parent can follow up by pointing out differences in light and shadow at different times of day, recalling the book while watching where the sun is in the sky as the light changes.

McCloskey, Robert. *Time of Wonder.* Puffin, 1989.

McCloskey's book illuminates in words and pictures a child's experience of late summer in Maine. Weather is a factor to be reckoned with, and the children in the story pick up the adults' apprehension about the approaching hurricane, but they also observe their parents' knowledgeable preparation for it and their sturdy survival of the storm. Coziness and family security are the themes. Awareness and enjoyment of nature pervade the book, along with respect for its power and wonder at its mysteries. Where *do* hummingbirds go in a hurricane?

Although it is full of action, the book is also quiet and thoughtful, acknowledging the moods of children whether at play in the sunshine, singing to cover fear in a storm, or experiencing a bittersweet farewell as they leave for another school year.

Developing imagination; Drive to understand; Resilience. What are special places for you, as the coast of Maine is for the children in the book? How does it feel to know that you are standing where other children stood hundreds of years ago? Or to wonder over the age of a fossil? What other places or events or objects have caused you to wonder? What do you find to wonder about on a simple walk near your house? What does your family do when there is a big storm?

Micklethwaite, Lucy. *I Spy: An Alphabet in Art.* HarperCollins, 1996.

This most original alphabet book is a collection of well-known paintings by artists such as Jan van Eyck, Jan Vermeer, Georges Seurat, and others less familiar, now in private collections or in museums in the United States and Europe. In each, Micklethwaite has selected a detail to represent a letter of the alphabet, inviting the child to scrutinize the painting carefully to find, for example, a nest in a floral still life, or challenging the child to recognize an orange in a painting by Matisse.

Developing imagination; Drive to understand. This beautiful art book, whose only text is "I spy with my little eye…" provides a brilliant way to introduce fine art to young people. Using paintings to play "I spy" with her own children, Micklethwaite found that they frequently saw details she had not noticed before. She says, "By making these paintings accessible, I was enabling my children to build up a store of images in their own minds which must inevitably lead to some interest in fine art." By using this book, even parents who know little of art can help their children begin to appreciate it.

Milne, A. A. *The Complete Tales of Winnie-the-Pooh.* Illustrated by E. H. Shepard. Dutton, 2006 (80th anniversary edition).

This is a fine gift for the fourth birthday of a child who already has plenty of experience with books—but do not begin at the beginning. The dialogues in the introductory material and in the first chapter do not label the speakers, causing difficulty for young listeners trying to follow without benefit of punctuation. Rather, plunge right into one of the stories—each chapter can stand alone. Your child will learn them all and develop favorites, and the characters will become part of her imaginary menagerie.

Identity; Relationships with others; Resilience. This is a wonderful bedtime reader, full of wisdom, humor, and acceptance of self and others.

O'Brien, John. (Illustrator). *The Farmer in the Dell.* Boyds Mills, 2000.

The words are the same, but the pictures tell a different story—not a circle game, but the tale of a hapless farmer heading off to go fishing who does not watch the path ahead and falls into a dell, which is helpfully defined by a road sign: "DELL. A secluded hollow…." This dell is so deep that the farmer cannot climb out, so his wife reaches down to help. But she herself needs help, so she reaches for the nurse—and so forth. At first, the cheese stands alone, refusing to help, but then relents. Finally, the farmer is pulled out, only to tumble back in...so the song can begin again. The wit and humor in the faces of the characters and the detail in the pictures make *The Farmer in the Dell* worth revisiting, even for children who have heard it all before.

Developing imagination.

Ó Flatharta, Antoine. *Hurry and the Monarch.* Illustrated by Meilo So. Dragonfly, 2009.

Hurry is a Texas tortoise who is visited by a monarch butterfly migrating from Canada. After a brief conversation, the monarch flies on to Mexico as Hurry settles in to hibernate for the Texas winter. In the spring, the monarch stops again and lays eggs on a milkweed plant near Hurry before flying a little farther north, where it stops to rest for a while. "For a while becomes forever," because the migration requires several generations. But in Texas, Hurry watches an egg hatch into a caterpillar. The caterpillar forms a chrysalis and then emerges as a new monarch, eager to continue the migration north. The slow-moving, long-lived Hurry, happy in his garden, is a counterpoint to the monarch, with its short lifespan and wide-ranging habitat.

Drive to understand. The maps on the end papers of this book show the monarch migration path, and the afterword provides more information about monarchs for adults to share with children.

Schultz, Robert A. & James R. Delisle. *Smart Talk.* Illustrated by Tyler Page. Free Spirit, 2006.

Smart Talk is written for, about, and even (mostly) by gifted children from four to 12 years old. On their website, www.giftedspeak.com, the authors surveyed gifted children around the world, asking a range of questions in seven categories, including Fitting In, Expectations, School, and Home. They have published "some of the most common answers, as well as some of the most interesting and funny ones." The responses are insightful and revealing and should prove helpful to young readers who will surely find someone out there who answers as they would have. (Responders are identified only by gender, age, and state of residence.) In addition, there are brief biographies called "A Kid Like You" interspersed among the chapters. Sections in each chapter called "Reflection/Connection" offer suggestions for further thought and action.

Achievement; Aloneness; Identity; Intensity; Relationships with others; Using ability. This book is listed under each grade level represented in this chapter, but its application will vary according to age. It may be most useful as a discussion starter, in a group or after a child has read it alone. It can be read straight through or skimmed once and then referred to whenever appropriate. Parents and teachers may help children follow through on ideas offered under "Reflection/Connection." However it is used, this book promises greater self-understanding for gifted children and offers a valuable resource for adults working with them. For four-year-olds, begin by looking through *Smart Talk* for responses from children four years old or slightly older.

Tresselt, Alvin. *Hide and Seek Fog.* Illustrated by Roger Duvoisin. HarperCollins, 1988.

The fog approaches from the ocean and stays for three days, keeping the lobstermen and sailors off the water and children inside by the driftwood fire. The text and illustrations blend beautifully to evoke the calm, quiet, introspective mood induced by a heavy fog. If the book is read slowly, thoughtfully, and liltingly, both child and adult will pick up the mood of cozy settledness.

Aloneness; Identity. Conversation about this book can focus on the warm inside feel of a rainy or foggy day, the quiet pleasure of working alone on a favorite project, or the contentment of playing alone while knowing that there are people in the next room or coming home soon. The child who can appreciate such experiences is on the way to becoming a self-reliant person, capable of being at peace with himself.

Van Leeuwen, Jean. *Amanda Pig on Her Own.* Illustrated by Ann Schweninger. Puffin, 1994.

This book contains four stories about Amanda, whose older brother Oliver has just begun school. Amanda misses him but then learns that she is never *all* alone, and so she learns to be happy entertaining herself. She also learns how to feel better when sick in bed, the disadvantages of a messy room, and what a Bad, Sad, Mad Day is like. Young readers will recognize the feeling of frustration when nothing goes right.

Aloneness. Beginning readers can read this on their own, and it is a good book to remember when a child feels alone, or when a room is a mess, or when a day seems to go all wrong.

Identity. While Amanda learns to entertain herself and what it is like to have a bad day, she is also learning that she can handle daily difficulties—she is more capable than she thought. So is every child, but this is often not pointed out to them in so many words.

Resilience. Use this book to clarify your child's awareness of her own growth, connecting recent specific examples from events at home or preschool to Amanda's experiences.

Willems, Mo. *Leonardo, the Terrible Monster.* Hyperion, 2005.

Leonardo (a small, furry creature with blue eyes and tiny horns) wants very much to be a monster, but he is terrible at it. He lacks Tony's many teeth, Eleanor's huge size, and Hector's simple weirdness. Finally, he decides to do some serious research and then to find an appropriate victim—a scaredy-cat kid. Selecting Sam, Leonardo sneaks up on him hopefully and scares him so thoroughly that Sam cries. But when Sam tells Leonardo all the reasons that he is crying, beginning with his big brother stealing his action figures, the failed monster decides to adopt a different approach—better to be a wonderful friend than a terrible monster. This is a heart-warming story that is saved from sentimentality by the delightfully humorous creatures that Willems has created for his characters. Children will laugh at Leonardo's antics and then be ready to talk about his big decision.

Arrogance; Relationships with others; Using ability. Why does Leonardo want to be a monster? Why does it not work for him? When we use our abilities, how much do we need to think about using them to help others? What does this story tell you about why children who act like monsters do so? How does it help to know more about why Sam cried?

Early Elementary: Kindergarten to Grade 2

Abeel, Samantha. *Reach for the Moon.* Illustrated by Charles R. Murphy. Orchard, 2001.

Inspired by the works of an established artist, 13-year-old Samantha Abeel has responded with moving, insightful poetry and prose. Charles Murphy's watercolors are realistic but often have mystical overtones; Abeel's writings tell the story or reflect the emotion she perceives in each painting.

The story of how this book came to be is as inspirational as the book itself. Samantha Abeel is not only gifted but also learning disabled. For the first years of schooling, her inability to comprehend numbers, tell time, or make change overshadowed her insight and her verbal gifts. Recognizing Samantha's writing talent, her seventh-grade English teacher, Roberta Williams, chose to encourage her strength and to overlook difficulties with spelling, verb tenses, and due dates. At the request of Elizabeth Abeel, Samantha's mother (herself an artist), Williams arranged a summer writing program for Samantha based on the art of family friend Charles Murphy. The result is not only this book, it is also a success story for Samantha and a demonstration of what can happen when schools, parents, and mentors work together on behalf of a child who does not fit the mold.

Creativity; Differentness; Resilience; Using ability.

Alexander, Lloyd. *The Fortune Tellers.* Illustrated by Trina Schart Hyman. Puffin, 1997.

Alexander has created an original folktale, marked by gentle humor and just enough complexity to challenge perceptive four-year-olds. A disgruntled carpenter, hearing his fortune told, concentrates only on the promises and not on the very large "ifs" that the fortune-teller adds in warning. Nevertheless, things turn out exactly as he hopes when the fortune-teller disappears and the carpenter accidentally replaces him, hedging his bets by adding conditions to his predictions as the original seer had done.

The tale is set in Cameroon, home of the illustrator's son-in-law. The Caldecott Medalist's illustrations of the landscape, the marketplaces, the people, and the interiors of homes and shops are truly fine. Colorful, descriptive, and whimsical, they reflect the wit and humor of the text.

Drive to understand. Much can be learned from the illustrations alone. Ask the child to notice and identify details in the pictures. Follow the ubiquitous monkey through the book. Discuss the story-line and help the child understand the paradoxes in the fortune-teller's answers. For more mature children, find Cameroon on a globe or atlas.

Aliki. *Feelings.* HarperCollins, 1986.

This is not a story, but a book showing on each page a different familiar childhood event—a birthday party, a space capsule created of wood blocks and then destroyed, getting lost in a store, being bored—with the characters commenting on their positive and negative feelings.

Aloneness. Identify lonely or alone situations in the book (such as boredom). What do you do when you feel like that? What else could you do?

Identity. A calm, objective discussion of both good and bad feelings based on the book can help a child recognize and accept his own feelings later, after an episode in which emotions may run so strong that rational discussion is not possible. How would you feel if this happened? Why? What would you do? Are there other times when you feel the same way? How do you act when you feel that way? Is it all right to feel that way? Do other people ever feel the same way you do?

Relationships with others; Sensitivity. This book can be used to help children focus on how other people feel, as well as on how they themselves feel. How can you tell what these people are feeling? How can you tell when your friends feel angry, lonely, or happy? What do you do in those situations?

Anno, Mitsumasa. *Anno's Journey.* Paper Star, 1997.

This wordless book shows a man journeying on horseback through a medieval European landscape. The reader who looks carefully can identify a fair, a duel, a foot race, a ping-pong game, and many visual jokes—the book is full of details to observe and discuss.

Developing imagination; Drive to understand. A child can pore over this book for hours, continually finding something new. An adult can enrich the experience by questioning: What are they doing? Tell me a story about this. What do you think this is?

Bang, Molly. *Dawn.* Chronicle, 2002.

Dawn's father tells her the story of how, shortly after he found and rescued a wounded Canada goose, a young woman magically appeared and began to weave light, strong sails for the ships he built. He married her, and they had a child—Dawn. The sails that the woman made for their family boat were especially fine. A wealthy client demanded sails like them; she protested that it would take too much out of her to make more such sails, but when her husband insisted, she relented. Just as the sails were nearly finished, he impatiently opened the door of the room where she worked—and saw the Canada goose, pulling out its breast feathers, and weaving them into sailcloth. At his appearance, a flock of geese flew into the room and carried her off. At the end of her father's story, promising to find her mother and bring her back in the spring, Dawn sets off in the small boat that her father had made for the three of them.

Developing imagination; Drive to understand. Ask the child to imagine a sequel to Dawn's story. Or point out that *Dawn* is based on the Japanese tale of the Crane Wife, and suggest comparing the two stories.

Bang, Molly Garrett. *Tye May and the Magic Brush.* (Adapted from the Chinese). HarperCollins, 1992.

Tye May is a poor orphan who longs to paint. One night in a dream, she receives a magic brush from a woman who tells her to use it carefully. With her brush, Tye May paints birds and animals that come to life. Soon she paints for the poor: a loom for a weaver, an ox cart for a farmer. A greedy landlord, and then the Emperor, want Tye May to paint for them. She pretends to cooperate with the Emperor, but his greed causes disaster for him and his court. Some say that Tye May still goes from village to village, painting for the poor.

Moral concerns; Using ability. This is a read-alone book about the wise use of gifts. Why does the brush work well for Tye May and cause such trouble for the Emperor? What is the wise use of gifts—what does the woman mean when she says, "Use it carefully"?

Base, Graeme. *The Eleventh Hour.* Puffin, 1997.

For his eleventh birthday, Horace the Elephant plans a party. He invites 11 guests, whips up a feast of 11 treats, and plans 11 games. The guests arrive early and play games until the hour appointed for the feast: 11:00. Then—surprise and mystery!

But there have been clues. Each luscious illustration contains clues—and red herrings, in the form of anagrams, clocks, riddles, hidden creatures, mirror writing, and jumbled messages. In a sealed section at the end of the book, Base reveals the clues, all the while encouraging the reader to deduce the answer through careful observation.

Developing imagination; Drive to understand. The appeal of this book is not limited to just one age group. The verse, illustrations, and storyline will have great appeal to older preschoolers, and early elementary students must read to figure out the clues. Children of middle elementary age are fascinated by codes of any kind and will certainly enjoy the intricacy of Base's concoctions. Some clues—Egyptian cartouches and Latin inscriptions, for example—are probably beyond most readers of any age without explanation. Every reader will find plenty of challenge here.

Base, Graeme. *My Grandma Lived in Gooligulch.* Puffin, 2007.

When Grandma lived in Gooligulch, she made a practice of taming wild animals—Australian animals with strong rhythmical names that carry Base's rollicking verse along. A wombat pulled Grandma's gig (cart), while a bandicoot rode beside her. The night the emus came to dine, a great fuss ensued when a frill-necked lizard appeared. Finally, Grandma sails off to sea (by then it seems her only option), but the author suggests that Grandma is probably back in Gooligulch by now.

Base depicts 21 animals and Grandma on the fly leaf, with a chart to help the child identify each. Interspersed throughout the text, pages are gorgeously colored double spreads to give us a better view of the animals. Enticing as the pictures are, the text is equally memorable and challenging, full of names of Australian birds, animals, and plants and laced with an occasional Australian term (gig, two-up, petrol) for the child to add to her vocabulary.

Developing imagination. A child who hears Grandma's story read by one who has a sense for the rhythm will soon be reciting sections on her own. This book could easily lead to others, fiction and nonfiction, on Australia.

Base, Graeme. *The Sign of the Seahorse: A Tale of Greed and High Adventure in Two Acts.* Puffin, 1998.

In this tongue-in-cheek undersea environmental drama, a gang of Groupers forces Pearl's and Finny's father, "a fine, upstanding Trout," to sell the Seahorse Café, while the Soldiercrabs, led by Pearl's true love, Bert, leave to find the source of pollution that has killed a nearby reef. With the end of the Café, Pearl leads the local fish to a new reef, while Finny and his Catfish Gang stay behind to punish the Groupers. Overhearing that an open spigot on an oil barrel is causing the harm, Finny tries to close it and fails. But Bert succeeds, and then the Soldiercrabs return to capture the Groupers. Finally, all follow Pearl's secret Sign-of-the-Seahorse trail to the new reef, where Pearl and Bert are reunited and the miscreant Grouper Gang members are put to menial tasks at the new Seahorse Café.

The plot is complex, and much of the vocabulary would be considered beyond young children by any formal measure, but the lush illustrations and the flawlessly rocking rhythm of the verse carry young listeners along, holding their interest for reading after reading. For very bright children, in fact, the allure of all those fascinating words may be part of what holds their interest; another draw is the map of the ocean floor, with a key for the trails followed by various members of the cast. Certainly, the plot and level of language keep the adult reader alert. The quietly pervasive humor is appreciated by readers of any age. This is recommended as a read-aloud for children in the early elementary years.

Drive to understand. Because of the complexity of both plot and language, this book, like other Base offerings, presents a delightful intellectual challenge.

Moral concerns. Underneath the fun, Base presents a serious message about environmental pollution. How did those reeking barrels get there in the first place?

Relationships with others. Finny and his Catfish Gang present themselves as punk adolescents, yet they prove that their hearts are in the right place. While *The Sign of the Seahorse* can be appreciated simply for its artistry and humor, it would also be possible to use Finny as an example of the importance of judging people by what they do rather than how they look.

Brown, Laura Krasny. *How to Be a Friend: A Guide to Making Friends and Keeping Them.* Illustrated by Marc Brown. Little Brown, 2001.

With characters depicted as appealing dinosaurs, this is a simple, straightforward guide to how to be a friend (share toys, invite others to play with you) and, just as important, how not to be a friend (blame friends for something they didn't do, be a poor sport if you win or lose). Adult intervention is recommended in situations that children may not be able to handle on their own (anger that grows out of control, bullies), and an outline is provided for "Talking Out an Argument." This is a how-to book that will be especially helpful for bright children who may not be as socially intuitive as their peers but who respond well to direct information.

Relationships with others. Keep this book handy to guide discussion when needed—so many situations are included that it should be easy to find an appropriate bit of advice.

Brown, Ruth. *If at First You Do Not See.* Andersen, 1997.

A caterpillar goes off in search of food, but each time he thinks he has found a meal, he discovers that he has stumbled onto one creature or another who does not want to be eaten. At last, a scarecrow puts the caterpillar in his pocket where he can rest. When he awakes, the caterpillar has become a butterfly.

The illustrations carry the story. On each page, the text continues around the margins so that the book must be turned; when it is upside down (if the reader looks carefully), the creature who is reluctant to become dinner appears. Imbedded in the right-side-up picture of the grass or flowers that looked so good to the hungry caterpillar is an upside-down picture of a man or a witch, but we must work a bit to find it.

Developing imagination. In Brown's book, the child's imagination is called into play to make sense of both story and pictures.

Bryan, Ashley. *Turtle Knows Your Name.* Aladdin, 1993.

The little boy has a very long name, Upsilimana Tumpalerado. Eventually he can remember all of it, and on that day, his delighted Granny takes him to the beach, where they dance his name dance. As always, when there is a name dance, Turtle swims to the surface to hear the name and then dives to the bottom to spell it out in shells on the ocean floor. But though Upsilimana Tumpalerado knows his name, it is too long for his friends, and they still call him Long Name. One day, Granny challenges Upsilimana Tumpalerado to tell her *her* name, and he goes searching to find one who knows it—Turtle, of course.

Both the colorful illustrations and the story are full of joy in this retelling of a West Indian tale. Upsilimana Tumpalerado must have a firm sense of his place in the world, with his name written on the bottom of the sea, a Granny who patiently teaches him to remember it, and villagers who respond to his questions by circling around him, dancing and singing.

Identity. Remind the child of the various traditions that his family has developed to impart the same sense of place and foundation.

Bulla, Clyde Robert. *Daniel's Duck.* Illustrated by Joan Sandin. HarperCollins, 1982.

Growing up in a Tennessee mountain cabin, Daniel wants to learn to carve like his brother Jeff, who carves so well that his proud parents say that someday he may carve as well as Henry Pettigrew, a man widely known as the best wood-carver in Tennessee. Daniel's father gives him wood and a knife, and Daniel thinks for some time before he finally carves a duck looking backward. At the spring fair, where the family hopes to sell the handwork that they have made all winter, people stand in silence before Henry Pettigrew's carved deer, but they laugh when they see Daniel's duck. Mortified, Daniel seizes the duck and runs to throw it in the river. He is stopped by an old man who quietly explains that there are different kinds of laughter. People laughed at Daniel's duck because it made them happy. The duck is good, says the man—who is no other than Henry Pettigrew.

Creativity; Differentness; Using ability. Daniel's differentness is represented by his interest in carving animals merely for the sake of their beauty, while his practical brother carves useful dishes. It is Daniel's divergence that leads him to carve the duck looking backward. It would be worthwhile also to mention Henry Pettigrew's understanding. Daniel's work is better understood by older people than by children, indicating that he will "fit in" better when he and his peers are adults.

Intensity; Perfectionism; Resilience. For a child who already shows signs of being dissatisfied with work that is not perfect, Daniel's story offers a chance to talk about how one product is seen differently by different people. There is no one standard of perfection; the key is to do one's best and enjoy the result.

Sensitivity. Daniel displays two kinds of sensitivity—one through his period of thoughtfulness before beginning to carve, and the other through his assumption that the laughter was derisive. The first can be positive and productive; the second type of sensitivity can be damaging if not understood and counteracted.

Bunting, Eve. *Dandelions.* Illustrated by Greg Shed. Sandpiper, 2001.

Mama and Papa, with Zoe and her younger sister Rebecca, travel to the Nebraska Territory in a covered wagon to claim the land that Papa had found when he came here the summer before their journey. Papa is joyful, excited about beginning a new life, but Mama looks backward to the home they had left in Illinois. There are almost no trees here, and the horizon stretches as far as they can see. Even the soddie, the sod house Papa builds, seems to blend in with the waving grasses. Mama fears that Zoe and Rebecca will get lost if they stray too far; Mama worries about everything.

Eventually Zoe realizes that Papa worries, too, about Mama and about the baby that is coming in the fall. Then, on the way home from her first trip to town with Papa, Zoe finds dandelions growing along the trail. They stop and dig a clump to plant on top of the soddie as a gift to Mama—the gold of the dandelions will make their home stand out against the sameness of the prairie. The next morning, as the family gathers in hope that the newly transplanted dandelions will take hold, put down roots, and thrive in their new home, Mama realizes that they, too, are transplants who must be strong enough to thrive.

Drive to understand; Resilience. Some children will understand the metaphor of the dandelions, and some will read this book simply as a story of pioneers traveling to a new life. Either way, the sensitively-told story and the earth-tone illustrations, so appropriate for the story, convey a sense of what it is to leave home and go to a strange land—an experience still common to Americans from many places.

Bunting, Eve. *Train to Somewhere.* Illustrated by Ronald Himler. Sandpiper, 2000.

A relatively unknown part of our country's history is that, between the 1850s and the 1920s, "Orphan Trains" carried homeless children from the crowded cities of the East to the farms of the West. Many parents just arriving in the United States could not find work that would support a family, and some gave up their children in the desperate hope that the children would find a better life. Some children found loving homes, and some found endless work as field hands or housemaids in return for their room and board.

Train to Somewhere is set in 1888, when Marianne rides an Orphan Train with Miss Randolph and a group of children who need homes. West of Chicago, the train makes several stops at small towns where people gather to choose a child to take home. At every stop, Marianne searches for her mother, who had promised to come get her. Neither pretty nor old enough to be strong, Marianne is the only child left at the last stop in Somewhere, Illinois. The people waiting there are not what she wanted, and the people do not really want her because she is not a boy; nevertheless, they warm to each other quickly. Despite the heartbreak of the Orphan Trains, we know that Marianne has found a loving home.

Aloneness. The children on the Orphan Train must have felt very alone. How did they help each other to feel less lonely? Even though she is alone, how does Marianne know that her mother loves her?

Drive to understand. How did the need for Orphan Trains fit into American life at the time? What was life like in the cities? On the farms?

Moral concerns. How were the Orphan Trains a good solution for children whose parents could not take care of them? How were they not? Do you have ideas for a better solution? Or for how the Orphan Train solution might have worked better?

Relationships with others. Even though the children on the Orphan Train are in a difficult situation, there are many examples of kindness in the book. What are they? How do they help? What kindness have you shown recently? How do you think it helped? Do you know someone in a difficult situation whom you could help with kindness?

Resilience. How did Marianne maintain a sense of hope and optimism?

Cendrars, Blaise. *Shadow.* Translated and illustrated by Marcia Brown. Aladdin, 1995.

The French poet Blaise Cendrar's poem, "La Feticheuse," evokes an image that goes far beyond that cast by an object between the earth and the sun. It incorporates the idea of spirit, both haunting and enchanting, and the mystery of the African jungle. Brown's illustrations capture the mood of the text, conveying an eerie—but not at all frightening—sense of awe of the unknown that Shadow represents.

Developing imagination. The text, translated as it is from poetry, offers a challenge to young listeners and readers to comprehend it both intellectually and emotionally. The illustrations are original and abstract, enhancing the text to add to the total experience of the book.

Cleary, Beverly. *Ramona the Brave*. Illustrated by Alan Tiegreen. HarperCollins, 1995.

Trying hard to grow up, Ramona enters first grade, where calm, task-oriented Mrs. Griggs is not as exciting or as understanding of Ramona's idiosyncrasies as Miss Binney was last year. Ramona struggles with the consequences of crumpling the artwork of a student who copied her owl, with moving into a new bedroom and finding it scary to be alone, and with the need to create a slipper from a paper towel after she throws her shoe at a German shepherd that chased her as she walked to school. Throughout the book, she experiences the fears and triumphs of a first grader in a loving family with supportive teachers.

Creativity; Differentness; Relationships with others; Resilience. This book is just an introductory example of the work of Cleary, who is enormously popular because she knows exactly how to capture the vulnerabilities of children such as Ramona—gifted, creative, spunky, independent, always feeling different. Ramona's predicaments and solutions delight children who are always getting into scrapes and feeling misunderstood themselves. Cleary's books have been loved for many years, and even as adults, her readers remember how comforting it was to find someone like them.

Cooney, Barbara. *Island Boy*. Puffin, 1991.

A simple story of the life of Matthais Tibbetts, born the first of 12 children in the first family on Tibbetts Island (a fictional island off the coast of Maine) around 1900. The family flourishes on the island, but eventually all return to the mainland; even Matthais leaves the island to serve as cabin boy and then master on a sailing vessel. After 15 years, Matthais returns to the empty house, bringing his bride, Hannah. Their three daughters leave when they are grown, but after Hannah's death, Annie and her son, also named Matthais, return. Life continues on the island as the grandfather, daughter, and grandson sell vegetables and milk to vacationers on nearby islands. In due time, Old Matthais, the Island Boy, dies during a trip to the mainland on rough seas. Young Matthais may stay on the island—we do not know. We do know, though, that Old Matthais has lived a complete, fulfilled, and successful life.

Cooney's illustrations set the mood for this description of a life of hard work whose rewards are the simple enjoyment of family and the pleasures of making good use of the abundance provided by land and sea. Without preaching, Cooney speaks of these basic values and the satisfaction they bring. Her story is a strong statement of the richness to be found in a sense of family and place.

Drive to understand; Identity. For children who have no experience with living on an island or with the northeast coast of America, *Island Boy* provides a narrative of a way of life similar enough to their own to facilitate understanding, but different in time and place.

Dorros, Arthur. *Abuela.* Illustrated by Elisa Kleve. Puffin, 1997.

Rosalba tells of a day in the park with her *abuela* (grandmother). She imagines flying over New York City with her *abuela*, seeing the harbor, the airport, the streets and office buildings, the Statue of Liberty. Rosalba's narrative is sprinkled with terms in Spanish—her *abuela's* language—offering just enough challenge to invite an English-speaking child to become fascinated with the words. The illustrations are joyous, colorful, and rich in details to explore.

Developing imagination. Invite the child to imagine with you what you would see if you flew together over a familiar place. For a young child, begin with a small space, such as his own block; enlarge the area for older children.

Drive to understand. This is a delightful book to introduce a child to New York City and to another language. A glossary of Spanish terms is included.

Dragonwagon, Crescent. *Home Place.* Illustrated by Jerry Pinkney. Aladdin, 1993.

Hiking in the woods, a family comes upon remnants of a vanished homestead—daffodils, a chimney, a stone foundation. Digging just a little, the girl discovers a marble and part of a china doll. A family has lived here, and the hikers imagine how they lived, trying to reconstruct the ordinary daily events in the lives of unknown people long gone.

Developing imagination; Drive to understand. The book stretches our awareness of our own lives by imagining lives much like ours lived generations ago. The book evokes wonder about how things both change and remain the same, and it adds depth and meaning to our daily concerns, such as those about the weather and about a family meal—concerns that do not change over the centuries.

Ehlert, Lois. *Red Leaf, Yellow Leaf.* Harcourt, 1991.

In this excellent example of a nonfiction book for early readers, Ehlert describes planting and caring for a sugar maple tree. She tells how it grew in the woods before it was transplanted to a nursery, then to a garden center, and then to the hole already dug for it in the back yard, as well as how it changes through the seasons. The book is visually rich, with realistic and meticulously accurate details of maple flowers and roots, yet the illustrations are presented in close-up views so that the reader must supply the context mentally. Notes at the end of the book give information about the parts of the sugar maple, as well as instructions for selecting and planting a tree.

Drive to understand. This book answers questions that children of this age may never have considered. Discussion could raise more questions: How is planting a tree like planting a bean seed? How is it different? Why?

Relationships with others. For some children, discussion of pets or animals as friends may be a good introduction to the skills of friendship. Certainly, Ehlert considers trees her friends. Caring for a living thing, even a tree, is much like caring for a friend, requiring an awareness of what the friend needs to thrive and then supplying that as much as possible.

Ferris, Jeri. *What Are You Figuring Now? A Story about Benjamin Banneker.* Illustrated by Amy Johnson. Turtleback, 2001.

Benjamin Banneker (1731-1806) was a son of free black parents, a Maryland farmer who studied astronomy, clocks, and mathematics—matters of great interest at the time he lived, when ships sailed by the stars and there were only two books in many homes: an almanac and the Bible. His formal schooling lasted only four winters before he had to work full time on the farm. But when he was 20, he borrowed a watch, took it apart to analyze how it worked, and reassembled it. Then he used his drawings to build a clock out of wood, and he became famous as the man who built his own clock.

With his study of astronomy and skill at math, Banneker became a surveyor—so well-known that he was appointed by President George Washington and Secretary of State Thomas Jefferson to assist Pierre L'Enfant in laying out the streets of Washington, D.C. He decided to write an almanac, which required hundreds of mathematical calculations to predict the phases of the moon and eclipses, but his was known for its accuracy. Only after age 60 did he stop farming his 100 acres to devote himself to math and astronomy, still living in his cabin with his wooden clock.

Banneker constantly hungered for conversation concerning ideas about books, math problems, and what was happening elsewhere in the world. The emphasis on this, plus the fresh writing style and the ability of the author to compel us to truly care for Banneker, recommends it for intellectually curious readers.

Drive to understand; Intensity; Using ability. What quality kept Banneker going when he had no one to talk to? How was his family important to him? With whom do you talk about books or math or other favorite subjects? Why is it important to have someone to talk to about these things?

Resilience. How was Benjamin able to persevere in the face of little formal education and being an ethnic minority? How do modern-day boys and girls maintain and develop their curiosity?

Fleischman, Paul. *Glass Slipper, Gold Sandal: A Worldwide Cinderella.* Illustrated by Julie Paschkis. Holt, 2007.

We've heard that the Cinderella tale is told in different versions around the globe, but this book demonstrates how it is so. Fleischman tells the familiar story, incorporating elements from Mexico, Korea, India, Ireland—the map on the end pages shows 17 source countries, each contributing something from its own culture. (The glass slippers are from the French; in Iraq, they were golden sandals.) Meanwhile, Paschkis uses textiles from various countries to inspire the patterns and color combinations of her vivid folk-art designs, and she subtly labels the country of origin for the story element featured on each page.

For readers of all ages, this book is fascinating for the novelty of the conception, of great interest for the variations from different cultures, and deeply moving as we comprehend the universality of the Cinderella story—one more confirmation of our common humanity. For children who are growing up in a global society, this is a very appealing beginning.

Drive to understand. This version of the Cinderella story may inspire teachers and librarians to introduce a unit on folktales from around the world. What are the themes in this story that people everywhere recognize? Note the different names for the leader: king, magistrate, headman. What other differences do you find for ideas that are similar from one culture to another?

Fleischman, Paul. *Weslandia.* Illustrated by Kevin Hawkes. Candlewick, 2002.

He does not like pizza or soda or professional football. In fact, Wesley feels like an outcast from civilization. So when school lets out for the summer and he seeks a summer project, he devises his own civilization—he digs a garden plot and then learns how much he can do with the one type of plant that grows. Evoking early cultures around the world, the illustrations show Wesley using various parts of the plant to cook food, weave clothing, and build shelter. He moves on from the basics to inventing games and then an alphabet and a language to name the items that he has created. His schoolmates scoff, become curious, and then want to join in the fun. By fall, he has "no shortage of friends," Fleischman writes, while Hawkes pictures the neighborhood children following Wesley to school dressed in woven robes just like his.

Children who like to do things differently will find in Wesley a kindred spirit. The illustrations support Wesley's cheerfulness with humor; the book treats a serious subject with a very light touch.

Creativity; Developing imagination; Differentness; Using ability.

Fraser, Mary Ann. *I.Q. Goes to the Library.* Walker, 2005.

Following up on *I.Q. Goes to School* (2002), the little mouse named I.Q. is well settled in with the class when Library Week arrives. He joins the other (human) students on Monday for Reading Corner Day, when Mrs. Binder reads a book so funny that I.Q. spends the rest of the week looking for it. But each day the class is so busy learning about the library that it is not until Friday, when Mrs. Binder shows them how to use the computer to find where in the library a book is shelved, that I.Q. has his chance. He follows instructions, finds the book on the shelf, and after the classroom teacher vouches for him, he is able to check out his book. I.Q. is endearing, the illustrations add comedy, and through it all, I.Q.—and the reader—pick up good basic information about using the library.

Drive to understand.

Goble, Paul. *Death of the Iron Horse.* Aladdin, 1993.

On August 7, 1867, a group of Cheyenne Indians derailed a Union Pacific freight train in Nebraska to protest the railroads' incursions into their territory. After the derailment, the Cheyenne plundered the freight cars, taking not money but all they could carry of goods that their people could use. Goble's telling gives the story a mythic quality—the story is told as an old Cheyenne man, remembering years later, might have told it to his grandchildren. Simple but beautiful illustrations recall the destruction caused by conflict, with the majestic expanse of the West as a backdrop.

Drive to understand. Since this story is based on fact, discussion can lead to further exploration of the disruption of the various American Indian cultures.

Moral concerns. The book can be used as a springboard for discussion that examines both sides. Were the Cheyenne wrong? How can we determine whether they were or not? Then consider the story from the point of view of the men on the freight train. Were they wrong? In what way? Who was stealing what, and why, and with what justification?

Goble, Paul. *The Legend of the White Buffalo Woman*. National Geographic Society, 2002.

In this beautiful book, the author of many beautiful books about the Plains Indians tells their most important sacred legend: the story of how the Great Spirit, in a time of trouble, sent a white buffalo calf in the form of the White Buffalo Woman to give the tribes the pipe (often called the peace pipe) and a new way to pray. Goble begins with a creation story, then tells of the visit of the White Buffalo Woman, and concludes with a description of how the tribes found the red clay from which to make their pipes.

The illustrations are majestic and compelling, well-suited to the subject. An author's note sets the legend in historic context. At the end are precise drawings of several pipes, with an explanation of the meanings of some of the symbols used in making one, as well as a map showing the location of the Pipestone Quarry in Minnesota, now a national monument.

Drive to understand. Some children will approach this book intellectually, showing curiosity about the pipe and the history, perhaps wanting to visit the Pipestone Quarry. Others may respond simply to the beauty and mystery of the story and the illustrations. Adults should be sensitive to the individual response and use it as a guide for further discussion.

Godden, Rumer. *The Story of Holly and Ivy*. Illustrated by Barbara Cooney. Viking, 2006.

Ivy is an orphan who goes looking for an imaginary grandmother at Christmas. Holly is a doll in a toyshop who wishes for a girl to own her. Mrs. Jones wants to celebrate Christmas so much that she decorates a Christmas tree for the first time, and Mr. Jones is the policeman to whom Peter, who works at the toyshop, turns when he discovers that he has lost the key to the shop. Holly, Ivy, and Mrs. Jones are united, thanks to Peter, on Christmas Day, and each wish is granted. This story is told from three alternating points of view— Holly's, Ivy's, and Mrs. Jones'—so the reader must hold three separate stories in mind until they merge.

Drive to understand. In addition to the intellectual challenge, this is a heartwarming story with an implied appreciation for home and family.

Hall, Donald. *The Man Who Lived Alone.* Illustrated by Mary Azarian. David R. Godine, 1998.

The man who lived alone builds himself a camp near the farm of relatives where he had lived and worked as a boy. He is very much an individual, growing and canning his own vegetables, hunting for meat, working in town for a few days each year for cash to pay his taxes. He makes friends with an owl and takes pride in his mule. He can do anything with his hands: solder, build a house or a shotgun, shoe a horse or mule. He likes to keep his own hours, and he some-times works all night. His aunt and uncle, and then his cousin and her husband and daughter, are close enough for company when he wants it, and he often helps them out.

The man who lived alone is alone but not lonely; rather, he is resourceful, affectionate and generous. His life is not typical but it is self-sufficient, and he is content. This book's unusual theme provides assurance that spending time alone is not necessarily negative, and in its nonjudgmental reporting, it exemplifies tolerance for a different way of life.

Aloneness; Creativity; Differentness; Introversion. A reading of this book can lead to a conversation about people we know who live alone or who spend a great deal of time alone and are happy doing so. The idea is simply to indicate to the child that being alone can be done well and is potentially a positive experience.

Hall, Donald. *Ox-Cart Man.* Illustrated by Barbara Cooney Porter. Puffin, 1983.

The ox-cart man lives in New England at a time when embroi-dery needles still come on ships from England. In October, he and his family load all of the produce of their farm that they can sell onto the ox cart, and he walks 10 days to Portsmouth. There, he sells everything, even the cart and the ox. He buys a few necessities and walks back home, where he and his family begin preparing for next

October's trip. While the ox-cart man carves a new yoke and builds a new cart, his wife spins flax into linen, his daughter embroiders the linens, and his son makes brooms.

The story is about the self-sufficiency of the farm family, with everyone sharing in the work that sustains them. The illustrations carry much of the story, providing details for discussion, as well as evoking the New England seasons and the well-regulated, productive life that results from the family's work.

Drive to understand. The family makes use of everything available to them, some of which will be new to contemporary readers. For example, what does the farmer actually do when he splits shingles to sell? What does the child know about spinning flax into linen, making maple syrup, and shearing sheep?

This book can also be enjoyed simply by examining the pictures and discussing the many details of the hardworking family's life. Donald Hall lives in rural New Hampshire. He is also a poet, and in 2006, he was appointed our 14th Poet Laureate.

Hatkoff, Isabella, Craig Hatkoff, & Paula Kahumbu. *Owen & Mzee: The True Story of a Remarkable Friendship.* Photographs by Peter Greste. Scholastic, 2006.

After the 2004 tsunami in the Indian Ocean swept the shores of Africa, a baby hippopotamus was found separated from his mother and stranded on a coral reef near the village of Malindi. Villagers and visitors worked together for hours to rescue the frightened hippo, and then they found a home for him in Haller Park, a nearby animal sanctuary. When the baby was released at the park, he ran to the nearest familiar creature he saw: Mzee, a 130-year-old turtle—the shape and color of a mother hippo—resting in a corner of the enclosure. At first, Mzee did not want to be disturbed, but Owen would not give up, and soon the old turtle and the young hippo—a most unlikely pair—became inseparable friends, following each other around the enclosure and eating and swimming together.

This true story is now in book form because six-year-old Isabelle Hatkoff saw a photograph of the two animals and asked her father to help her write a book about them. Greste's photographs substantiate the validity of the almost incredible story.

Drive to understand; Relationships with others; Resilience. The story of Owen and Mzee can spark a number of areas of research for children ages five to 10. Pictures of the people who care for Owen and Mzee make Kenya seem not far away at all, and supplementary material at the end of the book provides information about Kenya, hippopotami, and Aldabra tortoises, as well as the 2004 tsunami. In addition to this intellectual approach, teachers and parents may want to explore the discussion guide based on *Owen & Mzee*, "Cultivating Resiliency: A Guide for Parents and School Personnel," at www.scholastic.com/discussionguides.

Heller, Linda. *The Castle on Hester Street.* Illustrated by Boris Kulikov. Simon & Schuster, 2007.

Julie is visiting her grandparents, listening to her grandfather tell stories about his journey from Russia to America. Grandfather's stories are fanciful, full of magic and wealth and fame. Grandmother counters with her stories of the realities: crowded ships, Ellis Island, and hard work as they raised their family.

Drive to understand; Resilience. Together, her grandparents give Julie—and the reader—a taste of Jewish immigration and the undaunted spirit that sustained the newcomers as they made their places in their new home. As a result, Julie receives the gift of her own heritage. For non-Jewish children, the book is a telling of history that incorporates painful fact, unquenchable humor, and the spirit of a people.

Hill, Elizabeth Starr. *Evan's Corner.* Illustrated by Sandra Speidel. Puffin, 1993.

Living in a two-room apartment with a family of eight, Evan wants a space of his own. His mother suggests that he choose a corner for his own place, and after doing so, Evan adds a picture, a plant, and a turtle. When his brother Adam asks why he wants a corner of his own, Evan says, "I want a chance to be lonely," and when Adam asks if he can come into Evan's corner, Evan helps him choose a corner for himself. But Evan is not entirely happy in his corner, and his mother understands why: "Maybe you need to step out now, and help somebody else."

Evan's story illustrates simply and beautifully the need to balance time alone and time with others—a lesson that gifted people must learn over and over. This book introduces the concept in terms that a preschooler can understand.

Aloneness; Introversion. Why does Evan want to have a chance to be lonely? What is good about being alone? How does he know when he has had enough time alone? What do you do when you need time alone? What do you do when you have had enough?

Drive to understand. Especially for children not familiar with cities, the illustrations in this book reveal the profusion of inner city life in details of home, streets, shops, and playgrounds. Evan finds a way to cope with it, and he is part of a stable, loving family.

Relationships with others. Why is Evan not completely happy in his corner? Will he want to go back there after he helps Adam decorate his corner? Why is it important to step out and help somebody else? How can someone who enjoys being alone also be a friend?

Hoban, Tana. *Shadows and Reflections.* HarperCollins, 1990.

This wordless, plotless book is simply a collection of photographs of buildings, animals, and people, showing them in shadow and reflection. Discuss this visual treat first with book in hand—What do we see in the picture? What do we see that is *not* in the picture?—and then again on a walk, looking for the beauty in the shadows and reflections all around us.

Developing imagination.

Hoff, Syd. *Who Will Be My Friends?* HarperCollins, 1987.

Looking for friends in his new neighborhood, Freddy finds that the adults are friendly but busy, and the children ignore him. Undiscouraged, Freddy plays alone, throwing and catching a ball in full view of the other children. When they notice how well he handles the ball, they ask him to join them.

The obvious messages in this book are that it is easier to be accepted if we have something to offer to others and that it is sometimes necessary to take the initiative in order to find friends. There are more subtle messages, however: Freddy does not force himself into the children's game; rather, he quietly lets them see what his skills are. He seems to understand their reluctance to accept him immediately without being hurt by it.

Aloneness; Relationships with others; Resilience. For a young gifted child who feels rebuffed, this book can demonstrate that if we offer ourselves and our skills to others without being presumptuous, it is easier for them to accept us. Conversation about this will require a light approach—just a suggestion by the adult and then listening for response from the child, which will guide the duration and direction of any further dialogue.

Isadora, Rachel. *Ben's Trumpet.* Live Oak Media, 1998 (paperback/cassette edition).

Ben plays an imaginary trumpet as he listens to the musicians from the Zig Zag Jazz Club. He plays for his family and himself until other boys tease him for having no trumpet. The trumpeter for the Jazz Club sees that Ben has stopped imagining himself playing and invites him to the Club, where he begins teaching him to play. Stunning black and white illustrations capture the art-deco style of the '20s, and the pages seem to vibrate with the music.

The intensity of his desire to be a musician sets Ben apart. Alone and different, he is vulnerable to the taunts of other children, especially when he allows his imagination to take over. But it is just this that catches the attention of a potential mentor—something that, in real life, may make all the difference.

Creativity; Differentness; Intensity; Resilience. Does the child know people like Ben (adults or children) who have interests so strong that they seem different from most people? If not, can you help the child meet such people? Point out that those who succeed in difficult fields such as music are often as dedicated as Ben. The difference is positive, although it is not always viewed that way by children.

Johnson, D. B. *Henry Hikes to Fitchburg.* Sandpiper, 2006.

Henry and his friend decide one summer day to go to Fitchburg to see the country, each in his own way. Henry will walk the 30 miles, and his friend will work until he earns enough money for the train ride. While Henry wades a river, gathers flowers to press in his old music book, and finds a bird's nest, his friend moves the bookcases in Mr. Emerson's study (that is Ralph Waldo Emerson, of course, though it is not spelled out in the book), sweeps out the post office, and cleans Mrs. Thoreau's chicken coop. At last he has earned enough, and he rushes for the train, the requisite 90 cents in hand, to arrive in Fitchburg in time for sunset. Henry arrives by moonlight, acknowledging with a smile that the train was faster and explaining that he stopped for blackberries, which he offers to his friend.

This gentle introduction to Henry David Thoreau and his ideas is based on *Walden*, in which Henry imagines a conversation outlining two ways to go to Fitchburg and explaining why he prefers his own. In vibrant illustrations, we see Henry savoring his plan and the friend enjoying his, with the reader left to make a choice—but it is clear that Henry has had the more adventurous day.

Differentness. The real-life Henry was different all of his life, apparently contentedly so. In this story, his friend follows the more usual method of travel, while Henry's choice is consistent with his wish to spend as much time as possible doing things that interest him. This lovely book may help a parent or teacher affirm a child who is concerned about having ideas that are different from the norm.

Relationships with others. Although Henry and his friend have very different approaches to life, they respect each other's choices and remain friends. In particular, it is helpful to note that Henry, the different one, is comfortable both with his own unusual path and with his conventional friend.

Joosse, Barbara M. *Papa, Do You Love Me?* Illustrated by Barbara Lavallee. Chronicle, 2005.

A Maasai boy asks his father the perennial question, and his father answers in terms inspired by the culture of the Serengeti. If the boy is hot, they will rest in the shade of a Greenheart tree. If the boy is thirsty, his father will teach him to find water in the ground. If the boy should fall asleep while guarding the animals, and if his birthright cow were killed?—then his father would be angry, but he would still love him.

In addition to the example of unconditional paternal love, this book offers an introduction to the animals, the customs, and the concerns of those living a traditional life in Kenya and Tanzania. A detailed glossary at the end of the book gives more information—explaining, for example, the role of the elders, the responsibilities of the herd boy, and the importance of the herds to the Maasai way of life. This is a companion to *Mama, Do You Love Me?* (1991), featuring an Inuit mother and daughter.

Drive to understand; Relationships with others.

Lyon, George Ella. *Who Came Down that Road?* Illustrated by Peter Catalanotto. Orchard, 1996.

A boy and his mother go for a walk along what his mother says is an "old, old, old, old road"—just a trace, really, a path that has been traveled for thousands of years. "Who came down that road?" he asks, and she answers that her great-grandparents came down that road soon after they were married. He asks again, and she goes back further, to when soldiers came down the road during the Civil War. Again he asks, and she tells him of pioneers before the soldiers, and Indians before the pioneers, and then back to the buffalo who came to the salt lick, and the mastodons, and then to the fish in the sea that covered this place and left the salt lick. Still the boy questions, until finally his mother speaks of "the mystery of the making place." As the text retreats in time, the illustrations become more dreamlike, with superimposed figures. On the last pages, as mother and son walk on, wondering, their footprints emerge from the crowded tracks of all who have gone before.

Developing imagination. George Ella Lyon lives near the buffalo trace that inspired this book. Other places, too, can inspire discussions like the one she imagines. Who lived by this lake? Who floated down this river? Who stood here, where we are, and looked up at the same stars?

Drive to understand. For older children in this age group, this book evokes a sense of history and our connectedness to it. It could easily lead to a timeline or to more books about any one of the travelers who came down the road.

Martin, Bill, & John Archambault. *Knots on a Counting Rope*. Illustrated by Ted Rand. Henry Holt, 1997.

Sitting with his grandfather in the glow of a campfire, an Indian boy asks the old man to tell him the story again—to "Tell me who I am." Grandfather wants Boy to learn to tell the story by himself, and speaking in turns, they trace the history of Boy's birth—he was a frail infant, born blind—and his learning to "cross the dark mountains"—a metaphor for when we feel afraid to do what we have to do. Boy learns to ride a horse, even to race his horse by counting the gallops and feeling the turns. As they finish the story, Grandfather ties another knot in the counting rope, marking Boy's growing confidence as he faces the challenge of blindness and of his Grandfather's aging. By the time his Grandfather dies, Boy will know with certainty who he is, what he can do, and that he will not be alone in crossing the dark mountains.

Identity. While few children have a story as dramatic as Boy's, this book can remind parents that every child needs to know that she is special, nurtured, and growing strong, as Boy learns from his Grandfather's story. Parents can create a personal story for their own child that will build her sense of identity. "Crossing the dark mountains" can become a useful metaphor in family communication.

Differentness; Resilience. His blindness makes Boy different, but with his Grandfather's encouragement, he faces the challenge without bitterness. He does not win the race, but his family is so proud of him for riding "like the wind" that winning does not matter. What is important is how well he handles his difference.

Martin, Jacqueline Briggs. *Snowflake Bentley*. Illustrated by Mary Azarian. Houghton Mifflin, 1998.

We have heard that no two snowflakes are alike, but how do we know that? Because a Vermont farm boy born in 1865 loved snow so much that he spent a lifetime studying it. Although practical Vermont farmers said that snow is as common as dirt and not worth studying, Wilson Bentley thought that snowflakes were beautiful, and he learned to photograph them, eventually developing a technique of microphotography that showed the world the intricate and endlessly variable design of snowflakes. His book, *Snow Crystals*, first published when he was 66 and still in print, is even now the beginning point for those who want to learn about snow crystals.

Drive to understand. Wilson Bentley demonstrates the drive to understand—he developed his own system for learning what he wanted to know. When you want to learn about something, how do you begin?

Intensity. Some people, like Wilson, care so much about a certain idea that they think about it all the time. Are you like Wilson? What ideas or topics have interested you so much that you wanted to learn everything about them?

Mora, Pat. *Tomas and the Library Lady.* Illustrated by Raul Colon. Dragonfly, 2000.

Not a full biography but a true and significant incident in the life of a real person, this is a story from the childhood of Tomas Rivera, who was born in Texas to a migrant family in 1935 and died in 1984 the chancellor of the University of California at Riverside. It begins with the family's annual drive through the summer heat to Iowa to pick corn. In Iowa, Tomas listens to his grandfather tell stories, and with Papa Grande's encouragement, he walks downtown to the library to find more stories. Noticing his reluctance to enter, a librarian kindly offers him a drink and brings him books. Tomas spends all day reading, and when the library closes, the library lady lets him take books home, checked out on her own card. All summer, Tomas goes to the library whenever he can, reading his library books to his family in English and teaching the library lady a few words of Spanish. At the end of the summer, Tomas teaches her a sad word: *adios.* He gives her a loaf of *pan dulce*, sweet bread, from his mother, and in the car on the way back to Texas, he reads his new book, a gift from the library lady.

Developing imagination. Imaginative readers can identify with Tomas's ability to see a dinosaur and to feel the warm neck as he holds on for a ride—to lose himself in books until the library lady lets him know that the library is closing.

Drive to understand. Although it skims over the difficulty and poverty of migrant living, this book introduces the concept to young readers, while offering an example of a real boy who had a very strong drive to learn and understand. For children who take easy access to plentiful books for granted, Tomas's story adds a new and valuable perspective.

Olsen, Susan Ulrich. *Just Not Quite Right.* Illustrated by Margaret Kjeldgaard. Mindset Press, 2000.

Despite the efforts of his loving parents, Elmer Eagle has a problem with flying—or rather, with landing. Something is just not quite right, and when his parents realize that Elmer does not see well, they mobilize their community of friends to prepare a landing field that Elmer will be able to discern.

Written by a special education teacher and beautifully illustrated, this book can be useful in many settings—for those with special needs, for the gifted, for anyone who feels different, for each of us when we do not fit in for one reason or another. The solution that Elmer's parents found—loving care and rallying the community— like the problem, is universal.

Differentness; Resilience; Using ability.

Parr, Todd. *It's Okay to Be Different.* Little Brown, 2004.

With bright colors and simple human and animal figures outlined in firm black lines, Parr suggests many ways in which it is okay to be different. He includes matters of appearance (it's okay to have a different nose, like the elephant in the picture), of disability (it's okay to have wheels, like the boy in the wheelchair), and so on. It's okay to have different moms, to be proud of yourself, to do something nice for someone, to get mad. He does not say that it's okay to learn fast, or to be interested in topics that do not interest others, or to work especially hard to do something well, but these ideas could easily be added.

Differentness; Identity; Using ability.

Pennypacker, Sara. *Clementine*. Illustrated by Marla Frazee. Hyperion, 2006.

Third grader Clementine is in the gifted program for math, but she also exhibits other traits of gifted children, such as a high level of creativity and physical activity, plus considerable verbal ability and a talent for getting into trouble for reasons that make perfect sense. In the week she describes in the book, she cuts off her friend's hair while trying to help, cuts off her own hair in sympathy, and spends an unusual amount of time in the principal's office—even for Clementine. Her warm heart and her real desire to know what is the right thing to do carry her through.

This episodic novel is an ideal early chapter book for children who can see some of themselves in Clementine. Reminding readers of Beverly Cleary's Ramona (see *Ramona the Brave*, above), this, too, is the beginning of a series, with *The Talented Clementine* (2007) and *Clementine's Letter* (2008) continuing the story of Clementine's adventures and mishaps.

Creativity. How does Clementine's creative thinking get her into trouble—and how does it help to solve problems? Do you have abilities that can be either helpful or a problem? How can you determine which way it goes?

Relationships with others. What can you learn about getting along with others from Clementine's friendship with Margaret?

Resilience. When Clementine thinks she is really in trouble, what is her solution? Do you think it was a good response?

Portis, Antoinette. *Not a Stick*. HarperCollins, 2008.

A pig, shown in spare line drawings, carries a stick while a disembodied voice, first admonishing him to be careful with the stick, asks a series of questions regarding what he is doing with the stick. Each time the pig responds, with increasing impatience and vehemence, "It's not a stick!" while the picture shows what he imagines it to be—such as a horse he imagines that he is riding or a paintbrush pointing toward Van Gogh's *Starry Night*. The adult continues to label it a stick, and finally the pig arrives at a statement of what it is instead of a stick: he announces definitively and triumphantly, "It's my Not-a-Stick!"

This book follows the author's *Not a Box* (2006), featuring a rabbit and an empty cardboard box. Both books celebrate the imagination of a child playing with a simple, makeshift toy, and both could lead to limitless experimentation inspired by the rabbit and the pig.

Creativity; Developing imagination.

Rohmann, Eric. *The Cinder-Eyed Cats.* Dragonfly, 2001.

This story, told in rhyme, is of a boy who sails through the sky to a tropical island where five sleek cats greet him. Boy and cats are joined in a dream-like sequence by ocean creatures, dancing underwater in the moonlight and around a campfire. With the dawn, boy and cats are alone on the beach; the boy sails off and the cats slumber, waiting for the moon to come around again. While the poem provides the framework, it is overwhelmed by clear and detailed illustrations of benevolent cats—tigers, really—and colorful sea creatures of all kinds—a visual feast swirling through the tropical day and the mysterious night.

Creativity. For the imaginative child, this book offers much to ponder and to enhance with movement or music.

Developing imagination. For the more literal-minded child, the story issues an invitation to fantasy, while the elegant cinder-eyed cats and the brilliant and varied creatures of the deep offer an opportunity to enjoy beauty for its own sake.

Rumford, James. *Sequoyah: The Cherokee Man Who Gave His People Writing.* Translated into Cherokee by Anna Sixkiller Huckaby. Houghton Mifflin, 2004.

A family visits the redwoods of California, and the 10-year-old boy asks about the Giant Sequoia trees: Where did the name come from? His father tells him the true story about the Cherokee Indian man who lived "when the United States was new." Sequoyah was a crippled metalworker who did not know how to read—the Cherokee language had no writing system—but he did not want his people or their voices to disappear. So when he was about 50 years old, he decided to invent writing for the Cherokee people. Many believed that he could not do it; some feared that his symbols were evil. They burned his cabin down, destroying the symbols that he had created, but Sequoyah began again, with a better idea. When his six-year-old daughter learned to read Cherokee, others quickly learned to read it, too.

The beautiful written Cherokee language, which is still in use, is demonstrated on every page in Huckaby's translation. The final pages include a chart of the Cherokee syllabary (not an alphabet, but a symbol for each syllable in the spoken language), a history of the naming of the Giant Sequoia trees, and a few facts of Sequoyah's life.

Creativity. After seeing how many different symbols Sequoyah created, young readers may want to try making their own writing system—something very few people in human history have accomplished.

Drive to understand. Children in this age group may not have thought much about how a language is constructed—or about how important their own language is to any group of people. Sequoyah was born in Tennessee and died in Oklahoma—the forced migration of the Cherokee people, which they called the Trail of Tears, took place during his lifetime, but it is not mentioned in this book.

Say, Allen. *Kamishibai Man.* Houghton Mifflin, 2005.

Feeling nostalgic for his old craft, the long-retired kamishibai (paper theater) man decides to go back to the neighborhood where he used to entertain the children, telling stories illustrated by pictures carried in a box theater on the back of his bicycle. He finds the neighborhood changed, the trees cut down for more buildings, and he reminisces about the children who would gather and the stories he would tell. But then television came along, and the children stopped coming. Suddenly he realizes that a crowd of adults is gathered now—the grown children are delighted to see him again. That night when he returns home, his wife tells him that she has been watching his story on the evening news.

Allen Say remembers kamishibai from his childhood in Japan. In a foreword, he describes how the kamishibai man worked; in an afterword, a scholar of Japanese folklore reviews the place of kamishibai in

Japanese culture. This is a beautiful book with a fascinating story to tell.

Creativity; Developing imagination; Drive to understand.

Schultz, Robert A. & James R. Delisle. *Smart Talk*. Illustrated by Tyler Page. Free Spirit, 2006.

Smart Talk is written for, about, and even (mostly) by gifted children from four to 12 years old. On their website, www.giftedspeak.com, the authors surveyed gifted children around the world, asking a range of questions in seven categories, including Fitting In, Expectations, School, and Home. They have published "some of the most common answers, as well as some of the most interesting and funny ones." The responses are insightful and revealing and should prove helpful to young readers who will surely find someone out there who answers as they would have. (Responders are identified only by gender, age, and state of residence.) In addition, there are brief biographies called "A Kid Like You" interspersed among the chapters. Sections in each chapter called "Reflection/Connection" offer suggestions for further thought and action.

Achievement; Aloneness; Identity; Intensity; Relationships with others; Using ability. This book is listed under each grade level represented in this chapter, but its application will vary according to age. It may be most useful as a discussion starter, in a group or after a child has read it alone. It can be read straight through or skimmed once and then referred to whenever appropriate. Parents and teachers may help children follow through on ideas offered under "Reflection/Connection." However it is used, this book promises greater self-understanding for gifted children and offers a valuable resource for adults working with them. Begin by looking through *Smart Talk* for comments made by younger children with experiences close to those of students in kindergarten through second grade.

Sendak, Maurice. *Outside Over There*. HarperCollins, 1989.

A fantasy told with pictures as much as with words, this is the story of Ida, who rescues her baby sister from the goblins—who turn out to be babies, too. Ida is intuitive, resolute, and brave, a girl of about six who knows her own mind and does what needs to be done. The illustrations are full of details to be pored over and discussed.

Developing imagination. With its fairy-tale quality, this book is recommended for its potential to stir the child's imagination, both visually and verbally.

Identity. The impact of this book is emotional rather than intellectual. The strengths in Ida's character may speak for themselves, but adults might wish to reinforce the child's awareness by mentioning what is admirable about Ida, how her baby sister and father feel about her, and why. Perhaps a time can be recalled when the child showed some of Ida's qualities.

Shulevitz, Uri. *How I Learned Geography.* Farrar, Straus, & Giroux, 2008.

The author remembers when war came and he fled with his family to another country far to the east, leaving everything behind. There, they lived in a small, bleak space with little food. His father went to the bazaar to buy bread but came home instead with a map. The boy went to bed hungry and angry, but the next day, his father hung the map of the world on the wall, bringing color into the room and giving the boy a source of endless learning and wonder. Bread would have fed his body for a day, but the map nourished his imagination for all the time they lived there.

In a new genre, memoir as picture book, Shulevitz describes in words and pictures a formative experience from his childhood. The pictures, especially of his imagined flights to other lands, are beautifully fanciful; this is a 2009 Caldecott Honor Book. An author's note adds a brief history of his family's experience during World War II and more pictures, demonstrating the deep impact that the map had on him.

Developing imagination. An award-winning writer and illustrator of children's books, Shulevitz reveals in simple, moving words and pictures an early influence on the development of his own prolific imagination.

Drive to understand. This book could be used for informal discussion or to introduce a study of maps and geography, for K-2 students or older ones.

Steig, William. *Sylvester and the Magic Pebble*. Simon & Schuster, 2005.

This is the much-loved story of how Sylvester the donkey finds a magic pebble and then, frightened by a lion, wishes in panic to be a rock. And he is. His parents and all of the creatures of Oatsdale search long and hard for Sylvester, but no one recognizes that the rock is the object of their search. Winter comes, and Sylvester falls into a long, hopeless sleep, while at home, his parents grieve. In the spring, determined to cheer themselves up, they picnic at the very spot where the magic pebble lies on the ground next to the rock that is Sylvester. His father admires the pebble and places it on the rock. Sylvester wishes to be himself again—and instantly, he is.

Told with simple dignity and moving dialogue, the story is memorable for the purity of the emotional experience of parents who lose a beloved child—softened by the fact that we know that Sylvester is alive and unharmed. We are deeply concerned about how he will become a donkey again, but not frightened. Young children can find security in seeing how much parents love their children without being asked to deal directly with the concept of death. And should anyone miss it, the ending states the moral. Sylvester's family may want to use the magic pebble for a wish someday, but not now. Reunited in their home, the three hug each other—"What more could they wish for? They all had all that they wanted."

Identity. A child who understands that his parents, too, would search diligently for him and would grieve like Sylvester's parents if he were Sylvester will gain awareness of his own importance as a valued member of his family.

Sensitivity. Readers cannot fail to be touched and moved by the worry and love that shine through this story. An overly intellectual child may gain a measure of softness and awareness of emotions through a story such as this one, while a sensitive child may find it a vehicle for feelings that otherwise remain felt but unexpressed.

Steinberg, Laya. *All Around Me I See*. Illustrated by Cris Arbo. Dawn, 2005.

After a rain, a family goes on a nature hike to the rhythm of a poem full of metaphors. The young girl sees the rain as a drink for the earth, a rock as an island for a frog, a leaf as a boat for a beetle, a branch as an owl's point of view...and then her point of view changes as her imagination takes her high above the earth and finally back to her parents' campsite: "The earth is a home for me." The illustrations are realistic; it is the girl's imagination that soars.

Developing imagination; Sensitivity.

Viorst, Judith. *Alexander and the Terrible, Horrible, No Good, Very Bad Day*. Illustrated by Ray Cruz. Aladdin, 1987.

The youngest of three brothers, Alexander goes through a day that includes finding nothing in his cereal box (his brothers find treasures in theirs), having the only cavity when they go to the dentist, and learning that the store has sold the last sneakers of the color he wants. The day goes from bad to worse, and the only solution seems to be to move to Australia. But, says his mother, some days are like that—even in Australia.

Despite Alexander's undeniably awful day, when he rolls over to go to sleep, the reader knows that tomorrow will be better. Some days are like that, indeed, and even young children can learn that when they have a day like Alexander's, it does not mean that something is wrong with them.

Relationships with others; Resilience. Parents can talk about their own bad days. Recognizing the phenomenon and learning that tomorrow probably *will* be better is a step toward maturity.

Viorst, Judith. *Rosie and Michael*. Illustrated by Lorna Tomei. Aladdin, 1998.

Michael tells why Rosie is his friend, and Rosie, in parallel terms, tells why Michael is hers. There is no plot here, but a lot of understanding of what friendship is: tolerating imperfection, plotting (and accepting) friendly pranks, sharing fears and sorrows, keeping secrets, forgiving mistakes, and tolerating idiosyncrasies.

For a gifted child who feels rebuffed and is puzzled about how to be a friend, discussion could grow out of each page of this book. What exactly are Rosie and Michael doing for each other here? The analytical power of intellectually gifted youngsters should help them to generalize, or to follow adult generalizations, from the situations that Viorst presents.

Relationships with others. Do you know any friends who treat each other this way? Does anyone do this for you? When did you last do this for someone else? Can you plan to do this for someone tomorrow? Tell me how it turns out.

Whelan, Gloria. *Hannah.* Illustrated by Leslie Bowman. Random, 1993.

Hannah is nine in 1887 and is very excited when the new teacher comes to board at her family's farmhouse in northern Michigan. Hannah has never gone to school—she is blind, and her mother has kept her at home, saying there is no point in sending "poor Hannah" to school. Miss Robbin is the first person to show Hannah around the farm, encouraging her to touch, feel, and smell the farmyard animals and the flowers growing in the northern woods. When Miss Robbin asks if Hannah can go to school, her mother reluctantly assents.

The first day does not go well; Carl, the oldest boy in school, teases her and trips her, and she gets lost trying to find her way home alone. Hannah is ready to give up, but Miss Robbin and her father encourage her. The teacher creates an abacus so that Hannah can learn arithmetic, and she tells Hannah's parents about the new Braille system that enables the blind to read and write. Hannah is eager, but the Braille device costs five dollars—too much for her parents to spend. Then comes the potato harvest, with a prize for the person who gathers the most potatoes. The contrite Carl, who has won the prize for the last two years, has an idea that surprises Hannah—while she has gathered potatoes, enjoying for the first time the pleasure of doing what everyone else is doing, others have helped fill her basket over and over. Hannah wins the prize; soon she will be able to write about it.

With an accurate historical sense for her northern Michigan setting, Whelan has written a moving story that young readers can enjoy independently. Hannah's keen observation of life around her through careful listening enhances the reader's perception of the mental life of a person who does not see.

Differentness. How is Hannah made to feel different from others? How is she made to feel that she is like others? In what ways have you helped someone who is different feel comfortable in a group? In what other ways could you do so?

Relationships with others. Sometimes people do not say exactly what they mean. Hannah's mother is an example of this. What are all of the reasons you can think of that Hannah's mother does not want her to go to school? Do you know of someone who sounds gruffer than he or she actually is? Why did Carl act as he did, both on Hannah's first day of school and at the potato harvest? What does Hannah do that helps people like her?

Resilience. How was Hannah able to keep herself so strong-minded and able to overcome obstacles?

Sensitivity. What exactly happens at school that causes Hannah to try to go home alone? How could she have reacted differently?

Wiesner, David. *Free Fall.* HarperCollins, 2008.

The plot line is scant in this wordless picture book. A boy merely sleeps and dreams, waking in the morning to his familiar room. The book's strength is in the surreal illustrations, which for adults call up a wealth of associations: *Alice in Wonderland, Gulliver's Travels,* and the art of Dali.

The jacket carries a brief poem describing a dream—an optional text which can be used to follow the pictures, which do progress from one to another in a dreamlike way. It is a journey of strange but familiar images, with a safe return. *Free Fall* is a Caldecott Honor Book for 1989.

Developing imagination. A child can follow the poem or choose to make more (or less) of the pictures, according to her experience and imagination.

Wood, Douglas. *Old Turtle*. Illustrated by Cheng-Khee Chee. Scholastic, 2007.

In the early days, when animals and fish and stones and mountains and stars could all speak and understand one another, an argument began as each of the beings of the world described God in terms familiar to themselves but foreign to the others: "'God is gentle,' chirped the robin. 'He is powerful,' growled the bear." The argument grew louder until Old Turtle, who seldom spoke, called for silence. Old Turtle said that God is all that the others had said, and more. And, said Old Turtle, a new creature is coming who will be a reminder of all that God is. But when the people came, they, too, began to argue. They hurt one another, and they hurt the earth. Then one day, another voice called for silence, and the mountain, the ocean, the stone all spoke of seeing God not only in themselves, but in one another as well. Finally, the people heard, and they, too, learned to see God in the beauty of the earth and in each other.

Drive to understand; Sensitivity. On one level, Old Turtle is about views of God drawn from nature—a good choice for parents who want their children to have a sense of the sacred without doctrinal overtones. But on another level, it is not about God so much as it is about the fact that people have, and regrettably argue about, differing *views* of God. Full of metaphors for God, the story is a metaphor in itself. The storyline is told simply enough for a kindergarten child to follow, yet the concepts will challenge older children as well. The illustrations are lush watercolors with an abstraction that well suits the subject.

One of the characteristics of gifted children is an early interest in God, with questions that go beyond the stories introduced in religious training. Regardless of a family's religious perspective, this is a beautiful book to develop an understanding of the differences and potential similarities in expressions of religious insight.

Yolen, Jane. *Owl Moon*. Illustrated by John Schoenherr. Philomel, 2007.

On a cold, moonlit, winter night, a little girl and her father go owling. Leaving the warmth of the farmhouse, they cross snowy fields and enter the dark woods—silently, for when you go owling, you must be quiet. In a clearing, they stop, and Pa calls to the owl. At last the owl answers, swooping overhead through the tall trees. Pa's flashlight beam catches the owl as it settles onto a tree branch above them, and for long minutes, they look into its eyes. Then it rises and glides away.

Developing imagination. Yolen's prose is very close to poetry, and Schoenherr's illustrations give us moonlight on the snowy fields and woods of his own farm. Both words and pictures reflect the sense of awe that are part of the unique experience of quiet and respectful eye contact with a wild creature. A three-year-old who has learned quiet gentleness can feel this, but *Owl Moon* is appropriate for older children, too.

Upper Elementary: Grades 3-5

Alexander, Lloyd. *The First Two Lives of Lukas-Kasha*. Puffin, 1998.

Lukas is a vagabond and a scamp in an unspecified town in 15th-century Persia. A wandering magician's trick transports him to Abadan, where he is immediately greeted as king. It soon becomes obvious that he is only a puppet king, and Lukas finds himself caught up in palace politics and then in the imminent war with the neighboring country of Bishangar. Refusing to use bloodshed to solve problems, Lukas manages to bring peace, growing up considerably in the process.

This is a light and lively story, with the gradual maturing of Lukas handled so deftly that it is quite natural and believable that a vagabond could act like a king. Nur-Johan, the Bishangar captive who turns out to be Queen, presents a contrast to Lukas in her youthful purpose and determination, yet Lukas can teach her how to recognize when using one's wits is more effective than her direct and literal approach might be.

Identity. Point out places in the story when you knew Lukas was growing up. Describe Lukas and Nur-Johan and how their backgrounds determine their character and behavior. How did each change? Lukas says of his having been sent to Abadan, "I'll have to make my own sense" of the situation. That's a profound statement.

Are there situations in your life that are hard for you to explain or understand? Have you made your own sense of them? Could you? How does Lukas do it?

Moral concerns. How does Lukas confront the moral dilemma of war? In what other situations—international or domestic—would his approach work, and how?

Avi. *The Fighting Ground.* HarperCollins, 1994.

Jonathan is 13, tilling the fields with his father near Trenton, New Jersey, when the bell from the tavern a mile and a half distant sounds an alarm. It's April 3, 1778; his father is recovering from a war wound, and Jonathan is sent to learn the news—but then, both parents order, he is to return home immediately. Learning that 15 Hessians are marching from Pennington, Jonathan, eager to fight, disregards his parents' directive and joins the hastily-gathered band of colonists under the command of a zealous and not entirely trusted corporal. All is confusion when they meet the enemy on the road; Jonathan flees and is captured by three Hessians. Neither Jonathan nor they know who won the battle, and although they speak only German (translated in the back of the book), making verbal communication impossible, Jonathan begins to feel a degree of comfort with them.

They find an abandoned farmhouse for shelter, and when Jonathan enters a shed for a bucket to milk the cow, he discovers a young child, a boy who will not speak to Jonathan but who, when Jonathan asks "Mama?" points to where his parents lie shot. In the night, as the Hessians sleep, Jonathan escapes with the boy and runs through darkness, stumbling upon the remnants of the colonial band. A Frenchman in the group speaks to the child, who in a torrent of French tells of his parents' deaths and shrinks from the Corporal, who wants to return to the house to kill the Hessians. The Corporal insists that Jonathan lead the way, but it becomes clear that the Corporal has been there before—it was he who killed the boy's parents because they were informers. In an agony of indecision, Jonathan switches loyalties from the Corporal to the Hessians and back, but he is finally forced at gunpoint to aid in the killing of the Hessians. He returns home just 24 hours after he left, changed forever.

The chapters in this book are titled by the time of day, highlighting the brevity of this period that changes Jonathan's life. There is a complete lack of the glory that Jonathan had expected; he experiences only fear and confusion and uncertainty as to what the colonists are doing and why. Germans, Americans, and French are all good and bad by turns—human, sympathetic characters with flaws. Avi has written a story of how war takes over, ignoring human values.

Drive to understand. Discuss the differences between what Jonathan expected and what he found. How does the reality of Jonathan's experience square with what we see of war—or any kind of violence—on television? Analyze how representatives of each nationality are admirable and despicable. What is Avi saying by depicting them in this way?

Moral concerns. How did Jonathan's view of his father change? Did any of your views change as a result of reading this book? How do the ideas in this book affect your thinking about the wars going on now?

Blumberg, Rhoda. *Shipwrecked! The True Adventures of a Japanese Boy.* HarperCollins, 2001.

Born in 1827, Manjiro was a poor fisherman trying to support his family by the time he was nine years old. When he was 14, his little fishing boat was blown out to sea by a storm, and Manjiro and four others were shipwrecked on a deserted island. Months later, they were rescued by an American whaler, but they could not go home— the isolationist policies of Japan prevented anyone who left the country from returning. On the ship, Manjiro quickly learned English and began learning seamanship and whaling. Impressed with his intelligence, the ship's captain added Manjiro to the crew, and he became the first Japanese person to visit the United States. He returned to Japan years later, defying the isolationist laws, but government officials recognized the value of his experiences and honored him as a samurai. Manjiro played an important role in helping Japan become open to other countries.

Manjiro's story is well-known in Japan but not familiar in the United States outside of Massachusetts, where he lived with Captain

Whitfield and was educated. Blumberg's carefully-researched book is her bid to change that. In the process, she covers a range of topics, including the importance of the whaling industry before oil was discovered and 19th-century Japanese and American history and culture. The book is illustrated with sketches and woodblock prints from the period, some of them by Manjiro himself.

Drive to understand. Compare the isolationism of Japan with the openness of Europe and America at the time. Japan had a long period of peace, but with very strict rules. Why did Japan have so many more rules at that time than Europe and America had? What has changed since then?

Resilience; Using ability. What innate abilities enabled Manjiro to rise from poor fisherman to samurai? Beyond natural ability, what aspects of character helped him to survive and thrive?

Brink, Carol Ryrie. *Caddie Woodlawn*. Illustrated by Trina Schart Hyman. Aladdin, 2006.

Caddie is 11 in 1865, growing up in a pioneer family in Wisconsin. A tomboy, she fords the river and runs through the fields with her brothers, while her older sister, the sedate Clara, learns more lady-like ways. From her father, Caddie learns to repair clocks and to respect the Indians who still live near the Woodlawn farm, and she risks her father's anger in a sudden decision to ride to the Indian camp to warn them of danger. She also learns from her father to value the wisdom of strong women—and to aspire to become one.

Brink's novel is a compilation of stories that the real Caddie Woodhouse told to her granddaughter, the young Carol Ryrie. Caddie is remembered and her story is loved by many grown women who saw themselves in the active, assertive girl when they were young.

Differentness; Identity; Intensity. How has Caddie's unusual childhood helped her to become a strong and good woman? What people do you know who are like Father, Mother, Cousin Annabelle, Tom, or Caddie's teacher? What are you learning from other people in your life?

Moral concerns. Caddie faces some choices in the course of this book that could lead to a discussion of decision-making. Ask what those decisions are and why Caddie chose as she did.

Byars, Betsy Cromer. *Summer of the Swans.* Illustrated by Constantinos Coconis. Puffin, 2004.

Since their parents' divorce, Sara and her older sister Wanda and younger brother Charlie have lived with Aunt Willie. Charlie has been mentally disabled since he was ill at three, and Sara is fiercely protective of him. At 14, she is also concerned about her moods, her appearance, the size of her feet, and Joe Melby, who seems to have taken Charlie's watch. Then Charlie gets lost, and in the search for him, which Joe joins, Sara develops a new perspective.

The characters are especially well drawn in this book, and Sara and Joe in particular will stand as models of empathic and caring behavior in situations in which impatience might be expected. Byars' descriptions of Charlie's thinking can help children who have been ignorant or afraid of the mentally disabled to develop a sympathetic understanding. This understanding can be generalized, with sensitive guidance, to a tolerance and valuing of all others who are not as quick as a gifted child.

Relationships with others. How do the different characters treat Charlie, positively and negatively? How did you feel about the different ways he was treated? How can we understand those who tease? How and why does Sara help Charlie? Why is she able to understand so well how he feels? Is there someone you know who needs your help? Are you the kind of person who offers help when it is needed? Why or why not?

Byrd, Robert. *Leonardo: Beautiful Dreamer.* Dutton, 2003.

This book is a lush presentation of the life of Leonardo da Vinci, who was a model of intellectual overexcitability (as described in Chapter 2). Using facts, anecdotes, and da Vinci's notebooks to convey the personality and enthusiasms of Leonardo, Byrd has provided his text with illustrations that burst with energy, reflecting the curiosity and intellectual vitality that governed his subject's life. Leonardo explored astronomy, optics, botany, hydraulics, and geology; he was also a painter, a sculptor, a mathematician, and an architect. Byrd touches on all of this. With as much to learn from the illustrations, sidebars, and end papers as from the main text, this is a book to be read and read again.

Byrd's biography of the Renaissance genius, beautifully enhanced with the author's illustrations, is a trove of information presented verbally and visually. Each page features a large highlighted section presenting the narrative of Leonardo da Vinci's life, while the margins are crowded with Byrd's versions of Leonardo's paintings and designs, as well as one or more small panels giving details of his ideas and inventions. The effect is to draw us into the mind of Leonardo, with many large ideas fighting for space—as they did in Leonardo's notebooks.

Do not be deceived by the picture book format of this book. Written for older children, it is likely to be cherished by bright, curious readers who will enjoy not just reading, but really studying all of it—including the fine print on each page. Adult readers will surely find more here than they knew; this is an excellent choice for like-minded children and adults to read together.

Drive to understand. A long timeline and bibliography at the end of the book will provide ideas for more inquiry into history, art, biography, flight, and architecture—a list as rich and varied as Leonardo's areas of investigation.

Using ability. When Leonardo was old, he doubted the worth of what he had accomplished. Think of one of his projects that failed, and then think about what he did accomplish in working on that project. See if you can apply this idea to a project of your own.

Conly, Jane Leslie. *Racso and the Rats of NIMH.* Illustrated by Leonard Lubin. HarperTrophy, 1991.

In this sequel to her father's popular book *Mrs. Frisby and the Rats of NIMH* (listed under O'Brien, below), Conly continues the story of Jenner, one of the dissenting rats from the earlier book. Jenner has left the rats to return to the city, and from there, his restless son Racso sets out to join the colony that the rats of NIMH have founded at Thom Valley. Insecure about how he will be accepted and endowed with a false sophistication from life in the city, Racso resorts to lies and boasting to win a place in the colony. The quiet competence, humility, tolerance of hard work, and cooperative spirit of the other rats gradually have an effect on Racso. As they work together to prevent a dam from flooding their valley, Racso learns how to contribute to the group effort, and eventually he becomes the hero he has wanted to be.

Racso displays the bravado that many uncertain children exhibit. Both those who are like Racso and those who are annoyed by children like him will understand how Racso feels about his own behavior. Discussion can emphasize how important the patience and understanding of others is in changing Racso.

Arrogance; Identity. Why does Racso lie, steal, and boast? What is more effective behavior when joining a new group? Why is it hard to do? What qualities in Nicodemus help Racso? Do you know someone who has those qualities? What is that person's effect on you?

Relationships with others. What situations can make anyone feel as Racso does about himself? How does this affect how people get along with others? What can help?

Dahl, Roald. *Danny the Champion of the World.* Illustrated by Quentin Blake. Puffin, 2007.

Danny's whole purpose in telling his story is to let us know that his father, without a doubt, is the most marvelous father a boy ever had. He is very convincing. Danny's mother died when he was a baby, and his father is raising him alone. They live in a gypsy wagon next to the gas station that his father owns somewhere in rural England.

Danny's early years are filled with engines and car repair, and by the age of five, he is a fine mechanic. His father tells fascinating stories and walks Danny to school every day. All of this is wonderful, but the real excitement begins when Danny is nine and wakes one night to find his father gone. He soon returns, and Danny learns that for the first time since his mother died, his father has gone to Mr. Hazell's wood to pursue an old passion: poaching pheasants. Danny is appalled, but as he learns more about the tradition, the reasons for it, and the many others who share his father's passion for it, Danny and the reader see this activity in a different light. Danny becomes

Champion of the World by contributing a new and creative idea that eventually involves the entire community. But first, he uses his precocious skill and ingenuity in a courageous night-time rescue when his father is in trouble.

Danny is exactly the sort of character that children of this age love to read about. He is living a life of freedom that many would envy, his father respects his ability to learn and teaches him grown-up, real-world skills, and his considerable creativity is appreciated by all. In addition, Dahl uses English terms that present a mild challenge for good readers, and Danny's father explains to Danny—and to the attentive reader—a number of very interesting things about engines, the natural world, and the political issues surrounding pheasant hunting. Above all, Dahl writes with an intelligent humor that will have children laughing aloud as they get the joke embedded in the narrative.

Drive to understand. Discuss the new things that you learned from this book: about life in England, gypsy wagons, hunting and fishing, etc.

Moral concerns. How do you feel about poaching pheasants from Mr. Hazell's wood? How would the same arguments for or against it apply (or not apply) to poaching wildlife in the United States?

Resilience. Who do you know in your own life who has overcome tragedy and poverty as Danny did?

DeClements, Barthe. *Nothing's Fair in Fifth Grade.* Puffin, 2008.

When Elsie Edwards joins their class, the fifth graders groan. Elsie is not just fat; she is gross. She scrounges food at lunchtime because her lunchbox contains only broth, a carrot, and a pear. Then lunch money begins disappearing from desktops, and they realize that Elsie steals money to buy candy. But as Jenifer and her friends gradually get to know Elsie better and learn that her need to eat stems from problems at home, they see past her appearance to a real person with feelings that they can relate to. Jenifer resents Elsie's A's in math, until Elsie helps her understand fractions and Jenifer realizes that Elsie is an excellent teacher. A scary hitchhiking incident brings all of the friends together, and finally they join in an effort to help Elsie get through the rest of the school year without getting into trouble so that she can come back next year.

A former school counselor who has now published several books for children and young adults, DeClements has a firm knowledge of upper elementary children and creates believable characters of all ages. This book was originally published in 1981; some of the references may be outdated, but the theme is timeless.

Differentness. In what ways is Elsie different from others in the class? In what ways is each of the students different from his or her friends? What things do all of them have in common?

Identity. Sometimes it is easy to discount the value of a person who is overweight. What good qualities does Elsie have that Jenifer and her friends would not know about if they had not made the effort to get to know her better? How might this change your assumptions about anyone you know?

Relationships with others. Jenifer and her friends would be called mean from the point of view of a new child in their class. What causes them to behave this way at first? What causes them to change their minds about Elsie? What can you learn from this to apply to a situation in your life?

Resilience. What is there to admire in the way Elsie handles the situation?

DiCamillo, Kate. *Because of Winn-Dixie.* Candlewick, 2000.

Ten-year-old Opal Buloni rescues the dog that has somehow invaded and partially destroyed the produce department of the Winn-Dixie store in Naomi, Florida. Opal needs a friend as much as the dog does, because she has just moved to Naomi with her father, the preacher, and because she is thinking about her mother, who left when Opal was three. To her surprise, her father agrees that Winn-Dixie can stay, and from then on, the dog—who makes friends easily—accompanies Opal wherever she goes. That summer, Opal and Winn-Dixie meet and befriend Miss Franny, the librarian; Gloria Dump, an old woman called a witch by local boys; Otis, who hires her to work at the pet shop so she can pay for a collar and leash for Winn-Dixie; and eventually, some children her age. Hearing their stories, Opal begins to understand that everyone carries sorrow. The story ends with a party in which all of these lonely people, each with a story, come together—and although much of the credit goes to Opal, there is a sense in which it is all because of Winn-Dixie.

With Winn-Dixie as a catalyst, her father begins telling Opal about her mother. We understand from his story that her mother will not return, and eventually Opal's father confirms that he knows this, too; this helps Opal begin to grow toward acceptance. The author provides a creative metaphor in Miss Franny's gift of lozenges from her family's defunct candy company, which taste sweet but with a touch of sadness that can be recognized by those who have known sorrow. Far from just another tale of a winsome dog, Opal's story of Winn-Dixie is rich with humor, sadness, love, and understanding.

Relationships with others; Resilience. Opal makes friends easily with people older and younger than she is, but she has more difficulty with those her own age. When and how do *people*—not just Winn-Dixie—help her to make friends? What guidelines for making friends are suggested in this book? Do you agree with them? How would you change them? What would you add?

Sensitivity. What does Opal say or do that tells you how sensitive she is—how aware she is of the feelings and needs of other people?

Erdrich, Louise. *The Birchbark House*. Hyperion, 2002.

Erdrich's first novel for young people opens with a vignette; a group of voyageurs finds a baby girl, the sole survivor of the smallpox that has killed her Ojibwa family, alone on an island in Lake Superior. Fearing that she, too, is sick, the men paddle away, but one of them tells his wife of their discovery. The fearless Old Tallow rescues the infant and brings her back to her home island, where she nurses the baby to health and gives her to a family to raise. The story follows Omakayas (Oh-MAH-kay-ahs) and her family through the year that she is seven.

Omakayas admires her older sister, is annoyed by her younger brother, and deeply loves her baby brother, Neewo. Helping her mother and grandmother with the gardening, rice gathering, food preservation, and making of clothes from animal skins, she also realizes that she has a special relationship with wild creatures, especially with Andeg, her pet crow. Her grandmother watches for further signs that Omakayas will be a healer. This one eventful year includes the winter of 1847, when another smallpox epidemic changes their lives. Omakayas learns much about death as well as life; especially after she learns the truth about her origins from Old Tallow, she begins to understand her unique powers.

A member of the Turtle Mountain Band of Ojibwa, Erdrich researched the history of her own family and found ancestors who lived on Madeline Island in Lake Superior, the island in the story. Her descriptions of daily life—the tasks and the stories—are woven into the storyline, and Ojibwa words are seamlessly included, with a glossary for more detail. Her illustrations enliven and expand the story: those who have gathered stones on the shores of the largest Great Lake will immediately see that the six small stones in one illustration are not generic; they are clearly Lake Superior beach stones. But beyond the authenticity, Erdrich has created in Omakayas a compelling character—a strong, loving, intuitive girl with an intensity and love of life. We want to know more about her, and we look forward to following Omakayas and her family in subsequent books in this projected series. For young readers who love Laura Ingalls Wilder's stories of American pioneer life, Erdrich's series illuminates the same period in history through the eyes of an Ojibwa girl.

Drive to understand. There is so much information embedded in the story that this book can easily be used to enhance curricula. Questions might be based on contrasting life on this Lake Superior island with life in Boston in 1847, or on learning more about the mission schools, the treaties that Fishtail wants to be able to read, and methods of cooking—parents and teachers can generate many ideas to help children learn more about American Indian life in the 19th century. See also Marrin's *Sitting Bull and His World* in the Middle School listing.

Identity. How does the combination of what Omakayas learns from her grandmother and what she learns from Old Tallow help her understand herself? How does this strengthen her sense of who she is—her identity? She is only seven at the time of this story—why does she seem so mature?

Intensity. Consider all the ways in which Omakayas shows her determination and love for what is important to her—for example, holding Neewo so long when he is sick. What is it in your life that you care so much about? How do you know?

Relationships with others. Think about the ways in which Old Tallow is both tough and tender. How is it hard for her to live with her toughness, and how does it help others? Who do you know who appears to be tough but might have some tenderness, too?

Erdrich, Louise. *The Game of Silence.* HarperCollins, 2006.

The sequel to *The Birchbark House* opens in the summer of 1850, with Omakayas watching from shore as six canoes struggle to reach her beautiful Lake Superior Island. They carry starving refugees— friends and relatives who have been forced from their homes by Lakota and Dakota people. The newcomers bring disturbing news: the president of the whites has declared that the Ojibwe must leave their homes and move west. In the year that follows, as they await confirmation of this order, adults teach the children the game of silence—the winner is the child who can be silent the longest. Omakayas continues to learn from her grandmother, who teaches her about medicines and healing; she also has portentous dreams. On her spirit quest, her dream prepares her for the unbearable pain of leaving her beloved home, giving her hope for the future. When finally the family must pack what they can in canoes and paddle west over the big water, and then up a river in a new land, the game of silence becomes a matter of life and death.

As Europeans and Americans moved west across the continent, they pushed American Indians ahead of them, forcing eastern woodland groups into the Great Plains. People whose survival depended on their familiarity with their environment were forced to leave what they knew, inevitably encroaching on the land of others who understandably did not welcome them. In this second book in her series, Erdrich establishes with heartbreaking clarity the deep knowledge and inexpressible love of the Ojibwe for the beautiful land and waters that sustained them. *The Game of Silence* is a winner of the Scott Odell Award for Historical Fiction. It is followed by the next in the series, *The Porcupine Year* (2008).

Drive to understand. Learn more about the movements of American Indians as the United States government changed its policies, about the use of native plants for food and medicine, and about the skills involved in making maple syrup and storing food for the winter. For example, what local foods are available in the winter in the northern part of the United States?

Relationships with others. Living in a small group requires accepting difficult behaviors in others. How did Omakayas accomplish this with Pinch? With Two Strike? What examples of this do you see around you?

Fitzhugh, Louise. *Harriet the Spy.* Yearling, 2001.

Harriet spends her after-school time spying on neighbors. She keeps a notebook filled with comments, not always flattering, on them and on her classmates. Shortly after Harriet's nurse, Ole Golly, leaves the family to get married, the other sixth graders discover Harriet's notebook and form a plan to get revenge. The loss of Ole Golly and her two best friends causes Harriet to respond with the sturdy independence that got her into trouble in the first place. Her parents and teachers, though, eventually help her use her keen powers of observation and her writing ability in positive ways. Gradually, Harriet softens enough to apologize, and her friends return.

Harriet is a prickly person who comes to realize at the end of the book that she is intelligent. She has never known what to do with her precocious insights and has used her ability in negative ways. This problem is really only pointed out, not solved, in this book.

Arrogance; Relationships with others. Why is Harriet's notebook so important to her? Why does she write so many stinging comments? How does her intelligence get her into trouble? How can it help her get out of it? If you were writing a sequel to this book, what would you have Harriet do to make and keep friends but still be herself? When is it all right not to be popular?

Differentness; Identity; Using ability. Harriet has been using her special ability in ways that have given other people good reason to dislike her. Do you know anyone who does this? Why do people behave that way? What are the disadvantages of doing so? What do people who act like this need from others to help them change? What can they do for themselves to change? What will enable Harriet to use her ability more positively?

Fleischman, Paul. *The Half-a-Moon Inn.* Illustrated by Kathy Jacobi. HarperCollins, 1991.

In a setting very similar to the England of an earlier century, Aaron Patrick's mother leaves him at home alone for the first time when he is 12—he was born mute and until now has never been away from her. She has taught him to read and write, but she worries because he cannot call for help. A blizzard keeps her away too long, and Aaron sets out over roads he has never seen to search for her. Lost, he finds that his writing is of no use—no one he meets can read. He is turned into a servant boy by the pickpocket proprietress of Half-a-Moon Inn and later escapes only through his wits. This story is part fantasy, part mystery, and much suspense, heightened by the drawings—all elements that children of this age love to find in fiction.

Differentness; Drive to understand. The setting and Aaron's muteness add interest and information to this challenging adventure story.

Fleischman, Paul. *Seedfolks.* Illustrated by Judy Pedersen. HarperTeen, 2004.

In a decayed section of Cleveland, a young girl from Vietnam plants six lima beans in a sheltered spot in a vacant lot in memory of her father. An elderly Romanian woman sees her return to care for them and alerts her neighbor, the school janitor, who waters the beans when the weather turns too hot. An old man who speaks no English begins a garden, building on his knowledge of farming in Mexico. A lonely Korean widow finds community among the gardeners. A young African-American man tries to win back an old girlfriend by planting her favorite—tomatoes. An English nurse brings her patient, a stroke victim, in his wheelchair, and he chooses to plant only flowers.

Fleischman tells the story in the words of 13 people—gardeners and observers—whose lives are affected by the neighborhood garden that they all cherish—a garden that creates a community not without problems. *Seedfolks* speaks of individuals overcoming fear, prejudice, and emotional shells as they work in their separate garden plots. At first they work alone, but eventually they begin surmounting language barriers to help each other and share their harvest.

Drive to understand. Advanced readers may enjoy Fleischman's ability to write in different voices, as he speaks through people with very different backgrounds. For example, compare the vocabulary and styles in the stories of Curtis, Nora, and Amir. What can you guess of their personalities from their choice of words?

Moral concerns. What does Sam mean when he says, "I smiled back. That's my occupation"? What is Sam's role in this book? Think of someone who plays the same role in your community. What can you learn from Sam and people like him?

Relationships with others. Tell an experience you have had like that of the woman who tells Amir, "Back then, I didn't know it was *you*...."

Fritz, Jean. *Where Do You Think You're Going, Christopher Columbus?* Illustrated by Margot Tomes. Paper Star, 2000.

This lively biography tells much more than that Columbus sailed to what was to become America in 1492. Fritz follows Columbus on all four of his voyages, describing his bravado and his stubbornness, his successes and his failures, and providing along the way glimpses of the late 15th-century European view of the world.

The contrasts are instructive. Columbus was a good seaman but a poor governor. He returned to Spain from his first voyage to a royal welcome, but from 1493 to the end of his life, he faced one disappointment after another. Although he was clearly intelligent, the qualities that carried him through these difficulties were persistence and faith in what he was doing. This book offers a way of demonstrating the importance of these characteristics to gifted students who may be trying to rely too much on native intelligence alone.

Drive to understand; Resilience; Using ability. What words would you use to describe Columbus's character? What qualities made him a good explorer? A poor governor? Why do we hear only of his successes? Do you know of other famous people who failed as well as succeeded? What characteristic was most important to Columbus's success? Do you share any of his traits? What are the advantages of having these traits? What are some disadvantages? How can you enhance the advantages and overcome the disadvantages?

Galbraith, Judy. *The Gifted Kids Survival Guide for Ages 10 and Under* (3rd ed.). Illustrated by Nancy Meyers. Free Spirit, 2009.

This guide to giftedness offers a wealth of information for gifted children about what "gifted" is and means; what works and does not work in school gifted programs; what to do if there is no gifted program; how to avoid boredom; about perfectionism, social issues, high expectations, and resources—and it includes several websites where gifted students under the age of 10 can find more information. Interspersed are results of surveys of gifted students, as well as questionnaires and checklists for readers to fill out—such as "20 Questions to Identify a GT."

The author writes to children in a comfortable, conversational tone, and the format makes extensive use of graphics to add impact. Children respond well to both, so they are able to make use of the information and suggestions on their own. At the same time, lists of potential adult helpers are offered, with encouragement to seek assistance when needed. Advocacy, by children as well as adults, is recommended, with supporting information and resources. This survival guide can be read through or dipped into as interest dictates; it can be used in a group, one-on-one with a gifted child, or by the child alone, with discussion as appropriate. It focuses on many of the categories covered in this bibliography.

Achievement; Aloneness; Creativity; Differentness; Identity; Perfectionism; Relationships with others; Using ability.

Greene, Constance C. *A Girl Called Al.* Illustrated by Byron Barton. Puffin, 1994.

Al(exandra) has an extraordinary IQ, but she doesn't work to capacity and is a nonconformist. She explains all of this when she meets the narrator (a girl of Al's age who is never named) shortly after she moves into the same apartment building. Al is also lonely and is defensive regarding her weight and her parents' neglect. The narrator introduces her to Mr. Richards, the building janitor, and he very gently works to help Al lose weight and to relieve her loneliness.

Although giftedness is mentioned just once, it is clear from her conversation and her insights that Al is gifted. The emphasis of the book is three-fold: on the gradual development of sensitivity to the feelings of others, on the common courage of people facing loneliness, and on the way in which friendship can compensate for lost family ties. This book is better used with third and fourth graders than with older gifted children.

Aloneness. What sets Al apart and contributes to her loneliness? What does she offer to the narrator and her family, and to Mr. Richards? What does the narrator offer Al? How will Al become less lonely over time?

Differentness; Identity. Why is it important to Al to think of herself as a nonconformist? How does her nonconformity increase her problems? How does it help her with them? How does her intelligence help her to cope? How do you know that she is lonely, even though she never says so?

Relationships with others. Al is a very strong character—clearly the leader in the girls' relationship. Discussion can begin with this relationship: What do the two girls have to offer each other despite their differences? What does Al need from other people? Would you be willing to give it to her? What would make it difficult for you to do so?

Greenspon, Thomas S. *What to Do When Good Enough Isn't Good Enough: The Real Deal on Perfectionism: A Guide for Kids.* Illustrated by Michael Chesworth. Free Spirit, 2007.

Based on his experience as a psychologist who works with children and families, Greenspon writes directly to children between ages nine and 13 about issues related to perfectionism. He describes it so that a reader can consider whether, or to what degree, the term applies to him or her. Greenspon explains the distinction between trying to do well and perfectionism, offers suggestions for lightening the burden of worry, describes some sources of perfectionism, and offers ideas for thinking differently about oneself and for seeking help from parents and other adults. In the second part of the book, he presents basic information about some emotional disorders that are different from perfectionism but sometimes coexist with it. He closes with a chapter about what it's like to see a counselor or therapist, followed by a note to adults about how they can help.

Perfectionism; Using ability. This informative and encouraging book can be recommended to a child who can read it alone and then discuss it with an adult, or adult and child could read it together and talk about it as they read. Whatever the approach, the book will be much more effective if a trusted adult is available to support a child who needs to take steps to lighten the burden of perfectionism.

Hannigan, Katherine. *Ida B:…and Her Plans to Maximize Fun, Avoid Disaster, and (Possibly) Save the World.* HarperCollins, 2006.

After a bad beginning in kindergarten, Ida B's parents promised that they would homeschool her, and she has had four happy years of learning and living on the land that will be hers someday, including enjoying her conversations with special trees in her family's orchards. But when her mother develops cancer, financial need dictates that some of the land must be sold, and Ida B must go to public school for fourth grade. Ida B's sense of betrayal, her anger and rebellion, are mighty forces indeed—but so is her understanding of what is happening (she says that her heart hardens and shrinks) and where she goes wrong. An empathic teacher and the constant love of her parents carry her through this difficult year.

Ida B listens to the trees and to the brook and finds wisdom in what they tell her. Clearly, she is one who operates on a metaphorical level, and her intuitive understanding of the powerful emotions that sweep over her while her mother is sick is often expressed in metaphor. At the same time, her mind has an analytical bent; she approaches a problem by creating a plan, with variations designed to cover any eventuality that she can imagine. Her mother's cancer is a catalyst, not the main thread of the story; but it is well handled here, and the book could be helpful to a child who is experiencing similar turmoil. Briefly put, *Ida B* is an excellent book to help bright, sensitive children recognize and explore complex emotions at a safe distance.

Developing imagination. What do you think really happens when Ida B hears the trees respond to her? Have you experienced anything like this? Would you like to? How do you think Ida B does it?

Intensity. About what parts of her life does Ida B care the most? How can you tell? What is difficult about caring so much? In what ways is it a good thing? Do you know others—or are you—as intense as Ida B?

Relationships with others. What effect does her decision not to enjoy school have on Ida B's relationships with her teacher? With other students? What effect does it have on Ida B? What does this story say about the effect of a person's attitude on how they get along with others? Does this message make sense to you? What would you add to it?

Resilience. How can nature help one maintain a personal balance in the face of stress and turmoil?

Sensitivity. How is it that Ida B is so aware of her own feelings? Do her descriptions sound right to you—have you experienced any of the feelings that she describes? Why is it important to be aware of how your feelings affect your behavior?

Henkes, Kevin. *The Zebra Wall.* HarperCollins, 2005.

At 10, Adine is the oldest of the five Vorlob girls, followed by Bernice, Carla, Dot, and Effie. The new baby's name will begin with F, and the wall in the nursery is ready, newly painted with a mural featuring flowers, frogs, ferns, fish, and a fairy. But this time it is different: Aunt Irene comes for a visit and gives every evidence of staying—in Adine's room. The baby's arrival brings surprises and a change in plans, but the Vorlob family is flexible and up to the challenge.

Unhappy as Adine and her sisters are with Aunt Irene's presence, they manage to hold their tongues and accept their parents' decision to welcome her. Very gradually, Adine learns to see the situation from Aunt Irene's point of view and moves toward her own acceptance.

Relationships with others; Resilience. What makes Aunt Irene's visit difficult for Adine? How does Adine warm up toward her aunt? What surprised you about Aunt Irene? Think of someone with whom you are not comfortable. What surprises might they have for you if you knew them better?

Hest, Amy. *Love You, Soldier.* Illustrated by Sonya Lamut. Candlewick, 2000.

Katie is seven when the war comes and her father leaves in an olive green uniform. She and her mother stay in their New York City apartment, her mother working in the hospital and Katie spending hours in the public library. Her mother's friend Louise comes to live with them, since her husband Jack is in the army, too, and soon Louise has a baby. Katie loves Rosie, but then the worst possible news comes: Katie's father has been killed in the war. Katie and her mother stay on in the apartment with Louise and Rosie until the war ends and Jack and Louise's brother Sam come home. Then there are more changes, which Katie is reluctant to accept. But their elderly neighbor, Mrs. Leitstein, encourages her, saying, "Love is risky, but it's worth it."

The challenges of developing an identity are intensified for Katie, who must learn to adjust, accept, and risk more than most growing children. She is helped in doing so by the love around her—from and for her parents, Louise, Rosie, Mrs. Leitstein, and finally Sam, the cause of the greatest risk. We are confident that despite the loss of her father and the unknown future, Katie will be fine.

Identity; Relationships with others. In what ways does Katie grow up from age seven to the end of the book? What and who helps her to grow well?

Huck, Charlotte. *The Black Bull of Norroway.* Illustrated by Anita Lobel. Greenwillow, 2001.

Peggy Ann has said that she does not care how wealthy a husband she finds, so long as he loves her. She would even be content with the

Black Bull of Norroway, known to be a monster—and indeed, the Black Bull of Norroway appears when Peggy Ann sets out to find her fortune. Like Beauty's Beast, the Black Bull is kind, and Peggy Ann's fears subside. He takes her each night to a castle belonging to one of his three (human) brothers, where she is well-treated. On the third day, the Bull limps, and Peggy Ann lifts his hoof to remove a thorn. Her kindness breaks part of the spell, and the handsome young Duke of Norroway appears in his place—but only at night. Until the Duke defeats the Guardian of the Glen, he will be a bull during the day. There are more tests for Peggy Ann, but with loyalty, courage, and patience, she prevails.

Rather than writing modern fairy tales about girls, Charlotte Huck seeks traditional tales with brave heroines. This is a Scottish tale set in Norway—an author's note mentions an appearance of the "Black Bull o' Norroway" in Scottish literature in 1549, and the tale has appeared in several anthologies since the mid-19th century. It is a sophisticated, satisfying story, with richly colored illustrations in a folk-art style.

Developing imagination; Drive to understand. Some students in this age group may be ready to approach a folktale in two ways: to enjoy the emotional appeal of the story itself, and then to step back and see it as part of the history of literature. Because it will be new to most readers, and because it incorporates elements from other, more familiar tales, this book lends itself to both possibilities.

Jarrell, Randall. *The Bat-Poet.* Illustrated by Maurice Sendak. Harper-Collins, 1997.

The bat stays awake during the daytime and wants the other bats to do so, too, to see all of the wonders that he sees. They will not, so he makes up poems to tell them about the day. They do not understand. He tells his poem to the mockingbird, who comments on the rhyme scheme and the meter but misses the feeling altogether. Only the chipmunk will listen. The bat makes more poems, and finally one about bats that he wants to share with the other bats. But when he goes to the barn to find them, they have gone to sleep for the winter.

Older elementary children will appreciate the storyline, which parallels Plato's story of the man who left the security of the cave and, when he returned, could not make the others understand his descriptions of the wider world. Both stories can be used to help gifted children understand the uniqueness of their perceptions and why those perceptions are not always shared by others.

Creativity; Differentness; Intensity; Sensitivity. The bat-poet never found another bat who would listen. How did he feel about that? What did he do about it? Have you ever felt that you wanted to say something that no one else could understand? How did you find someone to listen? If you couldn't find anyone, what did you do instead?

Juster, Norton. *The Phantom Tollbooth.* Illustrated by Jules Feiffer. Random, 2000.

Milo, who is so bored with life that he never knows what to do with himself, drags home from school one day to find a large package in the living room. Opening it, he finds One Genuine Turnpike Tollbooth. Milo assembles it, drives his small electric car up to the booth, and pays the toll. The road beyond takes him to the Kingdom of Wisdom and the two rival cities, Dictionopolis and Digitopolis, founded by the king's quarrelling sons. Two daughters, Sweet Rhyme and Pure Reason, had kept the peace until they were banished. Milo sets off to find the sisters, accompanied by the Watchdog, Tock, and the Humbug. They drive through the Forest of Sight (where the city of Reality has disappeared because people were too busy to look) and the Valley of Sound (which is silent because people became too busy to listen). Beyond the Mountains of Ignorance, they find Rhyme and Reason in the Castle in the Air and return them to the Kingdom of Wisdom. When Milo returns home, he finds that his adventures have made him aware of how much there is to see and do in the world—he will not be bored again.

New thinking is called for in this book, not only by the symbolism in the plot, but also by the language, which is full of puns (which are a favorite language game for children of this age) and literal interpretations of verbal expressions—as when Milo and his companions inadvertently "jump to (the Island of) Conclusions." Frivolous as it all sounds, Milo does change during the course of the book. The refreshing use of language, the symbolism, and Milo's boredom should all appeal to gifted readers.

Drive to understand; Using ability. Describe Milo at the beginning and the end of the story. How did he change? What changed him? How did the trip help him know what to do with himself? Is this book silly or serious? How is it silly? How is it serious? Why did the author write it? What is the value of silliness? What serious messages lie behind the story? Did it make you think of words, numbers, and spending time on unimportant tasks in a new light? How? Does Milo's story change your ideas about boredom?

Kaufman, Gershen, Lev Raphael, & Pam Espeland. *Stick Up for Yourself! Every Kid's Guide to Personal Power and Positive Self-Esteem.* Free Spirit, 1999.

Adapted from materials written for a college-level psychology course so that children from eight to 12 years old can use it on their own, this book is also accompanied by a teacher's guide. General issues of self-esteem, labeling feelings, naming future dreams (and how to get there), and developing relationships with others are especially useful. The difference between role power and personal power, for example, can be a helpful concept as hypercritical youngsters learn how to be effective in their criticism of authority figures.

Identity. Information on self-esteem can be adapted to the particular needs of highly able children learning to come to terms with exceptional talent.

Relationships with others. Pointing out that fostering good relationships with others is a necessary step toward developing self-esteem, the authors include useful information on building such relationships.

Using ability. The section on naming dreams and how to get there offers suggestions that can be helpful in making good use of an outstanding ability.

Kehret, Peg. *Saving Lilly.* Aladdin, 2002.

Mrs. Dawson has arranged a surprise for her sixth-grade class: a field trip to the circus. But Erin and David, who have researched mistreatment of animals for a TAG (Talented and Gifted) project, do not want to go. When they ask their classmates to sign a petition to cancel the field trip, Mrs. Dawson, backed by the principal, overrides them. But after two television reporters from an animal rights group show a video of Lilly, the elephant, being prodded off of the circus truck with a hook, many sixth graders join Erin and David in remaining at their desks when the bus leaves for the circus; now they are supported by the principal and their TAG teacher. Then they learn that it may be possible to buy Lilly from the circus and send her to an elephant sanctuary. Almost the entire class joins them in raising the money. Mrs. Dawson and several parents offer expertise, but the sixth graders do the work.

The adults as well as the children in this story gradually become more aware and concerned as they learn about animal rights—and readers will, too. *Saving Lilly* appeals intellectually and emotionally, providing solid information while it makes us care very much what happens to Lilly. Though not emphasized, it is clear that Erin and David have many characteristics of gifted children—they are idealists who think outside the box, Erin is sensitive to the feelings that other classmates have regarding her success in school, and they are committed to determining what is the right thing to do and doing it.

Drive to understand. Peg Kehret is an animal lover herself, and she provides information for others to learn more—read the author's note, and follow up by checking on the websites that she recommends.

Intensity. Describe Erin's and David's feelings about not going to the circus. What does Erin mean when she thinks that the saying "Ignorance is bliss" is right? Do you agree?

Moral concerns. What moral decisions do Erin and David have to make regarding school rules? Regarding helping Lilly?

Relationships with others. How does being gifted change the way Erin interacts with her classmates? Do you have the same concerns? How does it affect your relationships with your classmates?

Kendall, Carol. *The Gammage Cup: A Novel of the Minnipins.* Illustrated by Erik Blegvad. Odyssey, 2000.

For 880 years, the Minnipins have lived in their valley in the Land Between the Mountains, isolated from the world and remembering the story of Gammage, who led them there, and Fooley, who floated away over the mountains in a balloon 440 years ago and returned with a few little-understood but well-revered artifacts. The Minnipins live tidy, well-regulated lives, with only a few exceptions: Gummy, who scribbles poetry; Mingy, the Money Keeper; Curley Green, who likes to paint; Walter the Earl, the only Minnipin who studies history from the few written records rather than relying on legend; and Muggles, who timidly at first but then more boldly thinks for herself rather than following the traditional ways without question. The story starts slowly and builds to an exciting climax as the five outcasts lead the other Minnipins in a brave and successful effort to save their valley from invasion.

Differentness. The theme of nonconformity can lead to discussion about rules—spoken or unspoken—that are difficult for some to follow. What conformities do we expect, like the green doors on (almost) every house in Slipper-on-the-Water? When is it appropriate not to conform to expectations? When is it inappropriate?

Identity. Why does Muggles change from being like everyone else in Slipper-on-the-Water to being just herself? How does she do it?

Relationships with others. How do we treat people who do not conform? What happens to Muggles when she stops following others' expectations and begins saying what she thinks? How does she avoid offending others when she speaks out?

Kendall, Carol. *The Whisper of Glocken: A Novel of the Minnipins.* Illustrated by Imero Gobbato. Sandpiper, 2000.

In this sequel to *The Gammage Cup*, the Watercress River floods, forcing the Minnipins in Water Gap to flee upstream. Reaching Slipper-on-the-Water, Glocken, who is bell-ringer of Water Gap, realizes his dream of meeting the Old Heroes of the Gammage Cup. Glocken finds them living quite ordinary, settled lives—but the Old Heroes hail Glocken and the four Water Gapians who have fled with him as the New Heroes who will find and repair the source of the flooding. So five very ordinary Minnipins from Water Gap set out on their own adventure, discovering their latent heroism as events require.

The writing in this book is more subtle and demanding than in *The Gammage Cup*, with vocabulary, metaphor, and proverbs to challenge the upper elementary reader. Imagination is called into play as the reader creates the Minnipin world from vivid description. Each of the five New Heroes, despite insecurities, peculiarities, and weaknesses, manifests true, self-sacrificing heroism at one time or another, and they offer tolerance and support to each other as they work to free the Watercress and save their Land Between the Mountains.

Creativity; Drive to understand. For good readers who love to read, this is an excellent introduction to fantasy.

Knowlton, Jack. *Maps and Globes*. Illustrated by Harriett Barton. HarperCollins, 1986.

Beginning with ancient maps drawn on clay or silk cloth and Polynesian stick chart maps, the author moves quickly on to Magellan's voyage and the advent of more accurate globes. In the section on geographical terminology, he introduces and defines words like *latitude* and *longitude*, *elevation* and *depth*. Then he demonstrates various kinds of maps: physical, political, and specialized maps that show features such as metal deposits and stagecoach lines. He concludes by suggesting a visit to the library to explore atlases.

Barton's illustrations are clear and closely tied to the text, which goes directly to the point, providing much information cleanly and efficiently. Providing satisfying initial information while at the same time opening the door for future learning, *Maps and Globes* is a model nonfiction book.

Drive to understand. Many concepts are introduced which the child may wish to explore further, and the invitation to the library makes it clear that there is more to learn. The information given here is excellent background for reading maps, even (perhaps especially) for those who are more familiar with searching Google Earth than with using a good world atlas in book form.

Konigsburg, E. L. *From the Mixed-Up Files of Mrs. Basil E. Frankweiler*. Aladdin, 2007.

Claudia Kincaid persuades her younger brother Jamie, who has enough money to finance the project, to join her in running away.

Following Claudia's careful plans, they hide in New York's Metropolitan Museum of Art for a week. At first, Claudia's reasons for running away are unclear even to her, but as she becomes fascinated by the mystery of a statue that the museum has purchased, she realizes what she wants to accomplish before she returns home.

Drive to understand. Written with a light touch, this is nevertheless not a frivolous book. It gives children who do not live in New York much incidental information about the city, the Metropolitan Museum, and art. In addition, it portrays inquisitive children who have had superb educational opportunities and are appealing models for lively, intellectually curious young people.

Differentness; Identity. Why did Claudia want to run away at first? What is her reason by the end of the book? Why does she want to be different? What are some advantages to being different? How could someone like Claudia accomplish the same thing without running away?

Introversion. What does Mrs. Frankweiler mean when she talks about having some days when, rather than learning new facts, it's good to "allow what is already in you to swell up until it touches everything"?

Konigsburg, E. L. *Jennifer, Hecate, Macbeth, William McKinley, and Me, Elizabeth.* Aladdin, 2007.

Jennifer and Elizabeth become friends on Halloween of Elizabeth's first year at William McKinley School. Jennifer says she is a witch, and she does some mysterious things that make it seem possible that she is. Elizabeth becomes an apprentice witch, and all winter, the girls meet at the library on Saturdays to study witchcraft, planning to make a magic potion that will enable them to fly.

Elizabeth is lonely at first in the new school. Jennifer, being gifted and African-American, is different and is not included in the school's social life, but she seems unconcerned about it. A subtheme is Elizabeth's gradual separation from Jennifer's influence—with Jennifer's help—so that the friendship becomes more equal than the original follower/leader relationship.

Aloneness; Introversion. Do you think that Jennifer is lonely? Why or why not?

Differentness; Identity. Why does it not seem to bother Jennifer that she is not popular at school? Do you think she is happy just as she is? Why or why not? How do you know when Elizabeth begins to do more thinking for herself? Why does this happen?

Relationships with others. Why is Elizabeth uncomfortable at the birthday party? Do you agree with her behavior? Why is she more comfortable with Jennifer? Why does Elizabeth finally pull away from Jennifer? How does this affect their friendship? What does each girl offer to the other?

L'Engle, Madeleine. *A Wrinkle in Time.* Aladdin, 2007.

Fourteen-year-old Meg Murry, her younger brother Charles Wallace, and Calvin O'Keefe travel through time and space in search of Mr. Murry, a scientist who disappeared while experimenting with a tesseract—a wrinkle in time. When they find him, they must use all of their strength to free him and themselves from the force of evil.

Almost all of the characters in this story are very intelligent, and the three children respond in different ways to the difficulties that this causes them in relating to others. L'Engle creates a world in which it is psychologically safe to be gifted and in which the characters care for and challenge one another.

Drive to understand. Like many of L'Engle's books, *A Wrinkle in Time* features an entire cast of gifted characters. For one thing, they each exhibit the drive to understand, a trait that an intellectually curious reader will easily recognize. What is more, they show that such a drive adds meaning and purpose to living. The book is intellectually satisfying to gifted children also because of frequent references to math, science, literature, and music. Challenging discussions based on the book could begin with the question, "What do you think about life on Camazotz?"

Differentness; Identity. How are the children different from their schoolmates? How does each feel about being different? How do we show that we do or do not value differences among people?

Levine, Gail Carson. *Ella Enchanted*. HarperTrophy, 1998.

When Ella was born, Lucinda, the sentimental and impulsive fairy, bestowed her gift—without sufficient thought, as usual: obedience. Ella would always be obedient. Growing up in the home of a wealthy merchant, Ella was protected from her gift by the watchful caring of her mother and Mandy, the cook. But the Lady Eleanor dies when Ella is 15, and Sir Peter sends Ella to finishing school. There, the envious Hattie learns that Ella is compelled to obey every order, and she uses the knowledge to make Ella's life miserable. When Ella flees to find Lucinda and beg her to take back her gift, she survives a near-fatal encounter with ogres and meets kind elves and friendly giants, but she fails to gain freedom from the fairy's gift. The adventure forces her to realize how dangerous the gift is, both to herself and to those she loves—even to the prince.

Ella is intelligent and high-spirited, and her struggle to be herself and to make her own decisions is the story of this book. Gradually the reader realizes that it is also a modern retelling of the Cinderella story. *Ella Enchanted* is a delightful book to read simply for the pleasure of it, but it also offers ideas for discussion. The climactic inner battle in which Ella finally wins freedom from Lucinda's influence is especially worth attention if adults and children can articulate it as a metaphor for growing up—a struggle which in real life must happen more than once.

Identity. Why is it important that Ella learn how not to be always obedient but to make her own decisions? Why is it important for Ella, as well as for Char and Kyrria? Why is it important for anyone? How is Ella finally able to overcome the effects of Lucinda's gift?

Moral concerns. What are the advantages of being obedient? What are the disadvantages? What guidelines can help you decide when it is best to be obedient, and when not?

Relationships with others. What qualities in Ella make her a good friend for Char? What role does Ella's friendship with Arieda play? Hattie and Olive are caricatures, as is often the case in fairy tales—what kind of "friendship" do they represent?

Lindgren, Astrid. *Pippi Longstocking.* Translated by Florence Lamborn. Illustrated by Louis S. Glanzman. Puffin, 2005.

A series of vignettes tells about Pippi, who has come home to Villa Villekulla after sailing with her father; she lives alone in the family home and is wonderfully free. Very strong, with no parental restrictions and the freedom to do just as she likes, Pippi goes from one adventure to another, following her own unique logic—to the amusement of neighborhood children and the huge enjoyment of the reader.

Using ability. Pippi provides fantasy material and plenty of independence and divergent thinking for beginning readers, girls and boys alike. Adults who met Pippi decades ago still light up when they talk about her, putting Pippi Longstocking in the same category as Caddie Woodlawn—a timeless heroine.

Lindgren, Astrid. *Ronia, the Robber's Daughter.* Peter Smith, 1994.

On the night Ronia is born, a fierce storm brings lightning that cracks Matt's Fort, her father's castle, in two. Matt, his wife Lovis, and his band of robbers, rejoicing over the birth of this dark-haired daughter, are not concerned. They simply abandon the north half of the castle and continue to live in the south fort. The high-spirited Ronia grows into a fearless explorer of the forest and the mountains around Matt's Fort.

One day, exploring Hell's Gap—the fissure between the two parts of the old castle—she meets Birk, son of Borka, the other robber chieftain in the area. Soldiers have come too close to Borka's territory, so he and his band have taken up residence in the north fort without the formality of asking permission. From then on, Ronia and Birk explore the forest together, coming to depend on each other for company and safety among the forest folk, like the gray dwarfs and harpies. As their affection for each other grows, the inevitable conflict between their fathers builds. When it reaches its climax, the independent Ronia chooses Birk, leaping Hell's Gap as evidence of her decision. Soon Ronia and Birk leave their families, unable to accept the hatred between their fathers and unwilling to pursue the robber's life. Sweet reconciliation comes eventually, after they have spent an idyllic summer in the Bear's Cave. The two bands of robbers join forces, but the soldiers make the robbing life ever more difficult. When they grow up, we know, Ronia and Birk will lead the band toward a more lawful life.

Ronia is as strong-minded as Pippi Longstocking, but her story is a strong narrative rather than a collection of loosely-linked incidents. Ronia is a memorable heroine, and Birk, too, is an independent thinker. The deep friendship between them is a very moving love, with no thought of the future except the simple certainty that they will always be together. Swedish author Lindgren displays her love for the atmosphere of the northern forest in every season, and this, along with the presence of the folkloric forest creatures, adds a uniqueness to the setting that suits Ronia's character completely. With its distinctive writing style and unusual names, this book may need more introduction than most, but once children have an understanding of the setting and characters, they will be eager for more. This is a book that parents and teachers may want to read aloud—for their own pleasure as well as that of their children.

Arrogance. Why do Matt and Borka talk to each other as they do? What purpose does it serve? When they change, toward the end of the book, what has brought about the change? Why are they no longer arrogant?

Moral concerns. Why are Matt and Borka robbers? Why will Ronia and Birk not be? What are the reasons for the change?

Relationships with others. Describe Ronia's personality, and Birk's. What personal traits do they have that enable them to become friends even though their families are enemies? What traits do you have that help you make friends?

Lowry, Lois. *Anastasia Krupnik.* Bantam, 1998.

In her green notebook, 10-year-old Anastasia records her favorite words, important private information, and a list of "Things I Love!" and "Things I Hate!" When she learns that her mother will have a baby boy in March, she adds "my parents" and "babies" to the Hate list, but she stops short of running away when her father suggests that she give the new baby whatever name she chooses. Anastasia writes a horrible name in the green notebook. Over the next few months, she considers becoming a Catholic and changing her name, learns how to listen to her 92-year-old grandmother, falls in and out of love, decides that she likes her name—and records all of this in the green notebook, occasionally moving an item from the Hate list to the Love list. Eventually even "babies" appears on the love side of the ledger.

Anastasia is a bright, inquisitive, sensitive girl who is doing her best to make sense of the world and the process of growing up. She vaguely dislikes her teacher without knowing the reason—which is clear to the reader when the teacher rejects a poem that Anastasia has written that does not rhyme. Later, her teacher makes a special effort to be kind, and Anastasia moves her name to the Love list. Anastasia's parents are models of support and understanding for a gifted child. There are no major issues here, only Anastasia becoming more aware of herself through her own efforts and with her parents' help.

Identity; Relationships with others. How do people get moved from the Hate to the Love list? What do they all have in common? Describe the difference between the college students' and Anastasia's attitude toward Wordsworth. Do you know people who have the students' attitude? What are the consequences? (If it seems appropriate, discussion leaders may want to add questions related to Anastasia's knowledge of and attitude toward her own giftedness.)

MacLachlan, Patricia. *Arthur, for the Very First Time.* Illustrated by Lloyd Bloom, HarperCollins, 1994.

When he is 10, Arthur goes to stay with Great-Aunt Elda and Great-Uncle Wrisby for the summer because his parents are fighting. In addition, Arthur believes that his mother is going to have a baby, which he does *not* want. Life is very different with Uncle Wrisby and Aunt Elda—they live on a farm, so they teach Arthur about nature and farm life. Their pet chicken, Pauline, sleeps in the kitchen, and their pig, Bernadette, will give birth to piglets soon. In addition to the animals, Elda and Wrisby also have neighbors, including Moira (who becomes Arthur's friend) and her grandfather, Moreover, the local veterinarian. Moira calls Arthur "Mouse" (reflecting Arthur's timidity, but in a caring way) as they become friends, and Arthur learns that her family problems are more troubling than his are.

Nevertheless, Moira is a positive person who urges the timid "Mouse" to do something—and Arthur does.

This is a story of friendship and of Arthur's growing sense of purpose, nascent self-understanding, and eventually the shift in his attitude toward a baby, which is directly due to his experience with Bernadette's piglets. The book includes Aunt Elda's story, which will remind readers of MacLachlan's later and better-known *Sarah, Plain and Tall.*

Identity. What did Arthur do? Why? How has he changed? So much is unresolved at the end of this book that some discussion can center on what the reader thinks will happen next. How will Arthur be different when he returns to his parents? How will his family be different?

Montgomery, L. M. *Anne of Green Gables.* New American Library, 1991.

As an 11-year-old orphan, Anne is adopted by a 60-year-old Prince Edward Island farmer, Matthew Cuthbert, and his sister, Marilla. Anne is red-haired, bright, and eager to please, but above all, she is impetuous and imaginative. Despite her best efforts, she is forever getting into trouble. The story follows her for the next five years, through friendships, problems at school, and misunderstandings. The reader watches as Anne learns to tame her romantic nature, growing more mature and thoughtful in the process.

First published in 1904, this book is such a favorite that it has been adapted for various reading levels. Try to find a version at or slightly above the reading level of the child. This is an excellent choice for mother-daughter reading aloud, which would permit a higher reading level with more challenge and more interest. The story is refreshingly old-fashioned and idealistic in comparison to today's lighter novels for this age group. Contemporary readers may be surprised by the emphasis on Anne's efforts to "be good" and Marilla's efforts to avoid spoiling her, but the underlying desire to make something good of one's life is worth considering, and it is well done here. Perhaps it is just the distance in time that allows this book to make the point without preaching.

Identity; Using ability. Anne has no problems with recognizing and using her intelligence, so she can be a positive example. In what ways are you like Anne? In what ways could you be like her if you had lived in her time? Who are kindred spirits for you? Might Anne be one? Why or why not?

Resilience. In what ways does Anne demonstrate resilience? Is there anything that you can learn from her?

Moser, Adolph. *Don't Feed the Monster on Tuesdays!* Illustrated by David Melton. Landmark, 1991.

Subtitled *The Children's Self-Esteem Book*, this nonfiction book is designed to be read by parents and children together. Psychologist Moser explains how children can replace negative feelings about themselves with positive ones. Imagining a monster inside our heads that makes us feel bad about ourselves—others call it "bad self-talk"—he suggests that on Tuesdays, children avoid feeding the monster by saying only nice things to themselves and others. This will become easier on Wednesday, and then every day—and the rewards, in the responses sure to come from other people, are great. Moser touches on perfectionism, making the point that to feel good about oneself, it is not necessary to win every time; it is only important to do one's best.

This is one of a series of books by the same author for children from ages nine through 12, each addressing a different issue in healthy psychological development. Besides self-esteem, the series covers stress, anger, grief, and lying. In each book, Moser describes and defines the problem in terms familiar to children, making it clear that others experience it, too. Then he shows the way to solutions. Because the books are written in simple language with cartoon-like illustrations, they look like children's books, but my local bookseller shelves them with books on parenting, highlighting the importance of parent involvement in reading the books and helping the child deal with these issues. Parents will want to read them first and may be surprised to learn how serious these concerns are to their children.

Drive to understand; Identity; Perfectionism; Relationships with others; Resilience.

Naylor, Phyllis Reynolds. *Shiloh*. Illustrated by Barry Moser. Aladdin, 2000.

Eleven-year-old Marty Preston is walking through his beloved West Virginia countryside one Sunday when he comes upon a dog—a frightened beagle who clearly yearns to befriend Marty and who follows him home. But Marty's family can't afford to feed a pet, and his father returns the dog to its owner, Judd Travers, whose reputation for meanness is based in part on his mistreatment of his hunting dogs. When the beagle (whom Marty has named Shiloh) escapes and returns to the Prestons, Marty hides him, even from his family, while he tries to find a way to earn enough money to buy the dog. The crisis comes when Shiloh is attacked in his hiding place by a neighboring German shepherd, and Marty's parents—and Judd— discover Marty's secret.

Marty is caught in a dilemma in this Newbery winner because both the law and the weight of local custom conflict with his passionate desire to protect Shiloh from a cruel owner. Although his parents are supportive, they insist that Marty work the problem out on his own. His manner of doing so shows uncommon courage, maturity, and wisdom, along with a recognition of the need for compromise.

Identity. What is it in Marty that causes him to question rules that others around him follow easily? Imagine Marty in 15 years— what might he do then to protect a dog like Shiloh? How and why might Marty be different from his parents when he is grown?

Moral concerns. Did Marty make any decisions that you would not have made? Was his parents' position a good one? Why or why not?

Nivola, Claire A. *Planting the Trees of Kenya: The Story of Wangari Maathai*. Farrar, Straus, & Giroux, 2008.

Born in 1940, Wangari Maathai grew up in a peasant family at a time when Kenya was green with trees and families could grow the food they needed. When she returned to Kenya after just five years of study in America, she found most of the trees and small farms gone, pushed out by large farms growing food to sell elsewhere. Wangari began teaching the women how to grow trees to replace those they cut down for firewood. Thirty years later, 30 million trees had been planted in Kenya.

Wangari Maathai won the 2004 Nobel Peace Prize for her work empowering the women of Kenya, showing them how to care for their own land. Her story is timely and inspiring, embellished with Nivola's colorful, primitive-style, sweeping landscapes. Nivola also provides an author's note that will interest older readers.

Drive to understand. There is information here to begin learning about Kenya, about some of the effects of colonialism and of corporate farming, about the life of a Kenyan peasant girl who grew up to be a member of her country's Parliament, and about what one determined person can do to change the world.

Using ability. Wangari Maathai must be very intelligent, but that is not all she needed to accomplish what she has. What other traits have contributed to her success?

O'Brien, Robert C. *Mrs. Frisby and the Rats of NIMH.* Illustrated by Zena Bernstein. Aladdin, 1999.

Worried about the illness of her son Timothy, Mrs. Frisby goes to Mr. Ages, a wise older mouse, for medicine. Later, when it is clear that Timothy is too weak to be moved from their garden home before it will be destroyed in spring plowing, Mr. Ages sends her to the rats for help. Thus, she learns how the rats had been captured and groomed in a laboratory at NIMH, their intelligence enhanced until they learned to read. They finally escaped, and they set up their own civilization under a large rosebush on the Fitzgerald farm. Now they are planning to move again, this time to a remote valley where they can be self-sufficient, no longer dependent on Mr. Fitzgerald's grain. Mrs. Frisby also learns that her husband Jonathan, who had died the previous summer, had been a laboratory mouse who escaped with the rats; he died during an attempt to help them. The rats are therefore eager to help Mrs. Frisby, although they, too, are in danger.

The super-intelligent rats of NIMH are so different from other rats that they want to live differently, according to their own ideas and values, even though they do not entirely agree among themselves on those values. One basic question that the book raises is how much separateness is called for by a high intelligence, and why.

Differentness; Identity. After escaping from NIMH, the rats are uncomfortable with other rats, who edge away from them. If you have experienced this, how do you respond? What are advantages of the rats' separate civilization? What are the disadvantages? This story is an extreme: What examples of the same impulse to separateness do we see among people? What are the advantages and disadvantages? What compromises are possible? What is your preference?

Moral concerns. Nicodemus and others argue that a life made easy by machinery is too easy, causing the rats to lose a sense of purpose in meaningful work. What do you think? What could they do in the leisure time that machinery might give them that would justify the use of that machinery? How do people respond to this situation? How might we do better?

Paterson, Katherine. *Bridge to Terabithia.* Illustrated by Donna Diamond. HarperTeen, 2004.

Sensitive and interested in art, Jess is a misfit in his family and in school. When Leslie moves to Jess's rural area of Virginia and joins his class, her companionship frees Jess to play and learn in the country of their imagination, Terabithia. After Leslie dies in a flooded stream, Jess must face her death and his aloneness. Although he is still different from others, he realizes that he has gained strength from his friendship with Leslie and is comfortable being himself now.

Katherine Paterson wrote this book after the death of a special friend of her own son, and it rings with the truth of the relationship between two sensitive people who find strength and validation in their friendship. Many children can respond to that truth, whether or not they themselves have such a relationship, and this book is highly recommended for bright and sensitive upper elementary readers.

Aloneness; Introversion. Why do Jess and Leslie enjoy Terabithia so much? What other places could serve the same purpose? Do you have such a place? Would you like to have one? How would you find it? When would you go there? What would you do there? Would you go alone or with someone?

Differentness; Identity; Sensitivity. How is Leslie different from the other students at Jess's school? How is Jess different? How does each one feel about being different? What would happen if they tried to change in order to fit in better? If you could meet them, would you like them better as they are or if they changed in some way? Do you know anyone who seems different from the group but who is pretty good at being who he or she is?

Drive to understand. Describe the difference in background between Jess and Leslie. Why is the trip to Washington, D.C. so important to Jess? Have you had any such experience?

Relationships with others. How do Jess and Leslie recognize each other as potential friends? What does Leslie offer to Jess? What does Jess offer to Leslie to build a friendship? What do you offer to and gain from special friends?

Using ability. Why has it been so difficult for Jess to develop his artistic talent? What will he have to do to be able to use his talent? What traits will help him? What traits do you have that would help you, if you were in his situation? What talent do you have that you can develop? Is it harder or easier for you than for Jess? Why?

Rodgers, Mary. *Freaky Friday.* HarperTeen, 2003.

Annabel Andrews and her mother trade places, so Annabel goes through the day in her mother's body and sees herself as others speak to her "mother" about her. She learns that her brother loves her despite her impatience with him, that the housekeeper will not clean her room because it is so messy, that the boy she admires thinks she is ugly and awful, and that her teachers are frustrated with her under-achievement.

This book is sometimes hilarious as the reader follows Annabel's thoughts and reactions. The high point is her mother's interview with her teachers, in which Annabel learns that she has a high IQ and that her teachers are concerned about her lack of achievement. When she and her mother resume their own bodies, she finds that her mother has had her braces removed and her hair cut and has bought Annabel a new wardrobe. Instant transformation from an ugly duckling to a budding beauty—what every adolescent girl would love to have!

Achievement; Using ability. How will Annabel's behavior change as a result of the inner changes that take place in this story?

Identity. What is it about the interview with her teachers that makes Annabel want to change? How would Annabel describe herself at the beginning of the book? How would you describe her at the end? What inner changes have taken place? Why? Do you know anyone like Annabel? What do you think he or she is like inside?

Rumford, James. *Traveling Man: The Journey of Ibn Battuta, 1325-1354.* Sandpiper, 2004.

We know about Marco Polo, but probably few Americans are aware that in that age of exploration, a 21-year-old Moroccan named Ibn Battuta made his own daring and sometimes dangerous journey. From his home on the edge of the Ocean of Darkness (how strange to hear that name for our familiar Atlantic!), he traveled to the center of the known world—Jerusalem—and on to Arabia, Russia, India, and finally China. He even sailed on the Ocean of Ignorance, the Pacific, on his way home. There, he told his story to a court secretary, who wrote it down. The original document is now in the National Library in Paris.

This is a fascinating story wrapped in a beautiful book, with gilt illustrations and maps, as well as a glossary. Some of the illustrations include Arabic and Chinese calligraphy, with translations provided at the end.

Drive to understand. Opportunities abound for lesson plans based on Ibn Battuta's travels. How does his trip compare to Marco Polo's? How did the cultures of the two men differ, and what difference would that have made in their journeys? Try to imagine a world centered on Jerusalem—where is the geographical center of our world view?

Schultz, Robert A. & James R. Delisle. *Smart Talk.* Illustrated by Tyler Page. Free Spirit, 2006.

Smart Talk is written for, about, and even (mostly) by gifted children from four to 12 years old. On their website, www.giftedspeak.com, the authors surveyed gifted children around the world, asking a range of questions in seven categories, including Fitting In, Expectations, School, and Home. They have published "some of the most common answers, as well as some of the most interesting and funny ones." The responses are insightful and revealing and should prove helpful to young readers who will surely find someone out there who answers as they would have. (Responders are identified only by gender, age, and state of residence.) In addition, there are brief biographies called "A Kid Like You" interspersed among the chapters. Sections in each chapter called "Reflection/Connection" offer suggestions for further thought and action.

Achievement; Aloneness; Identity; Intensity; Relationships with others; Using ability. This book is listed under each grade level represented in this chapter, but its application will vary according to age. It may be most useful as a discussion starter, in a group or after a child has read it alone. It can be read straight through or skimmed once and then referred to whenever appropriate. Parents and teachers may help children follow through on ideas offered under "Reflection/ Connection." However it is used, this book promises greater self-understanding for gifted children and offers a valuable resource for adults working with them.

Sperry, Armstrong. *Call It Courage*. Simon Pulse, 2008.

When Mafatu was three, his mother was killed at sea. Mafatu survived, but his childhood experience left him afraid of the sea in an island culture and a coward in the Polynesian world where courage is everything. Rejected by all, Mafatu finally leaves Hikueru, his home island, and sails to a deserted island where he must depend only on himself for survival. While providing food and shelter and building a new canoe, he also kills a shark, a wild boar, and an octopus. Finally, he must flee the island, pursued by a band of men from a nearby island. Having so abundantly proven his courage to himself, Mafatu returns home to the welcome of his people.

This fast-paced adventure will hold children's attention and give them a vivid picture of life in another part of the world. Mafatu's journey is the classic quest story, and he sets for himself tasks that correspond to the rites of passage marking the beginning of manhood in many societies. Although younger gifted children can read *Call It Courage* with enjoyment, those in the upper elementary grades are at a more appropriate age to respond to the story of Mafatu's search for identity.

Identity; Resilience. Why did Mafatu leave Hikueru? Why did he explore the island he found, even though he suspected it might be one of the dark islands? Why did he go to the plateau instead of leaving the island when he heard the drums? Describe Mafatu's character. What traits helped him survive psychologically (survive the teasing and rejection of his people)? Physically (survive the dangers of sea and island)? What challenges do young people in the United States face in growing up that these traits will answer? How can you use the traits that Mafatu had or developed?

Stanley, George Edward. *Geronimo: Young Warrior.* Illustrated by Meryl Henderson. Aladdin Paperbacks, 2001.

This volume of the *Childhood of Famous Americans* series is especially interesting, if only because Geronimo, who was born in 1829, grew up in an Apache village learning skills and traditions that have largely disappeared. The author emphasizes the values that Apaches held and taught their children—values that may be surprising in light of the standard and limited view of Apaches as stereotypically fierce and warlike. Geronimo's story is told in a series of incidents from his childhood, skillfully woven together with vignettes of members of his family and his village. They tell of the steps toward becoming a brave and then a warrior—the tests and challenges involved in the upbringing of an Apache youth—along with some of the myths and stories that encompass and pass along the wisdom of the people.

Throughout the book, there is enough information about past and potential war with the Mexicans in the south, as well as the Americans beginning to move in from the east, to tie Geronimo's village to the wider world. The last few pages tell of the simultaneous deaths of Geronimo's mother, wife, and children at the hands of Mexicans, of failed peace treaties between Apaches and Americans, and of Geronimo's appeals to the United States government to find a healthy place for Apaches to live. Eventually the Apaches settled near Fort Sill, Oklahoma, where Geronimo was buried after his death in 1909.

Drive to understand. What skills did Goyahkla (Geronimo's child-hood name) need to learn that you are not learning? What are you learning that he did not? Why is his list so different from yours? When he was older, Geronimo had to learn many other skills—things you are learning now—in order to get along with the Americans who were moving into Apache lands. If you had to get along with people so different from you, what difficulties do you think you would have?

Relationships with others. Think about how Goyahkla was taught to behave toward other people—older people, his family and friends, and Apaches from other villages. How is this like what you have learned about how to treat others, and why? How is it different, and why? How would what he learned in his village have helped Geronimo as an adult talking with Americans?

Thomas, Joyce Carol. *Brown Honey in Broomwheat Tea.* Illustrated by Floyd Cooper. HarperCollins, 1995.

In this collection of a dozen lyrical poems, National Book Award winner Thomas writes of home and loving family, as well as of family trees broken by the journey from Africa. Mostly she speaks of the beauty and strength of African-American identity in lilting, thoughtful poetry, reinforced by earth-toned illustrations that celebrate strong and loving family relationships.

Drive to understand. Children who do not share Thomas's African-American heritage may derive new understanding from poems that address it, even obliquely: "Brown Honey in Broomwheat Tea" and "Family Tree."

Identity. Children of this age can enjoy poems that speak of self-worth and self-confidence, such as "Cherish Me," "I Am a Root," and "Becoming the Tea."

Using ability. The beginnings of a decision to use ability may be found in "Magic Landscape."

Van Draanen, Wendelin. *Shredderman: Secret Identity.* Illustrated by Brian Briggs. Knopf, 2004.

Nolan begins by describing the bully of the fifth grade, Bubba Bixby. School would be a whole new place without Bubba, who (among other things) assigns hurtful nicknames to everyone. Nolan's nickname is Nerd, but his teacher has written a note congratulating him on his perfect math test: "You shred, man!" So when Nolan comes up with an idea for a project that involves his digital camera, creating a website, and catching Bubba in some of his nefarious acts, he chooses "Shredderman" for his domain name. The website is a success, but more important are the changes in Nolan. As he plans a way to confront Bubba, he also gently but firmly confronts his other classmates, politely calling them by their real names and asking them to call him Nolan.

The solution that the author presents may be unrealistic, but the problem is very real, and Nolan's adventures with the website add humor and suspense to the story. On another level, the spirit of the resolution rings true. Nolan learns to be assertive and gains some understanding of how Bubba learned to be mean.

Relationships with others. Think about what Nolan did—with Bubba and with his other classmates—and how you could accomplish the same thing in different ways. Why does Nolan suddenly want to *defend* Bubba? Create one more chapter, telling what happens after Bubba returns to school.

Whelan, Gloria. *Miranda's Last Stand.* HarperCollins, 1999.

After Miranda's father is killed in the Battle of Bull Run, she and her mother stay at Fort Lincoln, where her father had been stationed, and Mama supports them as a laundress for the soldiers. Growing up at the fort, Miranda is taught to hate Indians, especially Sitting Bull, who led the Sioux at the Battle of Bull Run. When Miranda is 10, Mama receives a letter saying that Miranda has inherited her grandparents' farm. They long to move, but first they must save enough money to last until the first crops come in. Then Buffalo Bill Cody hears of Mama's skill as a painter, and he asks her to travel with his Wild West Show and paint backdrops of the West. In Buffalo's Wild

West Show, there is an entire Indian village, including three children who become Miranda's friends and, later, Sitting Bull himself. When Miranda hears Sitting Bull tell the story of Bull Run from his point of view, she realizes that she must give up her hate, even though she knows Mama cannot.

Miranda's story is set first in the Dakota Territory in 1886 and then moves from Chicago to Washington, D.C. and around the northeastern states. The description of life in Buffalo Bill's Wild West Show and of the people—including Mr. Cody, Annie Oakley, and Sitting Bull—is a wonderful example of historical fiction for this age group. The beautiful descriptions of the land give evidence that Whelan traveled the routes she describes. She raises a complex question and handles it smoothly in a fashion well-suited for children of Miranda's age, making this book an excellent introduction to a balanced picture of one of the most dramatic and misunderstood events of United States history in the late 19th century.

Drive to understand. The Battle of Bull Run was such an emotional event that only recently have children's books begun to appear with a balanced view. For older students in this age group, this book can be used along with Marrin's *Sitting Bull and His World*, in the Middle School section.

Identity. Miranda finally realizes that she is a person who can "climb out of herself." What does she mean? Can you do that? If you have not done it yet, can you learn how to?

Moral concerns. Was Miranda right or wrong to hide her mother's money? To give Sitting Bull's medicine to her mother? How did you reach your answers to these questions—what factors did you consider?

Relationships with others. It seems unlikely that Miranda and Quick Fox could become friends, but they do. What do they have in common? What does each one of them do to overcome the barrier between them? What personal qualities did it take for each of them to be able to do this? Which of these qualities do you have, and when have you used them in this way?

Willard, Nancy. *A Visit to William Blake's Inn: Poems for Innocent and Experienced Travelers.* Illustrated by Alice & Martin Provenson. Voyager Books, 1982.

This collection of poems about a visit to an inn hosted by poet William Blake is enhanced by pictures of the inn's interior, with one wall cut away like a dollhouse so that readers see everything on several floors and the roof. Each poem creates an imaginative world of its own, but all are tied together by the mystical spirit of William Blake and the poetry he wrote 200 years ago.

Drive to understand; Using ability. Willard's poems should be read aloud and enjoyed. Some lines could be memorized for the sheer pleasure of knowing them by heart. The illustrations can be examined for the unexpected surprises on every page. A few poems written by Blake could be read aloud, too. Willard has used some of Blake's rhythms, and children will enjoy comparing them.

Winter, Jeanette. *The Librarian of Basra.* Harcourt, 2005.

In a true story of dedication and courage, Winter tells of Alia Muhammad Baker, the librarian in Basra, Iraq, who saved the books when the library was about to be destroyed. As war came closer to Basra, she began taking books to her home for safekeeping. When it arrived, she enlisted neighbors to help move the remaining books to a nearby building, just nine days before the library was burned to the ground. Then she hired a truck to move them to even safer places in the homes of friends—and waited for a new library to be built.

Without too much detail for young children, the illustrations are striking, and the pictures of Alia's face are moving studies in anguish, worry, and patience. The story puts a human face on war, as it is clear that books are important to people everywhere. The name of the invading country is not mentioned. Cementing the reality of the story, part of the proceeds from this book will go to help rebuild the Basra library.

Drive to understand. Discuss the books that were in the Basra library—some of them ancient. How old would "ancient" be in Iraq? How old are most books in libraries in the United States? Does this matter? If so, why?

Wisniewski, David. *Golem.* Sandpiper, 2007.

More than 400 years ago, the Blood Lie, a rumor that Jews used the blood of Christian children to make Passover bread, swept over the city of Prague. Christians who believed this story threatened the lives of the Jews of Prague. According to legend, in seeking a way to avoid violence, Rabbi Loew created a Golem, shaping a man out of clay and bringing the clay figure to life with words from the Cabala. Rabbi Loew explained to Golem that it had been created to protect the Jews by night and to serve in the synagogue by day. When the Jews were no longer in danger, Golem would return to the earth. Eventually the enemies of the Jews rioted at the gates of the Jewish ghetto. In protecting the Jews inside, Golem grew to enormous size and strength, raging out of control and causing too much destruction. After this, the emperor guaranteed the safety of the Jews, and Rabbi Loew caused Golem to return to clay. This was a poignant moment, for Golem had learned to love life. The legend concludes with the possibility that, when needed, the Golem could come to life again.

The Golem legend raises questions of good and evil and the gray area between the two, in which humans sometimes lose control over forces too strong for them. Wisniewski illustrates his version of the Golem legend with forceful cut-paper collages, so compelling that this book earned the Caldecott Medal in 1997. A long author's note at the end summarizes the history of the Golem, the Cabala, Rabbi Loew's historical connection to the story, and a brief history of the persecution of the Jews. It compares the Golem story to the Frankenstein story and ends with the suggestion that the impetus for the Golem, protection for the Jews, lives in the nation of Israel.

Drive to understand. Why were rumors like the Blood Lie started?

Moral concerns. What characters in this story represent evil? In what way? Who represents good? In what way? Which does the Golem represent, and how? Name characters in other stories who represent both good and evil. How is this true of people?

Relationships with others. Relationships between two groups of people in this story—the Jews and the Christians—were very bad indeed. How did individuals in the story work to bring peace? When two individuals reach the point of telling untrue stories and threatening each other, what can be done to improve the situation? Have you ever done anything to improve such relationships? If so, what?

Wojciechowska, Maia. *Shadow of a Bull*. Illustrated by Alvin Smith. Aladdin, 2007.

Manolo's father was once the greatest bullfighter in Spain, and everyone expects Manolo to be like him. When Manolo is almost 12—the age when his father first fought a bull—a group of men who have been watching him since his father's death begin training him to become a toreador. Manolo is not sure that he wants to be a bullfighter, and he assumes that his fear means that he lacks courage. He sets for himself the task of learning to be brave. Two people help clarify his hopes for the future: Juan, who passionately longs to become a bullfighter, and the doctor who has spent his life repairing bodies broken in the bullring.

Manolo is trapped by the expectations of others and confused by his own definition of courage. The decision that he eventually makes reflects both self-knowledge and moral courage.

Drive to understand. This well-written story conveys with respect the historical tradition behind bullfighting, but it also raises inevitable questions, without giving any definitive answers. Manolo's answer, as it should be, is only for himself, leaving room for discussion.

Identity; Intensity. How does Manolo feel about himself? How would you describe him to someone else? How does Manolo define courage? How does he show it? How would you have defined it before reading the book? How about after reading the book? Do you see examples of moral courage in others? In yourself?

Using ability. What advice would you give Manolo? Manolo's mother says that what his father did was "for himself, most of all for himself." Is that all right, or is it selfish? Why? What does Manolo do for himself? Is it selfish? What do you do for yourself that is not selfish?

Yee, Lisa. *Millicent Min, Girl Genius.* Scholastic, 2004.

Millicent is 11 years old, will be a high school senior in the fall, and has talked her parents into allowing her to take a college course in poetry this summer. In turn, to her dismay, they have signed her up for volleyball—to give her "a more normal and well-rounded childhood," as the school psychologist advised them to do. Worse, they agree that Millie will tutor Stanford Wong in English, with the hope that he can pass sixth grade after all. Stanford's interest is in basketball, not academics, and Millicent has only scorn for him, although their grandmothers are good friends. During the summer, Millie meets Emily Ebers; the two girls quickly bond, and as Stanford develops an interest in Emily, his schoolwork improves. Afraid that it will make a difference in their friendship, Millie somehow never finds the right time to tell Emily about her outstanding academic record. When Emily finds out, she feels betrayed and is furious at both Millie and Stanford. Millie is slow to believe that Emily is upset, not because Millie is so bright, but because she was not honest with Emily, but eventually the three work things out.

Millicent carries her briefcase everywhere, tries to be helpful by pointing out faults, and tells her story in elevated/stilted language—and yet we empathize with her, because bright as she is, she is also clueless. At some level, she knows this is so, and her bravery in telling about her lack of friends is poignant. Emily likes her, not for her brain, but for herself—a revelation that Millicent will need to think about for some time before she will fully believe it. And Stanford is not unintelligent, which becomes clearer in *Stanford Wong Flunks Big Time*, a sequel book described below. Millie misunderstands him because she assumes that all gifted people are interested in academics. The story of Millicent Min is an exaggeration in that so few people are as smart as she is, but her dilemma rings true for many gifted and highly gifted children. For those who are not geniuses, Millie's story may provide insights that will lead to greater understanding and tolerance.

Aloneness; Introversion. Sometimes Millie is lonely, and sometimes she enjoys being alone. What makes the difference between the two for her? For you?

Arrogance; Differentness. Does Millie's writing make her sound arrogant to you? Do you think she is arrogant? If you know anyone who talks as Millie does, does her story make you think about that person differently?

Identity; Using ability. What different kinds of giftedness are exemplified by the characters in this book? Millie knows most about intellectual giftedness—how does this contribute to her cluelessness? What can you learn from her?

Relationships with others; Resilience. Is it better, as Maddie says, to be liked than right? How do you decide whether to be liked or right in different situations? Why is it difficult for Millicent to believe that Emily likes her for herself rather than for her brain?

Sensitivity. Although Millie is certainly accustomed to emphasizing her intelligence, she also has awareness of how others are feeling. When does her sensitivity show itself?

Yee, Lisa. *Stanford Wong Flunks Big Time.* Scholastic, 2007.

Written after *Millicent Min, Girl Genius* (annotated above) but telling the story from his point of view, Stanford sheds a different light on things. As we know from Millicent's story, Stanford must submit to her tutoring when his passion for basketball overshadows his interest in school and only summer school can save him. But also this summer, the arguing increases between Stanford's workaholic father and his mother, his beloved grandmother finally has to move to a retirement home, and Stanford is doing all he can to hide his summer school attendance from his friends. When Emily Ebers enters the picture, it is almost more than he can handle. Stanford matures considerably this summer, and he tells the whole story with feeling and humor.

This is a boys' book, but girls—especially after reading *Millicent Min*—will enjoy it, too. For both, *Stanford Wong Flunks Big Time* provides insights into the passion for a sport, the need for paternal attention, the capacity for tenderness with a grandparent, and the hopes and fears involved in finding a girlfriend that Stanford describes with a range of emotions as things appear to unravel and then come together again. And always there is humor to keep things lively. Each book can stand alone, but readers will probably enjoy them more if they read Millicent's story before Stanford's. Yee has also written Emily's version: *So Totally Emily Ebers* (2008).

Relationships with others. There are many well-described characters in this book: Stanford, each member of his family, the Roadrunners. Choose one, and think about how Stanford's relationship changes with that person during the summer. Why does it change?

Using ability. How does Stanford's passion for basketball compare and contrast with Millicent's passion for learning? Consider the role of balance in each of their stories.

Yep, Laurence. *Hiroshima.* Scholastic, 1996.

This short novella is the story of Sachi, a composite of several survivors who were children in Hiroshima at the time of the bombing and who later came to the United States. On the morning of the bombing, Sachi and her sister Riko walk together to their work for the war effort—Sachi to join her classmates in tearing down houses to form a fire lane, and Riko to answer telephones at army headquarters in an old castle. Meanwhile, the *Enola Gay* is flying toward Hiroshima with an 8,900-pound atom bomb, its American crew hoping that this bomb will end a terrible war begun four years earlier, when Japanese pilots attacked American ships at Pearl Harbor on a quiet morning like this one.

In spare prose, Yep reviews the attack and its aftermath, including statistics—which, he tells us in an afterword, were difficult to verify. No one really knows how many people were living in Hiroshima, how many were killed that day, or how many died later from radiation. Sachi survives by jumping into a river with many others, but her face is terribly disfigured, and 10 years later, she is one of 25 "Hiroshima Maidens" brought to the United States for 18 months of plastic surgery performed by volunteer American doctors. Now every year on August 6th, she is among the Japanese who place candles in boxes on the river in memory of those who died on that date in 1945. Every year, new names are added to the list, as survivors continue to die from radiation poisoning.

Drive to understand; Moral concerns; Resilience. This book is easy to read but may be difficult to discuss. The story is told without sentimentality, so it can be used simply as an informational piece. But Yep includes a chapter on efforts toward world peace since the bombing, and his book can also be a point of departure for discussion of current efforts to curtail nuclear weapons.

Yep, Laurence. *Later, Gator.* Hyperion, 1997.
Teddy is the unsentimental but imaginative older brother who gives the considerate and thoughtful Bobby practical gifts, like socks, partly out of his resentment at how much everyone likes Bobby. This time, he outdoes his own reputation for causing trouble: he gives Bobby a pet alligator named Oscar. To his astonishment, Bobby is thrilled, their mother falls in line, and the relatives are impressed. But their father, whose chicken dinner was fed to the alligator before he got home, announces that henceforth, Oscar will eat garbage. Suddenly, Teddy is helping Bobby find food for the alligator. Their search through Chinatown's restaurant garbage cans alarms the members of their father's club, who immediately assume that his business is failing and rally to help the boys find food. As the story plays itself out, Teddy realizes that Bobby is more perceptive than he thought, and he begins to feel protective and brotherly toward Bobby.

Basing his story on a childhood experience with an alligator named Oscar and a brother with whom he grew up in San Francisco, Yep closes with an afterword, stating that now that alligators have been declared endangered, he knows that it was wrong to buy one. But he has written a warm and funny story that will keep young readers laughing and give them something to think about regarding sibling relationships. At the same time, he gently reminds us that there is more to the lives of Chinese people in San Francisco than tourists see in restaurants.

Relationships with others. Bobby says, kindly, that it takes someone like him to handle their friends and someone like Teddy to handle their enemies. What does he mean by this? Which role would you play? What are Bobby's strengths? What are Teddy's strengths? What can they offer each other? What can they learn from each other?

Sensitivity. What examples of Bobby's sensitivity can you identify? Can you follow them? What examples can you give of sensitivity in your own recent experience?

Middle School: Grades 6-8

Adderholdt, Miriam & Jan Goldberg. *Perfectionism: What's Bad about Being Too Good.* Illustrated by Caroline Price Schwert. Free Spirit, 1999.

Many gifted teenagers are victims of perfectionism, harboring so strong a desire to do everything perfectly that they consider second place or a B a failure. Some go so far as to avoid risking that failure by refusing to accept a new challenge or to take an advanced course. *Perfectionism* speaks to these students, describing its effects on mind, body, and relationships and then prescribing practical steps toward becoming more realistic about expectations. Counselors, teachers, and librarians will find the book a useful tool for school-based discussions on giftedness, and parents can use it effectively in the home. The insights that it offers are as important for adults working with gifted youngsters as for the students themselves.

This book can be used independently by students in the middle grades or in senior high. For younger students, parents can gather ideas from the book and present them to their children in whatever way seems appropriate.

Perfectionism; Using ability.

Alexander, Lloyd. *The Iron Ring.* Puffin, 1999.

Tamar, the young king of Sundari, loses a game of dice to Jaya, king of Mahapura. The result is that Tamar, a member of the warrior caste to whom honor is everything, leaves Sundari to journey to Mahapura as Jaya demands. At the beginning, Tamar travels alone except for Rajaswami, his old tutor, but his retinue grows. In India's golden age, animals speak, and soon Tamar and Rajaswami are joined by a monkey king, an eagle, and by Mirra, a *gopi* (village milkmaid), whose cleverness and spirit contribute much in the struggle to reach Mahapura. The little group is drawn into a great battle, as several kings vie for leadership in the region. Tamar has reason to ask again and again what honor requires of him as he tries to be true to his *dharma*.

Alexander's fascination with Celtic mythology led to the *Prydain* series, set in Wales. Now he turns to the ancient mythologies of India and explores as well the nature of *dharma*, the meaning of honor, and the limitations of caste systems. *The Iron Ring* is a quest story, with forces for good pitched against evil, requiring Tamar to seek his own interpretations, as we all must in the process of growing up. A brief exploration of the old caste system in India would be useful before reading this book.

Drive to understand. In considering the questions under *Moral concerns*, look at them first from the Indian point of view and then from the American point of view. How do the answers change? How would you explain what Tamar learns from the chandalah?

Identity. How does one know what one's *dharma* is?

Moral concerns. How can Tamar justify leaving his subjects in Sundari to follow his idea of honor? Was Ashwara right to refuse to fight anyone except Nahusha? In what ways does Rajaswami change his ideas of right and wrong?

Perfectionism. What would be your advice to Tamar when he finds it difficult to follow his *dharma* exactly as he thinks he should?

Alexander, Lloyd. *Westmark.* Puffin, 2002. (The first book of a trilogy, followed by *The Kestrel* and *The Beggar Queen,* both published in 2002.)

A printer's apprentice who flees when his master's press is destroyed as a result of political upheaval, Theo meets a rich assortment of characters in quick succession: a street urchin; two "river rats"; a charlatan and his sidekick, a dwarf; revolutionary students, one of them a cartoonist and one a thief; courtiers and royalty—all of whom reappear as the trilogy unfolds. Ruled by a weak king who is controlled by a power-hungry chief minister, Westmark falls into war with a neighboring kingdom as civil unrest builds. The street urchin, Mickle, learns that she is Westmark's princess, and Theo grows to love her while he also joins the revolutionary students who help her army defend Westmark from the neighboring Regian army. Far from staying in the safety of the palace, Mickle proves to be a fine general. When the war against the Regians is won, however, she and Theo must address the civil unrest within Westmark and a further threat from the exiled chief minister.

This trilogy traces Theo's growth from a young and naive printer's devil to a thoughtful, complex young man who recognizes and regrets his own potential for violence. His loyalties are divided first between the monarch and the rebels who struggle for a republic, then between his natural pacifism and the raging desire for vengeance that rises when a friend is killed. At the same time, he tries to understand his motivations—to please one of the revolution's leaders, Justin, or to follow his own inner commands.

The writing in this book is deceptively simple and the plot perhaps too dependent on coincidences, but the ideas are demanding and require a thoughtful response. Intellectual challenge is also provided by frequent shifts in locale as different facets of the story come into play.

Drive to understand. Discussion related to intellectual curiosity will help the reader view the story from a socio-political level, looking, for example, at the causes of political unrest. Alexander has based his story on the history of the French Revolution. What are the similarities between pre-revolutionary France and Westmark? Why is Westmark ripe for rebellion?

Identity; Intensity. Readers can interpret the story at a personal level, exploring the development of Theo's character as he grows. What are the results of Theo's need to prove himself, both within himself and for others?

Moral concerns. What does Theo learn as he struggles with the pacifist and the warrior within his character? What contradictory values or impulses do you recognize within yourself? What can you learn from Theo's experience?

Using ability. How can Florian so steadfastly oppose his background, giving up his birthright? What motivates him?

Anderson, Laurie Halse. *Fever 1793,* Aladdin, 2002.

August of 1793 in Philadelphia is hot and dry, the air miasmic. When people begin dying of yellow fever, Matilda's family feels safe in their home and coffeehouse, which her father purposely built away from the lower ground near the Delaware River. But as graveyards fill, those who are able flee the capital city of the young United States to wait for the first frost—which will kill the fever—in less crowded villages and farms outside of Philadelphia. When her mother is stricken and Matilda and her grandfather finally decide to go to friends in the countryside, they find that the city has been quarantined, and they are denied passage on the road. Grandfather and then Matilda become ill, recover, and return to a nearly deserted and anarchic Philadelphia. Matilda survives by finding Eliza, the free black woman who cooked for the coffeehouse, and she supports Eliza's work with the Free African Society, which was formed to care for fever victims and survivors. Finally, in late October, the frost arrives and the fever abates. On November 10th, President Washington returns to the capital. By then, Matilda is already picking up the pieces of her life.

Spread by mosquitoes, the fever of 1793 killed nearly 5,000 people—10% of Philadelphia's population. This thoroughly researched and fast-paced novel evokes the fear and horror of the disease, but also the courage and sacrifice of people who helped each other survive. An appendix provides more information about the epidemic, medicine of the era, the Free African Society, how city residents lived, and how famous Americans—including George Washington, Dolley Madison, and Dr. Benjamin Rush—were affected by the fever.

Drive to understand. In the early years of our history as the United States, the Industrial Revolution had not yet reached America, and everyday life—providing food, housekeeping, labor, transportation—was much as it had been during the Colonial period. What changes would occur in Matilda's life by 1830 or 1840? What changes would occur in medicine to make an epidemic less likely?

Moral concerns. Was it right or wrong for the rich and powerful people to leave the poor and powerless behind in Philadelphia? Was it right or wrong for Matilda and Grandfather to leave her mother? How likely is it that Matilda and Eliza would form a business partnership? Do you think it would be successful? Why or why not?

Resilience. In what different ways did Matilda, her grandfather, and Eliza helped each other to be resilient? What did they learn from each other?

Avi. *Crispin: At the Edge of the World.* Hyperion, 2006.

In this second book of a planned trilogy, the action begins just where *Crispin: The Cross of Lead* (see the next book entry; you might want to read it first) ended. Crispin and the weakened Bear try to get as far from the city as possible before they rest, but Bear is recognized and wounded, and they must hide in the forest. There, Aude, a crone, nurses Bear with the help of Troth, a disfigured girl. Too soon, Bear and Crispin must flee again, this time joined by Troth. The three become a family as they continue trying to evade the men who are chasing Bear. A storm at sea and an encounter with a band of outlaw soldiers in Brittany provide the background as Crispin must take more responsibility. The ending is somber but not hopeless; readers will close this book already looking forward to the next one.

The growth required of Crispin is rapid—the strain shows when he reminds himself that he does not have to be a man yet; he only has to be himself—but he is equal to it. Crispin's theme in this book is his burning desire to be free and to learn what that means, while Bear struggles with the memories of his part in the long war between England and France as he senses his own approaching death. Troth is shunned because of her cleft lip, but Crispin and Bear quickly see past that and value her loyalty, intelligence, and sixth sense—she is a character who may be further developed in the third book. Avi's handling of the superstition surrounding both Troth's disfigurement and Aude's "old religion" is deft, and he supplies more information on pre-Christian beliefs and on the 14th century in an author's note.

Drive to understand. There is more emphasis here than in *The Cross of Lead* on the Hundred Years War between France and England, as well as continuing descriptions of peasant life in the turbulent 14th century. Try to imagine Crispin's mental picture of the world at the beginning of the book, and at the end—try to imagine not knowing what is at "the edge of the world." In what ways is that still true for us in the 21st century?

Relationships with others. We can say that the villagers who attacked Aude and the others who feared Troth were ignorant, superstitious, and prejudiced—but why were they so? What causes people to feel that way? How can we understand it? How can we change it? To what extent is this still a problem?

Avi. *Crispin: The Cross of Lead.* Hyperion, 2004.

The 13-year-old who has always been called simply "Asta's son" flees his feudal English village after his mother dies and the steward of the manor house accuses him of murdering the priest, declaring that he is a "wolf's head"—to be pursued and killed if possible. He has learned from the priest that his real name is Crispin, but he cannot read the writing scratched on the back of the lead cross his mother cherished, and he knows nothing of his father. Seeking a city and avoiding men from the manor who would kill him, he falls in with Bear, a wandering juggler who treats him as a son. In the city, Bear meets with fellow conspirators and is captured by the steward of the manor, who is still pursuing Crispin. Crispin learns why the steward wants him dead: the etching on the cross names him "Crispin son of Furnival"—the lord of the manor. Knowing that his identity only puts him in danger, the once diffident and frightened Crispin courageously makes his way into the dungeon where Bear is being held and bargains his birthright for Bear's release.

This multi-layered book, a Newbery Award winner, is a medieval adventure and a coming-of-age story, blended with well-researched 14th-century settings and hints of the unrest that led to the Peasants' Revolt of 1381—in which John Ball, a co-conspirator with Bear, played a part. The human touch that holds all of his together and makes it so memorable is the strength of the relationship that develops between two misfits, Crispin and Bear.

Drive to understand. Crispin lives in a feudal society—what does this mean? How does it affect his life? At the time of this story, people like Bear were trying to bring change. What do you imagine that

Bear and his friends are discussing? What specific complaints would serfs have about their lives? What do you know about what happened historically at this time in England? How did it relate to the founding of colonies in America, just over 100 years later?

Identity. Crispin has to learn who he is in more ways than one. How does his personality change through the book? What role does Bear play in this, and in what ways does Crispin bring about change in himself?

Relationships with others. Why was Crispin so afraid of Bear at first? When did you first notice that the relationship was changing? When did Crispin begin to trust Bear? What does each offer to the other?

Avi. *Nothing but the Truth.* HarperTrophy, 2003.

Philip Malloy is a high-spirited ninth grader, passionate about track and less interested in English. His English teacher, Miss Narwin, is passionate about literature and less understanding of the extracurricular interests of ninth-grade boys. Unable to take Jack London and *Call of the Wild* seriously, Philip earns a D in English and is stunned to learn that he cannot try out for the track team with a D on his record. Things deteriorate from here. Encouraged by a homeroom teacher who is casual about rules, Philip hums along with *The Star-Spangled Banner* after he is transferred to the homeroom of Miss Narwin, who takes literally the rule that students must "stand at respectful, silent attention" for the playing of the national anthem. She sends him to the office, and due to another rule that cannot be bent, Philip is suspended. Not listening to Philip carefully enough to understand all of the nuances of the situation, his parents encourage him to stand up for his rights. Because of similar partial understanding on the part of school authorities, each with his or her own agenda, the incident explodes into a national scandal. With one miscommunication after another, the situation spins entirely out of control; in the end, no one wins.

Written as a documentary, this book is entertaining as a satire on high school rules, but it is more than that. A sympathetic reading yields insight into the motives of each character. The ease with which a number of small, subtle shadings of the story build inexorably to major misunderstanding is instructive. Philip is not unlike many students who would score well on a test of intellectual ability but who lack the interpersonal ability to see from someone else's point of view.

Differentness; Identity; Relationships with others. Realistically, what could Philip have done to get along better with Miss Narwin? What in his background or personality prevented his doing this? When could Philip have asked for advice, and from whom? Why did he not do this? If you could advise Philip, what would you say? What have you learned from his experience that might be useful to you?

Moral concerns; Using ability. Choose a member of the school faculty or administration and consider whether he or she did anything wrong, and if so, why. Ask the same questions regarding Philip, Philip's parents, another student, and the media. What were the consequences for each?

Avi. *The True Confessions of Charlotte Doyle.* HarperCollins, 2004.

In the summer of 1832, 13-year-old Charlotte Doyle boards the *Seahawk* in Liverpool to rejoin her family in Providence. Though her father had planned carefully so that she would be accompanied, the other passengers do not arrive. Charlotte, a young lady taught to obey her elders and avoid informal contact with servants, sails with only Captain Jaggery and his rough, rebellious crew for company. She soon realizes that she is in grave danger and must decide where her loyalties lie. Because she has to, she learns to be a sailor, doing so well that she earns the crew's respect. The Charlotte Doyle who disembarks in Providence in August is very different from the girl who had left the Barrington School for Better Girls in June.

Appealing to both boys and girls, Charlotte's story is much more than good mystery and adventure, although it is certainly that. Charlotte must change internally, without guidance or model, in order to survive. When she joins her family, she is expected to change again— a challenge that she will not accept.

Arrogance. Charlotte would not have called herself arrogant, but readers of her story might. What role does arrogance play in her decisions?

Drive to understand. Avi's story offers readers a compelling picture of life in the early 19th century, providing plenty of opportunity for comparisons and further exploration.

Identity. Discussion can center around Charlotte's decisions. Why would she adapt to the sailors' life yet be unwilling to re-adapt to her family's? Which is more truly Charlotte, and why? In 10 years, will Charlotte have one life or the other, or a blend? If a blend, describe it.

Relationships with others. What can you learn from Charlotte's ability to get along with the sailors?

Resilience; Using ability. How will the social rules of her time affect Charlotte's future? Are there situations now that cause people to straddle two lives, two expressions of themselves? How is it done? Is it healthy for them?

Billingsley, Franny. *The Folk Keeper.* Aladdin, 2001.

On the Mainland and in the northern isles, Folk Keepers are those whose duty it is to feed and pacify the Folk—vicious cave creatures, mostly teeth and wet mouth, who eat only flesh—to keep them from harming animals and crops. To gain the power of a Folk Keeper, a post awarded only to boys, Corinna has disguised herself as "Corin." Lacking the opportunity for an apprenticeship, she learns the trade by native ability, wit, and a toughness that places the highest priority on personal survival, with a quickness to seek vengeance when she is threatened and a determination to retain the independence that she has won. When she is summoned by Lord Merton to go to his Manor house at Cliffsend far to the north, she refuses his first offer—that she will be raised as a lady (for she knows that ladies can be powerless)—and only later agrees to go on the condition that she be appointed Folk Keeper for the estate. At Cliffsend, she is treated as part of the family and befriended by Finian, heir to the Manor House and the estate. To protect herself from these northern Folk, stronger and fiercer by far than those she has known, she must learn who the Lady Rona was and why there is a tiny grave near the chapel. She finds that she must also protect herself and Finian from Sir Edward, who had hoped to inherit from Lord Merton. As she does so, facing darkness and danger, she also learns who she is, the source of the strange powers that she has always had, and how to regain one that she has lost: the power of The Last Word.

Drawn from the selkie legends of the Scottish islands, *The Folk Keeper* is told through Corinna's journal, marked by saints' days and solstice rhythms. It can be enjoyed simply as a good story or perhaps as an introduction to fantasy or to the folklore of the northern British Isles, but Corinna's story also serves as metaphor for finding ourselves. Corinna gains control over her own life only when she gives up the power she has known as Corin. Determined to follow her lonely path independently, she finds at the last minute that there is more promise and growth in sharing her destiny.

Arrogance; Use of ability. Early in the story, Corinna is proud of her position: "I control the Folk. Here I'm queen of the world." With her statement in mind, explain this: Arrogance is often the other face of fear. Give examples from your own experience. What happens to Corinna's arrogance as she learns more about her abilities?

Differentness. Corinna is different in many ways. How is this a problem for her? When is it not a problem? When it is not a problem, what factors make it unimportant that she is different?

Identity. "There is a price you pay for power," Corinna writes. What price has she paid? What does she gain when she gives up the power? Name others you know, in public or private life, who have traded something of their identity for power. For what asset besides power might one pay with a loss of personal identity? If you are doing this, what would you change? What would you gain if you changed?

Relationships with others. Corinna has a strong need to take vengeance when she feels wronged; Finian does not understand this. What is the reason for the response of each? What does Corinna learn from this, and how does she change?

Blos, Joan W. *Brothers of the Heart: A Story of the Old Northwest 1837-1838.* Aladdin, 1993.

Shem Perkins's family moves to Michigan in 1837, when statehood opens up the land. He is 14 and is called "the fiddler's crippled son" because he had been born with a malformed leg and foot. That summer, he leaves home and finds work in Detroit, but then is sent on a winter expedition to Mackinac Island and the wild western shore of Michigan. Left alone in a cabin, he expects to die. But Mary Goodhue, an old Indian woman known for healing, finds him. Nearing the end of her life, she stays with Shem and teaches him, eventually showing him how to return home.

As in her earlier book, *A Gathering of Days*, Blos captures the rhythms of the language of the time in this well-researched novel. She also tells the story of Shem's inner growth in a few short but difficult months as he transcends his disability. When he returns to southeastern Michigan, she says, "His stride was unashamed"—the limp not vanished by any means, but so outshone by Shem's personal strength, courage, and purpose as to be unnoticed.

Drive to understand. This book can be read for understanding the lives of early settlers in a new state, for appreciation of American Indian values, and for its tale of wilderness survival.

Identity. Why was Mary Goodhue able to help Shem overcome his difference when his parents could not? What traits do Mary's husband and Shem have in common? What traits do you have that enable you to compensate for other, less desirable traits?

Resilience. When does Shem show resilience, and what form does it take? How does he have the strength to be resilient?

Bond, Nancy. *A String in the Harp*. Aladdin, 2006.

Unhappily spending a year in Wales while his father teaches at the University of Aberystwyth, Peter Morgan finds on the seacoast a strange silver object—a tuning key for a harp. The key sings to him, enabling him to see events that happened hundreds of years ago—scenes which eventually Peter realizes are from the life of the 6th-century Welsh bard Taliesin, to whom the key belonged. As Peter concentrates on Taliesin's story, he becomes more distant from his family. His father and sisters, Becky and Jen, become more concerned about him. At last, with his sisters' support, Peter realizes what he must do about the key, and the family is reunited.

The fantasy story of Peter's visions of Taliesin is convincingly counterbalanced by the reality of the area of Wales in which the

Morgans live and the Welsh people who become their friends. Bond's sense for the setting—both geographical and psychological—is sure, and readers will feel that they have gained some important knowledge about the essence of Wales.

Aloneness. Jen thinks that perhaps Gwilym isn't "solitary from choice." Why, then, is he solitary? Is his aloneness something to worry about? If so, what should Gwilym do to improve the situation? What should others do to help him?

Drive to understand. This book is part realism, part fantasy. How can you balance the rational and irrational aspects of the story?

Identity. What differences are there in Jen's and Becky's responses to Peter's behavior? How do they correspond to the reactions of Dr. Owen and Dr. Rhys? Why do these people respond so differently?

Bruchac, Joseph. *Code Talker: A Novel about the Navajo Marines of World War Two.* Puffin, 2006.

When he was six years old, Kii Yazhi was taken from his family's hogan to a mission school where young Navajos were taught English and encouraged to forget their native language and traditions. Even his name was changed—to Ned Begay. Ned learned English easily but never forgot the sacred language of his people. In 1942, when Ned was still in high school, a Marine recruiter came to New Mexico seeking Navajos who could speak English. They were wanted for a special purpose—to create an unbreakable code for the war effort in the Pacific. Ned joined the Marines, and the story follows him and his fellow code talkers through the terrible battles for the Pacific islands of Bougainville, Iwo Jima, and Okinawa. Other Indian languages had been used in military codes in the past, but they had been decoded. For World War II, Navajos were wanted because theirs is a very difficult language for all but native speakers. The code that they created was never broken. Their service was invaluable, but it was kept secret until 1969, and until then, they received no recognition for their critical role in winning the war in the Pacific.

Author Joseph Bruchac's ethnic background includes Slovak and English blood, along with his American Indian heritage, which is not Navajo but Western Abenaki; his ancestors lived in what is now New

Hampshire and Vermont. Bruchac's passion for preserving native languages underlies Ned Begay's love of his language and his people. In an author's note, Bruchac speaks of his respect for the Navajos and the code talkers, as well as the irony of the mission school's efforts to eradicate the language, followed a few years later by the nation's recognition that that language could be extremely useful. "In some ways, this novel can be read as a parable about the importance of respecting other languages and cultures," Bruchac writes. He is a prolific writer of poetry and songs as well as fiction, drawing from stories of American Indian groups and other cultures.

Aloneness; Identity. In what ways did being a Navajo help Ned to survive the war, both physically and mentally? What steps did he take to ensure that? How can you structure your life to build or maintain your sense of identity? What is there in your heritage that you can use as a basis for that effort?

Drive to understand. Recall all that you learned from this novel about the Navajos' culture and their ways of treating others. How does it square with your previous mental image of the Navajo people? This novel provides solid historical information about the Pacific Theater during World War II—it would be helpful to read it with an atlas at hand. You may also want to read some of the other books about code talkers and World War II that are listed at the back of *Code Talker.* In addition, you may be interested in reading other books by Bruchac.

Cole, Brock. *The Goats.* Farrar, Straus, & Giroux, 1992.

They are called goats because they are scapegoats, the brunt of a cruel trick at an exclusive but poorly supervised summer camp. Left alone at night on an island, the boy and girl make their way to the mainland and to an empty cabin. They determine never to return to the camp, and for three days, they avoid the searchers. During this time, they fall in with a group at another summer camp, and these campers treat them with kindness and understanding. The boy and girl, Howie and Lauara, learn to care for and depend on each other, building feelings of trust that neither has known before.

These two youths see themselves as "socially retarded," as Laura puts it, because they do not fit in. But in a short time, they learn to relate well to each other—proving to themselves and demonstrating to the reader that those who don't fit in with the crowd do very well if they can find just one person to whom they can talk freely.

Aloneness. To build an understanding of why some people are isolated by the cruelty of others, discuss scapegoating. Why is it that some people are "goats"? What causes a group—a neighborhood, school, or nation—to find goats? What characteristics make individuals vulnerable and likely to become goats? Consider the consequences of scapegoating: What characteristics of scapegoated individuals might make them valuable to society? What effect will this incident have on Laura and Howie as they grow older, and in their adult lives? What changes will have occurred in them as a result of their experience? How will it affect their personalities, if at all? What effect will it have, if any, on what they contribute to society? To discuss scapegoating at a personal level, inquire: Do you know any goats? Can you see beneath the surface to the qualities they have to offer? Do you ever see yourself as a goat? How can you grow beyond it?

Relationships with others. To use this book to help children discover ways to cope with being alone, ask: Are some people "socially retarded" for their age, as Laura says she is? If so, how does this happen, and what can one do about it? What was the difference that made the second set of campers kind to Laura and Howie? What did Laura and Howie learn that would help them get along better with others?

Cooper, Susan. *The Dark Is Rising.* Aladdin, 2007.

On his eleventh birthday, Will Stanton learns that he is one of the Old Ones, called to struggle through the ages against the Dark. The Dark is rising this Christmas season in one of a series of attempts to dominate the world. Will's task is to search for the six Signs that the Old Ones will need in the final battle against the Dark. His search takes him to distant places and bygone centuries, while he learns, under the tutelage of Merriman Lyon, to use the powers of the Old Ones. Throughout, he remains an 11-year-old boy, living in the warmth of a large family.

This is the second book of Cooper's *Dark Is Rising* sequence. The first is *Over Sea, Under Stone*, and following *The Dark Is Rising* are *Greenwitch, The Grey King,* and *Silver on the Tree.* All five are good adventure stories, but they also hold much to ponder for those who continue to think about a book long after they have finished reading.

Drive to understand. A Newbery Honor Book, this well-written fantasy is excellent for good readers; it is challenging in structure, as Will travels from one century to another and meets some of the same characters in each. The sequence of books is steeped in the folklore of old Britain; some readers will want to know more about the body of lore that is so basic to much of our present heritage.

Cooper, Susan. *Dawn of Fear.* Illustrated by Margery Gill. Aladdin, 2007.

Living near London during World War II, Derek and his friends, Peter and Geoffrey, are thrilled by the excitement of bomb raids that interrupt their school days. Wishing they could stay outside and watch the planes flying overhead, they obey the air raid drills reluctantly. Nighttime raids, when they and their families must leave their warm beds and go to their shelters, are a nuisance but not really disturbing to them. Their main interest is the camp they that are building in a field near their homes, where they stow precious gear in case of an imagined attack, unconsciously imitating the family shelters. They are pleased when Tom, a 16-year-old who will soon join the Merchant Navy, offers to help. When a neighboring gang destroys the camp, Tom leads them in retaliation in the form of a mud-ball raid. But the mud-ball slinging ends in a serious stand-off between Tom and the leader of the gang, a boy older than Tom who is shirking his military duty. As the younger boys watch, they are overwhelmed by the reality of the anger that they see, which goes far beyond their games. They recognize the potential for real danger, and for the first time, all of them fear the power of violence. That night, before Derek has had time to come to terms both with the strength of the adult anger that he has witnessed and with his own fear, another raid brings the real war much too close to home.

Since most readers think of Susan Cooper as an author of fantasy (see above), it may be surprising to discover this earlier novel—a work of historical fiction written with clear insight into the psychology of very real adolescent boys. It is valuable because it is definitely a "boys' book" (although girls will be moved by it, too) and because it offers a view of another society in another time, as well as providing some vocabulary challenges. But it is also valuable because it so skillfully contrasts the glamour of the face of war with the truly frightening realities behind it. It can be used with early adolescents in discussing the strength of human emotions and the danger inherent in romanticizing them without respecting their dark side.

Drive to understand. How is the fight between Tom and Johnny connected to the war? Why do the younger boys feel fear as they watch the older boys fight, although they have not feared the bombs? Is it good or bad to feel fear? Why?

Identity. How does Derek change during the timeframe of this story? What more does he learn about himself? How will he be different in the future? What events in your life (including events less serious than Derek's experience) have caused you to know yourself better and to grow?

Relationships with others. What is the difference between Derek's friendship with Peter and with Geoffrey? When does it first appear that Geoffrey may be more "real" than Derek had thought? What will help them to become closer friends in the future?

Creech, Sharon. *Chasing Redbird.* Macmillan, 2001.

Zinny (for Zinnia) Taylor is somewhere in the middle of seven children, growing up on a farm near Bybank, Kentucky. Although—or because—she is part of a large and loving family, at 12, Zinny feels lost. Since her parents are always busy with the others, Zinny spends as much time as possible with Aunt Jessie and Uncle Nate, whose house "fits snug up against" Zinny's. Things are quieter on their side of the house—their daughter Rose, who was just Zinny's age, died of whooping cough caught from Zinny when the girls were four, and since then, they have loved to have Zinny there. Just recently, though, Aunt Jessie died suddenly, and Zinny is sure it was her fault.

And now Jake Boone has returned to Bybanks. When Jake brings gifts to Zinny, she is certain that he is trying to reach her older sister May through her. In the past, boys who have liked Zinny at first have always later switched to May—perhaps because Zinny has a prickly exterior. In any case, Zinny has no idea why Jake would like her. In short, she feels guilty and unlikeable, and she does not talk much. Then she discovers the slate stones that are the beginning of an old, long-overgrown trail which leads from Bybanks right through their farm. Zinny determines to clear the whole trail. As she does, working through the summer, she also uncovers her own tangled feelings, learns parts of her own story that she had forgotten, and even comes to believe that Jake might like her after all.

This is a story for the better readers in this age group—for those who are able to interpret metaphor and who will enjoy the figurative language that Zinny and her family use. Creech brings characters from one of her books into another—in *Chasing Redbird*, we hear about Zinny's best friend Sal, who has moved to Ohio—another loss for Zinny. Sal's story is told in *Walk Two Moons*, described next.

Identity. How does Zinny's compulsion to clear the trail relate to her search for her own identity, separate from the other Taylors? How aware does she become of her strengths, as well her weaknesses? How aware are you of your origins? Of your strengths and weaknesses?

Introversion. Zinny clearly needs time alone. What other evidence is there that she tends toward introversion? If she saw herself in this light, what would she do to accommodate that after she finishes the trail?

Relationships with others. Why does Zinny treat others as roughly as she does? Why does she not believe that Jake could like her? How would she treat him if she believed otherwise? What does this say about relationships, in general?

Sensitivity. How do Zinny's parents show their awareness of her grieving for Aunt Jessie? For what else is Zinny grieving? Would you call Zinny a sensitive person? Why or why not? How aware are you when others may be more sensitive to events than they show?

Creech, Sharon. *Walk Two Moons*. HarperTeen, 2003.

A little more than a year after her mother left Sal and her father on their farm in Kentucky, Sal and her grandparents set out to trace her mother's journey to Idaho. On the week-long road trip, Sal tells Gram and Gramps the story of Phoebe, a girl Sal met when she and her father moved to Euclid, Ohio, shortly after her mother's departure. Sal and Phoebe became good friends despite their differences— Phoebe's family is stiff and "respectable," in contrast to the simple warmth of Sal's father and Gram and Gramps. But Phoebe's mother disappeared, too, giving the girls something in common and helping Sal to put her own loss in perspective.

Although it is simply told, this winner of the 1995 Newbery Medal is a complex story—or rather two stories, of Phoebe and of the trip to Idaho—many-layered and offering opportunities for serious discussion. Both girls are surrounded by loving adults, including their mothers; this is a book in which the characters search for understanding rather than laying blame. As Sal tells Phoebe's story, her own is blended with it, and the reader watches Sal glean snatches of insight from her own words.

A striking feature of the plot is how strong the characters are in their impacts on each other. Because the book is for younger readers, character analysis of each individual is sketchy, but the interrelationships among the people in the story are compelling. *Walk Two Moons* invites immediate re-reading. In fact, that might be a good idea, with the following questions in mind.

Identity. In what ways does Sal grow up in the year that this story covers?

Relationships with others. What does Sal learn about her own situation from watching Phoebe's family? How does her experience help her be a friend when Phoebe's mother leaves? What does she see that Phoebe cannot see? Why? Why is Ben potentially a good friend for Sal? How do your feelings about Margaret change as you gain more information? About Ben? Mrs. Winterbottom? Mr. Winterbottom? Sal's mother? How does learning more about people affect our relationships with them?

Curtis, Christopher Paul. *The Watsons Go to Birmingham—1963*. Laurel Leaf, 2000.

Kenny Watson is nine, and his brother Byron is 13—"officially a teenage juvenile delinquent," according to Kenny. In this African-American family, their father has a terrific sense of humor, their mother is the kind of person who knows how to patch up a misunderstanding between Kenny and his best friend, and their little sister Joetta is so soft-hearted that she defends Byron no matter what he does. Against the background of this nurturing home life, both boys struggle with the dangers at school. Kenny has two major vulnerabilities—he is smart and likes to read, and he has a lazy eye—so he concentrates on defending himself against teasing and bullies. Byron is sometimes one of the bullies and sometimes not, but always, he is into more and more trouble.

Finally, their parents decide to take Byron to Momma's home in Alabama, where he will spend the summer with Grandma Sands, who has a reputation for toughness. Daddy readies the Brown Bomber—the 15-year-old family car—for the long drive from Michigan, and Momma carefully plans the trip for maximum economy, safety, and educational value. Byron turns sullen, and Kenny watches to see whether Grandma Sands or Byron, the two meanest people he knows, will win the epic battle he foresees. However, Grandma Sands turns out to be not big and mean, but old, tiny, quick, and so insightful and loving—but always in charge—that Kenny knows immediately that Byron will lose the battle. But in the few days of the Watsons' visit, they experience first-hand the racial tension that is growing all over the South; they no longer think that Byron will be safer in Birmingham than in Flint. When they return home, Byron has a new perspective on himself and his family; he has grown up enough to be a proper big brother for Kenny and to begin to mold his own future.

The story is told through Kenny's eyes, a true and consistent view of the world as seen by a fourth-grade boy. This first novel is both a Newbery Honor Book and a Coretta Scott King Honor Book for 1996 and holds a long list of other honors. Although entirely fictional, it is based on the bombing of the Sixteenth Avenue Baptist

Church in Birmingham on September 15, 1963, in which four teen-age girls were killed. Curtis has brought the impact of that bombing to life for the reader by making the Watson family real and then sending Joetta to church on the Sunday that a bombing occurs. In an epilogue, he outlines the story of the civil rights movement, placing the Watsons' trip to Birmingham in the center of history.

Aloneness. How does Kenny realize that he has been alone? What is his part in changing that? Is this an idea you can use?

Differentness. Kenny accepts the reality that he will be teased for being smart. Would this happen in your school? What is the best way to respond?

Drive to understand. This book can introduce children to the civil rights movement and to the need for it. Why does Momma plan so carefully for the trip? Why are she and the children frightened when they stop in Tennessee?

Identity. Kenny knows that he is smart and that he likes to read, but he often calls himself stupid. In what situations does he do this?

Moral concerns. The Watson children have apparently known little about racial tensions before they go to Alabama. What do you think will be their long-term response to what they learned there? What is your response?

Relationships with others. What is it about Kenny and Rufus that makes them good friends? What makes Byron change his behavior toward Kenny?

Sensitivity. Would you agree that Kenny and Bryon are sensitive people, but in different ways? Describe the differences.

Cushman, Karen. *The Midwife's Apprentice.* HarperCollins, 1996.

When the story begins, the only name that the girl knows is Brat. About 13 years old, she lives in medieval England without home or family and fends entirely for herself. Then the village midwife discovers Brat sleeping in a dung pile for the warmth. She calls her "Beetle" and agrees to provide food and shelter in exchange for work. The food and shelter are meager, and the midwife is stingy with her knowledge, too, but Beetle watches and learns as she can. As her confidence grows and she finds a place in the life of the village, Beetle changes her name again to one more fitting: Alyce. But she fails in her work one day and runs away, finding work in an inn. There, she learns that the one fault the midwife found in her was that she gave up. Alyce returns to the village, overcoming her timidity, and takes her place as the midwife's apprentice.

Winner of the Newbery Medal, this small book offers a vivid and unforgettable picture of medieval life. At the same time, it is a truly and simply told story of a complex process: the coming-of-age of a girl who at first has only her own resources for support. Alyce is plucky. She accepts help when it is offered, grasps at every opportunity to learn, adds a natural compassion to her increasing knowledge, and is willing to learn from her mistakes. Her story provides a good example for students who may be reluctant to do these things for themselves.

Achievement. What personal qualities does Alyce need in order to grow from being a homeless beggar to being a midwife's apprentice? Which of these are also needed by young people growing up in the 21st century?

Drive to understand. What other books have you read that are set in medieval England or Europe? Imagine a conversation between Alyce and a character in one of those books. How would their stories be alike? How would they be different?

Perfectionism. What was it in her background that caused Alyce to decide to run away? When someone you know has given up, how was that person thinking as Alyce did?

Resilience; Using ability. What factors does Alyce consider as she makes the decision to return to the village and pursue midwifery?

Danziger, Paula. *The Cat Ate My Gymsuit.* Puffin, 2006.

Shy, overweight Marcy Lewis is propelled into the small group of student leaders when a favorite teacher is dismissed and Marcy proves her ability and willingness to speak out in the effort to have the teacher reinstated. To her amazement, Marcy finds that Joel, the smartest, most self-assured boy in the class, likes her—and that Joel's family life, like hers, is not entirely happy. As the students work together, they come into conflict with some of the adult community, including Marcy's father, but Marcy's self-confidence grows.

It may be necessary to point out that this book was first published more than 30 years ago, at the beginning of the women's movement, and also to give some background on Marcy's mother's discomfort with speaking her own mind, since she may not seem credible to some readers. But this should not be a major problem for students. The characters line up so clearly on one side or other of the issue of firing the teacher that it is easy to discuss the real theme of the book: standing up for one's own beliefs against following the majority—a good theme for middle school students to consider.

Aloneness; Differentness. How does one decide when to be part of the majority and when to be different? Is it worthwhile for Marcy to be different? Is it worthwhile for you? Under what circumstances?

Identity. What makes shy Marcy speak up when Mr. Stone announces Ms. Finney's leaving? Why is Joel so self-confident? What does he mean when he says that when he grows up, he wants to be Joel Anderson?

Relationships with others. Marcy finds herself in a situation that gives her a chance to know other students better and gives them a chance to know her, too. How does that happen? What role does Marcy play in making it happen? In your own situation, what could you do to make it happen if you needed to? What are the rewards?

Dash, Joan. *The World at Her Fingertips: The Story of Helen Keller.* Scholastic, 2002.

This frank biography goes beyond the story of the epiphany at the well—when Helen made the connection between the letters tapped into one hand and the water flowing over the other—and presents Helen's lifelong fierce determination, her hard work, her loneliness, and her ultimate success as she became actively involved in the world she lived in. Helen Keller lived to 87; in her long life, she embraced Socialism and feminism, opposed the United States' involvement in World War I, struggled financially, and lectured on behalf of the blind around the world. She defied the assumption that disabilities are merely to be endured and provided an example of her ideal: a life based on self-help and self-respect, especially through productive work, within whatever limitations that disabilities impose.

Achievement; Using ability. How important is the controversy over how much Helen could do by herself and how much Annie did for her? What did Helen achieve? How much of what you have achieved has depended on help from others? Are you a helper to anyone else?

Differentness; Identity. At Radcliffe, Helen realized that she had been trying to be like everyone else instead of living her own life. Have you noticed ways in which you are trying to be like everyone else? Can you identify the positive and negative traits that make you the individual you are? What limitations are you working with, and how? What strengths are distinctively yours?

Drive to understand. Helen's story includes some difficult periods in U.S. history. What is your opinion about the restrictions imposed on the media then and now? What do you know about Socialism and the I.W.W.—and what happened to those movements? Are they relevant today?

Relationships with others; Resilience. Helen became independent of her family, but she was always dependent on others, sometimes frighteningly so. How did this enforced dependence affect her relationships with family and friends? How did she deal with it at different times in her life?

Dickinson, Peter. *The Ropemaker.* Delacorte, 2003.

Tilja is just learning that she has not inherited the magic powers that are usually passed down through the women of her family, so her beloved farm home will go to her younger sister, and Tilja will have to leave. But more important is the realization that the magic that has protected the Valley for 19 generations is weakening. To save it from the Empire's invasion, two elders of the Valley, Meena and Alnor, accompanied by their grandchildren, Tilja and Tahl, must find the magician who made the protective magic. As the four journey to the forbidding capital of the Empire and beyond, they encounter one danger after another, and Tilja slowly learns that she does indeed have power; it is different from what she expected, and it is the one most needed on this quest. She returns home aware of her unusual ability and full of confidence in her future.

In this many-layered story, the concept of time plays a central role, with the strong magic of the Ropemaker as its symbol. The characters are well-drawn as distinct individuals—including even the recalcitrant horse, Calico, who accompanies the four travelers and provides a bit of humor. The plot is complex, revealed piecemeal as the journey continues; it requires an attentive reader. Winner of a Printz Honor award, *The Ropemaker* can be enjoyed by thoughtful readers from about age 12 and up, including adults. It is followed by *Angel Isle*, published in 2007.

Differentness. Initially, Tilja resents being different from others in her family, but as she learns more about the special ability she has—and finds ways to use it—she values it. By the end of the book, she is eager to explore it further. Review how this process works for Tilja, and then consider how it might work for you, or think of ways in which you have seen it work for others.

Using ability. Tilja's power is related to magic. What powers—abilities, talents, strengths—do you have that you look forward to developing further? How will you do this?

Duble, Kathleen Benner. *The Sacrifice*. Aladdin, 2007.

It is 1692 in Andover, Massachusetts, and 10-year-old Abigail is in the stocks for the sin of lifting her skirt and racing with her cousin, Steven. Her mother is understanding and supportive of Abigail's high spirits, but the next day, her father has one of his "fits"—spells of paranoia and fear—and her grandfather, the minister, brings frightening news: several girls in nearby Salem Village are accusing neighbors of witchcraft. The panic soon spreads to Andover, and Abigail and her older sister Dorothy are accused and imprisoned. However, their resourceful mother develops a plan to free them: she insists that Dorothy and Abigail accuse her (after all, she is the only one who has the power to calm her husband during his fits; she might be a witch), and she will go to prison in their place. The plan buys time: their mother is pregnant and will not be hanged until after the birth of her child. But for strong-willed Abigail, lying is impossible; she speaks the truth so forcefully that she helps to stop the madness.

Duble draws a stark picture of the sisters' dilemma. The accusers cannot prove that they saw a witch, and the victims cannot prove that they are not witches, but the populace chooses to believe the accusers rather than the victims. If Abigail and Dorothy deny that they are witches, they will be hanged; if they "confess," they will be returned to the terrible conditions of the prison; if they say they were following someone else's instructions, they will free themselves but accuse an innocent person. So the poison spreads. An author's note adds verisimilitude to her story as she explains that it is based on her own family history.

Differentness. What enables Abigail to think and behave differently from others in her community? How does your environment support or prevent different thoughts and behaviors? It can be difficult to be different; what makes it worthwhile?

Drive to understand. This early introduction to the Salem Witch Hunts is well-written for younger readers, with plenty of information for an understanding of the issue blended with characters supported by a cohesive and loving family. Can we understand how people in the harsh world of the early English settlers could convince themselves of witchcraft? Why did some believe in it and some not? What beliefs in England at the time paralleled the New England experience? Where in the world is the same kind of thing happening now, if at all? What made it stop in New England; what might make it stop now?

Moral concerns. What personal and family resources gave Abigail the strength to speak the truth in her trial? Are there advantages to having people like Abigail in a community? What are the disadvantages?

Fenner, Carol. *Yolonda's Genius.* Illustrated by Raul Colon. Aladdin, 1997.

After one of her classmates is shot and some bigger boys introduce her six-year-old brother Andrew to drugs, Yolonda's mother moves her family from their Chicago neighborhood to Grand River, Michigan. Momma finds a good job and settles happily into a house with trees in the lawn, but Yolonda has more trouble adjusting to the slower pace of Grand River. It feels safe, and she misses the constant need to be alert to danger. Tall and heavy, smart and sharp-tongued,

11-year-old Yolonda has never been adept at the jump-rope games the other girls played—or at making friends. In Chicago, where most of the kids in her school were African-American, the social order had been clear. In integrated Grand River, it is murkier.

For Andrew, there are other problems. He has trouble reading and does not speak unless he must, but he expresses thoughts, feelings, and his considerable insight through the music that he makes on the harmonica his father had given him when he was still in his crib. When a friend asks Yolonda if she is a genius, Yolonda looks up the word in the library. None of the definitions fits her, but when she reads a quotation from John Hersey—"True genius rearranges old material in a way never seen before"—Yolonda suddenly knows that Andrew is the genius in the family. When the safety of Grand River proves to be illusory and Andrew and his music are in danger, Yolonda makes it her business to prove Andrew's genius to the world. A visit to Aunt Tiny in Chicago and to the blues concerts in Grant Park give her the opportunity she needs.

This Newbery Honor Book offers hints of many themes for discussion.

Achievement. Why does her mother object to Yolonda's dream of becoming a police officer? What do you think she should do? What do you think she will do?

Creativity. How does Andrew's musical talent help him? How might it be a problem for him?

Identity. Now that she has taken care of Andrew, what does Yolonda need to learn about herself?

Intensity. Why is Andrew so single-minded about his music? What are the advantages and disadvantages of this?

Relationships with others. Why is it hard for Yolonda to make friends? What does she need to learn?

Resilience. What personal characteristics help Yolonda retain her individuality as she adapts to life in Grand River? How does her family help her?

Ferris, Jeri. *Native American Doctor: The Story of Susan LaFlesche Picotte*. Carolrhoda Books, 1991.

Susan LaFlesche (1865-1915), daughter of Omaha Chief Iron Eye, was sent to the Elizabeth Institute for Young Ladies in Elizabeth, New Jersey, to the Hampton Institute in Virginia, and to Women's Medical College in Philadelphia. She returned to the Omaha reservation in Nebraska to work as doctor, interpreter, and political leader for her people. In telling Susan's story, Ferris includes much information about American Indians' difficult transition from traditional to European ways, and she gives an unflinching portrayal of white domination, including the illegal purchase of native land (making farming impossible for American Indians) and the greed-motivated sale of alcohol. Not fictionalized, this is a biography, with historical records used as sources for quotations. The illustrations are photographs taken during Susan's lifetime.

Resilience; Using ability. Susan had many advantages, but she also faced many obstacles. What personal qualities helped her overcome them in order to make good use of her abilities and her opportunities? What elements in her environment, family, and background were helpful to her? If you had been Susan, what would have been most difficult for you? How would you have handled it?

Fleischman, Sid. *The Trouble Begins at 8: A Life of Mark Twain in the Wild, Wild West*. Greenwillow, 2008.

We know that Twain wrote *Tom Sawyer, Huckleberry Finn*, and a few other books, and we know some of his witticisms—but how much do we really know about the life experiences behind his humor? As he sought a place and a fortune in the turmoil of the mid-19th-century American west, the young Clemens worked as a printer, on riverboats, as a gold prospector, and finally as a newspaperman. His adventures and exploits along the way provided rich material for the lecture circuit and novel writing which eventually became his career. Fleischman adopts a voice much like Twain's as he blends the story of Samuel Clemens' life with the persona that Twain created over time. This entertaining biography, as humorous as

Twain himself, is well-researched and beautifully illustrated with period photographs and memorabilia.

Drive to understand. This book has an abundance of "back matter" that will help you see how the author planned as he wrote it. In "The Truth, More or Less," notice how Fleischman tries to distinguish between what is historically true and what is myth created by Twain himself. Read "The Celebrated Jumping Frog of Calaveras County" and note how the humor depends on language—which may seem out-of-date now, but it gives you an idea of the kind of humor that helped Americans cope with the difficulties that they faced at the time. Finally, see how the author has used reference books to gather his material and how he documents where he found the illustrations.

Identity. Why did it take Clemens so long to learn what he did best? How were those early years an advantage to him? How were they a disadvantage?

Moral concerns. What is your response to Twain's negative comments about the morality of human beings? What caused his cynicism?

Using ability. Back matter, sometimes simply called an "Author's Note," is increasingly found in nonfiction books. It is always interesting and can be useful to anyone who is thinking of becoming a writer. Watch for it in other nonfiction books.

Freedman, Russell. *Confucius: The Golden Rule.* Illustrated by Frederic Clement. Arthur A. Levine, 2002.

With a well-researched narrative, beautiful illustrations, and selected "Sayings from *The Analects*" decorating the front and back flyleafs, this 48-page biography goes far beyond the denigrating "Confucius say" mottoes in common use and provides an introduction to the times, life, and thought of Confucius that will interest middle school students—and inform most adults as well. The author sorts history from legend and gives dates and place names. Rather than simply repeating that Confucius was a minor government official, he supplies enough information about China's history, government, and social conditions in 6th-century BCE to clarify the options open to Confucius and to explain both why he became a scholar and what difficulties lay in that choice.

In a final chapter, "The Spirit of Confucius," Freedman outlines the spread of the philosopher's ideas after his death, showing how Confucius' vision of government based on ability rather than privilege inspired political reforms in China and the rest of Asia, and then spread to Europe in the 16th century—and 200 years later, to America.

Drive to understand. Lines of inquiry based on this book could follow participatory government, Chinese history, the intellectual curiosity of Confucius and his teaching methods, or a comparative study of Confucius, the Buddha, and Socrates—all teachers who were part of the 5th-century BCE flowering.

Using ability. Confucius said that at the age of 15, he "set his heart on learning" and began to study—to follow the life of a scholar. How do you think he knew that this is what he wanted? Is this a decision that you have made or are likely to make? If so, what specifically would you do to make it happen?

Galbraith, Judy, & James R. Delisle. *The Gifted Kids Survival Guide: A Teen Handbook.* Edited by Pamela Espeland. Illustrated by Harry Pulver, Jr. Free Spirit, 1996.

This is the "revised, expanded, and updated edition" of a title that has been popular since 1983, written to and for teens and providing information about every aspect of giftedness that can be useful to them as they grow up gifted. After taking plenty of time to explain definitions of giftedness, intelligence, and testing, the authors discuss ways in which students can take charge of their own education. The final chapter, "On Being a Teenager," discusses adolescence in general, drugs and sex, and suicide among gifted teens, with suggestions for prevention. The authors are veterans in the field of gifted education, and the conversational tone of the book attests to their knowledge and comfort with gifted adolescents.

Arrogance. In discussing how students can ask for appropriate educational programs, sample conversational ploys are presented that can be generalized to help young people understand how they can avoid sounding arrogant.

Identity; Relationships with others. A chapter devoted to relationships includes helpful information on finding friends, handling teasing, developing conversational strategies, and getting along with parents.

Perfectionism; Using ability. A segment on perfectionism offers suggestions for mastering this potentially destructive characteristic.

Garfield, Leon. *Smith.* Illustrated by Antony Maitland. Sunburst, 2000.

A street urchin and pickpocket in 18th-century London, Smith steals a document from a man who is then murdered by men seeking the document that Smith has pilfered but which he cannot read. The murderers then pursue Smith. In his flight, he meets and guides home a blind judge who takes Smith into his home. The suitor of the judge's daughter accuses Smith of the murder, and Smith goes to Newgate Prison. With the suitor's help, Smith escapes, but he has been led into a trap. As Smith tries to protect his friend the judge, he discovers that he is being betrayed by a highwayman whom he has always admired. Eventually, the tangle of shifting friends and enemies is straightened out, with the suspense lasting until the very end.

Drive to understand. This exciting mystery, like all of Garfield's work, is well-written, challenging fare for good readers. Garfield provides a far better picture of the dangerous realities of the streets and highways in 18th-century England than any nonfiction description could. Most of the characters are rascals or worse, presented sympathetically but with no excuses offered for their behavior—good background for discussion of the social implications of poverty and the diversity of human character.

Giff, Patricia Reilly. *Pictures of Hollis Woods.* Yearling, 2004.

Hollis was abandoned at birth, and 12 years later, she has a history of running away from foster homes. Now, bonding with her latest foster mother Josie, a retired art teacher who recognizes Hollis's talent in the pictures that she draws, Hollis thinks she may stay for a while. But there is a shadow story, told in alternate chapters, of Hollis's recent placement with a family of three—a father, a mother, and her foster brother Steven. Clearly, something went wrong there, and Hollis fled from that home as from others. Unfortunately, Josie begins descending into forgetfulness, and Hollis knows that the agency will not allow her to stay with her. So she takes matters into her own hands, fleeing with Josie to the summer home of Steven's family, closed now, with the family in town nearby for the school year. Snowmobiling from town, Steven discovers that Hollis has returned and secretly provides food, allowing her time to sort out what she will do next.

Those who know Katherine Paterson's Gilly Hopkins will recognize the similarity: Hollis, too, is tough and sensitive, bright and independent, determined to take charge of her own life. Like Gilly, Hollis has not had enough experience with a setting that offers what she needs to recognize it when she finds it. Love abounds in this book, and Giff brings the two threads of the story together in a very satisfying ending.

Relationships with others; Resilience. What is Hollis afraid of? How do her fears affect her decision about staying with the Regan family? In leaving the Regans, where does Hollis misjudge, and why?

Sensitivity. Hollis and Steven are both very sensitive, but in different senses of the word. Describe Hollis's kind of being sensitive and the role it plays in the story. Then do the same for Steven. Think of times when you have felt or shown one or both kinds.

Gorrell, Gena K. *Heart and Soul: The Story of Florence Nightingale.* Tundra, 2000.

This biography dispels the romantic picture of "the lady with the lamp" and instead sets Florence squarely in her time and place, just a few years later than the period of Jane Austen's novels (which some good readers in this age group may be ready to enjoy). The daughter of a wealthy Victorian family, Florence grew up on English country estates and was expected only to marry well—but she was impatient with teas and parties, and she declined offers of marriage, wanting to do something important with her life. After years of struggle against the restrictions of her family and of society, she became a nurse just as the Crimean War broke out. Her work in the Crimea brought her fame and enormous popularity, but it also broke her health. For the rest of her long life, she lived quietly in England, continuing to fight for better health care and living conditions for soldiers, for those caught in the poverty and squalid living conditions of England's cities, for the poor in India—for these causes, she worked not as a nurse, but as a semi-invalid activist wielding influence through her writings and her connections with men of power in the British Empire.

As valuable as the well-rounded description of Florence—who was not sweet and tender but rather tough and demanding on behalf of those who could not speak for themselves—is the information about the age in which she lived: the restrictions on women, the power and flaws of the British Empire, the impact of the Industrial Revolution on England's commoners, and the lack of training for nurses. Florence Nightingale was a difficult, gifted woman who had to struggle for every accomplishment and always fell short—but her work established the beginnings of many of the institutions that we take for granted today.

Achievement. If you could talk to Florence Nightingale now, what could you tell her about the outcome of specific projects that did not succeed as she wished? What other people can you think of who began to create something or bring about change in society and did not live to see the final result? Consider whether you have the idealism or patience to work toward a goal if you might not see the result. What is an example of such a goal?

Differentness; Identity. What difficulties did Florence face in finding her own identity as a gifted person who wanted to use her abilities? How is this easier for women with dedication and energy now? How is it still difficult?

Drive to understand. This book provides good background reading for greater understanding of the 19th century—including the Industrial Revolution, colonialism, and the American Civil War—and for the contrasts between Great Britain and the United States in their approaches to issues such as the women's movement and to political unrest in the early 20th century.

Intensity. How did the intensity with which Florence approached the tasks that she set for herself affect her success, positively and negatively? What can you learn from her experience?

Relationships with others. How is it that Florence was so loved by the people and yet so lonely? If she had been an easier person to work with, would she have accomplished so much? Was this a choice she made? How would you choose?

Resilience; Using ability. Florence Nightingale was not the only woman among Victorian England's wealthy families who was bored by the life that women were expected to lead, but she was among the most successful in escaping it. What did it cost her to do so? What were her choices, realistically? How are these choices different now, and how are they the same?

Greene, Bette. *Summer of My German Soldier.* Puffin, 2006.

Patty Bergen's parents are cold and distant; her father, in fact, is physically abusive to her. Living in a small Arkansas town during World War II, the 12-year-old experiences the loneliness that results from an emotionally barren home and from the lack of friends to match her own highly verbal, quick-thinking nature. Only when visiting her maternal grandparents in Memphis, where the family's Jewish traditions are honored, does Patty feel at home.

When Anton Reiker, a German soldier, escapes from a nearby prisoner of war camp, Patty hides him in the apartment above the Bergen garage. The son of a history professor at the University of Goettingen, Anton had been a medical student in Germany before the war. He sees both beauty and value in Patty, and he is the first person that she has met whose wide-ranging interests and good educational background provide companionship for her. Anton risks his safety in a bid to protect Patty from her father's beating, but then he must leave to avoid detection and danger for Patty and Ruth, the family housekeeper who also protects Patty.

This book offers many themes for discussion: physical abuse, low self-esteem in both Patty and her father, the importance to Patty of Anton's caring for her and seeing good in her, and the distinction that must be made between "German" and "Nazi." And, of course, there's prejudice—against Germans, African-Americans, and Jews. Of all the characters in the book, Anton—the German soldier, the enemy, the POW—and Ruth, the African-American housekeeper, are the most prejudice-free and sympathetic.

Aloneness; Differentness. What qualities set Patty apart from others in the story? Why do some people see good in her? Why do others not? How do the reactions of others shape Patty's behavior? In what ways is she independent of their reactions? What is the basis of the courage that enables her to hide a POW?

Drive to understand. Explore the story of Anton's father's choice to be quiet and live—the evidence that there was opposition in Germany to Hitler's military policies.

Moral concerns. Consider the prejudice in the story against Germans, Jew, and African-Americans. Who is prejudiced against whom? Explain why.

Greenspon, Thomas S. *What to Do When Good Enough Isn't Good Enough: The Real Deal on Perfectionism: A Guide for Kids.* Illustrated by Michael Chesworth. Free Spirit, 2007.

Based on his experience as a psychologist who works with children and families, Greenspon writes directly to children between ages nine and 13 about issues related to perfectionism. He describes it so that a reader can consider whether, or to what degree, the term applies to him or her. Greenspon explains the distinction between trying to do well and perfectionism, offers suggestions for lightening the burden of worry, describes some sources of perfectionism, and offers ideas for thinking differently about oneself and for seeking help from parents and other adults. In the second part of the book, he presents basic information about some emotional disorders that are different from perfectionism but sometimes coexist with it. He closes with a chapter about what it's like to see a counselor or therapist, followed by a note to adults about how they can help.

Perfectionism; Using ability. This informative and encouraging book can be recommended to a child who can read it alone and then discuss it with an adult, or adult and child could read it together and talk about it as they read. Whatever the approach, the book will be much more effective if a trusted adult is available to support a child who needs to take steps to lighten the burden of perfectionism.

Grey, Christopher. *Leonardo's Shadow: Or, My Astonishing Life as Leonardo da Vinci's Servant.* Simon Pulse, 2008.

Chased as a thief until he falls from the top of a cathedral, Giacomo is saved by, and then taken to the home of, the great Renaissance artist Leonardo da Vinci. About eight years old and remembering nothing of his origins, Giacomo has no choice but to accept Leonardo's suggestion that he stay as a servant, although his impertinent manner indicates that he has not been accustomed to serving. For the next few years, he runs errands, puts off creditors, and worries about the slow pace of his Master's progress on his great painting, *The Last Supper.* He also develops friendships with a group of other servants and learns something of politics in Milan under the difficult Duke, who wants *The Last Supper* finished before the pope's visit.

This is mystery and adventure tied to history, to art, and to Renaissance politics and culture. The young and irrepressible Giacomo sometimes speaks when he should not, but he is loyal to his Master's interests, and as he becomes more aware of the forces moving around them, he gradually learns to monitor his impulses— that is, he becomes more self-aware and tailors his behavior accordingly, most of the time.

In fact, a precocious 10-year-old boy named Giacomo became a servant of da Vinci in 1490. He was a "lovable pest" who stayed with Leonardo until the Master's death in 1519. Giacomo inherited Leonardo's paintings. See the annotation of *Leonardo: Beautiful Dreamer* in the "Upper Elementary: Grades 3-5" section of this chapter.

Drive to understand. Grey's version of Giacomo's story is fiction, but much of Leonardo's story is fact. What subjects would you like to learn more about: da Vinci's drawings and inventions, Cecelia Gallarani, Duke Ludovico, *al fresco* versus *secco* painting, or some other topic that was new for you in this book? The more you learn about these things, the more you will know about how the author pulled fact and fiction together to write this book.

Relationships with others. Who were Giacomo's friends—of any age? How did he win friendships, and how did he keep them?

Hahn, Mary Downing. *Daphne's Book*. Sandpiper, 2008.

Jessica is dismayed when her seventh-grade English teacher pairs her with Daphne in a book writing and illustrating contest, but Mr. O'Brien will not change his mind. Daphne is the best artist and Jessica the best writer in the class, and together he expects that they will produce something really good. Jessica is losing her friendship with Tracey, and she is convinced that working with the silent and unpopular Daphne will accelerate that loss. As she gets to know Daphne, however, Jessica finds herself more comfortable with her than she was with Tracey. The two girls allow their imaginations to work, creating a fantasy world out of which comes their book.

As their friendship grows, Jessica visits Daphne at the home that she shares with her younger sister Hope and their aging grandmother. The grandmother's health and mental state are rapidly deteriorating, and Daphne fears that she and Hope will be sent to an orphanage if anyone knows this. Finally the situation becomes so bad that Jessica tells her mother, breaking her promise to Daphne. Daphne's grandmother is sent to a hospital where she dies, and Daphne and Hope go to a children's home. Daphne and Jessica are reconciled when Jessica visits to tell Daphne that their book has won the contest, and Jessica learns that Daphne and Hope will go to live with relatives of their mother whom the social worker has located.

The behavior of Daphne's grandmother and the old house in which Daphne lives are in disturbing contrast to Jessica's family, which is comfortable and stable, even though her parents are divorced and her mother about to remarry. Despite the differences, Jessica and Daphne come together because they find that they can talk to each other better than to anyone else. They are alone but for this one friendship, and for the moment, it is enough.

Aloneness. What reasons might Mr. O'Brien have had for pairing Jessica and Daphne, other than their talent? Why are they not popular? What qualities do they have that compensate for lack of popularity? Predict their futures.

Relationships with others. Why are Jessica and Tracey moving apart? What qualities in Jessica help her to be able to learn from this situation? In Jessica and Daphne's friendship, what does each girl learn about herself? Who benefits most from the relationship?

Hamilton, Virginia. *The Planet of Junior Brown*. Aladdin, 2006.

Junior Brown is obese, and he is an artist and a musician. The adults in his life are his mother (who wants Junior to be cultured but is not able to understand his art or listen to his music), his piano teacher (who is demented, but Junior cannot afford to recognize that), his absent father, and Mr. Pool, the school janitor. There is also Buddy, a fellow student who has no family and who is part of an underground network that helps homeless boys to survive in New York City. Buddy and Mr. Pool watch Junior slip toward insanity, and they are able to begin helping him back to reality.

Best for older students in this middle school group, this well-written book offers challenging reading and at least two themes that are useful for gifted students to discuss: the frustration of Junior's talent, symbolized by the silent pianos, and the challenge of getting along with others, exemplified by Buddy, a leader who progresses from teaching his boys to live for themselves to teaching them to live for others. In spite of his strength, it is clear that Buddy also needs help—a reminder that we are all interdependent, none of us completely self-sufficient.

Relationships with others. Why does Junior need Buddy? What does he offer to Buddy? How do Nightman and Franklin help each other? Identify a leader whom you follow. What do you offer to that person?

Using ability. What does Junior need in order to use his artistic and musical talents? What does Buddy need?

Hesse, Karen. *Stowaway*. Illustrated by Robert Andrew Parker. Aladdin, 2002.

Eleven-year-old Nicholas Young's mother is dead, he is not the scholar that his brothers are, and his displeased father has contracted him to a cruel butcher. To escape these troubles, Nick stows away on a British ship in August of 1768. Captain James Cook, master of the *Endeavor*, is secretly charged with discovering new lands for England; the gentlemen traveling with him are naturalists looking for specimens and artists who draw the new species of plants, birds, and fish that they find. When Nick is discovered and put to work, he shares in adventures and dangers while he learns seamanship, geography, and rudimentary medicine—and keeps his journal. He meets natives of the South Pacific Islands and befriends one of them. Three years later, he is one of the few original crew members to survive the journey and return to London.

Nicholas Young's presence on the *Endeavor* is documented in the journals of Captain Cook and some of the crew. The book takes the form of Nick's journal, which is fictional—written by Hesse for the benefit of young readers—but which faithfully follows what is known about the voyage. Hesse includes a roster of the ship's company, the itinerary, a glossary of terms, and "A New Map of the World with the Latest Discoveries," published in Boston just a few years after Cook's voyage. (The reader will benefit from having a current atlas at hand.) Hesse has gathered a wealth of detail about weather, food, islands, native peoples, and more to create a coherent and entirely credible description of the experience of the global explorers of the 18th century. With a story framed by history rather than plot, this book is not for everyone, but for the right students, it can be a door to a rich understanding of a different world.

Drive to understand. Consider all of the different areas of information covered in this book: history, geography, natural history, politics, anthropology, and so on. Which ones interest you most? What new information did you gain? How can you pursue this line of interest?

Identity. How did Nick's perception of scholarship change during the trip? What did you think when Mr. Banks said, "You have talent, boy," and Nick replied, "Aye, sir." What did Nick mean? What experiences caused him to reply in that way?

Hunt, Irene. *Across Five Aprils*. Berkley, 2002.

Telling the story of a southern Illinois family through the five years of the American Civil War, this book depicts the pain of families and communities divided by loyalties to both North and South. Jethro Creighton is nine when the war begins, and within a year, he has the responsibility of managing the farm that feeds the family members still at home. Through letters, the family follows the sons at war, and they face hatred and danger because one son has joined the Confederate Army.

The war is the main story, but a strong secondary theme is the growth of Jethro, whom his unlettered mother recognizes as having special talent. Encouraged by the schoolteacher before he goes off to war and by the newspaper editor in a nearby town, Jeth follows the war through newspapers and atlases and works to improve his crude country speech. He will be the first of the family to go to college.

Drive to understand. The book presents many ideas for discussion. In talking about giftedness, include the distinction between intelligence and education, the need to look behind poor speech patterns for a good mind, and the value of an education to those who cannot take it for granted.

Relationships with others. For what reasons do some people in this book criticize others? What is your own response to the criticisms, at the beginning of the book and at the end? In real life, what are your reasons for sometimes looking down on other people? What can you do to develop your own tolerance for people who are different from you? Is it worth the effort? Why or why not?

Using ability. What does Matt mean when he says that the replacement teacher has a "mean and pinched-in mind"? How does Shad encourage Jethro to learn without school? Give examples of people who have open, expansive minds. How can you cultivate that for yourself?

Kadohata, Cynthia. *Kira-Kira.* Aladdin, 2006.

Katie begins her story in 1954, when she was three and her sister Lynn was eight. Their parents' grocery store did not thrive in Iowa, where there were few Japanese, so the family moved to Georgia, where her uncle lived and her parents could work in a poultry plant. Katie and Lynn have an especially close relationship, and Katie writes of Lynn's love of the ocean, the sky, and of the first word that Lynn taught her: kira-kira—"glittering." From early in the book, the attentive reader understands that Katie is writing after Lynn's death, an awareness that adds a glow—kira-kira—to the years they have together until lymphoma claims Lynn's life before she finishes high school.

This is a quiet book, and not for everyone. Some will see it as slow-moving, even depressing. But others will come away with a sense of the warmth and courage of this family, the dedication of the parents, and the stamina that carries them through a time that is very difficult in many ways. The prejudice faced by Japanese people in this country in the years after World War II and the working conditions in even a well-run poultry plant may come as a surprise to many readers. The emotional turmoil of watching a loved one die is handled well, and Katie's story ends in acceptance and renewal.

Drive to understand. You may want to learn more about how Japanese Americans were treated during World War II in order to understand the prejudice that the Takeshima family encountered. Why did some of the workers in the poultry plant want to form a union? How have conditions in the poultry industry changed since then?

Relationships with others. How does the relationship between the two sisters change over time? How does thinking about this help you understand relationships in your own life?

Sensitivity. Uncle Katsuhisa is introduced as a rather strange character, but he is more than that. In what ways does Uncle help Katie's family cope?

Karnes, Frances A. & Suzanne M. Bean. *Adventures and Challenges: Real Life Stories by Girls and Young Women.* Great Potential Press, 2000.

In a series of brief chapters, girls and young women ranging in age from 10 to 29 write their personal adventure stories. A sixth grader tells about her first rappelling experience; a young teen writes about organizing "Kids-4-Kids," a kids' run to benefit kids through America Reads; a college graduate describes a hard-won sighting of blue-throated macaws with a research team in the Amazon jungle of Peru and Bolivia—and there are 15 more stories. A separate section gives advice about planning one's own adventure, with heavy emphasis on planning, preparation, proper gear, and safety. Finally, a timeline lists adventurous women from 43 BCE to 2000 CE, with brief descriptions of their accomplishments. For girls who are adventurous, for those who aspire to be adventurous, or even those who would like to think about it for a while, this is an inspiring book.

Achievement; Using ability. What achievements described in the book would you like to consider for yourself? What would you need to do to make it possible for you? What did you learn about preparation for doing something you've never tried before? Where would you find help and advice?

Kaufman, Gershen, Lev Raphael, & Pam Espeland. *Stick Up for Yourself! Every Kid's Guide to Personal Power and Positive Self-Esteem.* Free Spirit, 1999.

Adapted from materials written for a college-level psychology course so that children from eight to 12 years old can use it on their own, this book is also accompanied by a teacher's guide. Discussion of general issues of self-esteem, labeling feelings, naming future dreams (and how to get there), and developing relationships with others are especially useful. The difference between role power and personal power, for example, can be a helpful concept as hypercritical youngsters learn how to be effective in their criticism of authority figures.

Identity. Information on self-esteem could be adapted to the particular needs of highly able children learning to come to terms with exceptional talent.

Relationships with others. This book includes useful information on building good relationships with others as a necessary step toward developing self-esteem.

Resilience; Using ability. The section on naming dreams and how to get there offers suggestions that can be helpful in making good use of an outstanding ability.

Kelly, Eric P. *The Trumpeter of Krakow.* Illustrated by Janina Domanska. Aladdin, 1999.

Joseph Charnetski is 15 in 1461 when his father's house and fields are destroyed; he flees with his parents to the busy medieval city of Krakow. There, they meet the alchemist and scholar Kreutz and his niece Elzbietka. Kreutz finds lodging for the family and work for Joseph's father as a trumpeter in the church tower. But those who destroyed the Charnetski's home have followed them to Krakow, seeking the Tarnov Crystal, which has been the responsibility of the Charnetski family for generations. Kreutz, too, is in danger. One of his students is systematically hypnotizing him to gain the secret of turning base metals into gold.

The setting of this book is one of its strengths, giving a picture of Krakow as a medieval center and of the 15th century as a time of transition from superstition to science. The story is suspenseful, and the subplot raises questions about the moral uses of knowledge. First published in 1928, it provides the intellectual challenge often found in older books.

Drive to understand. What situations can you name in which scientists are now asked to work for gain rather than for knowledge?

Moral concerns. What is the responsibility to society of anyone with unusual knowledge, ability, or intelligence?

Using ability. How valid are the arguments that Tring uses to persuade Kreutz to do the experiments that Tring wants him to do? In Kreutz's position, what would have been your attitude toward the general interest in making gold from base metals?

Klise, Kate. *Deliver Us from Normal.* Scholastic, 2006.

They live in Normal, Illinois, but 11-year-old Charles Harrisong is painfully aware that his family is too large, too poor, and simply too unusual to be normal. Super-sensitive, Charles wears his emotions close to the surface—his favorite book is *To Kill a Mocking Bird*, and he has not lived down the time several years ago when, as his class was reading *The Yearling*, he broke into tears when the deer died. His outgoing 12-year-old sister, Clara, is exploring a spiritualistic Protestant church with the accepting approval of her Catholic parents. The three younger children are also individuals who draw attention in various ways when the family is out in public. When the "in-crowd" responds in an especially cruel way to Clara's candidacy for president of the seventh grade, the Harrisong parents decide that the family will leave Normal. They drive to Alabama, where they trade their car and much of their savings for a very old houseboat. Now they are even closer to the edge of disaster than they were in Normal, and

Charles is convinced that it is his fault. But as they all work together to cope with the realities of their new situation, priorities shift, and Charles begins to relax into the warmth of his family.

Charles is precociously sensitive, aware, responsible, and anxious, as well as intelligent—readers like him will welcome a protagonist with whom they can identify. The children in the family run the gamut from extrovert to introvert, the family discusses various possible religious beliefs without rancor, and the parents each have their own strengths as well as obvious weaknesses. Though poor, this is a family that is powerfully bound together. The book is a comforting reminder that family support trumps school issues, even when the family seems less than perfect.

Differentness. Read *To Kill a Mocking Bird* and discuss why Charles identifies with Boo Radley. What similarities are there, and what differences?

Introversion. Discuss introversion and extraversion as exemplified in the Harrisong children. Does any of this relate to you?

Resilience. How important is mutual family support? In what ways is it evidenced here?

Sensitivity. Why did Charles and Clara have such different questions and answers regarding religion? If you had been part of their conversation, what would you have added? What is behind Charles' sensitivity? In what ways, if any, should he try to change it?

Konigsburg, E. L. *The View from Saturday.* Atheneum, 1998.

The Souls are a group of four students in Mrs. Olinski's sixth-grade homeroom, but only they know their name. They are also a winning Academic Bowl team. As they move through the finals and beat the seventh grade and then the eighth grade, Mrs. Olinski develops several answers to the repeated question, "How did you choose them for the team?" In truth, she is not sure herself. Readers understand gradually why these four belong together as they follow the story of each one, interlaced with Mrs. Olinski's story and with episodes from Bowl contests.

By accident, Noah Gershom is the best man at the wedding of Ethan Potter's grandmother and Nadia Diamondstein's grandfather.

By coincidence, Julian Singh sits next to Ethan on the bus on his first day at their school. While maintaining a socially safe distance from the new boy, Ethan surreptitiously supports Julian—who, in addition to being new, speaks politely, quietly, and with a British accent—as he faces classmates' teasing. Soon Julian invites Ethan, Nadia, and Noah to tea, served on Saturday afternoons at the bed-and-breakfast that his father is establishing. From then on, the four are drawn together through compatible interests, shared values, and complementary abilities. As they become more comfortable with each other, they decide that they need a project, and Julian suggests that they help Mrs. Olinski, who has returned to teaching after an accident that left her a paraplegic. Julian proposes that they help her gain confidence in coping with students who might take advantage of her—the same students who teased Julian. The Souls find ways to do this so subtly that it is only after Mrs. Olinski has chosen them and they have won the final contest that she realizes they have also chosen her.

This book is not for everyone, but there are those who will cherish it. As the narrators take turns telling their stories, interspersed with vignettes from the Academic Bowl contests, the location shifts from Florida to New York, and we meet the same secondary characters in different stories and settings. The structure in itself makes this a challenging book, but these four sixth graders have much to offer, each in his or her unique way. The level of their language will be very comfortable for verbally gifted children who too often monitor and tone down their language. The Bowl questions, too, are challenging, and the author thoughtfully provides the answers at the end. Finally, the main characters are insightful, thoughtful, clever, and motivated. The Souls are young people who do not fit the mold and might well have been lonely if Julian had not invited them to tea. Together, they are unbeatable in more ways than one.

Aloneness. Consider all of the ways in which Mrs. Olinski feels alone. Why was Julian the first to mention helping her? Which of the others also feel alone? How does this change during the book, and why?

Arrogance. What examples of arrogance do you see among the Souls? How do the others make allowances? Why do they do so? Do you see this happening in the people around you?

Creativity. Describe ways in which the main characters are creative. Are you creative in any of the same ways? In what other ways?

Differentness. Julian is different; Ethan knows instantly that he will be teased. If this happens to newcomers in your school, who tries to change it? What personal qualities are required to change it?

Identity. Each of the Souls is comfortable with who he or she is, even though they are all different from most sixth graders. How did they achieve this level of comfort?

Introversion. What role does Ethan play? How does his quiet, observant manner help? What other positives are there in being somewhat introverted? The first time they have tea, Ethan says he has gained something and lost something. What does he mean? Consider the same questions for the other Souls.

Perfectionism. Mrs. Olinski does not want to choose honor roll students for her team because they don't want to risk making mistakes. What is the problem with not wanting to take risks?

Relationships with others. Consider what Nadia and her father mean about giving a "lift" and "switches." What does Ethan mean when he comments, "Sometimes silence is a habit that hurts"? How are the four Souls an example of the statement: "Friends are people who are different but who complement—fill in for—each other"?

Sensitivity. What examples are there in the story of people being sensitive to the feelings of others? What examples are there of people who are more easily hurt than most of their peers expect them to be? What examples can you give from your experience of each kind of sensitivity?

Using ability. What does Mrs. Olinski mean when she says that she is looking for team members who say "Now what?" instead of "So what?" Which do you say? What difference does it make in your use of the special abilities that you have?

Lasky, Kathryn. *Beyond the Burning Time.* Scholastic, 1996.

In 1692, Mary Chase is helping her widowed mother, Goody, work the farm while her brother Caleb is apprenticed to a master ship builder in nearby Salem. That winter, several girls in Salem Village begin acting strangely, seeing spectral figures and having fits. Seeking causes, some people come to believe that they are afflicted by the devil. In the theocracy of Massachusetts—tightly run by Puritan ministers but without a civil government—it is not long before some are crying witchcraft, and the afflicted girls are encouraged to name the witches. Mary watches in growing fear as pious church members are arrested as witches, while her mother fiercely but calmly assures her that the charges are nonsense. Then the inevitable happens: Goody Chase, too, is arrested and taken to prison. Caleb takes Mary to Boston, finding work for her in an inn, before she herself is accused. Then brother and sister begin a desperate search for a way to save their mother.

This work is extensively researched historical fiction. Many of the characters in the book—but not the Chase family—are historical figures. In addition to documenting the background of mass hysteria and ignorance, Lasky points out how the residents of Salem Village (now Danvers, near Salem) were divided along lines of family and property ownership and how the families of many of the accusers stood to gain through the disappearance of rival landowners. In an author's note, Lasky clarifies how the vacuum in government, left when a former governor of Massachusetts revoked the colony's Charter in 1684, jeopardized titles to land and left property ownership open to question, setting the stage for the uncertainty and lawlessness that erupted seven years later. This book has a large scope, many characters, and much historical detail—it could easily prove overwhelming for many readers, but it will provide thought-provoking challenge for gifted students.

Aloneness. Consider the different ways in which people experienced being alone during the witch trials in Salem. How do they compare to ways in which people feel alone in our present society? Which of them have affected you? How have you responded?

Drive to understand. What does this event in our history tell us about the importance of the separation of church and state?

Moral concerns. What does Mary's metaphor of the sun and the moon and the eclipse mean to her? How did she change, and what brought about those changes? How can you explain the story of Mary Esty's appearances after her death, and her search for vengeance? Are Mary and Caleb guilty of the death of Constable Dewart?

Latham, Jean Lee. *Carry On, Mr. Bowditch.* Illustrated by John O'Hara Cosgrave. Sandpiper, 2003.

Nathaniel Bowditch grew up in Salem in the age of sailing ships. He had a quick mind, especially in math, and it was clear that he should go to Harvard. But there was no money, so instead, he was indentured for nine years. People who recognized his brilliance offered the use of their libraries, and Nat never stopped learning. He taught himself languages, mathematics, and astronomy, and when he went to sea, he learned navigation. Soon he was teaching others, and before he was 30, he had written a book on navigation which is still a standard text.

This biography is a story of both physical and intellectual adventure. In addition, it includes several themes related to giftedness: Nat's thirst for learning and the necessity of persistence, the eagerness of uneducated sailors to learn and Nat's commitment to teaching them, and Nat's commitment to accuracy and the importance of risking a new approach, trusting new knowledge rather than traditional methods. Nat's zest for learning and his disregard for obstacles shine throughout the book.

Drive to understand. This story could be read simply for the pleasure of learning how Nat navigated through days of fog, finding the harbor through the sheer power of mathematics.

Identity. People think of Nat as a "brain." What is your response to that?

Resilience; Using ability. Have you ever felt as though you are "stumbling on other people's dumbness. And—you want to kick something"? What traits does Nat have that enable him to overcome this while continuing to use his brain? What can you learn from Nat?

Le Guin, Ursula K. *Gifts.* Harcourt, 2006.

The families of the Uplands have distinctive and destructive powers, or gifts, that run down through generations. They employ these powers in feuds among themselves and in occasional forays into the Lowlands. Gry's family has the gift of "calling," but she will not use it as intended—to call animals to the hunt. The males in Orrec's family have the dire power of "unmaking"—destroying utterly—with a glance, when they will it. But in Orrec, this gift is slow to manifest, perhaps because his mother is a Lowlander. When it appears, it seems not merely unusually strong, but uncontrollable—a "wild gift"—so Orrec's father blindfolds him to keep him from harming others against his will. Tensions between neighbors lead to tensions between Orrec and his father, and finally, having learned more about his gift, Orrec removes his blindfold in a climactic confrontation with his father.

This book is fantasy, but the world that Le Guin imagines is earthy, very like that of the early days of the Celts in the northern British Isles—a society based in strife and cattle raids. The mood is quarrelsome, foreboding, and finally hopeful. The story may seem to end a little too neatly, but readers can look forward to more about Orrec and Gry in *Voices*, the second book of the *Annals of the Western Shore* series. For those who see metaphor beyond the plot, the story of Orrec and Gry raises several of the questions that gifted youngsters must answer for themselves.

Differentness; Identity. Orrec struggles through most of the book to understand the true nature of his gift. Who helped him to find it, and how? What gifts or talents of your own do you recognize, and what might be latent in you? What steps can you take to learn about them? How might others help you?

Moral concerns. Review the conversation between Orrec and Gry in which they try to discern the origin of the various Upland powers. How can a gift or ability be positive and also negative, healing and also destructive? How does this conversation help each of them understand himself or herself? How does it lead to their decision to leave? Can you offer a moral argument for their staying in the Uplands? For their leaving?

Using ability. Gry decides at an early age not to use her gift to call animals to the hunt, although she gradually learns how she can use it in her own way. For Orrec, it is more difficult; his father reminds him that he has a responsibility to his people to use his gift for their protection, saying, "To have the power is to serve the power." Orrec says that he feels the power when he is making a poem. Do you have a similar experience—that is, do you create anything that enables you to understand what Orrec means? In our real, modern world, what examples do you see of people questioning conventional ideas about how power should be used? How do Orrec's and Gry's responses to this question influence your thinking?

Lobel, Anita. *No Pretty Pictures: A Child of War.* Greenwillow, 1998.

Known to many young readers for her award-winning children's books, author and illustrator Anita Lobel here tells, for older readers, the story of her childhood. She was born to Jewish parents in Krakow, Poland, in 1936—"In a wrong place at a wrong time." Soon her father disappeared, leaving before the Nazis came; her mother had false identity papers, so she was safer in Krakow, and she could work. As deportations began, Anita and her younger brother were sent with "Niania," their Roman Catholic nanny, to Niania's family's home in the country. For five years—when Anita was five to 10 years old—the children moved from one "safe" place to another in Niania's care, until the Nazis found them and took them to Ravensbruck, a concentration camp. Always Anita kept her brother close to her and protected him, sizing up the intentions of the adults around them and making life-and-death decisions. After the war, they were taken to Sweden and finally reunited with their parents.

The story is told from the point of view of the child that Lobel was at the time. Simply-constructed sentences relate devastating realities and reveal her partial understanding of events around her. The impact on readers who know more of the story than she did at the time is profound—her description of the liberation of Ravensbruck and the journey to Sweden is especially moving. Sixteen pages of photographs are included, with the notation that those taken before 1945 survived because her father took some with him when he fled, and her mother hid others in the seams of her clothing.

Achievement. See the list next to the title page of awards that this book has won, and look up other awards that Lobel has earned. Despite the trauma of her childhood, Lobel has had a very successful career. How did she overcome her wartime experience to achieve so much? How did that experience hinder or help her?

Drive to understand. There are many stories of children surviving the Nazi period in Eastern Europe, but few are nonfiction. What difference does it make to you as a reader to know that this is a true story? What did you learn about the Jewish experience in the Nazi period that you had not known before? What more would you like to learn?

Resilience. Discuss ways in which Anita was resilient, and then ways in which her brother, her parents, and Niania showed resilience. Think back to when you were five or seven or 10—how do you think you would have handled the situations that Anita faced? What would have been hardest for you? What strengths do you have that would have helped you?

Lutz, Ericka. *The Complete Idiot's Guide to Friendship for Teens.* Pearson, 2001.

In the breezy *Idiot's-Guide* style, Lutz conveys solid and sensible information for teens about how to make and keep friends. She goes beyond the basics to a number of subtopics, including best friends, groups of friends, getting too close and then moving apart, helping a friend in trouble, and coping with the end of a friendship. In addition, she discusses boys and girls as friends and in a romantic relationship, writing frankly but always with a light touch.

For some gifted children, friendship does not come naturally. Although they may have learned the rules in elementary school, they find that the game changes in various ways in middle school and high school. Lutz's book will be useful for older middle schoolers and with high school students.

Relationships with others. Some, including most introverts, may prefer to read and reflect on this book on their own and not discuss it at all. For others, discussion will be most effective if it focuses on a section that covers an immediate concern rather than attempting to cover the whole book at once. Many single paragraphs in the book could be a starting point for valuable discussion at the right moment with the right person. Because it considers events that normally occur over time—spanning several years—this is a good book for a teen to have in his or her room as a reference.

Macauley, David. *Cathedral: The Story of Its Construction*. Houghton Mifflin, 1981.

By giving specific dates and names, Macauley adds authenticity to this book of fiction—a story of how the people of a French town worked together for 86 years to build "the longest, widest, highest, and most beautiful cathedral in all of France." The illustrations show in exquisite detail how the land was cleared and foundations built, how the buttresses, piers, stairways, vaults, windows, even bells were constructed—and how the village grew around the cathedral over the years. Correct architectural terminology is used, and a glossary provides definitions.

Drive to understand. Cathedral is used here to represent others of Macauley's books (*Castle, Underground*, etc.) which answer questions that most curious children have asked, if only to themselves. Macauley writes with respect not only for the object constructed, but for the people who do the work, and he never writes down to his audience. His books are a good introduction to serious work in the adult world.

Marrin, Albert. *Sitting Bull and His World*. Dutton, 2000.

The Lakota Sioux chief Sitting Bull was born in 1831 and died in 1890. During his lifetime, the traditional way of life of the Plains Indians virtually disappeared. He led his people as the U.S. Army, the railroads, and gold prospectors moved into the Plains and as the buffalo, mainstay of the Indians' existence, were driven close to extinction. After he participated in the defeat of George Armstrong Custer at the Battle of the Little Big Horn in 1876, Sitting Bull was portrayed as a savage warmonger in the popular press; yet he was a charismatic leader of his people—a warrior who defended the tribal lands with courage and vision—and he was called the greatest Indian of his time by a former adversary. Rather than enter a reservation in the United States, he led his band to Canada after Little Big Horn but had to return because as the buffalo diminished, the people began to starve. Ultimately, the book relates not only the eradication of the Indians' hunting grounds and villages, but also the elimination of their religious ceremonies, their heritage, and their way of life—in Marrin's term, ethnocide.

Marrin's biography is a balanced story, alternating the American Indians' view of events with that of the whites. Complementing the history of Sitting Bull's life, the author describes the American West in the 19th century, especially the profound differences between the white and Indian cultures. Neither white nor Indian is seen as blameless, but the reader does come to understand how economic and political pressures both in Washington and in the Army resulted in the killing of the buffalo and the destruction of the way of life of a whole people. Sitting Bull stands out unforgettably as a man of courage, character, and integrity.

Drive to understand. How does reading a book like this change your understanding of the American Indians, or the whites, or any other people with a culture different from your own?

Identity. By the time Sitting Bull was 38, the Lakota people said that he "owned himself." What does this phrase mean to you? Whom do you know who owns himself or herself in this sense? What qualities do these people have that may have helped them own themselves? What steps would you have to take to own yourself? What obstacles would you have to overcome? What would be the advantages of this to you?

Moral concerns. Given the vast difference in the cultures of the whites and the American Indians, how could the advance of the Europeans across the continent have been better managed? Have the changes in ways of thinking in the last 150 years made it easier to understand and handle a situation like this? In what ways do the same mistakes continue, here and elsewhere?

McCaffrey, Anne. *Dragonsong.* Simon Pulse, 2008.

Menolly is growing up on the island of Pern during a time of threadfall, of spores periodically falling from the sky and consuming all living matter not under shelter. Her father is head of a fishing village which is protected from threadfall by tradition and by the dragons that live on the island. However, the main theme of this book is not the conflict between dragons and threadfall, but between Menolly's unusual musical gifts and the tradition, strongly held in her village, that says women cannot become Harpers. Forbidden her music, Menolly flees the safety of the village to live alone, escaping threadfall as she can. When she is caught without shelter in a threadfall, she is rescued by a dragon and its rider and taken to the dragons' weyr. There, among the dragons and their riders, she finds shelter, friends, and finally, recognition of her talents and encouragement to use them.

Dragonsong is the first book in the author's Harper Hall Trilogy, and it is followed by *Dragonsinger* and *Dragondrums*. This is not the high fantasy of Cooper or Le Guin, a mighty struggle between good and evil, but rather a tale of a more insidious struggle much closer to our daily reality. Menolly's gentle enemy is the tradition-bound close-mindedness of Yanus, her father, who is a good man, a solid and reliable leader, a hard worker—but not a man of vision, not one who accepts change. Her mother, Mavi, accepts and reinforces Yanus's rule; only Menolly's brother, Alemi, understands her, but he has no power to help. The Harper Elgion, who serves the role of village pastor, is a force toward enlightenment, but change will be too slow for Menolly and her passion for music.

Creativity; Intensity; Using ability. What experience in your own life helps you understand the strength of Menolly's desire to use her music? Was she right to leave the Sea Hold? What else could she have done?

Drive to understand; Moral concerns. Where do we see too close a following of tradition, superstition, and slowness to change affecting our world? In what ways does it prevent people from growing? What balancing forces (like Alemi, Elgion, and the weyr) do you see today?

North, Sterling. *The Wolfling*. Illustrated by John Schoenherr. Puffin, 1992.

Growing up in rural Wisconsin in the 1870s, Robbie Trent leads a rigorous life, lightened by the companionship of his pet, a wolf cub, and by the friendship of his teacher, Hannah Hitchcock, and his neighbor, the Swedish-American naturalist Thure Kumlien. His hardworking and demanding father expects Robbie to end his education at the eighth grade and work for him until he is 21. Robbie must buy his time from his father if he hopes to continue his education, and he is encouraged by others to do so. He needs this encouragement, because it is difficult for him to see a way out of the obligation imposed by his father.

Robbie's story is based on the life of the author's father, with the historical accuracy documented in a separate section. It is particularly useful for discussing the difference in values between parents and children, as well as the need for children to be encouraged by other caring adults. Robbie's father is not uncaring, and he is sympathetically depicted as careworn with the shortsightedness that often goes with a daily struggle for a livelihood.

Drive to understand. How does Robbie feel about his father? What causes his father to feel as he does about Robbie's education? Are there stories in your family about the struggle of earlier generations for an education? What might the young Sterling North have learned from Thure Kumlien, who emigrated to the United States in 1843 and purchased land in Wisconsin—woodland rather than farmland so that he could observe the wildlife? What more can you learn about Kumlien?

Using ability. Why is it important for Robbie to continue his education? What traits does Robbie need to develop in order to do so? What traits does he already have that will help him? Do you think he will succeed? If you were in Robbie's situation, what person do you know would help you as Thure Kumlien and Hannah Hitchcock helped Robbie?

O'Dell, Scott. *My Name Is Not Angelica.* Yearling, 1990.

When she is 15, Raisha and others from her African village are captured by another tribe and sent to the Caribbean island of St. John to be sold as slaves. Raisha, renamed Angelica, becomes a house slave, but the others, including Konjo, who is Raisha's betrothed and their village leader, endure much harsher conditions working in the fields. Konjo soon escapes to head a group of runaways in planning a revolt. Joining the escapees, Raisha witnesses the climax of this small band's role in a general slave revolt.

Based on the slave revolt of 1733-34, this book meets the high standards that we expect in O'Dell's work. Raisha is strong, independent, and self-sufficient, like the young women in other O'Dell books. The book is well researched, and the reader feels both the justice and the hopelessness of the cause. The oppressing whites are shown with some sympathy, too, enmeshed in a system that inevitably enslaves the masters. This is a fine historical novel that clarifies the issues and tells the story on a very human level.

Aloneness. What examples do we have here of people standing alone for something that they believe is right? What gives them the inner strength that enables them to be so brave?

Drive to understand; Resilience. How is Raisha like Karana in O'Dell's *Island of the Blue Dolphins* and Bright Morning in his *Sing Down the Moon*? What common threads do you see in O'Dell's books about conquered and oppressed people? How can you tie these themes to current events?

Moral concerns. Why did some whites respond to slavery as Governor Gardelin did and some like Preacher Gronnewold? What justifies the disobedience of authority that culminates in rebellion? When is rebellion *not* justified?

Paterson, Katherine. *Come Sing, Jimmy Jo.* Puffin, 1995.

Eleven-year-old James Johnson belongs to a family of professional country music singers. Their new agent, upon hearing the child sing, urges him to join the family on stage. His feeling for the music helps James overcome his initial fear, but he finds that it is not as easy to become comfortable with the new identity that comes with performing. He does not want to become "Jimmy Jo" instead of James, he does not want school friends to know that he appears on television each Friday night, and he is not happy about the rivalry that his popularity sets up between him and other members of the family.

The stability in James's life comes from his grandmother and his father. Family relationships and tolerance of difficult personalities are well portrayed. Grandma encourages James to sing, saying "You got the gift…. It ain't fittin' to run from it…. The Lord don't give private presents." James's challenge is to use his gift while at the same time remaining himself.

Identity. Why is it so important for James to remain *James*? Why does it not bother his mother to change herself for the sake of publicity? How would you feel if you were James? Why? Why does James feel that he betrayed his grandma? Do you agree that he did? What could you say to help him feel better about that?

Using ability. How is James's gift a "burden" to him? ("Sometimes the gift seems more like a burden.") What are the rewards that he gets from singing? Are they worth the sacrifices? Identify a gift or talent of yours. What would be the sacrifices and rewards of developing it fully? Do you want to? How would you? Discuss Grandma's statement that "The Lord don't give private presents." To what extent do gifted people have a responsibility to use their gifts? If you think there is no responsibility, what other reasons are there to use gifts?

Paterson, Katherine. *Jacob Have I Loved.* Scholastic, 2009.

Growing up on an island in Chesapeake Bay, Louise is convinced that everyone despises her and loves Caroline, her beautiful, musically talented younger sister. Not until she is 17 does Louise recognize that she is gifted intellectually and capable of doing anything she chooses. Others are willing to help, but she must make the choice.

A Newbery winner, this complex book has several themes other than giftedness, and a thoughtful teenager will find much here to think about, including sibling rivalry, responsibility for one's own decisions, tradition-breaking and respect for tradition, and going one's own way despite feeling uncomfortable about being different.

Differentness. How could Louise have responded more helpfully to her feelings of being different?

Identity. How do Caroline's and Louise's pictures of themselves affect their behavior? Their decisions? How accurate are their pictures of themselves? How does being gifted affect each girl's childhood? What difference does it make (in personal happiness, in career choices, in the way you treat other people) to know that you have a special ability?

Relationships with others. Louise has what might be called a prickly personality. What makes her that way? How does her personality complicate her life? What role does her giftedness play? What can happen to people like this as they become adults? What keeps Louise from turning into a prickly adult? If you could talk to Louise as a teenager, what advice would you give her?

Resilience; Using ability. Why is Louise able to make use of her intelligence? What is the turning point for her? What could other possible turning points be for someone like her? How might the book have ended so that Louise would take more command of her own future?

Peck, Robert Newton. *A Day No Pigs Would Die.* Peter Smith, 1999.

Robbie tells of his thirteenth year growing up in a Shaker family in Vermont, and especially of his father, who was both illiterate and wise. Peck offers a series of vignettes that reveal the daily concerns of a rural community in which a Shaker family is even more traditional than most.

Rob grows up knowing that he is different and valuing his own family, even as he sees the disadvantages of their way of life. He is different because of his religion, not because of giftedness, but the principle is the same: the need to recognize and value the strengths of his family and himself, and to be able to accept both himself and his father in spite of their differentness.

Differentness. What factors help Rob accept his and his family's difference? Is this story outdated, or is it relevant today? How so? Generalize: What are the advantages and disadvantages of being different? How can people decide how and when to accept being different?

Identity. How is growing up a Shaker an advantage to Rob? How is it a disadvantage? Will he overcome the disadvantages? How? What does Rob admire in his father? What do you admire in Rob? In his place, what would you have done differently? Would you have rebelled? When? Why? Was Rob wrong not to?

Perkins, Lynne Rae. *Criss Cross.* Greenwillow, 2005.

At the beginning of the summer she is 14, Debbie wishes that something would happen—and a lot does happen this summer, as

Debbie and the friends that she has known all her life metamorphose into the young adults that they are becoming. Changes are subtle—mostly internal, slow, and rich with small surprises and with budding self-awareness. Debbie imagines a romance with a handsome football player and then develops a real friendship with a boy who is visiting his grandmother for the summer. Hector decides that he wants to learn to play guitar, and by the middle of the summer, he is writing songs, though his technique still needs work. Having shifted "from bookworm to gearhead" some time ago, Lenny solidifies his identity as a mechanic while maintaining his friendships with college-bound classmates. At the end of the summer, we know that something has happened when Debbie, who has been shy and sometimes unsure of herself, looks in her mirror at her frizzy-haired, frowning reflection and suddenly begins to laugh—and she likes the girl who is laughing.

This Newbery winner is so beautifully written that it is recommended for highly verbal students who are writing journals, poetry, or fiction on their own by now. We can see Perkins enjoying herself as she presents a chapter entirely of dialogue, with the speakers not always identified; another chapter in which two parallel stories are placed side by side like newspaper columns; and the "Japanese Chapter," much of which is written in haiku ostensibly made up on the spot in a conversation between Debbie and her friend Patty. But the author gives us much more than a demonstration of pleasure in language. Her description of the developmental dilemma and prospects of Dan Persik, the handsome but shallow athlete, is a blend of insight, sensitivity, and perspective. As the title suggests, *Criss Cross* is about connectedness and not-connecting, how paths cross and criss-cross, and where they may lead. At 14, these are fundamental concerns for Debbie and her friends.

Aloneness; Differentness. When and how does Debbie feel alone and/or different? What does she do about it? How does it change by the end of the summer? Consider the same questions for Hector.

Identity; Using ability. What different kinds of high ability does Lenny have? Do you think it is a good thing for him to be in the vocational-technical track? If not, how could it have been—or could it be—different? If so, how will he blend that with his intellectual curiosity? What do you think he will be doing in 10 years? Will this be all right, or would you like to change it?

Relationships with others. What did you learn from Dan Persik's role in this book?

Pfeffer, Susan Beth. *Life as We Knew It.* Harcourt, 2008.

Through entries in her journal, Miranda describes her family's response after an asteroid strikes the moon with enough force to bring its orbit closer to Earth, causing catastrophic tides, earthquakes, and volcanic eruptions, as well as loss of communication with the world beyond their rural home in northeastern Pennsylvania. Thanks to her mother's quick response, Miranda's family has food, and her brothers cut trees to burn in the wood stove. But storms are violent, police and health services gradually break down, and disease spreads. Miranda records the incremental losses and the stress of living in close quarters with no idea of when, if ever, this bleak period will end. At the end of the book, there is a little hope, but life will never be the same.

The disaster that Pfeffer imagines in this dystopian novel is plausible, and the effect on the reader is sobering in the extreme as one by one, the trappings of normal life are stripped away and options become more limited—due not to human folly but to an event over which we have no control.

Moral concerns. Was it right or wrong to hoard food? Should Peter have stayed at the hospital or moved in with Miranda's family to help them? Should Miranda's mother have helped the neighbor whose wife was ill? Why does the family become more insulated as the book goes on, connecting less with neighboring families? Was this a good plan? On what do you base your answers? What other moral questions occur to you?

Relationships with others. Consider each of the children in the story: Matt, Miranda, and Jonny. In what ways does each one grow through their experience? What resources help them to remain cooperative?

Resilience. How do the children react to the stress, both negatively and positively?

Rand, Ayn. *Anthem*. Boomer, 2007.

In a future collectivist society, Equality 7-2521 is out of place because he is more intelligent than most. Assigned to be a Street Sweeper, he discovers a tunnel which becomes a hiding place where he writes and experiments, eventually discovering electricity. When he presents his discovery to the Scholars, they reject him, and he flees to the Uncharted Forest, finding there an abandoned house from the Unmentionable Times (the 20th century). Here, he finds manuscripts and reads in them his heritage, including the forbidden, lost word: ego—I. Recognizing the possibilities of individualism, he resolves to begin a new life and a new political order.

This novel was written for the purpose of extolling individualism over collectivism. Middle school students with lively intellectual interests are enthusiastic about it. They understand the political message, see a need for balance between the individual and the community, and identify with Equality's urge to know and his frustration at being repressed.

Differentness. How can people who are different cope in our society without leaving, as Equality did?

Identity. Does anything like the Scholars' rejection of Equality's idea ever happen to students in school or to teenagers in their families? How do they react? How should they react?

Moral concerns. How can people like Equality, who are different from or brighter than others, manage to be themselves and yet fit into a community?

Relationships with others. Do you agree with Equality that "we have no need of our brothers"? Under what conditions might Equality recognize the need for other people?

Resilience; Using ability. Can you explain why Equality so strongly wants to study and to experiment? What personal qualities make him able to do so, while others cannot, although they wish to do so?

Schultz, Robert A. & James R. Delisle. *Smart Talk*. Illustrated by Tyler Page. Free Spirit, 2006.

Smart Talk is written for, about, and even (mostly) by gifted children from four to 12 years old. On their website, www.giftedspeak.com, the authors surveyed gifted children around the world, asking a range of questions in seven categories, including Fitting In, Expectations, School, and Home. They have published "some of the most common answers, as well as some of the most interesting and funny ones." The responses are insightful and revealing and should prove helpful to young readers who will surely find someone out there who answers as they would have. (Responders are identified only by gender, age, and state of residence.) In addition, there are brief biographies called "A Kid Like You" interspersed among the chapters. Sections in each chapter called "Reflection/Connection" offer suggestions for further thought and action.

Achievement; Aloneness; Identity; Intensity; Relationships with others; Using ability. This book is listed under each grade level represented in this chapter, but its application will vary according to age. It may be most useful as a discussion starter, in a group or after a child has read it alone. It can be read straight through or skimmed once and then referred to whenever appropriate. Parents and teachers may help children follow through on ideas offered under "Reflection/ Connection." However it is used, this book promises greater self-understanding for gifted children and offers a valuable resource for adults working with them.

Sebestyen, Ouida. *Words by Heart.* Yearling, 1997.

Lena's Papa has high hopes for his daughter, so he moves his family from the post-Reconstruction South to the more open West, where a black family may have a better chance. But Papa's willingness to work brings resentment from Mr. Haney, who loses his job to Papa, and Lena learns that not everyone rejoices with her when she wins the scripture-reciting contest. It is clear that prejudice here is merely subtler than it is in the South, and the family will still need extraordinary fortitude to survive.

Racial prejudice is the theme of this book, with Lena's giftedness adding emphasis to the need of African-Americans for opportunities to grow and develop. Talented blacks can see a version of their own struggle in Lena's story, and all talented students can recognize Lena's and her father's acceptance of the responsibility to use one's gifts, even against difficult odds.

Differentness. What does Papa teach Lena that will help her to survive? What else do you think she will need to get through the next few years?

Identity. If you were in Lena's position, do you think you could make it? What would be your greatest asset? Your greatest liability?

Resilience; Using ability. What did Papa teach Lena, both by what he said and by the way he lived? What is there in that which could be useful to you? If your own life is easier than Lena's, how might that make it more of a challenge for you to grow up to be a productive person, making full use of the abilities that you have? How are you doing so far?

Skelton, Matthew. *Endymion Spring.* Delacorte, 2008.

The narrative begins in 15th-century Mainz, Germany, where Endymion, a mute young servant of Johann Gutenberg, is witness to mysterious events that threaten to interfere with the invention of the printing press. In the second chapter, the story shifts to modern Oxford, England, where Blake and his sister entertain themselves in the Bodleian Library while their mother studies. Blake finds mystery in the form of an ancient book, *Endymion Spring*, on whose blank pages letters appear and then vanish, spelling out messages that only Blake can see. As the chapters shift between Mainz and Oxford, the two stories slowly converge. There is danger in both Mainz and Oxford, and the suspense continues to the end.

For booklovers, *Endymion Spring* offers some of the history of bookmaking, medieval settings and scholarship, the Bodleian Library, and a hint of the coming of digital books. For those who love fantasy and mystery, there is plenty here of both. And for those who wonder how much of the book is fact and how much is fiction, the author has added a short "Historical Note." There is also a section of "Questions for Discussion," as well as "A Conversation with Matthew Skelton," in which he talks about the process of writing the book. All of this extra material continues to draw the reader in after the story ends, providing yet more to think about. My local bookseller says that children come back into the store to thank her for recommending both *Endymion Spring* and *Leonardo's Shadow* (annotated earlier in this section), saying to her, "I might not have found it on my own."

Drive to understand. Although this is a book of fiction, it is possible that you gained quite a lot of information in reading it. What new knowledge do you have about life in Germany 550 years ago? About Johann Gutenberg? About others involved in the invention of the printing press?

You may also have gained impressions that you will hold while you gather more information from future reading—for example, as a result of reading this book, what is your current mental picture of the Bodleian, or of Oxford University, or of academic life? In addition, you may be doing some critical thinking. What more would you need to learn in order to transform your impressions into solid information about these things? How do you distinguish between the two? How does the author blur the line between fact and fiction in his historical note and acknowledgments?

These are questions about *how* you are thinking about the book. For questions more directly related to the plot, see the excellent list of questions at the end of the book.

Speare, Elizabeth George. *The Witch of Blackbird Pond.* Laurel Leaf, 1978.

Kit Tyler grew up with her grandfather in Barbados, but upon his death in her sixteenth year, she sails to Connecticut to live with an aunt whom she has never met. Kit does not fit in with the Puritan Connecticut of 1687, but she finds a few kindred spirits: Nat, first mate of the ship in which she sailed; Prudence, a downtrodden child hungry to learn; and Hannah, the outcast Quaker who lives by Blackbird Pond and who is thought to be a witch. Kit's friendship with Hannah leads to the accusation that Kit herself is a witch.

Characterization is excellent in this book. Kit is accepted, if not understood, by her Puritan relatives, and she comes to respect her stern uncle's fairness and sense of justice. Several characters—Kit, her uncle, Hannah, Nat, the young minister-in-training, and even Prudence—provide examples of standing alone for their own beliefs and the consequences (both the difficulties and the rewards) of doing so. The book also offers examples of ways in which people need and support each other.

Differentness. Consider each of the people who take a stand for their beliefs. What characteristics do they have that put them in this position? How do they find the strength or courage they need? What sustains them?

Drive to understand. This book is often recommended simply for the insight it gives into the lives of the New England colonists.

Moral concerns. How would this story have been different if the people of the village had asked questions of Hannah before deciding that she was a witch? How can we avoid similar pre-judging—that is, prejudice?

Relationships with others. Consider instances in which one person supports another even without liking what that person is doing. Have you ever seen someone offer that kind of support to another? Why do people do this? Have you ever done it yourself? Can you think of an opportunity to do so? What would be the consequences, both positive and negative?

Spinelli, Jerry. *Smiles to Go.* HarperCollins, 2008.

Confirmation of the theory that protons decay precipitates a shift in ninth grader Will's worldview. As he copes with the day-to-dayness of his life—which includes Tabby, his irrepressible five-year-old sister, and his friends Mi-Su and BT, with whom he plays Monopoly and eats pizza every Saturday night—another part of his mind tries to come to terms with the dissolution of the universe, including himself. Will is a planner and a champion chess player—one who thinks seriously about life—but he cannot plan everything. Mi-Su is becoming more than a friend to him, and BT appears to be a rival for her affection. There is humor, provided by Tabby and by Korbet, the five-year-old boy next door who adores her; to his dismay, Will is driven to consult Korbet regarding matters of love. And there is the disturbing fact that the easygoing BT is a better brother to Tabby than is Will. A serious accident causes another shift—a positive one—in Will's worldview and in his relationships.

Spinelli's sprightly style and humor make this a pleasure to read, although, along with Will, the reader contemplates the end of the universe. The book has several threads and can be discussed on several levels.

Differentness. Describe ways in which you are like Will. Which of the things that Will thinks or worries about surprise you? What sort of conversation would you like to have with him?

Relationships with others. What has caused the disconnect between Will and Tabby? How much responsibility does Will have to change it? Tabby? Near the end of the book, Will says about BT, "I don't measure him against myself. He is who he is." What is the problem with measuring others against yourself?

Spinelli, Jerry. *Stargirl.* Laurel Leaf, 2004.

Homeschooled until now, a new girl enters Arizona's Mica High in the tenth grade. She is a mystery from the beginning, wearing long prairie skirts, playing the ukulele in the lunchroom, and calling herself Stargirl. Mica High is "not exactly a hotbed of nonconformity," comments Leo Borlock, whom Stargirl chooses to be her boyfriend. Other students are fascinated at first, and Stargirl is suddenly the most popular girl in school; she even becomes a cheerleader. But she cheers when *anyone* does well on the basketball floor—even someone on the other team—and Stargirl and then Leo are shunned. This is painful for Leo but seems not to touch Stargirl, whose innate friendliness remains. At Leo's request, Stargirl tries but fails to fit in. Throughout, Leo and his friends are guided by Archie, a retired teacher whose insights are enigmatic but accurate. It is Archie who finally helps Leo begin to understand Stargirl.

In a story of high school pressure to conform, Stargirl is almost mythical, while Leo is quite human in his struggle to mediate between the everyday and the ideal. Archie plays the role of the Greek chorus, stretching the minds and hearts of the students who come to him for understanding.

Differentness. Stargirl is more different than usual, but we can see in her story what happens to people who are different. What is lost when Stargirl leaves Mica High? Generalize from this: what is lost when we shun people who are different?

Identity. Consider how Stargirl, Leo, and Archie are each true to his or her own identity. What can you learn from them?

Relationships with others; Resilience. Why is it difficult for Stargirl to have a group of friends? Was she unwise in any of the choices that she made? Was Leo unwise? Realistically, what could he have done differently?

Stewart, Trenton Lee. *The Mysterious Benedict Society.* Little Brown, 2008.

His tutor at the orphanage encourages Reynie Muldoon to respond to the newspaper advertisement inviting gifted children to take a test to qualify for "Special Opportunities." Reynie passes and soon finds himself in a small group of children recruited by a kind, modest genius, Mr. Benedict, to carry out a dangerous mission. They are an extraordinary group: Reynie is a natural leader, the one most able to see the big picture and come up with a plan; Kate is athletic and game, capable of crawling through heat ducts and dropping down from ceilings; Sticky has a photographic memory and a gift for languages; and the smallest, tiny Constance Contraire—who indeed is constantly contrary—finally shows her stuff at the crucial moment. Because they have agreed to work together on Mr. Benedict's mysterious assignment, they call themselves The Mysterious Benedict Society, and they infiltrate a school run by a megalomaniac who wants to control the world by sending subliminal messages of fear, distrust, and compliance through radio and television broadcasting.

This is a page-turner with much material for discussion. Issues of mind control, abandonment, conquering fear, and group and family loyalty are embedded in the story, as well as the differing gifts of the children and their use of them for the common good. The complex story implicitly invites readers to join the four children in finding solutions to the puzzling problems and the moral challenges that confront them.

Creativity. What is creativity, as exemplified by Reynie, Kate, Sticky, and Constance? Give examples of creative problem solving in the story. How does this expand your definition of creativity?

Drive to understand. Sometimes authors give clues in the names of the characters—in this book, Constance Contraire is only the most obvious example of this. Can you find the meaning behind Reynie's name? Mr. Benedict's? Others'? What is your understanding of Mr. Curtain's project?

Moral concerns. Of all the moral questions that Reynie faced, which would be most difficult for you? Why?

Relationships with others. Consider all of the connections among the four children. What were their challenges in learning to work together? What did they learn from each other about how to get along with others?

Sturtevant, Katherine. *At the Sign of the Star.* Farrar, Straus, & Giroux, 2002.

In 1677, 12-year-old Meg is the motherless daughter of a London bookseller. As her father's heir, she hopes to be able to choose the man she will marry and continue working in the bookstore, enjoying the friendships that he has built with the well-known writers of late 17th-century England. When her father marries Susannah, Meg fears losing this future—she tries to sabotage the wedding and then resists her stepmother's efforts to teach her the womanly arts that her father wants her to learn. Subtly, over time, Meg absorbs lessons from a book, from friends, and even from Susannah. She realizes that she cannot know her future as surely as she once thought she could, and she achieves a new openness to the possible futures before her.

Sturtevant has carefully researched the period, including the writers of the day (such as John Dryden and Aphra Behn, the first woman playwright). In Meg, she creates a protagonist whose feminist leanings are recognizable today, but with limitations that are true to the period. Meg's story continues in *A True and Faithful Narrative* (described next).

Drive to understand. Meg's story is set at a time of great creativity among English authors, especially playwrights (William Shakespeare had died only 61 years earlier), and the customers who come into Meg's father's store are some of the most well-known and highly regarded writers of the time. To learn more about London in this period, and especially the writers, read Katherine Sturtevant's author's note at the end of the book—it may suggest topics of interest for further research.

Relationships with others. Meg has a quick wit, which is positive—but it is accompanied by a sharp tongue, which can be negative. What experiences lead her to eventually modify her thinking and soften her approach to others? How is it possible for her—and people like her—to retain a quick mind and also learn to speak less sharply?

Sturtevant, Katherine. *A True and Faithful Narrative.* Farrar, Straus, & Giroux, 2006.

Having reached the marriageable age of 16, Meg has relinquished her dream of owning a bookstore, but she hopes more than ever to become a writer—however unconventional that is for a woman in 17th-century London—and decides that the best plan would be to marry a bookseller. The apprentice in her father's bookshop, Will, seems a rational choice, so when Edward, the brother of Meg's friend Anne, comes to say that he is sailing to Italy on business and asks Meg what he might bring her, Meg is startled and appalled to realize that Edward is hoping to court her. She responds too quickly, thoughtlessly suggesting that he might be captured by pirates and write a memoir that her father could publish. But Edward's ship *is* captured, and he is enslaved in Africa. Deeply regretting her careless comment, Meg uses her skill with words to raise ransom money for Edward. When he returns, Edward brings her a journal of his enslavement, which at first included brutal treatment. But then he was sold to a kind Muslim master who valued Edward's expertise with languages and treated him like a son. As she works with Edward to shape the journal for publication, Meg sees how much his experience has changed him. Not the dull businessman that she thought he would be, he brings an enlightened view of a larger world—larger even than the world that Meg knows in her beloved London bookshop.

In this sequel to *At the Sign of the Star*, Meg continues her struggle to reconcile the traditional role of women with her overwhelming need to write, even in the face of her father's disapproval. Her deep chagrin over her comment to Edward, her concern about Anne's unhappy marriage, and the possibility of marrying Will all contribute to the mix that chastens and eventually softens Meg as she grows into a young woman. In the end, her decision is not rational, but it is wise.

Differentness. Meg is very different from her family and friends, yet she has their love and respect. In what ways does she accommodate others' needs and interests? How does she accomplish this without giving up her uniqueness?

Using ability. There is not much question about whether Meg will use her ability; she cannot avoid writing. But how does her drive to write threaten other aspects of her life? Can you give modern examples of the same situation that Meg faces? What factors in her story, and in herself, help her avoid negative results?

Sutcliff, Rosemary. *The Sword and the Circle.* Puffin, 1994.

For her retelling of the Arthurian legends, Sutcliff draws stories from several sources and weaves them into a whole—a collection of stories of Arthur and Guenevere, Lancelot, Gawain, Tristan and Iseult, Merlin, and others, all of the Fellowship of the Round Table. Sutcliff has written often of this period and others in British history, and her sense for language and place enhances the tales to create an experience of wonder and imagination for sensitive readers.

Drive to understand. The author's note will intrigue readers who want to know more of origins—who was the historical Arthur, for instance? Sutcliff's stories come from history, poetry, and legend; some readers may want, now or later, to read the earlier versions. Especially inquisitive readers may also want to compare Sutcliff's retelling of the Arthurian legends with that of others.

Sutcliff, Rosemary. *Sword Song.* Farrar, Straus, & Giroux, 2005.

At 17, Bjarni Sigurdson is banished from Rafnglas, the Viking settlement that has been his home since he and his older brother left Norway. Out of impulsive anger, he has committed a murder, and Rafn, the chief of the settlement on the west coast of Britain, gives him a sword and orders him to be on the merchant ship leaving for Dublin in the morning. For the next five years, Bjarni must find his own way in the constantly shifting fortunes of the Viking Age. He becomes a mercenary, hiring out his sword arm to one chieftain after another. His impulsiveness carries him into trouble more than once, as leaders such as Onund Treefoot and the wise Lady Aud watch, correcting and encouraging him with care and concern. Finding adventure as soldier and sailor, he gradually proves his fierce loyalty to his chief, and he grows from boy to man during his banishment. On his return to Rafnglas, alone after leaping from a ship in a storm, he faces his greatest challenge: protecting a young woman who is struggling to keep her ancestral farm from those who believe her to be a witch.

Sword Song is Sutcliff's last book, left in second draft when she died suddenly in 1992. Because her language is true to the time—her vocabulary full of words that the people of the British Islands used before Chaucer—it is both challenging and fascinating to read. Sutcliff provides insight into the hardships of daily life, the everpresent danger of sudden death, and the mingling of cultures and religions as Vikings meet Picts, and Christianity meets the old religion of the Norsemen. Her research is trustworthy; this is a fine example of how history can be learned through fiction.

Drive to understand. Much discussion could be built around the Vikings' way of life. As we would expect, Sutcliff depicts them as warlike, but what else does she show us that does not fit the stereotype? For example, despite language barriers and constant warfare, the different peoples of the Scottish islands attempt to understand each other's customs and strive not to offend. Why was this important to them? Why is it important to us?

Tolan, Stephanie. *Surviving the Applewhites.* Harper Collins, 2003.

After running through all other school options, juvenile delinquent Jake Semple arrives at the "Creative Academy" at the chaotic Applewhite home in rural North Carolina. The Applewhites are all eccentric artists except E.D.—a misfit as the only organized member of the family—who is charged with teaching Jake. Jake is accepted as just one more member in a family of individuals, and gradually he takes an interest in the family's projects—especially when E.D.'s father, directing "The Sound of Music," casts Jake in a singing role. The chaos and genius of the eccentric Applewhite clan reaches its zenith when the production must be moved to the Applewhite barn, and E.D.'s organizational ability saves the show.

The zany humor throughout keeps this story moving. We see the other characters alternately through Jake's and E.D.'s eyes, and we watch as Jake discovers his potential and E.D. sees the value in her own special talent—all done with a light touch.

Identity; Relationships with others. When and how does Jake begin to change? How does the way the Applewhites treat him help Jake become more himself? Why does it work that way, in your opinion?

Voigt, Cynthia. *Izzy, Willy-Nilly.* Simon Pulse, 2005.

Izzy is a sophomore—a pretty, popular cheerleader—when she accepts Marco's invitation to a party, not because she especially likes him, but because he is a senior. Marco drinks too much, and the accident on the way home results in the amputation of Izzy's right leg. As she recuperates, Izzy watches her friendships change. Marco never calls, even to apologize. Lauren, who plans to be a model, withdraws from Izzy, overwhelmingly appalled at physical imperfection. Suzy's habit of lying becomes a too-familiar brand of false friendliness. Even Izzy's strong and loving parents, who deal efficiently with the practical aspects of her handicap, are not available to recognize her emotional vulnerability. Only Roseamunde, who is seen as weird and is rejected by Izzy's popular group, comes forward as a friend who can accept and reflect what Izzy is experiencing, though she does so awkwardly at first. The daughter of an artist, Roseamunde is more intellectual than the others and different in her own right—and she says exactly what she feels, a trait that enables her to reach Izzy in her isolation. When Izzy returns to school, she finds that she is still well-liked, but now she is on her way to becoming an individual.

Voigt offers an absorbing storyline with a psychological depth that continues to merit thought and discussion long after the reading is done. A teacher, she records the high school atmosphere accurately, and even the weaker characters are sympathetically drawn. Roseamunde is especially memorable, with her social awkwardness combined with the sensitivity, maturity, penetrating insights, and direct honesty characteristic of many bright and introspective people.

Identity. What does Izzy learn about herself from Roseamunde? From the accident? In what other ways can high school students become individuals beyond the high school scene? Why is it so important to Izzy that Roseamunde is so direct? Why does Roseamunde seem rough, and Izzy smooth, in being honest? Why is Roseamunde more developed as an individual by the age of 15 than Izzy is?

Relationships with others. What did Roseamunde see in Izzy that led her to believe she could be a friend? What do Roseamunde and Izzy have in common with each other that they do not share with Lisa, Lauren, and Suzy? What can they continue to learn from each other?

Resilience. How do the various characters try to cope with adversity? How effective are their different styles?

Voigt, Cynthia. *Jackaroo.* Simon Pulse, 2003.

Gwyn is a 16-year-old innkeeper's daughter—in medieval Wales, to judge from the names. Times are hard, and although the innkeeper is prosperous and his family better off than most, Gwyn feels intense sympathy for the poor, so distant from the concerns of the ruling lords. In this hard winter, a lord and his son stop at the inn, and when they leave suddenly, they request a servant for each of them. Gwyn and the manservant Burl attend them, but the four are separated in a blizzard, and Gwyn and the lordling spend many days snowbound in an abandoned stone cabin. Gradually they become friends, despite the awkwardness of the lord/servant relationship, and the lordling teaches Gwyn to read. Cleaning the cupboards of the stone cabin one day, she finds an old pair of thigh-high leather boots, a plumed hat, and a tunic—the costume worn by the legendary Jackaroo, who rides to aid the people in difficult times. Gwyn has never believed the legends, but later she finds the costume useful. In its disguise, she is able to dispense some of the gold pieces, given to her by the lord when she returned his son safely to him, to people who desperately need help. More importantly, riding as Jackaroo enables Gwyn to fully feel her strength and independence, until she realizes that she cannot follow the narrow choices open to her at the inn or in the nearby village.

Voigt captures language patterns and medieval mores and restrictions well, describing vividly the lives of common people living in a period that most literature depicts only through the eyes of the nobility. Many readers will identify with Gwyn's sensitivity to the needs that she sees around her, as well as with the sense of differentness it engenders. The love story of Gwyn and Burl is slow and subtle, a long friendship developing before Gwyn recognizes it as love.

Differentness. What restrictions did medieval living patterns impose on "different" people like Gwyn and Burl? If the Earl had not intervened, what could they have done? What restrictions do present living patterns and unwritten rules impose on people like them? What options do such people have now?

Identity. How did playing Jackaroo help Gwyn clarify her own identity? Why was it dangerous? What was Win warning her about? How would you have advised her about marriage? Why?

Sensitivity. Why is Gwyn so much more aware of others' needs than most people in the story? Why is Burl aware?

Whelan, Gloria. *Goodbye, Vietnam.* Yearling, 1993.

Thirteen-year-old Mai and her family live in the Mekong Delta of Vietnam in the early 1990s, after the conflict there. Life for them is difficult under the new government, even after the return of her father, who had been taken away by the police many months before. Mai has been out of school for two years because her family needs her to work to keep from starving. Much of the rice harvest is taken by the government, food prices rise daily, and now Mai's grandmother will be taken away soon because she will not give up the old ways of healing. But Mai's uncle and his family have escaped by boat to Hong Kong; they send a card saying that they hope to get to Chicago.

One day Mai's mother tells her that they will be leaving their village, the home of their ancestors, to try to find a new life elsewhere. They walk for two nights through swamps and forests, then find passage on a small and vastly overcrowded boat—thanks to the fact that her father has a secret skill as a mechanic, and the boat's old engine needs constant attention. During the thousand-mile voyage, both Mai and her father act quickly to save other refugees; in each case, the people they save bring talents that are beneficial to all. When they arrive in Hong Kong, they spend weeks in a crowded refugee camp, hoping that they will not be among those sent back to Vietnam.

Whelan's story is well researched, full of detail, and sparely written. Without sentimentality, she leaves the reader newly aware of the strength of the human spirit—in facing hardship, danger, fear, and sickness, bolstered by courage and by the determination to find a better life—and of the interdependence that characterizes the human condition.

Drive to understand. Mai's story sheds light on a particular moment in history, but her family's experience in general is that of refugees in many times and places. Why do people become refugees? Should other countries accept them, even if there are no jobs? What solutions are there to this problem?

Moral concerns. In fleeing without the proper papers, and in bribing the police officer with a duck, Mai's family is doing something illegal. What is your response to this? If it is all right in their situation, why is that so? How can you decide a question like this?

Relationships with others. Why is it so important that the people crowded onto the boat get along with each other? How do they manage to do so, even under such difficult conditions? How does their culture help them? How would what you have been taught help you?

Resilience. What personal characteristics enabled the refugees to face the challenges and risks? How did they help each other?

Using ability. Both the grandmother and Bac si Hong are willing to risk arrest to use their knowledge of healing. Why is it so important to them? What do you think might be that important to you, under circumstances like theirs? What would you have to offer?

White, David A. *Philosophy for Kids.* Illustrated by Cheryle Chapline. Prufrock Press, 2001.

After years of experience in teaching philosophy in colleges and universities, in 1993, the author began teaching philosophy in Chicago's public schools. In this book, he encourages "anyone 10 or over" to engage in philosophical thinking. White presents 40 questions about values, knowledge, reality, and critical thinking. After each question, he follows up with a brief discussion and an exercise suggesting approaches, possible answers, and a "quiz" that asks the student to think through his or her own response. This is followed by a section called "For Further Thought," which goes more deeply into the wider-ranging implications of various answers and includes references to related questions elsewhere in the book. The cover of this attractive book is Raphael's fresco *The School of Athens*; in a separate note, White names the philosophers depicted and what their position in the painting symbolizes.

All of this sounds serious, and it is, but White's good humor and joy in philosophy are infectious; they pervade the book. He has so much fun with philosophy that we know his students do, too. Sometimes they greet him with "Hey, philosophy dude!" He claims that he is "in no sense a 'dude,'" but he is pleased to interpret this as a suggestion that they think studying philosophy is "cool." At the end of the book, he provides suggestions for parents and teachers, with Teaching Tips for each of the 40 questions and suggestions for curricular integration. For students, there is a list of additional readings and a glossary.

Drive to understand. Studying philosophy must be the ultimate expression of this category—the Drive to Understand. This book is highly recommended—although it is not written solely for gifted children, they will respond to the ideas throughout the book, and especially to those in the "For Further Thought" sections.

White, Ruth. *Belle Prater's Boy.* Yearling, 1998.

When Gypsy Leemaster's Aunt Belle suddenly and mysteriously disappears, her cousin Woodrow—Belle Prater's boy—comes to live with their grandparents, next door to Gypsy in a Virginia mining town, and Gypsy and Woodrow become best friends. Woodrow has lived in a shack in the hills; he has few clothes, and his eyes are crossed. But he is well-liked immediately for his cleverness with stories, his humor, and his warmth toward people of every age. In contrast, Gypsy is the beautiful daughter of a beautiful mother, living in one of the nicest homes in Coal Station. Her strongest wish is to be able to cut her long blonde hair because she believes that people see only her hair, not the person underneath it; however, her mother promised her father before he died that she would never let Gypsy cut her hair. While Woodrow tries to explain to himself why his mother left, Gypsy's anger over her father's death gradually comes to the surface. Together they learn the story that they have not been told, and together they are able to transcend the tragedies of their parents' leaving.

This Newbery Honor Book is full of humor, of wisdom about the value of seeing through appearances to the person underneath, and about the truth that there is no escape from pain, even for people who seem to have everything. Setting her story in the 1950s, White has created warm parental figures in the children's grandparents, in Gypsy's mother and stepfather, and in the townspeople. Both the characterization and the setting are masterfully handled. Young readers will remember Gypsy's hunger to be known for more than her beauty and Woodrow's expert way of dealing with people for a long time.

Identity. What is behind Gypsy's desire that others should see who she is and not just her hair? Without saying anything about her physical appearance, how would you describe Gypsy? How would people describe you? How might you be misjudging someone you know because of a physical feature, whether it is beautiful like Gypsy's hair or unfortunate like Woodrow's eyes?

Relationships with others. What draws Woodrow and Gypsy together, beyond the fact that they are cousins? How do they help each other reach an understanding of what has happened to their parents? Consider the specific things they each do to help cheer up the other. What similar idea have you had to help a friend?

Yep, Laurence. *Dragonwings.* HarperTrophy, 1989.

Born in China, eight-year-old Moon Shadow travels to the "demon land"—America—in 1903 to join his father, Windrider, who has lived and worked in the Chinese community in San Francisco since before Moon Shadow was born. Life for the Chinese men working in California is uncertain and dangerous, as they struggle to learn a new language and new ways, sending much of their income home to their families. Moon Shadow works with his father in a Chinatown laundry, then moves to another neighborhood when his father takes a job with one of the demons. Windrider is a kitemaker whose imagination is caught by the Wright brothers' experiment with flying, and Moon Shadow is carried along on his father's dream of building an aeroplane. Despite setbacks and danger, and with the help of both Chinese and demon friends, they succeed for a moment.

Looking at the San Francisco of those years through Moon Shadow's eyes is sometimes jolting and always instructive, illuminating American and Chinese culture at once. The plot, based on the story of a Chinese immigrant who built a flying machine in 1909, gives Yep ample opportunity to explore the lives and struggles of the Chinese who came to America in the early years of the 20th century.

Differentness. In this book, we recognize how much more people are alike than different, and yet Moon Shadow is constantly faced with his differentness. Often, he expresses his opinion that the demon ways are wrong. Why do American ways seem wrong to him? On what basis can he—and we—judge when another is "wrong" or "right"? How does he know that he is doing the right thing, even though he is different? How can you adapt that to your own experience?

Drive to understand. Examine any stereotypical pictures that you may have had about Chinese immigrant workers in America. What have you learned from reading *Dragonwings* that might alter those pictures?

Relationships with others. Describe Moon Shadow's friendship with Robin. How is she different? Look at the friendship from her point of view. What does she bring to it, and what does she gain from it?

Resilience; Using ability. In learning to get along in a new country, the Chinese immigrants had to use every personal resource they could muster. What were some of the qualities that they displayed, good and bad? How many of those qualities do you have? What qualities or abilities might you develop further if you were challenged as much as they were to survive? How can you develop those qualities even though your survival is not an issue?

Senior High: Grades 9-12

Adderholdt, Miriam & Jan Goldberg. *Perfectionism: What's Bad about Being Too Good.* Illustrated by Caroline Price Schwert. Free Spirit, 1999.

Many gifted teenagers are victims of perfectionism, harboring so strong a desire to do everything perfectly that they consider second place or a B a failure. Some go so far as to avoid risking that failure by refusing to accept a new challenge or to take an advanced course. *Perfectionism* speaks to these students, describing its effects on mind, body, and relationships and then prescribing practical steps toward becoming more realistic about expectations. Counselors, teachers, and librarians will find the book a useful tool for school-based discussions on giftedness, and parents can use it effectively in the home. The insights that it offers are as important for adults working with gifted youngsters as for the students themselves.

This book can be used independently by students in the middle grades or in senior high. For younger students, parents can gather ideas from the book and present them to their children in whatever way seems appropriate.

Perfectionism; Using ability.

Auel, Jean. *The Clan of the Cave Bear.* Bantam, 2002.

This popular novel features several characters who stand out in their prehistoric clan because of their special abilities. The medicine woman of the Clan of the Cave Bear cares for a five-year-old girl from an unknown clan who was orphaned when an earthquake swallowed her home. As the young girl grows, the differences between the Cro-Magnon Ayla and the Neanderthal Clan people become apparent. The Clan is deeply traditional, relying on a mixture of instinct and knowledge from past ages. Ayla displays flexibility, intelligent curiosity, a drive toward individuality, and a willingness to take risks—all of which puts her at odds with the Clan people.

These differences between Ayla and the people who surround her are analogous to the differences that a highly talented student may sense between himself and many of the people around him.

Understanding how Ayla feels and seeing her responses to the situation can help him understand and respond constructively to his own situation.

Identity. How does Ayla come to recognize her differences? How does she feel about them? What is her self-concept, and how does it affect her behavior? How does it change as she learns more about herself?

Relationships with others. How does Ayla compromise her abilities in order to fit in with the Clan, and how does she decide when not to compromise? What mistakes does she make? Can you go on from this to draw a set of criteria to determine when compromise is adaptive and when it is nonproductive? What would be Ayla's definition of personal integrity? What is yours?

Bauer, Marion Dane (Ed.). *Am I Blue? Coming Out from the Silence.* HarperCollins, 1995.

This is a collection of 16 original stories, each a different perspective on the experience of growing up gay or lesbian, or loving someone who is gay or lesbian. They include Lois Lowry's "Holding," about how Will finally tells his best friend that his father is gay; William Sleator's "In the Tunnels," told from the point of view of a young gay Vietnamese soldier; Francesca Lia Block's "Winnie and Tommy," in which Tommy comes out to his girlfriend; Nancy Garden's "Parent's Night," about Karen's struggle to tell her parents that she is lesbian and their courage in supporting her; and M. E. Kerr's "We Might as Well All Be Strangers," describing how Alison discovers that the person in her family who understands her best is her grandmother, who remembers the Holocaust. In "Michael's Little Sister" by C. S. Adler, Michael struggles against the recognition that he is gay until his little sister, Becky, relates Michael's difference to her own sense of being different—in her case, because she is more interested in learning about nature than about "silly parties and TV shows."

The award-winning authors, some gay or lesbian and some not, reach across boundaries of color, class, nationality, and religion. In every story, the focus is on the primary importance of relationship—and for the young people in these stories, how that is affected by sexual orientation. For gifted children, the primary focus is the same: how their relationships are affected—for them, by having exceptional talent. The underlying questions in *Am I Blue?*, although it is about a different way of being different, are the fundamental questions that gifted children have, spoken or not: "Can I be myself and still have friends?" "Will lack of understanding—my own and others'—defeat the relationships that I value?" And the answers, repeated often in this book, are the same: "You are not alone."

Discussion of these stories will depend in large part on whether the leader assumes that the students in the group are gay or lesbian, or straight, or some of each. The following questions—only a beginning, as always—are designed to discuss the book as a whole. Answers may be based on any story that seems relevant to the discussion.

Differentness. How do the characters in these stories respond to the feeling of being different? How are their responses similar to those of people who are different in other ways, such as heightened intellectual curiosity or special talent or interests?

Drive to understand. For students who know little of the issues that gay or lesbian teenagers must struggle with, this book is a multi-faceted source of information and fresh awareness. *Am I Blue?* could be used simply for this purpose—as a resource for the exploration of homophobia.

Identity. While determining one's sexual identity is a theme in many of the stories, other forms of identity-seeking are here, too: ethnic identity, role in one's family, individuality within the group. What others can you add from your own experience, based on having an unusual talent or interest? How do these many identity issues relate to each other? Notice in how many of the stories the answer to the character's identity questions are left open at the end. Why is this? Answer in general terms, considering all of the kinds of identity search that have been mentioned.

Relationships with others. Consider the stories in which the tone of an important relationship shifts with the revelation that someone is gay or lesbian. When love or friendship deepens, what factors cause that result? When distance enters the relationship, why is that so?

What universal factors can you discuss that cause relationships to either deepen or fall apart as individuals define themselves more clearly in regard to issues other than sexual orientation?

Becker, Jurek. *Bronstein's Children*. Translated by Leila Vennewitz. University of Chicago Press, 1999.

Hans was an East German Jew just finishing at the gymnasium and preparing for the university when he discovered his father and two other men torturing a former Nazi concentration camp guard whom they had captured. The book alternates in time between the present, as Hans recalls the events leading up to his father's death, and flashbacks to the two-week period when the guard was held captive, a year earlier. The small cast of characters includes Hans's girlfriend Martha and her parents, who take Hans in after his father dies, and his sister Elle, who is in a mental institution due to sudden violent outbursts dating back to the Nazi period.

The storyline is deceptively simple, the structure demanding, the mood somber. The questions raised are serious ones. They can be asked as limited to the Nazi period, but then asked again in broader terms, as they apply to victims in other situations, perhaps even to readers' own lives.

Aloneness. Hans is lonely, alienated, and left to work out his solution by himself. How does he do it? Why does it take so long?

Identity. Who are the victims? How long does one remain a victim? How does one stop being a victim, and how much control does one have? How does this apply to your development of your own sense of identity?

Moral concerns. How does one gain control over one's own life and destiny? How does one gather the strength and courage to act?

Blackwood, Gary. *The Year of the Hangman*. Puffin, 2004.

In 1777, Creighton is 15, taking advantage of his widowed mother's overindulgence and already assuming the life of the indolent English gentleman that he expects to become, when his mother—despairing of her ability to make him behave—arranges to have him kidnapped and shipped to South Carolina Colony, where her brother is a colonel in the occupying English army. The colonel proves to be cold, demanding, and possibly implicated in the death of Creighton's father in the recent unpleasantness between England and her American colonies. Now England has put down the rebellion, and Creighton joins the colonel when he is posted to West Florida. There, Creighton becomes an assistant in the printing shop of Benjamin Franklin and begins to see England and the war through the eyes of the Americans. Soon he must examine where his loyalties lie and whom he can trust—while at the same time, he questions accepted ideas about the value of war.

In this work of uchrony (alternative history), Blackwood imagines that George Washington was captured, the British won the war, and now some die-hard patriots are making plans to continue the rebellion. Creighton becomes involved in spying, code-breaking, and duels—the book is full of adventure, as well as real and imagined history. The "year of the hangman," 1777, was so-called because the sevens look like gallows, a common sight at the time.

Drive to understand. One of the challenges for readers is to know—or to learn—enough American history to find the line between history and alternative history in this novel. The author's note provides a start; readers may want to go further or to write a uchrony of their own.

Identity. At what point(s) did Creighton begin to realize that he might welcome a different life from the one that he had known in England? What do you think he will be doing in five or 10 years? What internal changes in Creighton have occurred in 1777 to make that possible for him? Can you imagine such a change in your own life? If so, describe and explain it.

Moral concerns. Read again the composite of Franklin's ideas at the end of the book. With what thoughts do you agree or disagree?

Bradbury, Ray. *Fahrenheit 451*. Ballantine, 1996.

In Bradbury's imagined future, firemen have become those who create fire—the censors who burn books (which have a conflagration point of 451 degrees Fahrenheit). In doing so, they are merely carrying out the will of the majority, who long ago scorned books, turning to the pseudo-world of television instead. Books, after all, cause dissension, since they don't agree with each other, and in any case, the populace is more docile when kept in the state of intellectual numbness induced by video.

But Montag is a fireman who questions. After his wife attempts suicide (a common occurrence in this world), he brings down the books that he has hidden in the attic and begins to read, looking for answers and meaning. In due time, the firemen arrive to burn his house and books, and Montag becomes a fugitive. As the war that has threatened throughout the book descends upon the city, Montag finds himself welcomed by a group of other questioners and dissidents, each carrying the treasure of a remembered book in his brain.

The author's afterword is a protest against publishers' attempts to remove passages thought to be offensive from Bradbury's works as they were considered for use in high school anthologies—effectively censoring this book on censorship. The Ballantine Del Rey edition of 1979 restored lost sections and printed the afterword—all of which is worth discussion in itself. Here, in addition to censorship, Bradbury anticipates the rampant growth of restrictions on thinking, speaking, and writing that resulted from the move toward "politically correct" expression.

Drive to understand. Follow Beatty's history of the end of books. What looks familiar? How far have we gone toward the future that Bradbury predicts? Will the end of the Cold War (which Bradbury did not foresee) change any of his forecasts?

Moral concerns. What is the role, the danger, and the future face of censorship in our time? What are the differing roles of the public and the government? How does censorship affect the development and appropriate use of your abilities? What are sources of censorship in your life? What is your personal responsibility regarding censorship? What is the impact of the events of September 11, 2001 on these issues?

Finally, have you read the works that the men have memorized? They make a good reading list.

Chatwin, Bruce. *Utz.* Penguin, 1999.

Kaspar Utz, the only surviving descendant of his wealthy grandmother, is able to bear life in Prague under Communism rather well. Through various understandings with the authorities, Utz retains and even augments his collection of Meissen porcelain. The narrator, an English historian of the Northern Renaissance, meets Utz on a research trip to Prague in 1967, just before the "Prague Spring" of 1968—that brief period when there was hope of relief from the Communist regime. He returns in the late '80s, years after Utz's death (but before the collapse of the Iron Curtain) to learn the fate of the Meissen collection. He pieces together more of Utz's story, especially the role of his servant Marta, but the reader is left to conjecture about the Meissen.

Written by an English writer and based on Eastern European history and culture, this book will prove a serious challenge to American high school students, but it is worth the effort. Some background reading on August the Strong, the history of Meissen porcelain, and Dresden will add to the pleasure and enable motivated readers to follow the story easily, preparing them to consider the philosophical questions raised in this brief novel.

Drive to understand. Consider the aspects of Western society that disgusted Utz. What causes the difference between his attitude and that of those who wanted to emigrate? How does his attitude toward the Western world square with his passion for porcelain? What is Chatwin saying about materialism? What implications, if any, do you see for the blending of Eastern and Western European (and American) culture after the events of 1989? What do you think happened to the Meissen collection? What *should* have happened to it? Why?

Moral concerns. Utz says that the collection ruined his life. If so, in what way? Is Utz's fascination with porcelain a form of idolatry, in your view?

Cole, Brock. *Celine.* Farrar, Strauss, & Giroux, 2003.

Celine is a junior in a Chicago high school, an artist living with her 22-year-old stepmother while her irresponsible father is on a European lecture tour. Jake is a young boy in the apartment across the hall whose artist father is separated from his mother. Celine copes with these disparate people as well as with typical high school problems—the paper on Holden Caulfield, the friend who uses Celine as a cover to attend a forbidden party, the unwelcome boyfriend—with a sense of humor tinged with a fine edge of irony and devastatingly clear self-awareness.

It is the writing rather than the plot that will appeal to mature readers of *Celine*. Cole provides a sample of the thinking of a talented high school girl as she deals gamely, without pretension or illusions, with the realities of daily living, including the shortcomings of herself and others. Despite the distractions, we know that Celine will prevail, if only because of her clear sense of herself as an artist.

Identity. Questions might include inquiry into the role that art plays in integrating Celine's life. What, if anything, does or could play such a role in your life?

Using ability. Explore the importance of knowing that there is something we do well, of pursuing something outside of ourselves that helps us keep perspective, as art does for Celine. What other qualities in Celine help her to stay on top of things? What pursuits and qualities in you help you—or could help you—in the same way?

Cormier, Robert. *I Am the Cheese*. Knopf, 2007.

Adam Farmer tells the story of a bicycle ride from Massachusetts to Vermont in search of his father. Interspersed between chapters about the ride are documents recording a therapist's interviews with Adam, during which his memories slowly tell the story of his childhood in a happy family with a terrible shadow looming over it. Adam's father, a reporter, had provided information on organized crime to the government, and since then, his family's life has been ruled by the governmental agency that protects witnesses who have put their lives in danger. They have been given a whole new identity. Adam discovers that he isn't even Adam Farmer—he was born Paul Delmonte. Finally he realizes that Brint, his "therapist," is trying to get him to remember further information—information that Adam's father never gave him. It becomes impossible to know whom to trust, and the chilling sense that this is so grows until, by the end of the novel, it is the point of the story.

This book is recommended for good readers because it is challenging—with flashbacks, alternating settings, and shifting loyalties—and because it presents new ideas and information which raise questions about the role of government in citizens' private lives. It lends itself well to conjectural discussion.

Moral concerns. Should Adam's father have given the information? What is Brint's motive? Mr. Gray's? How could the system be handled better?

Crutcher, Chris. *Ironman.* HarperTeen, 2004.

Bo Brewster is an Ironman, a triathlete who uses intense training in swimming, cycling, and running to help cope with the strained relationship between him and his father. Bo's coach and English teacher, Mr. Redmond, is much like his father, and angry outbursts at Coach Redmond result in Bo's forced membership in the Nak Pack, an anger management group of troubled boys (and one girl) who meet with Mr. Nakatani every morning before school. Feeling that he really doesn't belong in this group, Bo slowly learns the sources of the others' anger and begins to understand his own. He tells his story, with growing insight and pointed humor, in the form of unsent letters to TV talk show host Larry King, who, he reasons, listens to everyone, no matter how unlikely the story.

Recently published nonfiction books (*Real Boys* and *A Fine Young Man*) discuss some of the destructive ways in which parents may choose to turn boys into men. Crutcher's book addresses this as fiction—and does it well. Bo's manner is brash and flippant at first; his gradual move toward emotional awareness and vulnerability is always balanced by the extreme physical demands that he places on himself as a triathlete, and he remains believable. Readers find much to think about, particularly regarding the line between someone else's problem and one's own problem. Crutcher tells a story about introspection with a rapid pace and plenty of action.

Drive to understand. One point that Crutcher makes in *Ironman* is that everyone has a story, and most people use various kinds of defenses to hide their story from others. What examples do you see around you? How does it change your feelings toward a person when you consider the story behind his or her actions? Does the story excuse destructive actions or merely explain them? What is your role in these situations?

Relationships with others. Mr. Nak tells Bo that it doesn't need to be okay with Bo that Mr. S. is gay; it needs to be okay with Mr. S. What, then, is Bo's role? Does his relationship with Mr. S. change? By the end of the book, how has Bo's relationship with his father changed? What will happen in the future? Why? What will Bo's role be?

Curie, Eve. *Madame Curie*. Translated from the French by Vincent Sheean. DaCapo, 2001.

Gathering letters, family stories, and her own memories, Marie Curie's daughter wrote this biography shortly after her mother's death. She tells of Marie's childhood in Russian-occupied Poland and of Marie's intellectual isolation while she worked as a governess to send her sister to medical school in Paris. When she was 24, Marie was finally able to go to Paris for her own studies. The book tells of her marriage to Pierre Curie, of their partnership in the discovery of radium, of the lonely years of dedicated work after his death, and of the honors that she at last endured, having no talent for the life of a celebrity.

The book is a rich source for high school students whose interests are intellectual in nature. It presents the different worlds of well-educated children growing up in 19th-century Poland and of the life of scientists in Paris at the turn of the last century. Most stimulating for many readers is the glimpse of the excitement of intellectual life in Europe at that time; it made demands on Marie and Pierre which they gladly met. Marie's life is a ringing statement of the connection between hard work and accomplishment, as well as of the passionate absorption of a gifted adult in her work. Both she and Pierre were happiest in their laboratory, but they also had warm relationships with family and colleagues.

Drive to understand. This book is listed here because of the picture it provides of intellectual life in both Eastern and Western Europe before and after World War I. For gifted students whose only experience with meeting their intellectual needs and interests has been the contemporary American high school, this view of Europe can be both stimulating and inspiring.

Intensity. Discuss the contrast between play during Marie's youth in Poland and work during her adulthood in Paris. Did she make a bad choice, in your view? Why or why not?

Resilience. At what points in her life did Marie display resilience? What helped her to cope?

Using ability. How did Marie's childhood and youth prepare her for her life's work? How did specific incidents lead her to her career choice? How important was the influence of her family? What similar events have happened in your life?

Dickinson, Peter. *Eva.* Laurel Leaf, 1990.

Eva Adamson is 14, living in a future when burgeoning population has resulted in an almost complete take-over of the earth by humans, who are crowded into high rise buildings in sprawling cities and who rarely see a tree or an animal. Her father does research on the few remaining chimpanzees, all in captivity, and when Eva is critically injured in an accident, her parents consent to an experimental attempt to save her life—transplanting Eva's brain into the body of a chimpanzee named Kelly. Her human mind survives but receives some of Kelly's genetic memory, and Eva becomes more comfortable in social groupings of chimps than of humans. Convinced that humans are giving up—social systems are failing, no one is going into research, long-term planning has lost its viability—a brilliant young rebel arranges for Eva and a group of chimps to escape to one of the few remaining natural tropical forests.

Several controversial and discussable themes permeate this disturbing book, including the effects of overpopulation on the earth's ecology, the ethical questions of the use of animals in research, the impact of the media on human initiative, and the loss of will to communal progress.

Drive to understand. The basic question of the book concerns what it is to be human. Have we somehow gone beyond the best that is human, to our detriment? Has the human race peaked? How has the impact of the media on human initiative changed since 1990?

Moral concerns. If we could start over again, as Eva's chimps may, what changes would you make in history? In human nature? In what ways do we have the potential to make these changes? How can we prevent, even now, the future Dickinson projects?

Doctorow, Cory. *Little Brother.* Tor Teen, 2008.

Seventeen-year-old computer-savvy Marcus is with gaming friends near San Francisco's Bay Bridge when a terrorist attack destroys the bridge. The teens are caught up in a sweep of suspects, blindfolded, and taken to an island prison where they are interrogated under threat of torture. Daryll disappears and is presumed dead; the others are released but find that San Francisco is now under the control of an over-zealous Department of Homeland Security. Determined to thwart the frightening increase in surveillance, Marcus uses the Internet and his technological expertise to reach teens all over the city and encourage a rebellion against further insults to the Declaration and the Bill of Rights. The situation becomes tense and very dangerous, a romantic interest grows, and Marcus does not always know whom he can trust—but he remains steadfast and courageous in his opposition to restrictions on personal liberties.

The author and the two writers who provide afterwords, Bruce Schneier and Andrew Huang, are well-known among those who work with digital security and its impact on personal liberty. Adults may have concerns about this book, but many teens will appreciate it. It raises legitimate questions that all of us will have to face sooner than we might wish.

Drive to understand. Two threads in *Little Brother*—digital security and the effect on civil liberties of efforts to fight terrorism—offer much opportunity for discussion, which might begin with George Orwell's *1984*, in which Big Brother personifies the threats to individual rights as Orwell foresaw them.

Moral concerns. Going beyond the easy questions—Is Marcus right or wrong in his actions?—consider the larger picture by creating questions of your own. Exactly what are the issues that this book raises regarding both the use of technology and civil liberties? How will these questions be answered in your lifetime? What new questions are likely to be raised? How can we determine what is right? What will your role be?

Relationships with others. Discuss this statement: Both students and adults must remember that, although students may know more about technology than their parents and teachers do, there is still much that they can learn from the adults in their lives. How does this either change or affect your response to this novel?

Douglass, Frederick. *Narrative of the Life of Frederick Douglass, an American Slave.* Bedford/St. Martin's, 2002.

Born a slave in Maryland in 1818, Frederick Douglass escaped to the north 20 years later. He had taught himself how to read and write but was otherwise uneducated. Nevertheless, leaders of the abolitionist movement recognized his intelligence and eloquence, and by 1841, he was a public speaker for their cause. Later he became Recorder of Deeds for the District of Columbia and United States Minister to Haiti. Written in 1845, this narrative is the story of his years in slavery. He tells of being passed from one owner to another, how and why he was beaten, what happened to his family and friends, and how a kind mistress taught him the alphabet and a few words before her husband forbade her to continue, saying that reading would make him unfit to be a slave—thereby firing in Frederick the determination to learn to read. The fact that he gives no details of his escape, fearing that the information would close the route to freedom for fellow slaves, creates for the modern reader a startling sense of immediacy and authenticity.

Drive to understand; Moral concerns; Resilience. The contrast between the appalling descriptions of slavery on the one hand and, on the other, the clear evidence of Frederick's sensitivity, intellect, and ability to articulate experiences and feelings is deeply moving. The book is valuable both for understanding slavery and as the autobiography of a gifted writer who fought against overwhelming odds to realize his capacities.

Eco, Umberto. *The Name of the Rose*. Translated from the Italian by William Weaver. Everyman's Library, 2006. (This edition is in hardback, with text plus commentary, and is 600 pages.)

Set in a 14th-century monastery in northern Italy, this acclaimed mystery novel is told by Adso of Melk, a Benedictine novice assigned to serve William of Baskerville, a Franciscan monk whose mission it is to arrange talks between emissaries of the two popes—one in Rome and one in Avignon. This mission, however, is merely the background for the more immediate problem that Brother William faces: finding the causes of the mysterious deaths, one each day, of the monks in the Italian abbey where the talks are to take place. This mystery centers on the library, where manuscripts are kept in a labyrinth forbidden to all but a few and which William and Adso must therefore explore by night.

Eco is a philosopher, historian, aesthetician, and semioticist, and his story is laced with discussions that range over all of these fields. In addition to unraveling the mystery, then, the reader's mind is challenged by the theology, the logic, and the politics of the 14th century, amid the confusion of Italian civil and ecclesiastical intrigue just after Dante's time.

Drive to understand. Readers may wish to discuss questions which are raised or implied in the text. For example, Adso comments, "I had always believed logic was a universal weapon, and now I realized how its validity depended on the way it was employed.... [It] could be especially useful when you entered it but then left it." In a discussion of the allegorical value of the legend of the unicorn, he says, "Higher truths can be expressed while the letter is lying." In Adso's final discussion with William, they consider the role of laughter, and of evil as a perversion of good. If both leader and readers note such quotations as they read, they will gather plenty of material for discussion when they meet.

Elyé, Beatrice. *Teen Success: Ideas to Move Your Mind*. Great Potential Press, 2007.

A teacher, Elyé bases her book on a series of discussion-starters that she developed for her gifted students. Each chapter embraces a different topic, all of them relevant issues for bright teens. Examples are time management, conversational skills, organizing meetings, health, success, solitude, and mentors. In other words, this book encourages and guides young people to delve into a series of topics vital to their emotional, intellectual, and social development.

Each chapter begins with an essay on the topic and then goes on to suggest questions and activities that the reader may pursue. And each chapter closes with "Words of Wisdom"—quotations from an astounding array of people, including Janis Joplin, Abraham Lincoln, Katherine Mansfield, Eleanor Roosevelt, and Lucille Ball, to take a few from the chapter on self-esteem—and two blank pages for notes. The reader can roam through the book, selecting topics that appeal in any order, but the first chapter on "Personal Notebooks" might be a good place to begin. The remaining chapters will surely generate ideas that will fill several journals.

Aloneness; Identity; Relationships with others; Using ability.

Faulkner, William. *The Sound and the Fury.* Vintage, 1991.

This "tale told by an idiot" is related in four parts, the first told by Benjy, the mentally handicapped son of an old Mississippi family. Subsequent narrators are Benjy's brothers: Quentin, who tells of the day he committed suicide, and Jason, whose meager (and partly ill-gotten) savings are stolen by the brothers' niece, last of the family, when she runs off with a sideshow pitchman. Faulkner himself narrates the fourth part. The story, then, is of the decline and finally the demise of a family which traced its lineage to a Civil War general and a governor.

The book is technically complex, employing not only multiple narrators but shifting time sequences and Faulkner's stream-of-consciousness writing style. An American classic, it challenges and rewards good readers. It is worth reading if only for the pleasure of recognizing fine literature—some sentences are brilliant jewels describing internal experience. Beyond seeing it as a work of art, however, thoughtful high school students will find that it helps to focus questions of value and of what is to be done with one's life.

Drive to understand. *The Sound and the Fury* can be recommended to college-bound students with an interest in literature as an example of Faulkner's writing.

Using ability. Consider each of the major characters: Jason III and Caroline; their children Quentin, Candace, Jason IV, and Benjy; Candace's daughter Quentin; and the cook, Dilsey. What are the elements of familial decay, and what are their origins? What elements work against decay, nudging the family toward maintenance or even advancement of its viability? Which are inevitable, and over which do individuals have some measure of control? In your own life, can you identify negative and positive forces that may determine your future? Do you have any control? How are you using the opportunities you have to make the most of your circumstances?

Fleischman, Paul. *Breakout.* Simon Pulse, 2005.

Seventeen-year-old Del is breaking out of her latest foster home, out of Los Angeles, out of her former life—she is heading to the mountains of Arizona in her newly-purchased old car, eager to be away before her disappearance is detected, when she is caught in a traffic jam. In the several hours that she is stalled with thousands of others waiting for an accident to be cleared, Del fumes, then uses the time to begin adjusting to her new life. She cleans and organizes the car, observes and talks with other drivers, and joins in a spontaneous talent show, demonstrating her gift for improvisation. Interspersed with the story of her breakout, in italics, are scenes from a one-woman performance that she gives eight years later, describing her experiences in a traffic jam. From these scenes, we know that she has successfully made a new life, found a career, and created a family as Elena Franco.

The action in this unusual book is mostly Del's internal monologue as she waits for traffic to clear and then revisits the experience later. *Breakout* is more clearly a work of creative art than most novels, and it demands more from readers—but they will find it rewarding.

Identity; Resilience; Using ability. In starting a new life, does Del create a new person? How are Del and Elena the same person? How are they different?

Sensitivity. Re-read the last two pages, from Sartre's "Hell is other people" to the conclusion that the traffic jam was "an exercise in giving up control." In these words, Elena voices revelations that Del gained in the traffic jam when she was 17. What do they mean to you?

Fleischman, Paul. *Seek.* Simon Pulse, 2003.

In Rob's senior year of high school, his English teacher requires each student to write an autobiography. Rob writes a radio play of his life story told in dialogue, with parts played by his boy-self and his present self, as well as his mother, grandparents, aunts, friends, and anonymous radio announcers. The missing voice is that of his father, a late-night DJ who left before Rob was born. We learn that throughout his childhood, Rob sought his father by listening to the radio, "seeking" up and down the radio dial and hoping to pick up his father's new show, wherever he might be. At age 13, Rob gave up in anger and frustration and stowed the shortwave equipment in the attic. Finally, Rob stops waiting for his father to return, and later, after his father hears Rob's voice on the radio and calls, Rob moves beyond acceptance to understanding and maturity.

The novel-in-dialogue is a challenging format; it will be easier to follow if the reader turns first to the "Performance Notes" and "Cast" list at the end of the book. The characters are finely drawn simply through their words—Grandfather's sly and feisty humor is especially delightful, and the love and wisdom of Rob's mother and grandmother are constant. It is easy to visualize them on stage, reading their lines into a microphone. Contact information for performance rights of the radio play is provided.

Relationships with others. Describe Rob's side of his relationship with his father as it changed over time. What people or events brought about the changes? What role did Rob play? What of this can you generalize to other relationships?

Sensitivity. Consider ways in which the sensitivity of Rob's mother smoothed the way for him as he grew up. Consider this comment of hers to Rob: "Forgiving doesn't mean you approve of what someone did. It means you understand why they did it. Once you understand, it's easier to stop condemning and focus on the present instead." What does this mean to Rob? What does it mean to you, and how might it apply to your life?

Fleischman, Paul. *Whirligig*. Laurel Leaf, 1999.

Obsessed with doing just the right thing to gain popularity in his new school, Brent sets off a chain of events that concludes with the death of an 18-year-old girl. For atonement, the girl's mother asks that Brent bring joy to the world, as Lea would have. She asks him to build four whirligigs, placing one in each corner of the United States. Though Brent is unaware of the results of his work, the reader learns how his whirligigs change the lives of a schoolgirl in Maine, a streetsweeper in Miami, a parent in Washington, and a teenager in San Diego. Brent, too, is changed by his experience. He learns the meaning of *karass*, a group of people linked without knowing it, perhaps never knowing who is in their karass or why.

Fleischman begins his story with a picture that will be all too familiar to young readers, as Brent agonizes over what to wear and how to behave at a party. The rest of the book moves forward and backward in time, shifting from Brent's travels around the country to the stories of people affected by his whirligigs. One connecting thread is the story of Brent's gradual movement toward recovery from the tragedy. The vignettes from the four corners of the country also tie the narrative together,

Identity. Contrast Brent's knowledge of himself before and after the accident. How can one gain self-knowledge without the intervention of tragedy? How would Brent have dealt with the party after his journey?

Relationships with others. The Miami streetsweeper comments, "People are always in a group…. And whenever there's a group there's fighting…. That's how life is." Do you agree? If you know of a group with no fighting, explain how they make that happen. Should we try to stop the fighting, or accept it as the streetsweeper does?

Frankl, Viktor E. *Man's Search for Meaning: An Introduction to Logotherapy.* Translated from the German by Ilse Lasch. Beacon, 2006.

The first part of this book tells of Frankl's experience in Auschwitz and other concentration camps, where he spent three years as a slave laborer. A psychiatrist, he focuses on the psychological reactions that he observed in himself and in his fellow prisoners. From his experiences came logotherapy, sometimes called the Third School of Viennese Psychiatry, after Freud and Adler. (Frankl speaks of the will to meaning, in contrast to Freud's will to pleasure and Adler's will to power.) The final third of the book gives a brief explanation of logotherapy.

This will be a useful book for young adults concerned with developing a philosophy of life, and it may be especially helpful for those who experience existentialist depression. Here are a few ideas which may be particularly intriguing: While existentialist philosopher Jean-Paul Sartre says that we invent ourselves, Frankl asserts that we do not invent the meaning of our existence, we detect it. He speaks of the existential vacuum which often manifests itself in boredom. And he speaks of the need for each person not to ask the meaning of life, but to ask the meaning of his or her own life: "to life [we] can only respond by being responsible." For Frankl, the pinnacle of human existence is self-transcendence.

Drive to understand; Resilience. There is much material here for thought and discussion; the book can be read again years later for more depth. Adolescents will respond to those ideas for which they are ready. Leaders may do well to ask them to pose the questions for discussion.

Fuller, Iola. *The Loon Feather.* Harvest Books, 1967.

Oneta, daughter of Tecumseh, grows up on Mackinac Island, at the confluence of Lakes Michigan and Huron, in the early years of the 19th century, when Mackinac was a fur-trading center at which French and Indian cultures met. Her French stepfather sends her to school in Quebec, and when Oneta returns to Mackinac at age 24, she has learned to see the best in each culture and to understand reasons for conflict between them. Eventually, she chooses to return to her Indian heritage, but she does so by serving as a bridge for her people from the old ways to the new.

This book has been called one of the most popular books ever written about the conflict of alien peoples. In the person of Oneta, it gently compels the reader to look at two conflicting cultures with respect and understanding for each. Fuller masterfully evokes the natural beauty and atmosphere of a specific place, and the story is set in an accurately depicted historical period. Nevertheless, the theme of accepting the differences of others is a universal human challenge which Oneta and others meet with dignity and a sustaining sense of self. The book is recommended for its challenge to readers to hold two conflicting views at once, stretching their minds and sympathies.

Drive to understand. What qualities do you admire in Oneta? In Martin Reynolds? What knowledge of American Indians have you gained from this book? Have any of your attitudes changed as a result of reading *The Loon Feather*? Which ones, and how? What new understanding have you gained of other historical clashes of cultures? What applications to your own life can be found here?

Galbraith, Judy, & James R. Delisle. *The Gifted Kids Survival Guide: A Teen Handbook.* Edited by Pamela Espeland. Illustrated by Harry Pulver, Jr. Free Spirit, 1996.

This is the "revised, expanded, and updated edition" of a title that has been popular since 1983, written to and for teens and providing information about every aspect of giftedness that can be useful to them as they grow up gifted. After taking plenty of time to explain definitions of giftedness, intelligence, and testing, the authors discuss ways in which students can take charge of their own education. The final chapter, "On Being a Teenager," discusses adolescence in general, drugs and sex, and suicide among gifted teens, with suggestions for prevention. The authors are veterans in the field of gifted education, and the conversational tone of the book attests to their knowledge and comfort with gifted adolescents.

Arrogance. In discussing how students can ask for appropriate educational programs, sample conversational ploys are presented that can be generalized to help young people understand how they can avoid sounding arrogant.

Identity; Relationships with others. A chapter devoted to relationships includes helpful information on finding friends, handling teasing, developing conversational strategies, and getting along with parents.

Perfectionism; Using ability. A segment on perfectionism offers suggestions for mastering this potentially destructive characteristic.

Golding, William. *The Lord of the Flies*. Penguin, 1999.

A group of British boys is stranded on a coral island during an atomic war. Two leaders emerge immediately: the fair-minded Ralph, whose efforts focus on keeping a fire going to attract rescuers, and the militant Jack, who becomes a hunter and scorns efforts toward rescue. There is also the thoughtful Piggy, whose insight guides Ralph. As the days wear on, memories of civilization fade, and the boys adopt primitive ways related to the hunt, painting their faces for camouflage and dancing to stir up blood lust. Horrible accidents occur as these practices continue unrestrained, and the boys gradually divide themselves into followers of Ralph or of Jack, with the majority following Jack. The boys—and the reader—long for adult supervision, but of course, the world's adults are busy destroying each other. Rescue comes at last, but not before the author's point about the dark side of human nature has been made.

Nevertheless, this is not a depressing book. However overwhelmed they are by numbers, Ralph and Piggy never give up their faith in the group process or their search for what is right. Therefore, the human spirit is not destroyed by the reversion to savagery of the other boys—one independent spirit can make all the difference.

Arrogance. What role does arrogance—the assumption of one individual that he or she is superior to others—play in this story?

Identity; Introversion. In what ways might Piggy be considered a leader? How does his leadership style differ from Ralph's? Introverts are sometimes "leaders by example"—do you think Piggy tends toward introversion? How is his presence valuable? What can you learn from this about yourself or about others you know?

Moral concerns. How does Ralph keep going in the final hunt? Why does he not align himself with Jack to save himself? What less dramatic examples do you see of the same behavior around you, or in the news? Have you ever kept going when you were alone but right? What enabled you to do so?

Relationships with others. Describe and analyze Piggy's attitude toward being teased. How is it useful to him? How would you use his example to encourage an elementary school child to cope with teasing? (This question can be used to help high school students find a way to understand and accept painful teasing remembered from their own childhood.)

Greene, Bette. *The Drowning of Stephan Jones.* Laurel Leaf, 1997.

Living in a small Arkansas town, Carla Wayland has been raised to be an independent thinker and to oppose injustice. But now, what she wants most is to enjoy being the girlfriend of good-looking, popular Andy Harris. For a long time, she tries to overlook the dark side of Andy, including his blind hatred of Frank and Stephan, a peaceful gay couple who live in the next town. Andy is the leader when he and two friends attack Stephan one day, and he follows the attack with a series of harassing late-night telephone calls to Stephan and Frank, Carla all the while playing the adoring girlfriend—sometimes protesting, but all too gently. A Christian, and naively certain that a man of God will have compassion, Stephan persuades Frank that they should seek help from the minister of Andy's church. The meeting goes well at first, but when the Rev. Roland Wheelwright realizes that the two men are gay, his demeanor alters completely, and he angrily shouts that there is no compassion for them.

By spring, Frank and Stephan have their shop well-lighted and their phone tapped, so the attacks and telephone calls cease. Carla wants to believe that Andy has changed, but late on prom night, when Andy and Carla and four friends are driving home late and drunk, they meet Frank and Stephan walking home after their car has broken down. An appalling attack on Stephan follows, with Carla as a witness. The book ends with Carla's return to her primary values as she testifies at the trial.

While Greene (the author of *Summer of My German Soldier*, found in the Middle School section of this bibliography) has written on controversial topics in the past, her topic for this book carries more emotional charge for today's readers. She gives religious fundamentalists a spokesperson for their point of view through both Rev. Wheelwright and Andy, who has learned much from his minister, as well as from his father. In contrast, Carla's voice is timid, limited for the most part to silent wondering and to quiet questioning of Andy's motives and actions. Frank and Stephan do nothing to provoke attack; it is clear that they are hated for what they are. At this stage in our national awareness of minority rights, this is an important book for thoughtful young people to read.

Aloneness. In addition to the newcomers Frank and Stephan, Carla's mother Judith has often felt alone in Rachetville. How has she found the courage to defend her beliefs? How do you feel about her decision to move away?

Differentness. On page 2, we learn that Carla feels different—why does she? How does her feeling of differentness influence her actions? How is the experience of students who are different because they are gifted similar to the experience of students who are different because they are gay?

Drive to understand. What do you learn from this book? Do you assume that Greene has painted an accurate picture of the town? Of the situation? Why or why not? In what way might the situation have changed since Greene wrote the book, which was first published in 1991?

Moral concerns. Choose any character other than the victims and consider how that person could have prevented the drowning of Stephan Jones. What support would that person have needed to help him or her do so? Where can such support be found? If the people of Rachetville decide that they do not want something like this to happen again, what steps should they take? What is your own community doing to prevent such hate crimes? What are you doing?

Relationships with others. Trace Carla's relationships with others from the beginning of the book to the end. What has changed? What has changed within Carla? How will these events affect her future relationships with others?

Haddon, Mark. *The Curious Incident of the Dog in the Night-Time.* Vintage, 2004.

Fifteen-year-old Christopher Boone is enormously gifted mathematically but unable to read social cues because he has Asperger's Disorder. When the neighbor's dog is killed and Christopher is first accused and then released, he decides to find out who killed the dog, using techniques learned from his reading of Sherlock Holmes. The trail leads him to the discovery that his mother has not died, as his father told him, but is living in London. By the time Christopher takes the train to London to find her, we already feel sympathetic toward him; still, we are awed by the self-understanding, persistence, and courage he summons to make the trip successfully.

Christopher tells his own story, alternating narrative chapters with displays of his thinking, especially his mathematical obsessions and inquiries. Each chapter is given a prime number; Christopher will not eat yellow or brown food (he tells us why); he cannot read facial expressions or understand metaphor, though he knows and uses simile. There is gentle humor in the book, as his very logical observations point out the absurdities of many common expressions in English. Christopher needs to be alone, does not want to be touched, and takes everything very, very literally. Like everyone else, he wants to do his best. We can only admire him.

Drive to understand. Describe what you knew of autism (and other disorders such as Asperger's) and savantism before you read this book, and how your views have changed. What did you learn from Christopher that surprised you?

Sensitivity. Christopher gives us an extreme example of "twice-exceptional"—people who are gifted and also have a learning difference. How has this story changed your understanding of twice-exceptional people you may know?

Hamill, Pete. *Snow in August.* Grand Central, 1999.

Struggling through a Brooklyn snowstorm in the winter of 1946 on his way to serve as an altar boy at the parish church, Michael Devlin passes a synagogue and responds to a rabbi's request for help—and so begins a remarkable relationship between the 11-year-old Catholic whose father died at the Battle of the Bulge and the immigrant rabbi whose wife died in Europe during World War II. Michael helps the rabbi improve his English and explains baseball to him, and Rabbi Hirsch teaches Michael Yiddish and talks of the Kabbalah and Jewish life in pre-war Prague. But anti-Semitism is a part of neighborhood life, and Michael is an unwilling witness when a

Jewish shopkeeper is brutalized by a gang of Irish thugs. From then on, the threat of danger shadows Michael, finally erupting in a vicious attack on him, leading his mother to find a new apartment and make plans to move away from the neighborhood. When Rabbi Hirsch is even more seriously injured in another attack, Michael's response is to turn to the rabbi's stories of the Golem, creating an ending that can be read as a dream sequence, a miracle, magic, or a metaphor.

Michael's unusual intelligence, curiosity, sensitivity, and imagination is revealed as he listens to the rabbi's stories of Prague, and it is clear that he is not a good fit in his rough neighborhood. For this reason, gifted teens may find him a sympathetic character. *Snow in August* was selected as a Community Reads title; the 1999 paperback edition includes a guide for reading groups. The questions below have been developed without reference to that edition.

Developing imagination. What role do imagination, magic, or miracles play in this story? In a way, there are two suggested endings in this book. Discuss them. Which seems real and/or valid to you? Which do you find more satisfying? Which keeps you thinking more? How would you have ended the book?

Drive to understand. As a question separate from the story, consider what you learned from this novel: about post-war Brooklyn, Jewish life in Europe prior to World War II, Catholicism, Judaism, anti-Semitism, music, baseball, Jackie Robinson. What would you add to this list? Discuss other fiction books from which you have gained new information.

For another version of the Golem legend and more background information, see the annotation of David Wisniewski's *Golem* in the Upper Elementary (Grades 3-5) section of this chapter. Many of the questions suggested there could also apply to Hamill's book.

Identity. At one point, Michael considers going to college, something that none of his friends would do. How likely is it that he will be able to realize this dream? What do you see in the story that might point to his success?

Moral concerns. Michael learns from his mother and his friends that being an informer is seriously wrong. Rabbi Hirsch says that keeping quiet about a crime is as bad as committing the crime. How does Michael's choice work out? How could he have handled it better? What is the prevalent attitude in your school or neighborhood, and how do you deal with it? Consider whether the ending that Hamill develops is necessary—or is it unnecessarily violent? What role does, or should, the religion of the characters play in the way the story ends?

Hesse, Hermann. *Demian: The Story of Emil Sinclair's Youth.* Dover, 2000.

As the subtitle suggests, *Demian* is really not so much about Max Demian as it is about Emil Sinclair. Beginning with an incident that occurred when he was 10 years of age, Sinclair recounts the "steps that I took to reach myself," ending with his first year of university and the beginning of World War I. In the intervening years, there are long periods when he has no contact with Demian at all, but each renewal of the friendship is highly significant for Sinclair's development. One other person, the musician and religious seeker Pistorius, is also important, both for what he teaches and for the fact that Sinclair must grow beyond him.

This psychologically-oriented account of the growing up of a highly sensitive, introspective boy has appealed to thoughtful young people since its first appearance. Sinclair is tormented by issues of right and wrong, good and evil; he tries desperately to understand how to live his life. "I wanted only to try to live in accord with the promptings which came from my true self. Why was that so very difficult?" In a time when it is difficult even to learn to *hear* the promptings from one's true self over the raucous demands of advertising and peer pressure, this book can be both a stimulus and a solace for those who march to their own drumbeat.

Aloneness. Why does Sinclair separate from his parents, even though it was a loving home? In what way does he return? How does this apply to you?

Identity. Such a personal book calls forth responses on a very personal level. Several themes may be drawn out in discussion: What is your interpretation of the "mark of Cain"? What is your experience of a *daemon* or fate? What objections might others raise to these concepts? How would you discuss them with those who might consider them elitist? Why was Pistorius not suitable as a long-term mentor? How does Sinclair's story help you understand yourself?

Intensity; Introversion; Sensitivity. Students who give evidence of these characteristics may enjoy this book because they see themselves in Sinclair.

Moral concerns. What is your interpretation of Demian's assertion that "Others sense their own laws within them; things are forbidden to them that every honorable man will do any day in the year and other things are allowed to them that are generally despised"?

Using ability. Sinclair says, "Each man had only one genuine vocation—to find the way to himself." Do you agree? How does this pertain to career choice?

Hesse, Hermann. *Steppenwolf.* Picador, 2002.

Harry Heller, a lonely intellectual of 47, calls himself the Steppenwolf—wolf of the steppes—in acknowledgment of the uncivilized, animal part of his nature. Loneliness and existential suffering have become the dominant forces in his life, bringing him to the point of suicide. Then he meets Hermine, a beautiful young woman who takes him in hand, teaches him to dance, and introduces him to the life of the dance halls in the Germany of the 1920s. The story culminates in a masked ball, reminiscent of a Faustian revelry, which becomes mystical and symbolic. Harry emerges with a resolve to re-enter the game of life—this time to learn to laugh.

Even at 47, Harry still struggles to balance his intellectual interests—writing, classical music, and political theory—with more common concerns such as dancing, jazz, people, and laughter. The two parts of the story represent extremes: the mood is sober and depressed until Harry meets Hermine, then happy and wild to the point of unreality. Suicide, loneliness, and Harry's inability to fit in are themes throughout the book, yet the overall impact is not depressing because Harry learns that neither intellectualism nor socializing is sufficient in itself. There must be a balance, and he will continue to try to find it.

Steppenwolf is not easy reading and should be recommended for older, mature, high-potential students who are likely to be dealing with similar issues. Ask students to identify themes that they would like to discuss as they read the book.

Drive to understand. Themes for mind-expanding discussion include the concept that some people are "the suicides," or "those who see death and not life as the releaser"; Harry's dream of his interview with Goethe; his view of the bourgeoisie and of the immortals; Pablo's opinions on music versus Harry's; and Hermine's last talk with Harry, summarizing the views of both of them.

Identity. Consider with students the implication that Harry takes himself too seriously—that he needs to laugh at himself. If they have seen the film "Amadeus," compare and contrast Harry and his idol, Mozart, concerning laughter and taking oneself and one's work too seriously.

Introversion. Discuss Steppenwolf's search for balance between his natural introversion and his need to be with people. If this is an issue for you, how are you dealing with it at the present time? How might it affect your college and career choices?

Relationships with others. How can others be helpful to Steppenwolf? How might they be damaging? How should he act to make the most of relationships with other people?

Howe, James. *The Watcher.* Simon Pulse, 2001.

The summer that Margaret is 13, her parents rent a cottage at the beach; it is the first time that they have taken a month-long vacation. Margaret does not play on the beach but instead sits at the top of the steps leading down to the sand, watching. Chris, the lifeguard, is aware that she is watching, as is Evan, the older child in the family that Margaret likes to watch most. She believes Evan's family to be the perfect family, quite unlike her own. Spinning a romantic fairy tale, Margaret imagines that she is part of this perfect family, but she cannot stay with them because every night, she must return to the beast and the enchanted doll. In shifting scenes, Howe provides glimpses of Chris's and Evan's worlds, until finally they intersect with

Margaret's real and imagined worlds in a powerful, fast-paced, and satisfying conclusion.

We see Margaret only through the eyes of others and through her imaginative story-weaving, until the very end. By then, we have developed an understanding of Evan and Chris. The shifting narrations, including Margaret's fantasy world, require holding several stories in mind at once. In addition, Howe makes good use of metaphor so that, although the reading level is not difficult, fully understanding the story will stretch some readers.

Aloneness. Each of the three main characters—Margaret, Evan, Chris—has reason to feel alone; each needs to find someone to talk to. They respond to this need in different ways. What are these ways? Are these the best ways available to them?

Arrogance. Evan assumes that Margaret stays by herself because she thinks she's better than anyone else, but his mother has a different insight. Why is it easy to make the assumption Evan does? In what situations is it best to look further and be more understanding?

Differentness. Evan struggles with feeling different—"not cool." What is it about him that makes him feel this way? What ways do you know to deal with this feeling?

Relationships with others. Evan's mother says that we think we are entitled to perfection, and we think there is something wrong with us if we settle for less. How does this assumption affect our choice of friends? Our ability to be a friend?

Using ability. Jenny tells Chris more than once that he has more ability than he is using. What has kept Chris from realizing his potential? Will that change as a result of his part in helping Margaret? What more will he need?

Hunt, Irene. *The Lottery Rose.* Berkley, 2002.

When seven-year-old Georgie wins a rosebush in a grocery store lottery, it brings to life the beautiful gardens in books, which represent to Georgie a safe haven from his alcoholic mother and her boyfriend's beatings. When the neighbors finally call the police to stop a beating and Georgie is sent to a residential school, he takes his precious lottery rose with him. Georgie knows that Mrs. Harper's lovely garden across the street from the school is the perfect home for his rosebush, but when he plants it there without permission, Mrs. Harper is so angry that he fears her, even though he learns to love her father, Mr. Collier, and her mentally handicapped son Robin. Georgie's old school file labels him "retarded," "destructive," and "incorrigible," but in the accepting environment of the new school, with Mr. Collier teaching him to read and Robin looking up to him as a friend, Georgie starts to relax, and he begins to give as well as receive love and trust. Eventually, Georgie learns to trust Mrs. Harper, and then a tragedy brings them even closer together.

With a background in psychology, Hunt writes with knowledge and sensitivity about the strong and conflicting feelings of a victim of child abuse. Robin is depicted with love and respect, and Mrs. Harper's anger and grief are shown in ways that young readers can understand. No one in the book enjoys a perfect life, but the story shows how interdependence can lift people above the limitations of circumstance.

Relationships with others. What does Georgie need from other people? What does he give to them? Ask the same questions for Robin and Mrs. Harper. Why is it hard to ask others for that which we need? Who in the story gives without being asked? Do you know someone who does this? Do you know what it is that you need from other people? That you give to others?

Using ability. Why does Georgie think that he will never be able to read? Why can he learn so much more easily at his new school than at the old one? What factors, other than intelligence, affect how well children do in school? (For broader understanding, encourage readers to name more influences on success in school than those in this story.) Do you know anyone who is not doing as well in school as she could? What does she need to be able to do her best?

Jinks, Catherine. *Evil Genius*. Harcourt, 2007.

Cadel's genius is in understanding and manipulating systems, especially computer systems. By the age of seven, he has caused so much trouble that his adoptive parents take him to Thaddeus Roth, a psychologist who approves of Cadel's experimentation and allows him to use Roth's own office computer, merely cautioning him: "Next time, don't get caught." After making a mistake caused by his failure to consider possible human responses—for which he has developed no intuitive sense—Cadel begins to create a system that will predict human behavior. When Cadel graduates from high school at 14, Roth suggests that he work toward a degree in World Domination at the Axis Institute, founded by Cadel's real father, now in prison. The Institute is a dangerous place, and Cadel is taught to trust no one. His growing isolation is finally relieved by Kay-Lee, an online correspondent who shares Cadel's brilliance. Gradually, Cadel questions the morality of what he is being taught, and he finally realizes he cannot believe anything he has been told, even by Thaddeus Roth and his father. Cadel is a gifted loner with an amoral upbringing who has a growing sense for right and wrong and who is trying to learn where he fits in.

On one level, this is an absorbing detective story, with several mysterious deaths and with twists and turns that do not resolve until the very end—truly a page-turner. At another level, it will challenge gifted readers because of the intelligence of the characters and the complexities of the storyline. On a third level are questions about the rights and responsibilities of people with extraordinarily high intelligence.

Identity. Cadel's search for identity begins with who his father is, but it goes much deeper than that. How would he have defined himself if you had asked him who he is at age seven? When he enters the Institute? When he decides that he must leave? When he writes to Sonja at the end of the book? How would you hope he could describe himself five or 10 years later?

Moral concerns. As Cadel plans to remove faculty members, he tells himself more than once that he has "no other choice." Is this true? If so, explain why. If not, identify alternatives, and then explain why Cadel should or should not choose them. Is there validity to Phineas Darkkon's and Thaddeus Roth's views about two kinds of people? What are the uses and limitations of their ideas? When does Cadel question them—and how is he able to question, given his background? What role do other people play in Cadel's moral growth?

Does the title mean *Caleb* is an evil genius? Or is there such a thing as "evil genius"—genius that is evil?

Relationships with others. When Cadel decides that it would be useful to make friends in order to understand social systems, how does he go about it? How does Gazo demonstrate friendship at first? Why does it take Cadel so long to respond? What qualities draw Abraham to Cadel? Why is it so easy for Cadel to see past Sonja's appearance? What do you learn from this book about friendship among very bright people?

Using ability. At the end, it appears that Caleb is not going to be able to use his ability for some time. What are the factors (in him, and in others around him) that brought this about? How does this happen in real life in people you know or know of?

Kerr, Barbara. *Smart Girls: A New Psychology of Girls, Women, and Giftedness.* Great Potential Press, 1997.

This is nonfiction, a report of a research study done by Kerr as the result of a high school reunion. The gifted women in her class asked her to find out why they were pursuing typical careers or homemaking instead of being the world leaders that they had been told they would be.

In a readable style, Kerr discusses the developmental history of most gifted girls, the barriers to intellectual achievement, the family-career conflict, and ways in which gifted girls can be helped to aim higher. She includes several short biographical sketches of eminent women that illustrate her findings.

Gifted teenage girls should read this book as part of their task of recognizing how their intelligence affects their choices over the next few critical years. It may make them uneasy about choices that they have already made that could limit their futures, and it will be quite natural for them to set the book aside unless they talk with women who are old enough to give living examples of what Kerr is describing.

Identity. Where in the book do you see yourself? Your friends? Your mother or other relatives who are older than you? What changes would you like to see in the pattern? What obstacles do you see?

What suggestions would you have for young women who want to overcome the obstacles?

Using ability. What are the patterns of decision making by gifted women that you are aware of in yourself? What critical decisions will you be making in the next few years that may determine whether you can make maximum use of your abilities? What planning can you do to keep your options open as long as possible?

Klass, David. *California Blue.* Scholastic, 1996.

John Rodgers is a junior growing up in a mill town in northern California. His father's high school football record has not been broken, and John's older brothers were football stars. The youngest in his family, John is a serious runner but not a star. He is also a serious student with a particular interest in butterflies, and during one run through old-growth forest, he finds an unusual chrysalis which he takes home. When it hatches into a brilliant blue butterfly that he cannot identify, he takes it to his biology teacher, who alerts her professor at Berkeley. John's discovery is an unknown species whose habitat in the company forest threatens his father's job and the life of the little mill town. The uneasy relationship between father and son is strained to the breaking point, just as his father is undergoing treatment for leukemia.

While he has always felt very different from the people of his town, these events precipitate a crisis, forcing John to choose between what he knows and a future that he cannot even imagine. For the first time, he begins to understand who he is, separate from his family and his town. His biology teacher, the Berkeley professor, and an environmental activist provide glimpses of very different ways of looking at the world. Father and son are reconciled by the end of the book, and John's future is wide open.

John could be a role model for young people whose interests and intensity set them apart from those around them. Although it is not comfortable for him to feel so different, he chooses being himself over fitting in with the crowd, and the reader senses how clean and right this feels to him.

Differentness. John is very different from many people in this story, but he is quite similar to a few. What decisions can he make that will allow him to benefit from the friendship of those few?

Intensity. How do you think John has discovered and maintained his interest in butterflies in the absence of support from family and friends? Do you know of other examples, in books or in real life, of people with this kind of intensity? How does it affect their lives? What are some advantages of being so interested in a particular thing?

Moral concerns. How do you feel about John's determination not to break the law and about what follows? What would your decision be? At what point in the story would you have made it?

Relationships with others; Resilience. John's issues with his family, with peers, and with teachers make his life very complex during the time of this story. How can he sort it all out over the next few years?

Lagerkvist, Par. *Barabbas.* Translated by Alan Blair. Vintage Books, 1989.

Swedish intellectual Par Lagerkvist has written a fictional account of the life of Barabbas after he was selected to be freed and Jesus crucified in his stead. Stunned and inarticulate, Barabbas listens to Peter describe the crucifixion from his point of view, then goes to the tomb on Easter morning to see the stone rolled away. He finally leaves Jerusalem to rejoin his band of thieves but finds that he no longer belongs. Years of slavery follow, and when he is taken to Rome, he becomes aware of the Christians there. Still inarticulate, he is drawn toward them, finally joining them in his own way, without their knowledge or consent; he remains alone to the end.

This fine book demands the best of the reader and offers a journey inward. It can lead to discussion on many levels. One useful approach is the question of Barabbas's aloneness, so fundamental as to put the loneliness that most of us experience in a different perspective. Also important is the potential the book has to help focus the religious questions that many inquisitive people begin to raise in the senior high years.

Drive to understand. It might be helpful to talk of Barabbas not as a person, but as an archetype: the Barabbas story. What is universal here? How does he represent—potentially—the experience of all of us? What does his story tell us about being human? Is the Barabbas story a necessary part of the Jesus story? How? What do we learn of our own potential in pondering the Barabbas story?

Introversion; Moral concerns. These two categories, too, might be useful points of departure for discussion, depending on the students and the context.

Laney, Marti Olson. *The Introvert Advantage: How to Thrive in an Extrovert World.* Workman, 2002.

Gifted teens who enjoy time alone, prefer to think things through before contributing to a class discussion, or enjoy a few close relationships rather than a crowd of friends—in other words, who tend toward introversion—will find this book to be a real gift, helping them toward self-understanding at a new level. An introvert herself, Laney conveys solid information—stating that introverts and extroverts are on opposite ends of an energy continuum—and she gives practical advice, showing how this affects the behaviors of each and offering ways to cope with the differences. Citing Linda Silverman's statement that 60% of the intellectually gifted are introverted, Laney explains that they may nevertheless feel "not very smart" because they are simply not aware that they need to give themselves time to "sift, sort, and contemplate." And she demonstrates with diagrams how the brains of introverts and extroverts work differently, resulting in introverts' need for more time.

In an extroverted world, introverts may feel slow and inadequate, so Laney points out some advantages of introversion. These include the ability to focus well for a long time, to be persistent, to take many factors into account, to create in imaginative ways, and to be thoughtful and reflective. Laney also acknowledges disadvantages, offering suggestions for coping with, for example, fatigue and discomfort when it is necessary to "act like an extrovert" for a long period of time. Most of all, she urges introverts to embrace and nurture their introverted temperament.

Aloneness; Differentness; Drive to understand; Introversion; Relationships with others; Using ability. Meant for adults, this book can also be useful in group or individual counseling with students who tend toward introversion. Any or all of the categories listed could be discussed. It might also be given to an introverted teen to read alone, but with an adult available for discussion when needed or requested. Introverted adults can recognize themselves in the book and lead discussion based on those insights. *The Introvert Advantage* can profitably be read again a year or so after the first reading; different "Aha!" moments will stand out on the second reading.

Lewis, Barbara. *The Teen Guide to Global Action: How to Connect with Others (Near and Far) to Create Social Change.* Free Spirit, 2008.

With concrete information and encouraging success stories, this very practical guide addresses the needs of teens who are so concerned about world problems that they want to know what they can do to alleviate them. After an introductory chapter offering general suggestions for finding a cause, researching it, and planning before taking action, there is information on connecting with others by joining a group or forming one. Lewis then divides the heart of the book into seven areas in which action is needed: human rights, hunger and homelessness, health and safety, education, environment and conservation, youth representation (political action), and peace and friendship. For each of these concerns, she gives background information on the issues and then offers sections called "Keep it Local" and "Take it Global."

The Teen Guide to Global Action makes it clear that teens around the world are already finding solutions, and it smoothes the path for those who would join them.

Drive to understand. Reading the stories from around the world is a quick—probably surprising and certainly inspiring—education in global need and responses from young people. For those who want to pursue an idea or a cause, there are panels throughout the book listing relevant websites, so it will be easy to learn more.

Moral concerns; Using ability. The author includes many stories of teenagers in several countries who saw a problem and led the way for others to join them in creating a solution. Some of the attempts failed initially, but often failure was followed by progress within a few years.

Lipsyte, Robert. *The Contender.* HarperTeen, 1987.

Alfred Brooks has dropped out of school. He lives with a widowed aunt and her daughters and works in a small grocery store in
Harlem. His best friend, James, is using drugs and spending time
with older boys who jeer Alfred about his dead-end job. Only Henry,
crippled from polio, has a kind word. Henry, who works in a gym,
suggests that Alfred come to the gym to learn to box. After James and
his new friends are caught attempting to break in to the grocery store,
Alfred does go to the gym, where Mr. Donatelli begins by telling
Alfred what is ahead of him: no guarantees of championship, but a
good deal of hard work before he can even be a contender. "Every-
body wants to be a champion. That's not enough. You have to start
by wanting to be a contender." Despite discouragement and threats
from James's new friends, Alfred does become a contender, and he
uses his new self-confidence and self-discipline to reach out to others.

Drive to understand. This award-winning, long-time favorite is
tightly written, offering in brief vignettes a picture of the difficulties
of growing up in a ghetto. How and why have conditions changed
since the book was written?

Resilience; Using ability. What are the positive influences in
Alfred's life? The negative? Why does he choose in favor of the positive? What events discourage him, and what keeps him going? How is
boxing helpful to him? What qualities does he bring to it that make it
successful? In what areas would you like to be a champion? Are you a
contender yet? If not, what steps can you take to become one? What
might discourage you, and how will you keep yourself going in spite
of discouragement? Who are your models and possible mentors? And
whom can you help?

Lutz, Ericka. *The Complete Idiot's Guide to Friendship for Teens.*
Pearson, 2001.

In the breezy *Idiot's-Guide* style, Lutz conveys solid and sensible
information for teens about how to make and keep friends. She goes
beyond the basics to a number of subtopics, including best friends,
groups of friends, getting too close and then moving apart, helping a
friend in trouble, and coping with the end of a friendship. In

addition, she discusses boys and girls as friends and in a romantic relationship, writing frankly but always with a light touch.

For some gifted children, friendship does not come naturally. Although they may have learned the rules in elementary school, they find that the game changes in various ways in middle school and high school. Lutz's book will be useful for older middle schoolers and with high school students.

Relationships with others. Some, including most introverts, may prefer to read and reflect on this book on their own and not discuss it at all. For others, discussion will be most effective if it focuses on a section that covers an immediate concern rather than attempting to cover the whole book at once. Many single paragraphs in the book could be a starting point for valuable discussion at the right moment with the right person. Because it considers events that normally occur over time—spanning several years—this is a good book for a teen to have in his or her room as a reference.

Merkel, Jim. *Radical Simplicity: Small Footprints on a Finite Earth.* New Society, 2003.

In March of 1989, like millions of others around the world, military engineer and arms trader Jim Merkel watched television news reports of the Exxon Valdez oil leak and wondered who was responsible. Reflecting on how much his way of life depended on oil, he quickly concluded that he was among the responsible ones. After a weekend spent calculating how he could live simply and nonviolently using only his fair share of world resources, he quit his job and began a new life, deliberately setting his income "…below taxable level. Then not a single cent of mine would rain bombs and bullets on peasants who lived near coveted resources." This book is his guide for those who want to reduce unsustainable consumption—to live with "radical simplicity."

In compelling imagery, Merkel asks the reader to imagine that he or she is first in line at a potluck buffet that includes not only food, but also the materials for shelter, clothing, health care and education—for all the world's people (and other living creatures), who are waiting in line for the reader to fill his or her plate. He asks, "How do you know how much to take?" He goes on to tell his own story and to help readers determine how much of this path they can follow, including calculations and charts that support his conclusions. In 1995, Merkel founded the Global Living Project, "with a mission to discover how to live sustainably in North America." The GLP website, www.radicalsimplicity.org, provides more current information.

Drive to understand. Merkel says, "When the world seemed infinite, wasting time was of greater concern than wasting resources." In what ways do you save time but waste resources? How could you change your priorities from time efficiency to what Merkel calls "Earth efficiency"? What would you lose? What would you gain?

Merkel also outlines a sustainable and rewarding division of "life energy" (pp. 48-49). How is your life energy currently divided? What might you consider changing for better balance?

Recognizing that not everyone will choose to follow radical simplicity to the degree that Merkel does, what can you do to move in the direction that he describes? Do you want to? Look at the website to learn more. How might you become involved?

Millard, Candice. *The River of Doubt: Theodore Roosevelt's Darkest Journey.* Broadway Books, 2005.

After losing his bid for re-election for president in 1912, Theodore Roosevelt took on the last major challenge of his adventure-filled life. With a team of naturalists and a crew of *camaradas* (local young men hired to manage the hardest work of the trip), he explored an unmapped tributary of the Amazon River. Millard's book is a well-researched and detailed narrative of that perilous journey through the canyons, rapids, and waterfalls of the Rio da Duvida—the River of Doubt—from the highlands of western Brazil to its confluence with the Aripuana, from which point the combined streams flow northeast to the Amazon.

Never knowing what lay around the next bend, the group faced near-starvation, debilitating illness, a murderer within their own ranks, and the awareness that they were always watched by warriors of the Cinta Larga, a tribe of Indians who had never seen a white man. The Cinta Larga were cannibals who hunted with poisoned arrows, skilled at remaining invisible in the jungle, but their willingness to watch and wait rather than attack the strangers who traversed their territory in dugout canoes is probably the decisive factor in the survival of the expedition.

Drive to understand. For high school students, *The River of Doubt* may serve as an excellent introduction to a man, a period of history, and a place they know little about. Possible topics for discussion include the Monroe Doctrine and its relevance to the trip.

Relationships with others. How did Roosevelt's relationship with Col. Rondon (the guide assigned to the expedition by the Brazilian government) affect the outcome of the trip? What qualities in other men on the trip (for example, George Cherrie, Joao Lyra, and Kermit Roosevelt) had an impact on the outcome? Discuss Rondon's support of the Brazilian Indians and his insistence that his men be willing to die but never kill. The Cinta Largas' manner of self-government and rules for warfare are also rich subjects for thought and discussion.

Resilience. What other examples do you know of people enduring as much danger, hardship, and uncertainty as the Roosevelt expedition did? What personal resources helped them to survive?

Molière, Jean Baptiste Poquelin. *The Misanthrope.* Kessinger, 2004. (Written in 1666).

Set in Molière's contemporary and fashionable 17th-century Paris, this drama is one of the masterpieces of the great French comedian. Alceste values sincerity in communication with others so highly that he is uncomfortable with the flattery that is considered good manners in courtly drawing rooms. He becomes quite fanatical about it, ignoring and hurting well-meaning friends and finally resolving to withdraw from society altogether because, in his eyes, it is so dishonest.

Molière's genius is to draw the comedic and the serious very close together; as a result, this comedy offers material for thoughtful discussion. However, high school students may need some background to understand the excesses of the French court at that time. If the play is only read, the meaning will be clear, but the comedy will not come through as poignantly as it does on the stage.

Arrogance. What role does, or should, tolerance for human weakness play in establishing our expectations of others?

Intensity. How far can one sensibly go in standing up for one's values? How much is Alceste losing by being such an absolutist about his?

Perfectionism. What standards do you feel very strongly about? In what ways do you compromise? In what ways does reading this play cause you to reconsider?

Relationships with others. Is Alceste justified in hurting others in the name of standing up for his beliefs? How do we know whether and when to sacrifice honesty for politeness? How might Alceste have avoided the outcome that occurs at the play's end?

Mortenson, Greg & David Oliver Relin. *Three Cups of Tea: One Man's Mission to Promote Peace…One School at a Time.* Penguin, 2006.

In 1993, descending after a failed attempt to climb K2 in the Himalayas of northern Pakistan, Greg Mortenson wandered away from his guide. Alone and exhausted, he stumbled upon Korphe—he was the first foreigner ever to visit this remote high-altitude village. Offered lodging, food, rest, and kindness, he slowly recovered. One day, he asked to see the children's school and was appalled to see 82 children—only four girls among them—kneeling on the frosty earth, studying in the open air without a teacher. Mortenson promised the village chief: "I'm going to build you a school." He returned to California—where his belongings were in storage and his home was his Buick—rented a typewriter in a copy shop, and began to write fund-raising letters for his school.

Most of the story thus far is related in the first chapter. The rest of the book tells of Mortenson's return trips to Pakistan and then to Afghanistan to build schools. Travel is always hazardous; on a dangerous journey into tribal Waziristan, he was kidnapped; the Taliban were active in Afghanistan; the Islamabad hotel where he used to stay was destroyed by terrorists in 2008. Mortenson has become part of the volatile history of that part of the world, and *Three Cups of Tea* is an adventure story throughout.

In addition to the following questions, discussion questions for book groups may be found on the publisher's website at

http://us.penguingroup.com/static/rguides/us/three_cups_of_tea.html.
Readers who are especially interested may want to consider another
book about the same mountainous area: *Ancient Futures* by Helena
Norberg Hodge, who writes about the traditional life of the Ladakh
people (whose language she studies) and what they have gained—
and lost—with the arrival of globalization.

Differentness. What can you cite in Mortenson's background that
prepared him to make such a sudden change in the direction of his
life? What motivates him to continue a difficult struggle, with few
precedents to follow? Do you know, or have you read about, others
who have chosen a very different path? How are they like or different
from Greg Mortenson? Do you think that you are likely to decide to
do something this unusual with your life?

Drive to understand. How did this book inform or change your
ideas about the people of Pakistan and Afghanistan? About Islam and
Muslims? About Buddhism and Buddhists? What more would you
like to know about this part of the world and these people? What
plans do you have to learn more?

Intensity; Relationships with others. The intensity of Mortenson's
commitment to his project sometimes complicates his relationships
with his family and friends. Describe how this happens, as well as
how both Greg and those who know him have to compromise in
order to work or live together. Consider relationships among your
family or friends that are similar, and analyze how they function.
Does any of this apply to you? What can you learn from this line of
thinking?

Oneal, Zibby. *The Language of Goldfish.* Puffin, 1990.

For someone who resists change, adolescence can be a frightening time. Carrie Stokes is frightened, but she doesn't know why. She
is most comfortable on Saturday mornings in her art teacher's home,
but when confronted with symbols of growing up, such as junior
dancing class, she has brief spells of dizziness. Finally, she loses touch
with reality to such an extent that her concerned parents arrange for
her to meet with a psychiatrist. The combination of her talks with
him and her continuing pursuit of her artwork—plus her acceptance

of an unexpected change in her art teacher—bring Carrie to an acceptance of change in herself.

Gifted in math as well as in art, Carrie has the advantage of being in the advanced math class; nevertheless, she feels out of step. The critical times come when she is forced to do something that she is not ready to do by people who expect her to act 13 before she is ready to do so. She must be herself and have some control over her own rate of growth.

This book offers several insights into the pressures placed on young people to grow up at the rate that society dictates, the necessity of being oneself despite external pressures, and the experience of psychotherapy—something about which young people probably need more information than they presently have. It also brings out the fact that people respond to the same situation in different ways for entirely legitimate reasons.

Aloneness; Introversion. Why does Carrie withdraw from friends at school? How does she spend the time by herself that she gains by withdrawing? Is withdrawing or the wish to be alone good for her? What are your reasons for your answer?

Differentness; Identity. Why did Carrie respond the way she did to the pressures of growing up? Can Carrie's story help you to be more tolerant of responses that you may not understand in people around you? In yourself? What does Carrie learn about herself? What does she do to help herself get better? Which of her strengths help her cope with being different? Which of your strengths help you?

Relationships with others; Resilience. How do other people help Carrie get better? What does Carrie do to allow them to help her? Have you ever been in a situation in which others could have helped if you had allowed it? Why is it difficult to accept help? What are the rewards for people who can do it?

Peck, Richard. *Remembering the Good Times.* Laurel Leaf, 1986.

At 16, Buck Mendenhall looks back over the last four years to tell the story of his friendship with Kate Lucas and Trav Kirby. Coming from different backgrounds, they are brought together by the transformation of their rural area into an affluent suburb. Together they face the stresses of adolescence in a too-rapidly changing world. It is

Trav, the brilliant and wealthy one, who finally cannot cope with the combination of pressure at home and mediocrity and neglect in the new school.

This book is rich in characters, relationships, and issues for discussion, but paramount is the suicide of bright, intense, sensitive Trav. Discussion of suicide is difficult—but worth the effort. Leaders should be prepared with their personal answers to the questions that students will ask, however incomplete those answers may be.

Identity. Trav and Kate both have talent. What are the differences that make Kate stronger? Do you share Kate's sentiments when she says: "I'll never trust anything again. I'll never believe in anything or anybody. You can count on that"?

Resilience; Using ability. Why did Trav kill himself? Whose "fault" was it? How might it have been prevented? What could Trav have done to prevent it? How would you answer the questions he raised about "deteriorating conditions" and the lack of challenge in school?

Pirsig, Robert M. *Lila: An Inquiry into Morals.* Bantam, 1992.

The author of *Zen and the Art of Motorcycle Maintenance* continues to state his Metaphysics of Quality in the form of a novel. The storyline in *Lila* has Phaedrus sailing down the Hudson River, hoping to get to Florida before winter. In a bar in Kingston, he meets Lila, who joins him and becomes a focus for some of his metaphysical musings. In this book, it is Lila who slips toward insanity as Phaedrus watches with concern.

The real stuff of the book is the wide-ranging philosophy, and *Lila* is suitable only for those who will be intrigued by that—the storyline is too slight to hold interest by itself. But those who would like an informal glimpse of philosophy at work can watch Phaedrus's mind roam as he explores such topics as the state of anthropology, Indian versus Victorian morals, European values versus late-20th-century American values, and religion and science.

Drive to understand. Phaedrus's musings provide plenty of discussion starters. To avoid too much leader domination, readers could be asked to jot down page numbers when they find a topic that they would like to pursue with the leader. Or they might be encouraged to follow one theme—the Victorian, or the anthropological, for example—throughout the book. Victorians specialized in manners, 20th-century intellectuals in causes. What might be next? Another recurring topic is the opposing roles of society and the intellect. How does this conflict affect you? How does your response to it compare with Pirsig's? He says that intellectual patterns have won. Do you agree?

Moral concerns. Are Victorian moral codes returning? If we do not return to Victorian values, what might ultimately replace them?

Pollan, Michael. *In Defense of Food: An Eater's Manifesto.* Penguin, 2008.

Pollan's 2006 book, *The Omnivore's Dilemma*, challenged Americans to look squarely at what happens to food before it reaches our tables. Now he brings his argument home. With the first seven words of this new book, he summarizes: "Eat food. Not too much. Mostly plants." He goes on to assert that most of the Western diet is not real food, but "edible foodlike substances." And while *The Omnivore's Dilemma* put the focus on the ethical and ecological consequences of our food choices, this book highlights a more personal dimension: our health.

In Defense of Food is a consciousness-raising effort to help readers recognize that much of what we choose to eat—even those of us who try to pay attention—is factory-processed, not real, food. This simple message may seem unlikely to require an entire book, but fresh insights keep coming, right to the end. Pollan comments that with the recent rise of organic farming, farmers' markets, and a new emphasis on eating local food, it is possible to avoid processed food for the first time in decades. In the last section of the book, he fleshes out the advice in his first paragraph. A sampling: *Food* is what your great-grandmother would recognize as food; from *plants*, leaves are better than seeds; guidelines suggest how to eat *not too much*. With a background in journalism, Pollan has a succinct, breezy style that makes reading his book a pleasure. For teens concerned about eating well, *In Defense of Food* is a recommended resource.

Drive to understand. In Defense of Food offers inspiration and information to help in eating better, as well as a depth of information in several areas. If you are looking mostly for practical advice, you may want to concentrate on the Introduction and Section III, "Getting Over Nutritionism." Those interested in the chemistry of food will also want to read Sections I and II, especially "The Industrialization of Eating: What We Do Know." If you are intrigued by anthropology, read "The Western Diet and the Diseases of Civilization."

For more information on all of the above, locate your areas of special interest in "Sources," beginning on page 206. Some of the items listed may be too technical for your purpose, but others can guide you to avenues of further exploration.

Pullman, Philip. *The Golden Compass.* Knopf, 2001.

In this first book of a fantasy trilogy, Pullman introduces Lyra Belacqua, growing up in Jordan College, Oxford. Her education from the scholars is spotty at best, but she is a scrapper and a born leader, and she learns much from play with town children and gyptians who travel through, as well as from her daemon familiar, Pantalaimon. Her comfortable life dissolves abruptly when her uncle, Lord Asriel, returns from a journey to the North with news of mysterious experiments involving children and their daemons. It is clear to the reader—though not to Lyra—that she is destined to play a pivotal role in world-changing events.

The Golden Compass will challenge young adult readers and intrigue adults. The language is on the high level that we seek for good readers, and mystery is drawn through the novel, not really settled by the end of this volume but continuing on to the sequels, *The Subtle Knife* and *The Amber Spyglass* (the trilogy is called *His Dark Materials*). Lyra is uneducated but curious, intelligent, and highly intuitive; the story invites conjecture about this world and possible others. The scope of the trilogy is huge, and leaders will want to bring their own response to the creating of discussion questions. Following are only a few initial discussion possibilities.

Arrogance. Can Lord Asriel's arrogance be defended? What is the role of arrogance if one is pursuing a great idea? Is it a positive or a negative trait? Why do you think so?

Intensity. Compare the intensity of Lord Asriel with that of Lyra.

Moral concerns. Consider questions for the whole trilogy, including such topics as religion versus science and the value of research (for example, does the end justify the means)? Is it acceptable for Lyra to lie her way through her adventures as she does? Why or why not? Whose motives are evil? By what definition? What is the source of the evil in this book?

Relationships with others. How does Mrs. Coulter's manipulative nature differ from Lyra's? Is one worse or better than the other? Why do you think so?

Reade, Charles. *The Cloister and the Hearth.* Wildside Press, 2007.

Erasmus, the great Dutch humanist, scholar, and theologian, was born probably in 1466, apparently out of wedlock. The 19th-century British writer Charles Reade wove a long and carefully-researched novel around the imagined lives of Erasmus's parents. In Reade's fiction, the young Gerard Eliasson and Margaret a Peter are cruelly separated after an interrupted marriage ceremony, and Gerard, a gifted scribe and illustrator, flees Holland to seek his fortune in Italy, home of the arts. When he is told, falsely, that Margaret has died, he turns to the priesthood in despair. The real love story unfolds later, after Gerard returns to Holland and, finding Margaret and their son there, relives the anguish of separation. The young Erasmus grows up knowing both parents, though Margaret and Gerard continue to live separate lives, caring for each other from a distance and working together in providing for the poor people in their community.

This is a long, leisurely book, to be read not for a deadline, not to finish the book, but for the pleasure gained in the reading—a summer book, with much food for thought. Wonderfully versatile, Reade writes equally convincingly of the raw danger in medieval foot travel and of subtle psychological change, of theological reflection and domestic strife, and of friendship among men and among women. The language that he employs is an early form of modern English, sprinkled with bits of Latin, Greek, French, and German, in sentences graced by rhythm and framed in long cadences—a luxuriant style in refreshing contrast to the short, choppy sentences of mid-20th-century novels. There is humor based on understatement, as well as controlled outrage at the social injustices of the day. Altogether, this is a compelling picture of conditions during the late medieval period in the north and the Renaissance in the south of Europe, bringing the 15th century to life in the reader's imagination. Highly recommended, *The Cloister and the Hearth* is both a challenge and a pleasure.

Drive to understand. Erasmus appears in the book, but only as a child. A follow-up might be to read about Erasmus, read something by Erasmus, and then look for foreshadowing—has Reade attributed to Gerard any stirrings of ideas which Erasmus brought to fruition, perhaps in his correspondence with Martin Luther?

Moral concerns. Can we separate the 15th-century attitudes that Reade describes from the 19th-century attitudes in which he was steeped— attitudes toward women, toward the Church, toward German, French, Italian, and Dutch people?

Resilience. In this long novel, several characters must be resilient to survive. What examples do you see in Margaret? In Gerard? In the people Gerard meets on his travels? Are we, in the 21st century, required to be more or less resilient than those who lived in the 15th century? Why?

Richter, Hans Peter. *Friedrich*. Translated from the German by Edite Kroll. Puffin, 1987.

A series of vignettes tells the story of the friendship between the narrator, a Christian boy, and Friedrich, a Jewish boy, in Germany from 1925 to 1942. Friedrich's family lives in the apartment above the narrator, and the two families are distant friends. As pressure against Jews builds, the landlord arranges an attack on Friedrich's family, and his mother dies as a result. Eventually his father is arrested, and Friedrich finds a hideout elsewhere. Seeking a picture of his parents, he returns to the narrator's family's apartment just as the air raid siren sounds, but the landlord will not allow Friedrich into the air raid shelter. When they return to the house, they find Friedrich sitting on the stoop. He has been shot and killed.

From the early picture of joy and spontaneous fun between Friedrich and his mother as they play in the snow, the book moves relentlessly to the final scene, bringing the enormity of the Holocaust down to one family and one boy. This is an excellent example of the extensive body of literature written to acquaint young people with the events of World War II in Germany, but it is different from many others (and thus more representative of reality) in that Friedrich is not a survivor. The value of this literature lies in the importance of educating a new generation of leaders about these events and, insofar as can be understood, about the structures that allowed them to occur.

Drive to understand; Moral concerns. This story in itself will not provide enough information for a full discussion. Rather, it provides the emotional impact that prepares students to look at the situation from both sides. Discuss the growing reluctance of the narrator's family to help Friedrich's family. Include discussion of similar hostilities elsewhere in the world. Aim for some understanding of circumstances that might cause—or prevent—a recurrence in any country.

Roth, Philip. *The Plot against America*. Houghton Mifflin, 2004.

In this novel of alternative history, Roth imagines that in the presidential election of 1940, the man who won was not Franklin Delano Roosevelt, but Charles Lindbergh, the national hero who had flown solo across the Atlantic only 13 years earlier—but who was also an isolationist and a Nazi sympathizer. (Lindbergh's political leanings are not part of the alternative history; rather, they are known from well-documented but less popularly known historical evidence.) Roth explores what might have happened to the Roth family—his parents, his older brother, and seven-year-old Philip himself—and to his Jewish neighborhood under a President Lindbergh.

As the fictional candidate, Lindbergh promises to keep America out of the war in Europe. After he wins, his leadership strengthens Hitler's chances of winning World War II and encourages efforts to marginalize America's Jewish population. The most devastating result is the effort by the new government to relocate Jews across the United States, thereby weakening long-held ties among families and friends, including the Roths. The result is a chilling and suspenseful narrative as Philip's family unravels in the face of divided loyalties and geographical separation. Life will not be the same again, even after the stunning conclusion relieves the tension.

Roth incorporates historical figures, including journalist Walter Winchell, New York mayor Fiorella La Guardia, and manufacturer Henry Ford, adding to the plausibility of his fiction. A postscript includes a chronology of these and other historical figures who appear in the book, the text of Lindbergh's 1941 speech at a rally of the America First Committee, and a brief quotation regarding Lindbergh's political views from A. Scott Berg's 1998 biography, *Lindbergh*. This book offers a wealth of opportunities for discussion with students who have a sufficient grasp of real history to appreciate this alternative version.

Drive to understand; Moral concerns. How likely is it that history could have turned out as Roth imagines? If these events had occurred, in what ways would America be different now? What role does the American culture of hero worship play? What is the role of racism and suspicion of minority groups in Roth's story? What is their role in contemporary America, as you consider whether this could happen now?

Singer, Isaac Bashevis. *A Day of Pleasure: Stories of a Boy Growing Up in Warsaw.* Farrar, Straus, & Giroux, 1986.

The son of a Hasidic rabbi, Singer writes here of his boyhood in the poor, Yiddish-speaking quarter of Warsaw in the early years of the 20th century. Each chapter relates a specific incident, described with increasing understanding and depth as he grows older and unrest in Europe builds toward World War I.

Critics rightly place this winner of the National Book Award for Children's Literature with young adult literature rather than with children's books. The writing style is plain enough for children, but high school students who are unfamiliar with Eastern Europe will find plenty of challenge in the cultural, political, and social history that Singer reveals as a byproduct of the stories he tells so well.

Drive to understand. Teachers of a variety of subjects will find material for questions related to a wide range of topics touched on in this book. Examples are: Hasidism, Yiddish language and literature, ghettos, poverty, the partition of Poland, czarist Russia, "Nicky and Willy" (Czar Nicholas II of Russia and Kaiser Wilhelm II of Germany), the unrest that led to World War I, Sarajevo, the creeping modernization that lured children like Isaac's older brother (and eventually Isaac, too) away from family traditions— and, of course, this book could be useful background for Singer's novels and other stories.

Creativity; Identity; Sensitivity. The book can also be seen as an expression of Singer's search for his identity as a writer, although his formal education was limited. How did this come about? What factors or people influenced him, and how? What personal characteristics did he describe that might have predicted his future as a writer? What are you doing or thinking now that might lead to a career or a satisfying avocation for you?

Smith, Huston. *The World's Religions.* HarperOne, 2009.

In this classic work, now in a 50th anniversary edition, the son of missionaries to China and professor of philosophy at Massachusetts Institute of Technology has written descriptions of seven great religions: Hinduism, Buddhism, Confucianism, Taoism, Islam, Judaism, and Christianity. His aim is to convey "the meaning these religions carry for the lives of their adherents." Accordingly, he writes little of doctrine and less of history (both of which are to be found in other sources) but reveals for each "why and how they guide and motivate the lives of those who live by them." In the final chapter, he presents a sound argument for accepting the validity of each faith for the people who follow it.

Thoughtful young people seeking meaning for their lives will find here seven different broad approaches to the question of meaning, each of which has stood the test of time. Moreover, while acknowledging the triviality and violence to which religion can descend, Smith describes each religion in its highest, most intellectually challenging and spiritually refined form. Readers will find stimulus for thought in each of these religions, and they will also gain a greater understanding of their followers.

Drive to understand. Senior high students who are beginning their personal religious search find this book useful, especially appreciating Smith's objectivity, which frees them to reach their own conclusions. The objectivity is balanced by a respect for each religion and its people—a human perspective which prevents the material from ever becoming intellectualized or dry.

Spiegelman, Art. *Maus I: A Survivor's Tale: My Father Bleeds History.* Pantheon, 1986.

Spiegelman, Art. *Maus II: A Survivor's Tale, II: And Here My Troubles Began.* Pantheon, 1992.

In his first book, this son of survivors of Auschwitz tells the story of his parents' meeting and the early years of their marriage in Poland, up until the time they arrived at Auschwitz and were separated. The second volume continues the story with their experiences in Auschwitz and after the war, including insights into the long-term psychological effects of the Holocaust on one survivor, his father, Vladek Spiegelman, and on his relationship with Art. (Spiegelman's mother, Anja, committed suicide in 1968, leaving no note.)

Spiegelman bases his story on taped discussions with his father and tells it in cartoon form, drawing Jews as mice, Nazis as cats, Poles as pigs, and Americans as dogs. The scene alternates between Poland in the 1930s and 40s and Rego Park, New York, where Art interviews his aging father and tries to maintain their uneasy relationship. The harrowing wartime experiences of Polish Jews, combined with evidence of the lasting impact on Vladek Spiegelman's personality, told with simple words and cartoon illustrations, create a vivid impression of the terror of those years like no other literature of the period.

Drive to understand. What new information or feelings about the Holocaust did you gain from this story? What part does the cartoon treatment play in your new understanding?

Moral concerns. Does the cartoon format trivialize the subject matter? Why or why not?

Relationships with others. Describe Vladek Spiegelman in a brief character sketch. Why is he so complex a person? How did Vladek's experiences affect his personality, which affected his relationship with his son, which affected his son's personality? Relate this domino concept to other intergenerational relationships you know.

Stewart, Mary. *The Crystal Cave.* Eos, 2003.

For those who love the Arthurian legends, here is Mary Stewart's story of one of the more mysterious characters: Merlin, the magician who took the infant Arthur and reared him, safe from the turmoil at court. This novel begins well before Arthur's birth, telling of the childhood and youth of Merlin, whose mother, the daughter of a king, would not reveal who Merlin's father was. Merlin grew up ignored as a bastard in his grandfather's court until he escaped during a period of strife and found himself in a position to change the course of British history.

Stewart paints a picture of the education of a young man gifted with the Sight—the ability to see what will come. But Merlin does not control his gift. It comes when it will; he can only prepare. We see in Merlin a lonely boy who discovers how to learn from everyone he meets. We also gain an understanding of the struggle between the native Britons and the invading Saxons, and of a time when three religions competed for the loyalty of the people who became the English. The historical background of the story is made clear in Stewart's explanation of place names that we can find on today's maps.

Drive to understand. Readers may want to find other versions of the Arthurian stories or nonfiction accounts of the search for the historical Arthur. How does Stewart's version of the story help us see why a historical Arthur might have become a legend?

Identity. Describe how Merlin feels about his gift and how he talks about it to others. What can a person with intellectual or artistic gifts learn from Merlin's example?

Using ability. What kind of life must Merlin lead in order to make the most of the Sight? How does he learn this? What does he do to make it happen? What environment do you need to make the best use of your abilities?

Storr, Anthony. *Solitude: A Return to the Self.* Free Press, 2005.

A Clinical Lecturer in Psychiatry at Oxford, Anthony Storr suggests that post-Freudian psychological theories place too much emphasis on interpersonal relationships as a sole foundation of human happiness. He argues instead that, especially for the creatively gifted, solitude may be essential to a contented, productive life. Certainly, the desire for solitude is not to be thought of as pathological. "If it is considered desirable to foster the growth of the child's imaginative capacity, we should ensure that our children…are given time and opportunity for solitude…. The capacity to be alone…becomes linked with self-discovery and self-realization." Storr explores the role of solitude in learning, thinking, creativity, and self-knowledge, as well as in grief work and religious insight, and he suggests that individuals can find life's meaning in interests and ideas as well as in intimate relationships. Indeed, for some gifted individuals at some times, ideas may be more important than relationships.

Chapters on solitude and creativity late in life may not appeal to teenage readers, but Storr's extensive use of biographical material to illustrate his point undoubtedly will. The book should prove reassuring to those students—the highly gifted and very introspective in particular—who are more comfortable alone than with others.

Aloneness; Introversion. How do you feel about alone time? How do those around you feel about it? How well do you use it? If you need more, how would you get it?

Relationships with others. In your own life, what is the present balance between interests and relationships? Are you happy with the balance? How would you change it?

Using ability. What implications does this idea of balance between ideas or interests and interpersonal relationships have for your career choice?

Tashjian, Janet. *The Gospel According to Larry.* Holt, 2001.

In a prologue, the author is approached in a grocery store parking lot by a young man who convinces her to read the manuscript that he hands to her. What follows is the manuscript—Josh Swensen's story of how his life changed after he built a website to protest consumerism: www.thegospelaccordingtolarry.com. Josh is bright and thoughtful, a critical thinker with a sense of humor and a serious goal: to make a contribution, to change the world. But the website takes on a life of its own as it gains a national following. When a contributor who objects to Larry's anonymity learns who Josh is and alerts the press, the resultant media frenzy tears Josh's world apart. He must re-evaluate his goals and literally change his life.

Josh makes a contribution by fighting materialism, but he also struggles with issues of loyalty to his stepfather, an advertising executive who strongly opposes everything that Larry stands for; with continuing grief over his mother's death three years ago; with his friendship/romance with Beth; and with his sense of identity and alienation. A very good read, this book also offers plenty of material for discussion.

Aloneness; Introversion. In what ways does Josh recognize, accept, and take care of his tendency toward introversion? What was your response to his comment, "We are meant to be alone in Nature. The word *lonely* never comes up"? How does he use alone time?

Differentness; Identity. What strengths in Josh's character help him to go forward after the media learn that he created the website? In what ways is his differentness a strength? How is he able to be so comfortable with it?

Drive for understanding. Each part of Josh's manuscript begins with a verse from one of the Gospels. Consider how each verse fits the part it introduces.

Intensity. If you are as intense about your interests as Josh is, you may find it useful to think about his comment that he has been "caring more about my message than about the people in my life."

Moral concerns. At the end of the book, Josh has a new definition of contributing. How does it compare to the way he contributed as Larry?

Relationships with others. Re-read the story at the end of the book, in which a sick person is asked, "What was left unsaid?" What insight does it give you regarding your relationship with important others in your life?

Thomas, Joyce Carol. *Marked by Fire.* Hyperion, 2007.

Growing up in the African-American community of an Oklahoma town, Abby Jackson learns wisdom and strength from her mother, from Mother Barker, from the rural rhythm of nature and the sudden devastation of a tornado, and from the cruelty of some of her neighbors. After an assault, she stops using her lovely singing voice. Mother Barker and her mother help her to gradually regain her sense of self, and she reaches adulthood with a deep, sure sense of her own uniqueness and a commitment to use her healing abilities, as well as her voice, for others.

The style of this book moves imperceptibly between prose and poetry. Evocations of the rhythms of speech in the singing and story-telling of the women of the community are especially powerful. There is a haunting quality in the writing style and in the person of Abby herself that makes this a beautiful book to read.

Identity. Abby's parents are Patience and Strong. How does Abby develop and use these qualities? Why are they especially useful for a sensitive person like Abby? Are you aware of using or developing these qualities in your own life? How do you know when to use which?

Relationships with others; Resilience. What examples are there in the book of the acceptance of human failings? Is it a strength or a weakness to be so accepting? Why? How is it related to Abby's acceptance of her special talents?

Using ability. Will Abby become a doctor? Should she? Why or why not?

Thomas, Rob. *Rats Saw God*. Simon Pulse, 2007.

Leaving his father's house in Houston after a disastrous junior year, Steve York continues his use of drugs as he begins his senior year in San Diego. But it is being named a National Merit Finalist, not substance abuse, that lands him in the office of counselor Jeff DeMouy. Steve cannot graduate unless he makes up his failing grade in English III, and DeMouy offers him a way to do this while avoiding summer school: write a 100-page paper. The alternating chapters of *Rats Saw God* track Steve's senior year in San Diego, interspersed with his paper about his sophomore and junior years in Houston. Gradually we learn why Steve moved to his mother's house, and we watch as he works out a new vision of his future in his writing. (We also learn how the title makes sense.)

Thomas writes as Steve would think, beginning with an over-written, swaggering, in-your-face style designed to impress observers with his intelligence and cynicism. It slowly evolves into a still-intelligent but more straightforward style as Steve becomes more comfortable with himself and with his father, whom he calls "the astronaut"—because he is one, and because he is more astronaut than father in Steve's eyes. The author clearly knows teens and sees past hair styles and body piercings to the anxiety and potential that lies underneath. Characterization is excellent, and the narrative commands attention as the plot unfolds chapter by chapter. The end is bittersweet but, like the rest of the book, realistic.

Arrogance. Is Steve arrogant? How would he appear to be so to most students at both of his schools? What purpose does this attitude serve for him? When and why does it diminish?

Relationships with others. What qualities does Steve seek in friends? What part does intelligence play in this search, consciously or otherwise? How would you answer these questions for yourself?

Using ability. What are Steve's strengths? How well does he use them in high school? How might that change in the future? How did you feel about his not choosing Harvard?

Tillich, Paul. *The Dynamics of Faith*. HarperOne, 2001.

Tillich examines the phenomenon of faith—objectively, analytically, and apart from specific doctrinal content, so that although he is one of the 20th century's great Christian theologians, followers of other religions, too, can read this book for greater understanding of their experience of their own faith. Defining faith as "ultimate concern," he considers what it is and what it is not. He also looks at the symbols of faith and at different types of faith. Sections on mythology and humanism as they relate to faith may be of particular interest to gifted high school students.

Drive to understand. This book is suggested as an introduction for questioning young people to religious thinking at its highest and most challenging—and therefore potentially most interesting—level. Whether the readers are among those who take religion seriously, those who question whether religion has any value at all, or those who read simply for exposure to a new field, interested high school students would do well to meet Tillich. This book is a good introduction to his thought.

Tolan, Stephanie. *Welcome to the Ark*. HarperTeen, 2000.

Varying family circumstances bring four child prodigies together at a residential home for disturbed children in upstate New York. Elijah, Taryn, Miranda, and Doug range in age from six to 17 and in talent from clairvoyance to extraordinary abilities in math and languages. Selected for a new program called the Ark, the four children move to a family setting in a group home, joining two psychologists who want to learn whether, through computer networking, they can help other child prodigies around the world. The networking soon surpasses computer capabilities as the four prodigies become so attuned to one another that they dream the same dream and experience each other's memories, eventually concluding that they share a quest, the exact nature of which they must determine. Sharing also a horror of violent acts, they begin testing ways in which, with their psychic abilities, they might end violence peacefully. As their networking reaches out to children in other countries, the director of the residential home fears losing control and closes the Ark, separating the children. Eight years later, Taryn, Miranda, and Doug meet again, apparently by coincidence. The sense that they share a quest returns as the book ends.

Like Susan Cooper's *Dark Is Rising* fantasy sequence for younger readers, Tolan's book explores the response of children with special talents to the forces of evil, and it raises the question of whether these children bear some responsibility to combat these forces. The sense that they may have such a responsibility gives meaning to the lives of the gifted children, overcoming the pain that their gifts have brought to them in the past.

Aloneness; Introversion. Considering Elijah, Taryn, Miranda, and Doug each in turn, what role does "alone time" play in the lives of each of them? When is it healthy, and when is it not—or is it always healthy?

Identity. Again considering each of the main characters in turn, how aware are they of being gifted? How does their gift affect their decisions? How has it been a negative in the past, and how have they dealt with that?

Moral concerns; Using ability. What is the connection between the abilities of the children of the Ark and their quest? In your view, do they have a responsibility to pursue their quest? Why or why not? What would be the consequences of a decision to pursue their quest? What would be the consequences of their deciding *not* to pursue it?

Relationships with others. A major theme of this book is that highly gifted people often appear to others to be misfits, even mentally unbalanced. What is your response to this? What can be done to increase understanding?

Voigt, Cynthia. *The Runner.* Simon Pulse, 2005.

In this prequel to *Homecoming*, Voigt tells the story of Bullet— Samuel Tillerman—at 17, a high school junior in 1967. The war in Vietnam is a distant struggle, not nearly as threatening as the conflict in Bullet's home, where his father's tight control has already sent Bullet's older brother and sister away for good. Only Bullet and his mother are left, she to endure, and Bullet to mark time until he, too, can leave. The discipline of running hardens Bullet—but running also brings him into contact with Tamer, an older black student. Tamer and Bullet's boss force him to look at himself with the same insistence on truth that he turns on the rest of the world. The book is beautifully written and demands much of the reader. Those who have read *Homecoming, Dicey's Song,* and *A Solitary Blue* will gain greater understanding of the children's grandmother, Abigail Tillerman, in this book. Those who have not read any of Voigt's *Homecoming* series will want to start here.

Drive to understand. What is Bullet's major inner conflict? Leaving his mother? Coaching Tamer? Facing his prejudice? Why do you choose the one you do?

Identity. Of the men Bullet knows, which is the best mentor for him, and why? What qualities make him a good mentor?

Moral concerns. Why would Bullet urge Tamer to stay out of Vietnam but not do so himself?

Vonnegut, Kurt. *Slaughterhouse-Five.* Dial Press, 1999.

Twenty-four years after the city of Dresden, "the Florence of the Elbe," was firebombed by the Allied Powers, Vonnegut published this novel based on his experiences as a prisoner of war and survivor of that massacre. As is fitting for an event too awful to look at straight on, the narrative dances around the bombing, foreshadowing the terrible event that we know is coming but then glancing off to focus instead on the story of Billy Pilgrim, the chaplain's assistant who plays Vonnegut's role. Billy is a time-traveler; his consciousness shifts easily from awareness of present to past and future scenes of his own life. His understanding of time as a continuum (whatever has been always is) rather than as made up of discreet moments is enhanced when he is kidnapped and taken to the planet Tralfamadore to be exhibited in a zoo. His story parallels the events leading up to the firebombing, setting it in a context of confusion and chaos.

The form of this novel is a kaleidoscopic mix of events, places, and people, not a chronological narrative at all—emphasizing the impossibility of comprehending Dresden through a logical, linear approach. It can only be approached sideways, out of the corner of one's eye. Today's students may need to be reminded that the book first appeared during another event that challenged comprehension: the Vietnam Conflict.

Differentness. Discuss Billy's differences in seeing what others do not see and how he copes with that.

Drive to understand. Vonnegut's method of telling the story could be considered in light of random versus sequential thinking. What does this approach tell us that a historical chronology would not? For what other subjects would this style be appropriate? What do you consider sequentially, and what holistically or spatially? Why?

Moral concerns. Learn more about the reasons for the bombing of Dresden. What is the other side of the story? What does the historical event of Dresden have in common with other 20th-century massacres? How does it differ? What have we learned?

Wolfe, Tom. *Bonfire of the Vanities.* Picador, 2008.

Sherman McCoy is a Wall Street whiz of the high-flying '80s, a junk bond "Master of the Universe," until he stumbles over the belief that he deserves to have even more. An accident in the Bronx with his mistress in his car brings Sherman devastating publicity—which transforms inexorably into notoriety—and acquaints him with a reality that is as harsh as his upbringing has been privileged.

Wolfe skillfully draws a wide range of characters and requires the reader to remember each throughout the long novel as he pulls the cast closer together toward the final court scene. As the story progresses, Sherman undergoes psychological changes that provide a good beginning for discussion.

Arrogance. How does the tone of the book change after Sherman is stripped of arrogance? What is the effect of this on you as the reader?

Drive to understand. How does Sherman's story relate to the sharp decline in the global economy that occurred in 2008, about 20 years after the period of this book?

Identity. Sherman is a decent person who shrinks from anything that he considers to be ill-bred. What acts are moral or immoral in his view? Where is the line between morality and a good upbringing?

Moral concerns. Why does Sherman have difficulty regarding the tapes? Would you? Why or why not? How could this theme be treated with someone such as yourself as the main character? What temptations could cause you to rise so high and fall so far?

Using ability. In order to have become a "Master of the Universe," Sherman must be of above-average intelligence. Why then does he get into so much trouble? What are the uses and limits of high intelligence as a guide for living?

Wolff, Tobias. *This Boy's Life: A Memoir.* Grove Press, 2000.

Prize-winning fiction author Tobias Wolff turns to nonfiction for this story of his boyhood, which is also the story of the masking and creation of an identity. Born in Alabama in 1945, Wolff moved with his mother to Washington State after his parents separated when he was 10. "Jack," as he calls himself, spends most of his teenage years in Seattle and then in a small mountain town, now with a volatile stepfather. He is a discipline problem, his friends are unsavory, and an almost schizophrenic split develops between who he believes he is and how others see him. A very strong core of undeveloped self-knowledge enables him to avoid being defeated by the difficult circumstances of his life; he is also aided by a renewed contact with his older brother, who had stayed with their father when the family separated. We do not see the completion of his growing up in this book, but we do see a major act of deception (which stops short of self-deception) that gives him an escape from the limitations of his early years.

This Boy's Life raises questions about who we are, who we think we are, who others think we are, and who we may become. One of Wolff's achievements is to make it possible to see with unusual clarity the lines between those four facets of self-understanding and self-creation. Evidence of the dichotomies in his self-perception appear throughout the book; toward the end of the book, we see introspection directly related to this theme.

Achievement. How does high potential complicate Wolff's boyhood?

Identity. Describe Wolff as he is, as he thinks he is, as others see him, and as a potential adult. Now do the same for yourself, and then for some other person you would like to understand better. How do the circumstances of your life make the development of your identity a different task from Wolff's? How does the book help you understand someone you know?

Moral concerns. How does Wolff use the words "citizen" and "outlaw"? What prevents him from "trying to be a citizen"? Which is the better route, and what is the cost of each? How are you choosing and why?

Zusak, Markus. *The Book Thief.* Knopf, 2007.

Liesel Meminger is nine in 1939, when her mother takes her to a foster home in a small town near Munich in Hitler's Germany. Her six-year-old brother dies on the way; at the cemetery, the illiterate Liesel picks up a book dropped from a gravedigger's pocket—she has become a book thief. Hans Hubermann, her gentle foster father, uses this book to teach her to read. Without money to buy books, in the next four years, Liesel steals five more, most of them from the home library of the emotionally devastated wife of the mayor, who tacitly enables Liesel to take them. As Liesel and her best friend Rudy grow into adolescence, the ugliness of Nazi Germany comes closer, first as Max, a young Jewish man whose father had been a friend of Hans, comes to their home seeking refuge, then in the news of neighborhood soldiers fighting in Stalingrad, and finally in bombing raids that come to Munich.

The narrator of Liesel's story is Death, who speaks with little emotion but with deep understanding, and with a mixture of horror and admiration of the work of humans. Many of the characters— Liesel, Hans, Rudy, and Max—are unforgettable. For readers who are aware of language as a value in itself, *The Book Thief* is filled with unusual combinations of nouns and verbs ("a voice stooped out and ambled...") and imagery (teeth "like a soccer crowd, crammed in"). This book will first challenge readers (the prologue will not become clear until later) and then captivate them, as the action moves forward and the power of words—Liesel's and Max's medium—gives it all meaning.

Drive to understand. First published as an adult book and now marketed for young adults, this is a more sophisticated work on Nazi Germany than others listed in this chapter. It could be used in a literature curriculum—especially for students who may become writ-ers, in a history curriculum, or in a combination of the two.

Moral concerns. Stealing, whether books or fruit, is taken rather lightly. What is your response to this? Does the context matter?

Using ability. As Liesel reads to the others in the bomb shelter, she thinks, "This is my accordion." Consider what she means by this—how does she know? What is there in your life that might be analogous?

Recommended Books from Earlier Editions

Following is a list of books found in earlier editions of *Some of My Best Friends Are Books* but removed from this edition to make room for new titles. Some of the books listed below may be hard to find; if so, they may be located in school or public libraries, through interlibrary loan, or through an online book search service. The publishers and dates given below are valid as this book goes to press.

Preschool

Very Young
Brown, Demi. *What Can You Find? Around the House.* DK Preschool, 1993.
Hoban, Tana. *Red, Blue, Yellow Shoe.* HarperFestival, 1986.
Stone, Erika. *Baby Talk.* Grossett & Dunlap, 1992.

Two and Three Years Old
Crews, Donald. *Carousel.* Greenwillow, 1982.
Crews, Donald. *Freight Train.* Harpercollins, 1992.
McCloskey, Robert. *Blueberries for Sal.* Puffin, 1976.

Four Years Old

de Gerez, Toni. *Louhi, Witch of North Farm*. Illustrated by Barbara
    Cooney. Puffin, 1988.

Gerrard, Roy. *Sir Cedric*. Farrar, Straus, & Giroux, 1984.

Lionni, Leo. *Frederick*. Dragonfly, 1973.

MacDonald, Golden. *The Little Island*. Illustrated by Leonard Weisgard.
    Dragonfly, 1993.

Sharmat, Marjorie Weinman. *I'm Terrific*. Illustrated by Kay Charao.
    Holiday House, 1992.

Steptoe, John. *Stevie*. HarperTrophy, 1986.

Early Elementary (K-Grade 2)

Aardema, Verna. *Who's in Rabbit's House?* Illustrated by Diane Dillon.
    Puffin, 1992.

Alderson, Sue Ann. *Ida and the Wool Smugglers*. Illustrated by Ann
    Blades. Groundwood, 1999.

Baker, Jeannie. *Where the Forest Meets the Sea*. HarperCollins, 1988.

Bunting, Eve. *The Man Who Could Call Down Owls*. Aladdin, 1994.

Carrick, Carol. *Stay Away from Simon!* Illustrated by Donald Carrick.
    Sandpiper, 1989.

Carrick, Carol. *What Happened to Patrick's Dinosaurs?* Illustrated by
    Donald Carrick. Sandpiper, 1988.

Clifton, Lucille. *Everett Anderson's Friend*. Illustrated by Ann Grifalconi.
    Henry Holt, 1992.

de Paola, Tomie. *Tomie de Paola's Book of Poems*. Putnam, 1988.

Gilks, Helen. *Bears*. Illustrated by Andrew Bale. Houghton Mifflin,
    1993.

Goble, Paul. *Iktomi and the Berries: A Plains Indian Story*. Orchard,
    1992.

Kellogg, Steven. *Best Friends*. Dial, 1986.

Larry, Charles. *Peboan and Seegwun*. Sunburst, 1995.

Lobel, Arnold. *On Market Street*. Illustrated by Anita Lobel.
    HarperCollins, 1989.

McDermott, Gerald. *Anansi the Spider: A Tale from the Ashanti*.
    Henry Holt, 1987.

Rappaport, Doreen. *The Boston Coffee Party*. Illustrated by Emily
    Arnold McCully. HarperCollins, 1990.

Steptoe, John. *Stevie.* HarperCollins, 1986.

Ward, Lynd. *The Silver Pony.* Sandpiper, 1992.

Wisniewski, David. *Elfwyn's Saga.* HarperCollins, 1990.

Yolen, Jane. *Bird Watch: A Book of Poetry.* Illustrated by Ted Lewin. Philomel, 1990.

Upper Elementary (Grades 3-5)

Arkin, Alan. *The Lemming Condition.* HarperOne, 1989.

Evan, Cheryl, & Anne Millard. *Usborne Illustrated Guide to Norse Myths and Legends.* Illustrated by Rodney Matthews. EDC, 1987.

Greene, Bette. *Philip Hall Likes Me. I Reckon Maybe.* Illustrated by Charles Lilly. Scholastic, 2000.

Hermes, Patricia. *Heads, I Win.* Illustrated by Carol Newsom. Pocket Books, 1989.

Honeycutt, Natalie. *The Best-Laid Plans of Jonah Twist.* Camelot, 1989.

Hunter, Mollie. *The Mermaid Summer.* HarperCollins, 1990.

Koch, Kenneth, & Kate Farrell. *Talking to the Sun: An Illustrated Anthology of Poems for Young People.* Metropolitan Museum of Art and Holt, Rinehart & Winston, 1988.

Phelps, Ethel Johnston. *The Maid of the North: Feminist Folk Tales from Around the World.* Illustrated by Lloyd Bloom. Topeka Bindery, 1999.

Smith, Janice Lee. *The Kid Next Door and Other Headaches: Stories about Adam Joshua.* Illustrated by Dick Gackenbach. Trophy, 1986.

Speare, Elizabeth George. *The Sign of the Beaver.* Yearling, 1984.

Stolz, Mary. *A Dog on Barkham Street.* Illustrated by Leonard Shortall. HarperCollins, 1988.

Stolz, Mary. *Go Fish.* Illustrated by Pat Cummings. HarperTrophy, 1993.

Tolan, Stephanie. *A Time to Fly Free.* Aladdin, 1990.

Yolen, Jane. *The Boy Who Had Wings.* Illustrated by Helga Aichinger. Crowell, 1974.

Middle School (Grades 6-8)

Conford, Ellen. *And This Is Laura*. Archway, 1978.

De Kruif, Paul. *Microbe Hunters*. Harvest Books, 2002.

Fox, Paula. *The Village by the Sea*. Yearling, 1990.

Garfield, Leon & Edward Blishen. *The God Beneath the Sea*. Illustrated by Charles Keeping. Orion, 1992.

Hunter, Mollie. *A Sound of Chariots*. Trophy, 1994.

Konigsburg, E. L. *Father's Arcane Daughter*. Aladdin, 1999.

Konigsburg, E. L. *(george)*. Aladdin, 2007.

L'Engle, Madeleine. *The Arm of the Starfish*. Laurel Leaf, 1979.

Matas, Carol. *Code Name Kris*. Aladdin, 2007.

Matas, Carol. *Lisa's War*. Aladdin, 2007.

Mayne, William. *Earthfasts*. Hodder, 1995.

Sullivan, Charles (Ed.). *Imaginary Gardens: American Poetry and Art for Young People*. Abrams, 1989.

Sutcliff, Rosemary. *Flame-Colored Taffeta*. Sunburst, 1989.

Tolan, Stephanie. *A Good Courage*. HarperTrophy, 1998.

Voigt, Cynthia. *Building Blocks*. Aladdin, 2002.

High School (Grades 9-12)

Holman, Felice. *Slake's Limbo*. Aladdin, 1986.

Hunt, Irene. *William*. Ace, 1984.

Le Guin, Ursula. *Very Far Away from Anywhere Else*. Harcourt, 2004.

Levitin, Sonia. *The Return*. Fawcett, 1988.

Strasser, Todd. *The Wave*. Laurel Leaf, 1981.

Thomas, Elizabeth Marshall. *Reindeer Moon*. Pocket Books, 1991.

Webb, James T., Elizabeth A. Meckstroth, & Stephanie S. Tolan. *Guiding the Gifted Child*. Great Potential Press, 1982.

Endnotes

Introduction
1 Winner, 1996, p. 233

Chapter 1
1 Buescher, 1985
2 Ravitch, 2000
3 Mendaglio, 2008, p. 13
4 Pyryt, 2008, p. 179
5 Daniels & Piechowski, 2009, p. 9
6 Silverman, 2008b, p. 158
7 Lind, 2000
8 Webb et al., 2005
9 For ongoing work with Dabrowski's theory of positive disintegration and with his concept of overexcitabilities (including how they impact the lives of gifted adults), see Daniels & Piechowski (2009).
10 Piechowski, 2002, p. 29
11 Silverman, 1994
12 See Mendaglio, 2008
13 Morelock, 1992
14 Winner, 1996
15 Williams, 1992, p. 33
16 Laney, 2002. Laney's second book, which is also of interest, is *The Hidden Gifts of the Introverted Child* (2006).
17 Kiersey & Bates, 1984

18 Gladwell, 2008; Goertzel, Goertzel, Goertzel, & Hanson, 2004; Kerr, 1997. Gladwell reports that top-level musicians spend about 10,000 hours practicing before they reach eminence—a figure that represents many hours of alone time.

19 Jarvis & Jarvis, 1999

20 Kerr, 1997

21 Kerr & Cohn, 2001

22 Pendarvis, Howley, & Howley, 1990, p. 234

23 Kerr, 1991, p. 125

24 Maslow, 1954, 1971. Maslow originally proposed five needs. His early work on the hierarchy of needs has been updated in Maslow & Lowery (1998) and now comprises eight levels: four basic needs and four growth needs.

25 Cross, 2005. Cross has found that even by first grade, some gifted students have "begun to engage in behavior patterns that reveal their discomfort with the gifted student label" (p. 64). As one way of addressing this issue in schools, Cross recommends differentiation in the classroom. For more on differentiation, see Chapter 2 in this book.

26 Kerr, 1997

27 Davis, 2006

28 Silverman, 2008a

29 Greenspon, 2002

30 Adderholdt & Goldberg, 1999

31 For students who have learned that they can stay current by "listening with half an ear" in class, the wake-up call is most likely to come around seventh or eighth grade in a math or a language course for which daily attention is required to keep up with the concepts or the vocabulary.

32 Winner, 1996. See also Kerr, 1997.

33 Kerr & Cohn, 2001

34 For more on this difficult problem, see Davis & Rimm (2004); Kerr (1991); Rimm (2008a, 2008b); Webb, Gore, Amend, & DeVries (2007); and Whitney & Hirsch (2007).

35 Kerr, 1991

36 Kerr, 1990

37 Vaillant, 2002. Lewis Terman of Stanford University began a longitudinal study of gifted students in 1922. Eighty years later, Vaillant included the women of Terman's study in his compilation of three longitudinal studies for a book on healthy aging. Vaillant interviewed one Terman woman who lived her entire life below the poverty line and did not have an opportunity to go to college. When Vaillant asked "Joy" whether her intelligence was a blessing or a burden, she replied, "Oh, a blessing! I read Shakespeare, Plato, and Freud for pleasure instead of to impress others." She had found that high intelligence made her life easier—everywhere she worked, she was a valued employee "because I could do everything without any help." Joy is a brilliant example of

how other factors (in Joy's case, supportive, loving parents; high emotional intelligence; a consistent positive attitude; and initiative in continuing to learn throughout life) can build resilient individuals who overcome circumstances that would leave others devastated.

Chapter 2

1   Ravitch & Finn, 1987
2   In Tennessee, for example, the Metropolitan Nashville Public Schools' Encore program includes a preschool component, which identifies gifted children at the age of three and provides programs for them until they enter the regular Encore program in kindergarten. For more information, go to www.mnps.org/ Page46.aspx.
3   For more information on the Center for Gifted Education at the College of William and Mary, go to http://cfge.wm.edu/. An introduction to a portion of the William and Mary curriculum is available at http://cfge.wm.edu/ curr_language.htm and also in a concise PowerPoint chart developed by Dr. Susannah Richards at www.iusd.k12.ca.us/parent_resources/gate/documents/ IrvineTalented20072page.pdf.
4   See www.nagc.org/index2.aspx?id=532
5   Office of Educational Research and Improvement, 1993, p. 13
6   Davidson & Davidson, 2004
7   Davidson & Davidson, 2004. See also Cross, 2005, p. 83
8   Webb, 1992, p. 12
9   Silverman, 1993, p. 10
10 Piechowski, 1979
11 Piechowski, 1979
12 Piechowski, 1979, p. 34
13 Piechowski, 1991, p. 287
14 Davidson & Davidson, 2004, p. 148
15 Halsted, 1998
16 Clark, 2007; Davis, 2006; Webb et al., 2007
17 Clark, 2007
18 James T. Webb, personal communication, December 17, 2008
19 Webb et al., 2007
20 Kerr, 1991, p. 23
21 Kerr, 1991, p. 22
22 Rogers, 2002; Ruf, 2005
23 Davis (2006) offers valuable descriptions of several methods for teaching thinking skills developed by well-known educators of the gifted. I am using just one of them, Bloom's Taxonomy, as an example here and again in Chapter 5.
24 Amidon, 1991
25 Office of Educational Research and Improvement, 1993

26 Davidson & Davidson, 2004
27 Karnes & Marquardt, 2003
28 Healy, 1999
29 Healy, 1999, p. 208 (personal communication from M. Russell Harter, researcher in reading and the developing brain at the University of North Carolina)
30 Healy, 1999, p. 214
31 Billington, 1990
32 Jarvis & Jarvis, 1999
33 Gardner, 2008. Gardner cites a study by the Pew Internet & American Life Project, which also found that nearly as many girls (94%) as boys (99%) play video games. In addition, it reported that teens who saw other teens using aggressive playing behavior often moved to stop the bad behavior.
34 Christopher S. Halsted, personal communications, September 28, 2008; October 20, 2008. Halsted's comments confirm the results of the Pew Internet survey reported by Gardner (2008).
35 Akst, 2008
36 Beers, 1998
37 Ravitch, 2000
38 Colangelo & Davis, 2003, p. 4
39 For other options for gifted children, see Clark (2007), Colangelo & Davis (2003), and Davis & Rimm (2004).
40 Kerr, 1991, p. 23
41 Kulik, 2003, p. 279
42 Robinson, 1990; Rogers, 2002
43 Robinson, 1997
44 Cross, 2005, p. 86
45 Colangelo, Assouline, & Gross, 2004. See also www.accelerationinstitute.org/ Nation_Deceived
46 Davis & Rimm, 2004
47 Assouline, Colangelo, Lupkowski-Shoplik, Lipscomb, & Forstadt, 2009
48 Webb et al., 2007
49 Ruf, 2005, p. 289
50 Tomlinson, 2001
51 Strip & Hirsch, 2000
52 Rogers, 2002
53 Gilman, 2008
54 Willis, 2009. Middle school teachers and parents may wish to look further into this book about how adolescent brains learn.
55 Archibald, 2004
56 Webb et al., 2007
57 Rivero, 2002
58 Ray & Wartes, 1991

59 Rivero, 2002

60 Shapiro, 2001

61 This series, by Judy Freeman, includes *More Books Kids Will Sit Still For: A Read-Aloud Guide (1990)*, *Books Kids Will Sit Still For: A Read-Aloud Guide, Second Edition* (1995), and *Books Kids Will Sit Still For 3: A Read-Aloud Guide* (2006).

62 Trelease, 2006

63 Based on her experience as a teacher, school librarian, bookseller, and children's author, Esme Raji Codell has written *How to Get Your Child to Love Reading: Activities, Ideas, Inspirations, and Suggestions for Exploring Everything in the World—Through Books* (2003). Parents can follow Codell's suggestions to help younger children choose a book, or they can offer it to older children to use independently.

Chapter 3

1 Reading interest inventories were common in the 1980s and 1990s. The findings on reading interests given in this chapter are derived from Hall & Coles (1997), Haynes (1988), Langerman (1990), Milliot (1998), Swanton (1984), and Whitehead (1984), as well as the authors specifically cited later.

2 Doiron, 2003

3 Gurian (2002) has been especially influential among teachers and school librarians who are planning reading programs for boys.

4 Sullivan, 2004

5 Engel-Smothers & Heim, 2008. In their book, Chapter 3, titled "Language: Getting Baby Ready to Read," is especially relevant to reading, but the entire book is recommended for parents interested in understanding optimal brain development.

6 Butler, 1998

7 Butler & Clay, 1991

8 Hall & Moats, 1999

9 This approach is perfect for toddlers, who delight in the sheer joy of language in cumulative tales such as "The House that Jack Built" or the rhythms of Dr. Seuss. Three- and four-year-olds love stories that allow them to join in on repetitious phrases or books without words that invite them to tell the story themselves.

10 Clark (1997) goes so far as to write, "I am convinced that reading is a natural, happy event if introduced during…this period [18 months to four years of age]. What we do at 6 years of age may be remedial reading." While she is not suggesting that parents engage in formal teaching, she does go on to say, "…if allowed the opportunity to play with words, if read to or shown any of the ways letters can be used to represent sound, children find their own way to learn. In an environment that responds *as the children direct* [emphasis added], that is rich in good language experiences, children enjoy learning in their own way. Learning to read is no exception" (pp. 120-121).

11 Guidance is available in Butler & Clay (1991). Pointing out the importance of parental sensitivity to any anxiety on the part of the parents or the child, the authors suggest a method of teaching that can be used by parents who decide that it is appropriate for their family. Hall & Moats (1999) urge parents to prepare preschoolers for reading instruction by promoting letter recognition and phonemic awareness so that the child recognizes the separate speech sounds in a word. Although the goal is preparation for learning to read in school rather than teaching preschoolers to read, some children may learn to read before they begin school with this much instruction at home.

12 Haupt, 2003. Haupt suggests that the upper elementary years are the time when children diverge, becoming either dedicated leisure readers or joining the ranks of those who may be able to read but choose not to.

13 Herald, 1997

14 Carlsen, 1980

15 Carter, 1982

16 Baskin, 1998

17 Samuels, 1998

18 The line between YA and adult literature is becoming increasingly blurred, with the decision often made by the publisher's marketing department, according to Michael Cart, a former president of the Young Adult Library Services Association and quoted by Rabb (2008).

19 Carlsen, 1980; Rakow, 1991; Samuels, 1998

20 Carlsen, 1980, p. 34

21 Carter & Abrahamson, 1998

22 Silvey, 2006

23 Herald, 1997

24 Romey, 2007

25 Estell, Satchwell, & Wright, 2000

26 Updike, 1989, p. 109

27 Swinger, 1989, p. 51. Alison's story is particularly appropriate as the introduction for a discussion of special characteristics of gifted readers. It will ring true for many readers of this book.

28 Recent studies of the reading interests of gifted children—especially gifted high school students—are rare. However, Romey (2000) interviewed eight gifted girls in an Alabama high school, grades 9-12, about their reading patterns, looking for implications for bibliotherapy. These girls preferred historical romance, mystery/horror, and science fiction; of primary importance to them was fiction with a strong female character. Interestingly, the girls discussed how being avid readers set them apart from their classmates so that the opportunity to talk with others who enjoyed reading was validating in itself—one of the benefits of bibliotherapy.

29 Nelson & Hauser, 1988

30 At www.hoagiesgifted.org/readinglists.htm, one can find links to lists of suitable books on various topics. Another helpful site is www.bertiekingore.com/gtchildreninlit.htm. These lists may include books with older copyright dates, but the books may still be in print. If not, they should be available through local libraries.

31 Nelson & Hauser, 1988

32 Helpful websites include www.bertiekingore.com/gtchildreninlit.htm and www.hoagiesgifted.org/readinglists.htm, as well as a book list created by Linda Silverman available at www.hoagiesgifted.org/featuring_gifted.htm.

33 Jarvis & Jarvis, 1999

Chapter 4

1 Cornett & Cornett, 1980, p. 8

2 Doll & Doll, 1997

3 Doll & Doll, 1997. For more information on clinical bibliotherapy, see Kaplan (1999) and Pardeck & Pardeck (1993). The Kaplan book is part of a series on bibliotherapy for troubled teens that focuses on six issues: family, identity, social concerns, abuse, health, and death and dying.

4 Lack, 1985. See also Zaccaria, Moses, & Hollowell, 1978, p. 29

5 For example, Brinson, 2005; Hébert, 1991; Hébert, Long, & Neumeister, 2001. A more recent study at Duke University found that after reading *Lake Rescue*, a novel for pre-teen girls that portrays the advantages of physical activity and good nutrition, girls aged nine to 13 showed a .71% decrease in body mass index. There were two control groups; the girls who read another book had a body mass decrease of .33% (attributed to reading instead of watching TV and being exposed to food commercials), while those in the control group that read no books showed a body mass *increase* of .05% ("Reading May Be a Way to Slim Down," 2008).

6 Schrank & Engels, 1981, p. 144. See also Schrank, 1982

7 Tillman, 1984

8 Riordan & Wilson, 1989

9 Hébert, 1991

10 Doll & Doll, 1997

11 Bernstein, 1989, p. 165

12 Hynes & Hynes-Berry, 1986

13 Slavson, 1950

14 Hunter, 1990, p. 28

15 Coles, 1989. Coles indicates that this holds true for college students as well.

16 Lerner & Mahlendorf, 1992, p. x

17 Spache, 1974, p. 242

18 Delisle, 1990, pp. 223-224

19 Reis & Dobyns (1991) offer a list of nonfiction and curricular material for use with gifted girls.

20 Hébert, 1995
21 Cross, 2005, p. 69
22 Coles, 1989
23 Dodson, 1997. In response to concerns about a decline in reading among boys, some schools are starting book clubs for boys. For more information, see "Boys and Books" (2006), Taylor (2004), and Wilson & Casey (2007).
24 Robinson, 1989
25 Stanley, 1999
26 Hébert, Long, & Neumeister, 2001. The authors suggest a number of follow-up activities that can be used most conveniently when a classroom teacher, counselor, or librarian is able to meet with the group over a period of time.
27 Stephanie Tolan, personal communication, n.d.
28 Hynes & Hynes-Berry, 1986, p. 58

Chapter 5

1 Alexander, 1991, p. 16, reviewing Barzun, 1991
2 Flesch, 1955
3 Chall, 1967
4 Children's backgrounds are very relevant to their approach to reading. Those from "high-literacy" homes, who have been read to and whose parents read often, do well with either method—about 5% can read when they enter school; most of the others quickly become independent readers after mastering the basics of phonics. In contrast, those from "low-literacy" homes may have half the vocabulary of students from high-literacy homes, may speak non-standard English, and may lack motivation for school, seeing teachers as working to change their language and their culture. For them, phonics may be an unsuccessful approach, while the whole language method encourages teachers to find reading materials that reflect their culture. See Rehner (2008).
5 Lynch-Brown & Tomlinson, 1999
6 Ravitch, 2000
7 Hall & Moats, 1999
8 Pressley, 2006
9 Kolker, 2006. Kolker's article traces the controversy over balanced literacy instruction (featuring strong emphasis on literature and a small supplemental program, Month by Month phonics), which was introduced in New York City's public schools in 2003 under Mayor Michael Bloomberg. At the time, new research had recently indicated that phonics is superior to whole language. Kolker points out that the reading wars can take on a political cast, with red states (and then-President George W. Bush) favoring phonics, while New York's Columbia University and Bank Street College promote whole language. Balanced literacy has since been modified, incorporating phonics in various

ways while keeping the whole language core, but Kolker concludes that New York City will most likely remain "a whole language town."

10 Kim, 2008, p. 372

11 Kim, 2008, p. 372

12 Nilsen, 2005. Professor of English and Director of English Education at Arizona State University, Nilsen is co-author of *Literature for Today's Young Adults*, a leading textbook on young adult literature.

13 For more on the effects of No Child Left Behind on gifted children, see Ruf (2005) and Whitney & Hirsch (2007).

14 Reis & Renzulli, 1989, p. 92, quoting Brown & Rogan, 1983

15 More information about the Center for Gifted Education's language arts curriculum for high-ability learners can be found at http://cfge.wm.edu/curr_language.htm. Teachers and homeschooling parents can contact the publisher (www.kendallhunt.com) for curriculum materials.

16 Flack, 2000

17 Dole & Adams, 1983

18 Clark, 2007

19 The following discussion is derived from Lehr (1991), who bases her comments on Applebee's (1978) use of Piaget's study.

20 Newman & Newman, 1983

21 Lehr, 1991

22 Baskin, 1998

23 VanTassel-Baska, 1989

24 Castiglione, 1987

25 Castiglione, 1987

26 Bloom, 1956

27 For optimum use with gifted readers, a Junior Great Books discussion should be modified for more openness, allowing opportunity for individualized responses. This requires leaders who bring to the task a lively intelligence, awareness of the characteristics of gifted children, and flexibility. When all of this is in place, the results are rewarding. More information is available at www.greatbooks.org.

28 Noe & Johnson, 1999

29 Hopkins, 1991, p. xiv

30 Bauer, 1991 (quotations are from pp. 112-115)

31 Rivero, 2002

32 Scales (n.d. As of September 21, 2008, this booklet was listed on www.amazon.com with a date of 1987. But it was "currently unavailable," with no publisher listed and "unknown binding.")

33 Colhoun, 2000

34 Colhoun, 2000, p. 8, quoting Jacqueline Hess of the Academy of Educational Development

Chapter 6

1   Paterson, 1989, pp. 68-69
2   Wells, 1990, pp. 129-131
3   Wells, 1990, pp. 129-131
4   Mockett & Welton, 1990
5   Baskin, 1998, p. 70
6   Freehill, 1961
7   Bloom, 1956

Chapter 7

1   D. G. Halsted, personal communication, September 5, 1992
2   Carter & Abrahamson, 1998
3   Flack, 1992
4   Bettelheim, 1977. Bettelheim also addressed fears that fairy tales may cause children to lose touch with reality, asserting that fairy stories are necessary for development, allowing small children to identify with the youngest, weakest character (note how often it is the third son or daughter who carries out the quest after the first two have failed) and respond with hope that they, too, will be able to make their way in the world. Bettelheim thought that the rich fantasy life fostered by fairy tales could protect children who otherwise might later seek psychological escape through drugs, astrology, or black magic.
5   The Jack tales are stories, generally from the British Isles, in which the main character is a boy called Jack.
6   May, R., 1991, p. 9
7   Dailey, 1991
8   Cook, 1969, p. 5
9   Wrede & Stevermer, 2003. The authors' *The Grand Tour* (2006) is a sequel.
10   Lynch-Brown & Tomlinson, 1999, p. 120
11   May, J. P., 1991
12   Rosenberg, 1986, p. 182
13   Nodelman, 1992
14   Livingston, 1990
15   Livingston, 1990, p. 208
16   Livingston, 1990, p. 131
17   Livingston, 1990, p. 132
18   Collins and Kooser are recent poets laureate. To find the names of American poets laureate, visit http://poetry.about.com/od/poets/l/bllaureates.htm.
19   Richards, 2008
20   Richards, 2007

Chapter 8

1   Ruf, 2005

References

Adderholdt, M., & Goldberg, J. (1999). *Perfectionism: What's bad about being too good?* Minneapolis, MN: Free Spirit.

Akst, D. (2008, August 29). Raising the bar: How parents can fix education. *Wall Street Journal*, p. W9.

Alexander, D. (1991, April 21). He told us so. *New York Times Book Review*, p. 16.

Amidon, S. R. (1991). Encouraging higher level thinking in the gifted adolescent. In M. Bireley & J. Genshaft (Eds.), *Understanding the gifted adolescent: Educational, developmental, and multicultural issues* (pp. 91-103). New York: Teachers College Press.

Applebee, A. (1978). *The child's concept of story: Ages two to seventeen.* Chicago: University of Chicago Press.

Archibald, G. (2004, Sept. 22). Public schools no place for teachers' kids. *The Washington Times.*

Assouline, S. G., Colangelo, N., Lupkowski-Shoplik, A., Lipscomb, J., & Forstadt, L. (2009). *Iowa acceleration scale: A guide for whole-grade acceleration K-8* (3rd ed.). Scottsdale, AZ: Great Potential Press.

Barzun, J. (1991). *Begin here: The forgotten conditions of teaching and learning.* Chicago: University of Chicago Press.

Baskin, B. (1998). Call me Ishmael: A look at gifted middle school readers. In K. Beers & B. G. Samuels (Eds.), *Into focus: Understanding and creating middle school readers* (pp. 65-79). Norwood, MA: Christopher-Gordon.

Bauer, M. D. (1991, January/February). An author's letter to teachers. *Horn Book, 67*, 111-116.

Beers, K. (1998). Choosing not to read: Understanding why some middle schoolers just say no. In K. Beers & B. G. Samuels (Eds.), *Into focus: Understanding and creating middle school readers* (pp. 37-63). Norwood, MA: Christopher-Gordon.

Bernstein, J. E. (1989). Bibliotherapy: How books can help young children cope. In M. K. Rudman (Ed.), *Children's literature: Resources for the classroom* (pp. 159-173). Norwood, MA: Christopher-Gordon.

Bettelheim, B. (1977). *The uses of enchantment: The meaning and importance of fairy tales.* New York: Vintage.

Billington, J. H. (1990, September). *The electronic erosion of democracy.* Paper presented at the Inaugural C. Walter and Gerda B. Mortenson Lecture, Urbana, Illinois.

Bloom, B. S. (Ed.). (1956). *Taxonomy of educational objectives.* New York: David McKay.

Boys and books: Boys' education stirs much debate, brings little consensus. (2006, August-September). *Reading Today, 24*(1), 1-2.

Brinson, S. A. (2005, Fall). Boys don't tell on sugar-and-spice-but-not-so-nice girl bullies. *Reclaiming Children and Youth, 14*(3), 169-174.

Brown, W., & Rogan, J. (1983). Reading and young gifted children. *Roeper Review, 5*, 6-9.

Buescher, T. M. (1985). A framework for understanding the social and emotional development of gifted and talented adolescents. *Roeper Review, 8*, 10-15.

Butler, D. (1998). *Babies need books: Sharing the joy of books with children from birth to six* (Rev. ed.). Portsmouth, NH: Heinemann.

Butler, D., & Clay, M. (1991). *Reading begins at home: Preparing children for reading before they go to school* (2nd ed.). Portsmouth, NH: Heinemann.

Carlsen, G. R. (1980). *Books and the teenage reader: A guide for teachers, librarians and parents* (2nd ed.). New York: Harper & Row.

Carter, B. (1982, Summer). Leisure reading habits of gifted students in a suburban junior high school. *Top of the News, 38*, 312-317.

Carter, B., & Abrahamson, R. F. (1998). Castles to Colin Powell: The truth about nonfiction. In K. Beers & B. G. Samuels (Eds.), *Into focus: Understanding and creating middle school readers* (pp. 313-332). Norwood, MA: Christopher-Gordon.

Castiglione, L. V. (1987). *Questioning methods for gifted students.* East Aurora, NY: DOK.

Chall, J. S. (1967). *Learning to read: The great debate.* New York: McGraw-Hill.

Clark, B. (1997). *Growing up gifted: Developing the potential of children at home and at school* (5th ed.). Upper Saddle River, NJ: Prentice-Hall.

Clark, B. (2007). *Growing up gifted: Developing the potential of children at home and at school* (7th ed.). New York: Merrill/Education/Prentice Hall.

Codell, E. R. (2003). *How to get your child to love reading: Activities, ideas, inspirations, and suggestions for exploring everything in the world— through books.* Chapel Hill, NC: Algonquin.

Colangelo, N., Assouline, S. G., & Gross, M. U. M. (2004). *A nation deceived: How schools hold back America's brightest students.* (The Templeton National Report on Acceleration). Iowa City, IA: University of Iowa Press.

Colangelo, N., & Davis, G. A. (2003). Preface. In N. Colangelo & G. A. Davis (Eds.), *Handbook of gifted education* (3rd ed., pp. xii-xiv). Boston: Allyn & Bacon.

Coles, R. (1989). *The call of stories: Teaching and the moral imagination.* Boston: Houghton Mifflin.

Colhoun, A. (2000, May 11-17). But—I found it on the Internet! *The Christian Science Monitor: MonitorWeek, 1*(16), 8.

Cook, E. (1969). *The ordinary and the fabulous.* London: Cambridge University Press.

Cornett, C. E., & Cornett, C. F. (1980) *Bibliotherapy: The right book at the right time.* Bloomington, IN: Phi Delta Kappa Educational Foundation.

Cross, T. L. (2005). *The social and emotional lives of gifted kids: Understanding and guiding their development.* Waco, TX: Prufrock Press.

Dailey, S. (1991). Folktales—The rainbow bridge between cultures. *Media Spectrum, 18*(4), 3-5.

Daniels, S., & Piechowski, M. M. (Eds.). (2009). *Living with intensity.* Scottsdale, AZ: Great Potential Press.

Davidson, J., & Davidson, B., with Vanderkam, L. (2004). *Genius denied: How to stop wasting our brightest young minds.* New York: Simon & Schuster.

Davis, G. A. (2006). *Gifted children and gifted education: A handbook for teachers and parents.* Scottsdale, AZ: Great Potential Press.

Davis, G. A., & Rimm, S. B. (2004). *Education of the gifted and talented* (5th ed.) Boston: Pearson.

Delisle, J. R. (1990). The gifted adolescent at risk: Strategies and resources for suicide prevention among gifted youth. *Journal for the Education of the Gifted, 13,* 212-226.

Dodson, S., with Baker, T. (1997). *The mother-daughter book club: How ten busy mothers and daughters came together to talk, laugh and learn through their love of reading.* New York: HarperCollins.

Doiron, R. (2003). Boy books, girl books: Should we re-organize our school library collections? *Teacher Librarian, 30*(3), 14-16.

Dole, J. A., & Adams, P. J. (1983). Reading curriculum for gifted readers: A survey. *Gifted Child Quarterly, 27*, 64-77.

Doll, B., & Doll, C. (1997). *Bibliotherapy with young people: Librarians and mental health professionals working together.* Englewood, CO: Libraries Unlimited.

Engel-Smothers, H., & Heim, S. M. (2008). *Boosting your baby's brain power.* Scottsdale, AZ: Great Potential Press.

Estell, D., Satchwell, M. L., & Wright, P. S. (2000). *Reading lists for college-bound students* (3rd ed.). Stamford, CT: Thomson.

Flack, J. (1992). Biography (Part I). *Understanding Our Gifted, 4*(4), 17-18.

Flack, J. (2000). The gifted reader in the regular classroom: Strategies for success. *Illinois Association for Gifted Children,* 22-30.

Flesch, R. (1955). *Why Johnny can't read—and what you can do about it.* New York: Harper.

Freehill, M. (1961).*Gifted children: Their psychology and education.* New York: Macmillan.

Freeman, J. (1990). *More books kids will sit still for: A read-aloud guide.* Westport, CT: Libraries Unlimited.

Freeman, J. (1995). *Books kids will sit still for: A read-aloud guide* (2nd ed.). Westport, CT: Libraries Unlimited.

Freeman, J. (2006). *Books kids will sit still for 3: A read-aloud guide.* Westport, CT: Libraries Unlimited.

Gardner, W. D. (2008, September 17). Video games are good for kids, experts find. *Information Week.* Retrieved September 19, 2008, from www.informationweek.com/story/showArticle.jhtml?articleID=210602159

Gilman, B. J. (2008). *Academic advocacy for gifted children: A parent's complete guide.* Scottsdale, AZ: Great Potential Press.

Gladwell, M. (2008). *Outliers: The story of success.* New York: Little, Brown.

Goertzel, V., Goertzel, M. G., Goertzel, T. G., & Hanson, A. M. (2004). *Cradles of eminence* (2nd ed.). Scottsdale, AZ: Great Potential Press.

Greenspon, T. S. (2002). *Freeing our families from perfectionism.* Minneapolis, MN: Free Spirit.

Gurian, M. (2002). *Boys and girls learn differently!: A guide for teachers and parents.* San Francisco: Jossey Bass.

Hall, C., & Coles, M. (1997). Gendered readings: Helping boys develop as critical readers. *Gender and Education, 9*(1), 61-68.

Hall, S. L., & Moats, L. C. (1999). *Straight talk about reading: How parents can make a difference in the early years.* Lincolnwood, IL: Contemporary Books.

Halsted, J. W. (1998). Keeping curiosity alive. In J. F. Smutny (Ed.), *The young gifted child: Potential and promise, an anthology.* Cresskill, NJ: Hampton Press.

Haupt, A. (2003). Where the boys are…. *Teacher Librarian, 30*(3), 19-24.

Haynes, C. (1988). Explanatory power of content for identifying children's literary preferences. *Dissertation Abstracts International, 49-12A,* 1317. (University Microfilms No. DEW8900468).

Healy, J. M. (1999). *Endangered minds: Why children don't think—and what we can do about it.* New York: Simon & Schuster.

Hébert, T. P. (1991, June). Meeting the affective needs of bright boys through bibliotherapy. *Roeper Review, 13,* 207-212.

Hébert, T. P. (1995, Spring). Using biography to counsel gifted young men. *Journal of Secondary Gifted Education, 6*(3), 208-219.

Hébert, T. P., Long, L. A., & Neumeister, K. L. S. (2001, Winter). Using biography to counsel gifted young women. *Journal of Secondary Gifted Education, 12*(2), 62.

Herald, D. T. (1997). *Teen genreflecting.* Englewood, CO: Libraries Unlimited.

Hopkins, L. B. (1991). Leave me alone! Cries the poem. *Perspectives, 7*(3), xiii-xv.

Hunter, M. (1990). *Talent is not enough: Mollie Hunter on writing for children.* New York: HarperCollins Children's Books.

Hynes, A. M., & Hynes-Berry, M. (1986). *Bibliotherapy: The interactive process: A handbook.* Boulder, CO: Westview Press.

Jarvis, J., & Jarvis, R. (1999). *The magic bookshelf: A parents' guide to showing growing minds the path to the best children's literature.* Atlanta, GA: Lorica.

Kaplan, J. S. (Ed.). (1999). *Using literature to help troubled teenagers cope with identity issues.* Westport, CT: Greenwood.

Karnes, F. A., & Marquardt, R. G. (2003). Gifted education and legal issues: Procedures and recent decisions. In N. Colangelo & G. A. Davis (Eds.), *Handbook of gifted education* (3rd ed., pp. 590-693). Boston: Allyn & Bacon.

Kerr, B. A. (1990). Career planning for gifted and talented youth. In S. Berger (Ed.), *Flyer files on gifted students.* Reston, VA: ERIC Clearinghouse on Handicapped and Gifted Children.

Kerr, B. (1991). *A handbook for counseling the gifted and talented.* Alexandria, VA: American Association for Counseling and Development.

Kerr, B. A. (1997). *Smart girls: A new psychology of girls, women, and giftedness.* Scottsdale, AZ: Great Potential Press.

Kerr, B. A., & Cohn, S. J. (2001). *Smart boys: Talent, manhood, and the search for meaning.* Scottsdale, AZ: Great Potential Press.

Kiersey, D., & Bates, M. (1984). *Please understand me: Character and temperament types* (5th ed.). Del Mar, CA: Prometheus Nemesis.

Kim, J. S. (2008, January). Research and the reading wars. *Phi Delta Kappan, 89*(5), 372.

Kolker, R. (2006, May 1). A is for apple, B is for brawl: Why New York's reading wars are so contentious. *New York, 39*(15), 42-46.

Kulik, J. A. (2003). Grouping and tracking. In N. Colangelo & G. A. Davis (Eds.), *Handbook of gifted education* (3rd ed., pp. 268-279). Boston: Allyn & Bacon.

Lack, C. R. (Spring, 1985). Can bibliotherapy go public? *Collection Building, 7,* 27-32.

Laney, M. O. (2002). *The introvert advantage: How to thrive in an extrovert world.* New York: Workman.

Langerman, D. (1990, March). Books and boys: Gender preferences and book selection. *School Library Journal,* 132-136.

Lehr, S. S. (1991). *A child's developing sense of theme: Responses to literature.* New York: Teachers College Press.

Lerner, A., & Mahlendorf, U. R. (1992). *Life guidance through literature.* Chicago: American Library Association.

Lind, S. (2000). Overexcitability and the highly gifted. *CAG Communicator, 31*(4), 19, 45-48.

Livingston, M. C. (1990). *Climb into the bell tower: Essays on poetry.* New York: Harper & Row.

Lynch-Brown, C., & Tomlinson, C. M. (1999). *Essentials of children's literature* (3rd ed.). Boston: Allyn & Bacon.

Maslow, A. H. (1954). *Motivation and personality.* New York: Harper & Row.

Maslow, A. H. (1971). *The farther reaches of human nature.* New York: Viking Press.

Maslow, A. H., & Lowery, R. (Eds.). (1998). *Toward a psychology of being* (3rd ed.). New York: Wiley & Sons.

May, J. P. (1991). *Lloyd Alexander.* Boston: Twayne.

May, R. (1991). *The cry for myth.* New York: Norton.

Mendaglio, S. (2008). *Dabrowski's theory of positive disintegration: A personality theory for the 21st century.* In S. Mendaglio (Ed.), Dabrowski's theory of positive disintegration. Scottsdale, AZ: Great Potential Press.

Milliot, J. (1998, September 14). PW/BEA survey finds some good news about reading habits. *Publishers Weekly, 245*(37), 10.

Mockett, S., & Welton, A. (1990, September 1). Picture books for the gifted. *Booklist, 87*, 63-66.

Morelock, M. J. (1992). Giftedness: The view from within. *Understanding Our Gifted, 4*(3), 1, 11-15.

National Commission on Excellence in Education. (1983). *A nation at risk: The imperative for educational reform.* Washington, DC: U.S. Department of Education.

Nelson, G. A., & Hauser, P. (1988). *Books for the gifted child* (Vol. 2). New York: Bowker.

Newman, P. R., & Newman, B. M. (1983). *Principles of psychology.* Homewood, IL: Dorsey.

Nilsen, A. P. (2005, January). The future of reading: An educator explains why she's worried and wonders what's next. *School Library Journal, 51*(1), 38-39.

Nodelman, P. (1992). *The pleasures of children's literature.* New York: Longman.

Noe, K. L. S., & Johnson, N. J. (1999). *Getting started with literature circles.* Norwood, MA: Christopher-Gordon.

Office of Educational Research and Improvement. (1993). *National excellence: A case for developing America's talent.* Washington, DC: U.S. Government Printing Office.

Pardeck, J. T., & Pardeck, J. A. (1993). *Bibliotherapy: A clinical approach for helping children.* Langhorne, PA: Gordon & Breach Science Publishers.

Paterson, K. (1989). *The spying heart: More thoughts on reading and writing books for children.* New York: Dutton.

Pendarvis, E. D., Howley, A. A., & Howley, C. B. (1990). *The abilities of gifted children.* Englewood Cliffs, NJ: Prentice Hall.

Piechowski, M. M. (1979). Developmental potential. In N. Colangelo & R. T. Zaffrann (Eds.), *New voices in counseling the gifted* (pp. 25-57). Dubuque, IA: Kendall/Hunt.

Piechowski, M. M. (1991). Emotional development and emotional giftedness. In N. Colangelo & G. A. Davis (Eds.), *Handbook of gifted education* (pp. 285-306). Boston: Allyn & Bacon.

Piechowski, M. M. (2002). Experiencing in a higher key: Dabrowski's theory of and for the gifted. *Gifted Education Communicator, 33*(1), 28-31, 35-36.

Pressley, M. (2006). *Reading instruction that works: The case for balanced teaching* (3rd ed.). New York: Guilford.

Pyryt, M. C. (2008). The Dabrowskian lens: Implications for understanding gifted individuals. In S. Mendaglio (Ed.), *Dabrowski's theory of positive disintegration.* Scottsdale, AZ: Great Potential Press.

Rabb, M. (2008, July 20). I'm YA, and I'm OK. *New York Times Book Review,* p. 23.

Rakow, S. R. (1991, January). Young-adult literature for honors students? *English Journal, 80*(1), 48-51.

Ravitch, D. (2000). *Left back: A century of failed school reforms.* New York: Simon & Schuster.

Ravitch, D., & Finn, C. E. (1987). *What do our 17-year-olds know? A report on the first national assessment of history and literature.* New York: Harper & Row.

Ray, B., & Wartes, J. (1991). The academic achievement and affective development of home-schooled children. In J. Van Galen & M. A. Pittman (Eds.), *Home schooling: Political, historical, and pedagogical perspectives* (pp. 43-62). Norwood, NJ: Ablex.

Reading may be a way to slim down. (2008, August 9). *Los Angeles Times,* reprinted in the *Traverse City Record-Eagle,* p. 8B.

Rehner, J. (2008). *The reading wars: Phonics versus whole language.* Retrieved December 18, 2008 from http://jan.ucc.nau.edu/~jar/ Reading_Wars.html

Reis, S. M., & Dobyns, S. M. (1991, April). An annotated bibliography of nonfictional books and curricular materials to encourage gifted females. *Roeper Review, 13,* 129-130.

Reis, S. M., & Renzulli, J. S. (1989, December). Providing challenging programs for gifted readers. *Roeper Review, 12,* 92-97.

Richards, S. (2007). *The talented readers: Who they are and what they need.* Retrieved May 15, 2009, from www.iusd.k12.ca.us/parent_resources/ gate/documents/IrvineTalented20072page.pdf

Richards, S. (2008, Winter). Beyond the Caldecott and Newbery: Awards and lists of books for the active reader and thinker. *Gifted Education Communicator, 39*(4), 48-50.

Rimm, S. B. (2008a). *How to parent so children will learn: Strategies for raising happy, achieving children.* Scottsdale, AZ: Great Potential Press.

Rimm, S. B. (2008b). *Why bright kids get poor grades and what you can do about it.* Scottsdale, AZ: Great Potential Press.

Riordan, R. J., & Wilson, L. S. (1989). Bibliotherapy: Does it work? *Journal of Counseling and Development, 67,* 506-508.

Rivero, L. (2002) *Creative home schooling: A resource guide for smart families.* Scottsdale, AZ: Great Potential Press.

Robinson, A. (1990). Point-counterpoint: Cooperation or exploitation? The argument against cooperative learning for talented students. *Journal for the Education of the Gifted, 14,* 9-27.

Robinson, A. (1997). Cooperative learning for talented students: Emergent issues and implications. In N. Colangelo & G. A. Davis (Eds.), *Handbook of gifted education* (2nd ed., pp. 243-252). Boston: Allyn & Bacon.

Robinson, D. (1989, September/October). Bibliotherapy discussions. *Ohio Libraries, 2,* 22.

Rogers, K. B. (2002). *Re-forming gifted education: How parents and teachers can match the program to the child.* Scottsdale, AZ: Great Potential Press.

Romey, E. A. (2000). *A study of common themes in reading selections of gifted girls: Implications for bibliotherapy.* Unpublished master's thesis, University of Georgia, Athens, GA.

Romey, E. A. (2007). *In a different place: Reading interests of gifted adolescent females.* Unionville, NY: Royal Fireworks Press.

Rosenberg, B. (1986). *Genreflecting: A guide to reading interests in genre fiction* (2nd ed.). Littleton, CO: Libraries Unlimited.

Ruf, D. L. (2005). *Losing our minds: Gifted children left behind.* Scottsdale, AZ: Great Potential Press.

Samuels, B. G. (1998). Creating lifetime readers: A novel idea. In K. Beers & B. G. Samuels (Eds.), *Into focus: Understanding and creating middle school readers* (pp. 347-362). Norwood, MA: Christopher-Gordon.

Scales, P. (n.d.). *Communicating through young adult books.* New York: Bantam.

Schrank, F. A. (1982, February). Bibliotherapy as an elementary school counseling tool. *Elementary School Guidance & Counseling, 16,* 218-227.

Schrank, F. A., & Engels, D. W. (1981, November). Bibliotherapy as a counseling adjunct: Research findings. *Personnel and Guidance Journal, 60,* 143-147.

Shapiro, J. F. (2001, Fall). Creating shared family memories. *Gifted Education Communicator,* 64-65.

Silverman, L. K. (1993). The gifted individual. In L. K. Silverman (Ed.), *Counseling the gifted and talented* (pp. 3-28). Denver, CO: Love.

Silverman, L. K. (1994). The moral sensitivity of gifted children and the evolution of society. *Roeper Review, 17*(2), 110-116.

Silverman, L. K. (2008a). Petunias, perfectionism, and level of development. In S. Daniels & M. Piechowski (Eds.), *Living with intensity.* Scottsdale, AZ: Great Potential Press.

Silverman, L. K. (2008b). The theory of positive disintegration in the field of gifted education. In S. Mendaglio (Ed.), *Dabrowski's theory of positive disintegration.* Scottsdale, AZ: Great Potential Press.

Silvey, A. (2006). *500 great books for teens.* Boston: Houghton Mifflin.

Slavson, S. R. (1950). *Analytic group psychotherapy with children, adolescents, and adults.* New York: Columbia University Press.

Spache, G. D. (1974). Using books to help solve children's problems. In J. R. Rubin (Ed.), *Bibliotherapy source book.* Phoenix, AZ: Oryx Press. (Original work published 1974).

Stanley, J. (1999). *Reading to heal: How to use bibliotherapy to improve your life.* Boston: Element Books.

Strip, C., & Hirsch, G. (2000). *Helping gifted children soar: A practical guide for parents and teachers.* Scottsdale, AZ: Great Potential Press.

Sullivan, M. (2004, August). Why Johnny won't read. *School Library Journal, 50,* 36-39.

Swanton, S. I. (1984, March). Minds alive: What and why gifted students read for pleasure. *School Library Journal, 30,* 99-102.

Swinger, A. K. (1989, Winter). Portrait of a gifted reader: Alison. *Ohio Media Spectrum, 41,* 46-51.

Taylor, D. L. (2004, December). "Not just boring stories": Reconsidering the gender gap for boys. *Journal of Adolescent and Adult Literacy, 48*(4), 290-298.

Tillman, C. E. (1984, May). Bibliotherapy for adolescents: An annotated research review. *Journal of Reading, 27,* 713-719.

Tomlinson, C. A. (2001). *How to differentiate instruction in mixed-ability classrooms* (2nd ed.). Alexandria, VA: Association for Supervision and Curriculum Development.

Trelease, J. (2006). *The read-aloud handbook* (6th ed.) New York: Penguin.

Updike, J. (1989). *Self-consciousness.* New York: Knopf.

Vaillant, G. E. (2002). *Aging well: Surprising guideposts to a happier life from the landmark Harvard Study of Adult Development.* Boston: Little, Brown.

VanTassel-Baska, J. (1989, November/December). The fine art of discussion (Part I). *Understanding Our Gifted, 2*(2), 5.

Webb, J. T. (1992). Assessing gifted and talented children. *Illinois Council for the Gifted Journal, 11*, 10-21.

Webb, J. T., Amend, E. R., Webb, N. E., Goerss, J., Beljan, P., & Olenchak, F. R. (2005). *Misdiagnosis and dual diagnoses of gifted children and adults: ADHD, bipolar, OCD, Asperger's, depression and other disorders.* Scottsdale, AZ: Great Potential Press.

Webb, J. T., Gore, J. L., Amend, E. R., & DeVries, A. R. (2007). *A parent's guide to gifted children.* Scottsdale, AZ: Great Potential Press.

Wells, R. (1990). The well-tempered children's book. In P. Zinsser (Ed.), *Worlds of childhood: The art and craft of writing for children.* Boston: Houghton Mifflin.

Whitehead, R. J. (1984). *A guide to selecting books for children.* Metuchen, NJ: Scarecrow.

Whitney, C. S., & Hirsch, G. (2007). *A love for learning: Motivation and the gifted child.* Scottsdale, AZ: Great Potential Press.

Williams, R. (1992). *Personality characteristics of gifted and talented students as measured by the Myers-Briggs Type Indicator and the Murphy-Meisgeier Type Indicator for Children.* Doctoral dissertation, East Texas State University, Commerce, TX. (Dissertation Abstracts International, 53(03), 762A; University Microfilms No. AAC92-22511).

Willis, J. A. (2009). *Inspiring middle school minds: Gifted, creative, and challenging.* Scottsdale, AZ: Great Potential Press.

Wilson, J. D., & Casey, L. H. (2007, Spring). Understanding the recreational reading patterns of secondary students. *Reading Improvement, 44*(1), 40-49.

Winner, E. (1996). *Gifted children: Myths and realities.* New York: Basic Books.

Wrede, P. C., & Stevermer, C. (2003). *Sorcery and Cecelia or the enchanted chocolate pot: Being the correspondence of two young ladies of quality regarding various magical scandals in London and the country.* Orlando, FL: Harcourt Magic Carpet Books.

Zaccaria, J. S., Moses, H. A., & Hollowell, J. S. (1978). *Bibliotherapy in rehabilitation, educational and mental health services.* Champaign, IL: Stipes.

Index of Authors, Titles, and Subjects (Chapters 1-7)

National Council of Teachers of English,
235
*National Excellence: A Case for
Developing America's Talent*, 49, 58
National Reading Panel (2000), 157
Nelson, G. A., 195, 510-11
Neumeister, K. L. S., 511-12
*New Oxford Treasury of Children's Poems,
The*, 227, 230
New York City, 512-13
Newbery Award, 234
Newman, B. M., 513
Newman, P. R., 513
Nilsen, A. P., 231, 513
No Child Left Behind legislation, 68,
157-8, 513
Nodelman, P., 514
Noe, K. L. S., 513
nonconformity, 56, 132-3
nonfiction, 72, 79-82, 88-9, 150, 202-8
criteria for selection, 203-8
for gifted readers, 206-8
in bibliotherapy, 117-19
Norse literature, 217
Norse myths, 213, 221
Northwestern University, 48
Norton, D. E., 231
Norton, Mary, 220
Norton, S. E., 231
Not a Stick, 187
Notable Social Studies Trade Book for
Young People, 235
Nye, N. S., 230

O
O'Brien, Robert C., 220
O'Dell, Scott, 77, 187
Odin's Family: Myths of the Vikings, 217
Odyssey, 214
Odyssey (magazine), 195
Office of Educational Research and
Improvement, 507
Old Ramon, 71
On the Road, 100

open-endedness, 54, 141, 153, 164,
170, 192, 203, 205-6
Ordinary and the Fabulous, The, 217
Orwell, George, 223
Out of the Dust, 228, 230
Outstanding Books for the College
Bound, 235
Outstanding Science Trade Books for
Children, 235
Over Sea, Under Stone, 222
overexcitabilities, 17-19, 32, 51-2

P
pace of learning, 57, 151-2, 158
Pardeck, J. A., 511
Pardeck, J. T., 511
parents
and discussing books at home,
125-8, 168-73
and gifted children, 35-6
and libraries, 177
and resistant readers, 98, 127
and teaching preschoolers to read,
82-3
as advocates for gifted children, 68-9
meeting intellectual needs of gifted
children, 69-72
See also enrichment; homeschooling;
reading aloud; reading guidance
Parent's Guide to Gifted Children, A, 56
Paterson, Katherine, 162, 184, 514
Pathfinder School, xiv
Pearce, Philippa, 220
Peck, Robert Newton, 187
Peeling the Onion: An Anthology of Poems,
230
peers
age, 12, 18, 29, 34-5, 42
finding, 32-3
intellectual, 54-5, 65, 139, 146,
148, 154, 160, 171
talking with, 154-5, 170-1
See also friendship; friendship skills
PEG, 52
Pendarvis, E. D., 32, 506

Index of Categories for Annotated Bibliography (Chapter 8)

Preschool (Up to Four Years Old)

Early Elementary: Kindergarten to Grade 2

Upper Elementary: Grades 3-5

Resilience

Sensitivity

Using Ability

Middle School: Grades 6-8

Achievement

Aloneness

Senior High: Grades 9-12

Index of Books for All Ages

Many of the following books can be used with readers older than the grade levels assigned in Chapter 8 as an introduction to a topic or simply for enjoyment of the information and the creativity that they represent. The art and poetry books may be used with readers of any age.

Index of Authors for Annotated Bibliography (Chapter 8)

Index of Titles for Annotated Bibliography (Chapter 8)

About the
Author

Judith Wynn Halsted, M.S., has worked with gifted children as a parent, teacher, librarian, and consultant. As the librarian for an independent school serving children from preschool through senior high, she was appointed director of the school's gifted program. She also taught Latin and assisted with college counseling. After retiring from teaching, she worked as an educational consultant, helping families find appropriate educational options for gifted students and guiding high school students with college decisions.

As her career evolved, her love for books and concern for gifted children—and especially for their social and emotional development—blended in the writing of this book. The first edition, *Guiding Gifted Readers*, appeared in 1988. This is the third edition under the current title. Nearly all of the vignettes in *Some of My Best Friends Are Books* come from her long experience with gifted students of all ages.

Halsted's commitment to libraries has continued. When her family moved to Traverse City, Michigan, the public library was housed in an inadequate 1905 Carnegie building. To improve public library services, Halsted joined the Library Committee of the League of Women Voters in 1988. She chaired the Committee as it worked to study library issues and then to raise public awareness of the need for a new building. The League's work led to the formation of Citizens for Libraries, a group of community leaders, with Halsted as one of the two co-chairs. This ad hoc group eventually numbered 1,000 volunteers who brought the library issue to a successful millage vote in 1996. The new Traverse Area District Library, which opened in 1999, is an exemplary library in a beautiful building and a focal point for many community activities.

Judith's life is enriched by family and friends, by being active outdoors (especially in Northern Michigan), and by music and reading. She lives with her husband in Traverse City, Michigan; they continue to learn from their two sons and their wives, and from their four grandchildren.